THE WOMAN AND THE DRAGON

THE WOMAN AND THE DRAGON
Apparitions of Mary

DAVID MICHAEL LINDSEY

PELICAN PUBLISHING COMPANY
Gretna 2000

*The word "Pelican" and the depiction of a pelican are trademarks of
Pelican Publishing Company, Inc., and are registered in the U.S. Patent
and Trademark Office.*

Library of Congress Cataloging-in-Publication Data

Lindsey, David Michael, 1955-
   The woman and the dragon : apparitions of Mary / by David Michael Lindsey.
      p. cm.
   Includes bibliographical references.
   ISBN 1-56554-731-4 (hc : alk. paper)
      1. Mary, Blessed Virgin, Saint—Apparitions and miracles—History. I. Title.
BT650 .L54 2000
232.91'7—dc21

99-054131

Printed in the United States of America

Published by Pelican Publishing Company, Inc.
1000 Burmaster Street, Gretna, Louisiana 70053

To the Blessed Virgin Mary, on whose nativity I was born.
And my parents, Herb and Rita, who made this book possible.

Contents

Illustrations

Preface

Devotion to Our Lady comes naturally for me. I was born on Mary's true birthday (August 5) and was named after my mother's favorite teacher, Sister Mary David. As a youngster I attended the Nativity of the Blessed Virgin Mary parochial school in Independence, Missouri, which was built the same year I was born (1955). I attend Mass at St. Mary's church, I wear Mary's Miraculous Medal, I have a life-size statue of Our Lady in my backyard, and on two occasions I've received the scent of Mary's roses at the Cathedral of the Immaculate Conception in Kansas City. Mary is my advocate and protectress; that's why I wrote this book. I want the world to know her and love her as I do, and to know at least some of the history surrounding her major battles with the devil, especially the battles she's fought within the last one hundred years.

Knowing the approximate time he would be chained up in hell for all eternity, the devil chose the twentieth century to attack the Church with all his might. According to Mary in Medjugorje, Satan appeared before God's throne one day and asked for an extended period of time to challenge the Church with all his power. God, who is just and fair, agreed to Satan's request and granted him one century, so the devil chose the twentieth—the last century before the third millennium in which he will be cast down to hell forever.

As history proves, the twentieth century has witnessed more death and destruction than any other century: hundreds of millions of lives have been lost in wars and famines, and millions more to deadly communicable diseases such as AIDS, which will soon be the number one killer in the world. No other century in the history of the world has known as much suffering and death as the twentieth century.

Alarmed at the horrible increase in evil in the world, people everywhere are wondering what on earth is going on. What's going on is a tremendous battle between the spiritual forces of light and dark; a real war being fought over the ownership of human souls.

Humanity must now make a choice between good and evil, between God and Satan. On the souls of the minority who are choosing God—including those who through no fault of their own don't know Jesus Christ—the sign of the Cross is being sealed, while upon the souls of the rebellious and unrepentant majority, the mark of the beast, 666, is being put.[1]

Ever since the 1960s, that rebellious decade containing the devil's number 6, Satan has become much more open and aggressive in his work because his time is growing short. No longer remaining in the dark shadows so as not to be seen, Satan has come out of hiding and is proudly operating in the open. For those with the spiritual eyes to see, the signs of his presence are everywhere. Unfortunately, most people prefer to live in the dark: whether they believe in the devil or not, these people are consciously following after him.[2]

This present generation is the evil generation that Jesus warned about in the Gospels, the generation of the "end times" when signs and wonders proceeding his Second Coming would abound.[3] Just take a look at the weather. Everywhere you look weather records are being shattered. It's as though the earth is trying to warn us that its Creator is about to punish the human race for its innumerable transgressions. According to several visionaries mentioned in this book, if it wasn't for the Blessed Virgin Mary, who restrains God's heavy arm, the world would have been severely punished a long time ago.

You'd think that with all the warning signs coming from God we'd repent our evil ways and turn back to him before it's too late, but we don't. Just look at the evils that are running rampant: school massacres, ethnic cleansings, civil and religious wars, terrorist bombings, racial hatred, broken families, child abuse, youth gangs, illegal drugs, pornography, legalized gambling, abortion, homosexuality, corporate downsizing, robberies, murder. Our love for God and our neighbor has grown cold, just as Jesus said would happen in the last days.[4]

Although the majority of people at the beginning of this millennium are choosing Satan over God, the Blessed Mother still stands—as she has throughout history—beside the One True Church, the Roman Catholic Church, as its advocate and protectress. When the Great Apostasy against the Catholic Church began in the sixteenth century, Our Lady of Guadalupe came to Mexico to replenish God's flock from the decimation of Protestantism. Then, when the twin Antichristian demons named Rationalism and Revolution were born in the eighteenth and nineteenth centuries, provoking intellectuals to declare Nature and Science their new gods, Mary came to Paris to give us the Miraculous Medal as testimony to the one true God. When famine ravaged Europe in 1846 and whole-scale revolution was about to break out on that continent, Mary came to La Salette, France, to warn the world of the imminent wars and disasters to come. In the spring of 1917, just before communism took over in Russia, Our Lady of Fátima appeared in Portugal to warn the world of its rise and spread. And two decades later, when Adolph Hitler ascended to power in Germany, approximately nineteen centuries after the death of Christ, Mary appeared in neighboring Belgium on two separate occasions, begging for the world's prayers and sacrifices. Most recently, in Rwanda and Bosnia, Mary appeared at least a decade before their civil wars started, pleading with the world to turn back to God before it's too late.

Time and time again, God has sent the Blessed Virgin Mary to earth to warn us that he is about to punish the world. If he could, Christ would gladly come back down from heaven and die on the cross again. But the Eternal Father won't let him, so he sends us his mother instead. Mary is the world's last warning. We must listen to her messages and warnings from God or face the imminent chastisement as his enemy. Very soon, there will be no more warnings and no more time left to repent because, according to the visionaries in Medjugorje, these are Mary's last appearances on earth. According to the visionaries mentioned in this book, Mary's prophecies concerning the very near future are extremely grave. All of them say the same thing: our time is running out and the world is about to be punished. God, through Mary, is telling us that we must convert while there's still time to do so, while mercy still exists. Afterwards, it will be a time of judgment, not mercy. Remember, God does not kid around; he makes no idle threats. He wants all men of all religions to convert and be saved. When he sends us his mother, he means for her to be taken seriously, not mocked and disbelieved. Please believe in what Mary has to say. Like it or not, your eternal destiny rests entirely on what you believe.

Within the last several decades there have been a glut of authors who have put out scads of books predicting a monumental event that will happen by Y2K, such as Christ's Second Coming, or the end of the world, or global financial anarchy and a third world war. When these false prophecies fail to materialize they will do tremendous damage to Christianity's believability. Many Christians will lose their faith because of them, and cynics and scoffers in the media will have a heyday. Be wary of people who claim something big will happen by a certain date, or of those who claim to have inside information from the Holy Spirit regarding the interpretation of Scripture, especially the Book of Revelation, which is very hard to decipher. There are many false prophets out there, who are all too eager to get rich by preying upon people's fears, ignorance, and gullibility.

The majority of false prophets, of course, are just making things up, but some may have received information from deceiving spirits. Be extremely careful of them, too. Also, there are many well-intentioned people who truly believe that what they say or write about the future comes from God and is the truth. Remember, only God the Father knows the exact hour and day of Christ's return and the end of the world, so live each day as if you will live to be a hundred, but be ready to die at any moment.

With all the lies being spread today about what is the truth, don't be discouraged if you no longer know who to believe. Time has a merciless way of proving false prophets wrong, and, sooner or later, they will all be found out. My advice is this: if you want to be sure of the truth, look to Mary for guidance.

The Woman and the Dragon is not a book about Marian apparitions per se— there have been enough of those written already—but an historical analysis of the Dragon's personal fight against Mary and the Roman Catholic Church, in relation to Mary's appearances on earth as symbolized in chapter twelve of the Book of Revelation. As a conservative Catholic, I hold to the traditional Catholic beliefs that Satan is a real, super-intelligent, preternatural being, who's the "Prime Mover" of all evil and disorder in the world, and not just a personification of our shadowy selves. I believe that he plans and evokes persecutions, heresies, schisms, apostasies, scandals, lies, and violence against the Catholic Church—both from within the Church and from without. This would only make sense on Satan's part if, indeed, the Roman Catholic Church is the One True Faith established by Jesus Christ two millennia ago. Contriving his diabolic schemes in his kingdom, hell, the Dragon holds a form of court that mimics that of heaven; in its hierarchy of authority from top down. As the "Monkey of God," Satan strives to imitate what he sees the Trinity doing, but in an evil, mocking, perverse way. Therefore, a better name for the devil might be Spite or Revenge or Negation. There is abundant evidence of this throughout history. For instance, God sent the Blessed Mother repeatedly to earth in the 1980s and 90s to preach repentance, conversion, holiness and sacrifice, while the devil sent his own anti-Madonna to the world to extol the six vices of materialism, greed, lust, envy, pride, and anger. Just two decades earlier, it was no mere coincidence that a bearded, long-haired, evil-eyed, psycho-babbling guru named Manson (Man's Son, or Son of Man) appeared in the City of Angels with his cadre of brainwashed disciples to wreak havoc on Hollywood by killing the wife and baby of the producer of *Rosemary's Baby*,[5] then killing the LaBiancas (whose name in Italian means "The Whites") to start a race war between blacks and whites. You see, Satan loves to choreograph his evil with sick parodies of Jesus Christ and Mary. That's the only satisfaction he has left. If you take the scales off your eyes and start looking at history spiritually, you'll soon discover many more examples of what I mean.

As mentioned, the premise of *The Woman and the Dragon* is about the interpretation of chapter twelve of the Book of Revelation as related to history, and contains controversial corollaries based on documented historical facts and apparitions of Jesus and Mary by credible visionaries, in conjunction with my own personal insights, and the prophecies and visions of numerous well-known Catholics throughout the last two millennia. The identities of the Dragon, the First and Second Beasts, the Antichrist, and the Whore of Babylon, who are revealed in the ninth chapter of this book, are based upon the revelations of a bed-ridden Italian invalid named Maria Valtorta during the Second World War, and are contained in her best-selling book *The End Times*, a book I highly recommend for students of prophecy

Let me warn you before reading *The Woman and the Dragon*: if you are looking for a feel-good book about a non-confrontational, New-Age Mary who doesn't exist, this book is not for you. I didn't write this book to tickle anyone's ears. This book contains admonitions and warnings from the true Mary of the Catholic Church, as they relate to my own personal opinions about evil. If you feel that you have to criticize me for expressing my Catholic beliefs you have that right, but remember, this country was founded upon the democratic principles of freedom of religion and freedom of speech. Publicly-funded artists have the right to display images of the Blessed Virgin Mary desecrated with elephant dung, and Hollywood has the right to produce movies and television shows that attack the teachings of Catholics. So I, as a Catholic apologist and member of the Catholic League, which fights for the rights of Catholics, should have the right to express my own beliefs from an orthodox Catholic perspective.

Finally, to those who may think that this book is too negative towards other people's religions and beliefs and is anti-ecumenical in subject matter, let me say that although I do criticize certain key historical figures who have done great harm to the Roman Catholic Church, I, like Mary, do not refrain from severely criticizing those within the Catholic Church who have brought scandal and apostasy to the Body of Christ. Quite frankly, I think that hell is well represented with the souls of unscrupulous priests, bishops, cardinals and, yes, even popes. Be that as it may, there are good and bad people in every religion, and members of other religions are no less children of God than Catholics and are destined to join their Creator someday in heaven if they have good will, love God with all their heart, soul, mind and strength, and obey the dictates of their consciences. It is only when you truly know Jesus Christ and consciously reject him that you risk judgment for rejecting the Way, the Truth, and the Life. God alone in his infinite wisdom decides upon the degree of responsibility that each individual must bear. To those who have been given much, much is expected. To those who have been given little, little is expected. Certainly all religions can't be equally true, but all men are created equal and salvation is open to everyone.

That said, here's a little interpretive history about Mary's epic battle against the Dragon, the Father of All Lies and Author of All Discord.

David Michael Lindsey

Introduction: The Doctrine of Mary

"My mouth shall speak wisdom, my heart shall offer insight."

Psalm 49:4

When Lucifer and his proud minions were cast down to earth for rebelling against God, the peace and harmony of heaven was totally disrupted. The remaining angels in heaven were left in a state of bewilderment, fearing that since they were spiritual creatures, like Lucifer, a vapor of pride might arise in them, too. Only when God the Father, the Eternal Thought, revealed to the good angels the full knowledge of his divine plan to create the purest, most humble of all his creatures—the Blessed Virgin Mary—did peace and consolation return to the heavenly hosts.[1]

The Blessed Virgin Mary, whom the archangel Gabriel greeted two thousand years ago as God's "Highly Favored Daughter[2] is truly the most blessed creature God has ever made; second only to him in perfection and beauty.[3] She had to be, for her womb, the "New Ark of the New Covenant," could not be tainted with the slightest stain of sin, original or personal. Otherwise, Jesus, the God-Man, would have inherited from his mother a sinful human nature. By a special grace from the Eternal Father, the Blessed Virgin Mary was created free from the impure nature we acquired from our first parents, Adam and Eve. Thus, Mary became God's "New Eve," restoring with her ever-virginal purity that Eve had lustfully lost when she, metaphorically speaking, ate the forbidden fruit in the Garden of Eden; thereupon, bringing Death upon the human race.

The doctrine of Mary's "Immaculate Conception," which is to be believed by all the Christian faithful, was dogmatically proclaimed by Pope Pius IX on December 8, 1854, in *Ineffabilis Deus*. In this bull, Pope Pius decreed that Mary was conceived without any sin:

" . . . by a singular privilege and grace from Almighty God and in view of the merits of Jesus Christ, [Mary] was preserved free from all stain of original sin."[4]

Belief in this dogma dates back to at least the eighth century, when an

21

observance of the Solemnity of the Immaculate Conception was first recorded.[5] The Virgin Mary herself confirmed the Church's doctrine of the Immaculate Conception four years after Pius IX's bull, when she appeared to a young girl, Bernadette Soubirous, in Lourdes, France, on March 25, 1858 (March 25 is the Solemnity of the Annunciation). After repeated pleas from Bernadette to identify herself, Mary announced to her, and thus to the whole world,

> "*Que soy era Immaculado Councepciou!*" ("*I am the Immaculate Conception.*")

For a long time, this truth of Mary's Immaculate Conception has been a heated point of contention between Catholics and Protestants. Some try refuting Mary's Immaculate Conception by quoting the Bible out of context: "All have sinned and come short of the glory of God,"[6] or, "There is none good but one, that is God."[7] Protestants contend that since Mary proclaimed that her "spirit rejoiced in God my savior"[8] then she must have been a sinner, and, therefore, could not be Immaculate. But, again, this contention is taking Scripture out of context. Mary rejoiced in God, her savior, not because she was sinful, but because of her humility, meekness, and subordination to her son, Jesus Christ, without whom no one, no matter how good they are, can enter heaven—not Abraham, not Isaac, not Jacob, not John the Baptist, not even Mary.[9]

Furthermore, in the Bible's Canticle of Mary,[10] the Blessed Mother presupposed the dogma of the Immaculate Conception by affirming to the whole world her fullness of grace and divine election. In this canticle, which was inspired by the Holy Spirit, Mary proclaimed:

> "*All ages to come shall call me blessed. God who is mighty has done great things for me.*"

Indeed, God has done great things for Mary. She is the only creature to receive a fullness of grace from God, so she deserves our highest veneration. By right, by election, by descent, and by her suffering,[11] Mary is seated in heaven at the right hand of Jesus Christ as the "Queen of Heaven,"[12] the "Co-Redeemer"[13] and "Co-Mediatrix"[14] of the world. (For those of you who are scandalized by this, the prefix "co-" means "with," not "equal to.") While, as we know from the Bible,[15] only Jesus Christ mediates between God and man, Mary, our heavenly intercessor, mediates between Jesus and man.[16] Now I ask you: what son, if he is truly good, can deny the requests of his mother, especially if that son happens to be the Son of God? Remember what Jesus did for Mary at the wedding of Cana, when she asked him to perform a miracle before his time had come to perform miracles—he obeyed her request.[17]

All too often, non-Catholics unfairly accuse Roman Catholics of worshiping Mary as a goddess because they bestow on her the honorific titles of "Queen of Heaven," "Co-Mediatrix," and "Co-Redemptrix." Nothing could be further from the truth. Catholics worship only God, and are not afraid of venerating Mary or making Jesus Christ jealous of his mother. Jealousy of Mary, the Woman of Revelation 12, is not a sin to be found in Jesus Christ but in Satan, the Red Dragon! Mary's "Do whatever he tells you"[18] leads us to Jesus, and Jesus leads us to God. She prepares; he fulfills. Without Mary there would be no Jesus. Without Jesus there would be no redemption. For this reason alone, Mary is worthy of our highest honor and devotion. Catholic invocations and supplications to Mary, the "Perpetual Virgin," do not in the least bit lessen our faith in Jesus Christ. Instead, they magnify it!

The Catholic Church has recognized Mary's perpetual virginity[19] as far back as the 2nd Council of Constantinople, in 553. Even before that, most of the early church fathers, such as St. Ambrose, St. Jerome, and St. Augustine, believed in Mary's perpetual virginity. And, as far as that goes, so did the early Protestant fathers, Luther, Calvin, and Zwingli. It's easy to understand why the early church doctors and early Protestant leaders believed in Mary's perpetual virginity: the doctrine can be understood from the Gospel of John, wherein Jesus gave his beloved apostle, John of Zebedee, custody of his mother before he died on the cross: "When Jesus saw his mother and the disciple whom he loved, he said to his mother, '*Woman, behold your son.*' Then he said to the disciple, '*Behold your mother.*' And from that hour on the disciple took her into his home."[20]

Now if Mary had other sons and daughters, it wouldn't have made sense for Jesus to give his mother away to a young man who wasn't even her relative. The fact is, Mary had no other sons or daughters. Those who claim that the Bible proves Mary had other sons and daughters because it mentions Jesus as having "brothers," are taking the word "brother" out of context. The Bible uses the words "brother" or "brothers" 750 times: 430 times in the Old Testament and 320 in the New. The word "brother" in the Bible often imputes kinsmen and followers, members of the same tribe or race, nephews and cousins, or relatives in general. In the common language that Jesus spoke, Aramaic, as well as in Hebrew, cousins were always called "brothers" because those languages had no separate word for "cousin." That's why Jesus' cousins—James, Joseph, Simon, Judas, the sons of Alphaeus (Jesus' uncle on St. Joseph's side)—are often mistaken by Protestants as the other sons of Mary.[21]

Similarly, the scriptural passage, "Joseph knew her not until Christ was born,"[22] is frequently misinterpreted by Protestants as meaning that Mary and Joseph had sexual relations following Jesus' birth. But that's not what the passage means. It simply means that Jesus was born of a virgin—nothing more, nothing less. Likewise, the reference to Jesus as Mary's "firstborn son"[23] does not infer that Mary had a second- or third-born son. The designation of "firstborn" was customarily given by the Hebrews for purposes of inheritance and consecration, regardless of how many children came afterwards—even if couples did not have any more children (as were the cases with Abraham and

Sarah, and Zechariah and Elizabeth). All firstborn Hebrew sons were required by Jewish law to be consecrated to the Lord on the eighth day after birth, at the time of their presentation and circumcision.[24]

In addition to Mary's perpetual virginity, Roman Catholic doctrine maintains that Mary was assumed into heaven at the time of her *dormition*, or falling asleep. Since about the sixth century, a feast day honoring the apostolic tradition of Mary's bodily assumption into heaven has been celebrated by the Catholic Church.[25] To affirm that long-held tradition, on November 1, 1950, Pope Pius XII officially proclaimed in the apostolic constitution, *Munificentissimus Deus*, the Catholic Church's infallible teaching of the Assumption of Mary. Besides the pope's proclamation, there is ample reason for Christians to believe in the Assumption of Mary, even though inference is not made to it in the Bible. Aside from the Old Testament precedents of Enoch and Elijah being assumed directly into heaven before death, Mary's assumption into heaven makes perfect sense. Jesus wanted to spare the virginal body of his mother, God's New Ark of the New Covenant, which was untouched by any man,[26] the indignity of being undressed and prepared for burial, and from having it suffer putrefaction in the grave. Corruption of the flesh after death is a fate reserved for the inheritors of original sin, which excludes the Blessed Virgin Mary. Archaeologically, even to this day none of Mary's relics have ever been found in any tomb or grave, lending further credibility to the Catholic dogma of the Assumption.

Regarding another controversial Catholic doctrine of Mary as the "Mother of God," this title didn't originate with Catholics but with the Jews. Even before Jesus was born, Mary was hailed by her cousin, Elizabeth, as the "Mother of my Lord."[27] Of course, God, who has no beginning or end, is in and of himself, and has no parents. It is the incarnate Jesus Christ, fully God yet fully man, who is referred to by the early church fathers as born of a woman. In the year 431, the Catholic Council of Ephesus affirmed this by naming Mary the *Theotokos*, or god-bearer—the Mother of God made Man.

In addition to being the Mother of God, Mary is also our "Mother of Perpetual Help." As Mary visited Elizabeth in her time of need, so, too, she visits us in our time of need. Whenever she sees that we are lacking in things that are important, Mary implores her Son Jesus to help us out. Even though his hour to perform miracles had not yet come, Jesus couldn't refuse his mother's charity at the wedding of Cana and changed the water into wine. So it remains with us today. Appealing to the most merciful heart of her son, Mary has the natural motherly influence to move her son to act on our behalf, especially against the never-ending wiles and cunning of the Dragon.

Chapter One

The Woman and the Dragon

"I will put enmity between you [serpent] and the woman, and between your offspring and hers; He will strike at your head, while you strike at his heel."

Gen. 3:15

"A great sign appeared in the sky, a woman clothed with the sun, with the moon under her feet, and on her head a crown of twelve stars. Because she was with child, she wailed aloud in pain as she labored to give birth. Then another sign appeared in the sky: it was a huge dragon, flaming red, with seven heads and ten horns: on his heads were seven crowns. His tail swept a third of the stars from the sky and hurled them down to the earth. Then the dragon stood before the woman about to give birth, ready to devour her child when it should be born. She gave birth to a son—a boy destined to shepherd all the nations with an iron rod. Her child was caught up to God and his throne. The woman herself fled into the desert, where a special place had been prepared for her by God; there she was taken care of for twelve hundred and sixty days.

"Then war broke out in heaven; Michael and his angels battled against the dragon. Although the dragon and his angels fought back, they were overpowered and lost their place in heaven. The huge dragon, the ancient serpent known as the devil or Satan, the seducer of the world, was driven out; he was hurled down to earth and his minions with him.

"Then I heard a loud voice in heaven say: 'Now have salvation and power come, the reign of our God and the authority of his Anointed One. For the accuser of our brothers is cast out, who night and day accused them before God. They defeated them by the blood of the Lamb and by the word of their testimony; love for life did not deter them from death. So rejoice, you heavens, and you that dwell therein! But woe to you, earth and sea, for the devil has come down upon you! His fury knows no limits, for he knows his time is short.'

"When the dragon saw that he had been cast down to the earth, he pursued the woman about to give birth to the boy. But the woman was given the wings of a gigantic eagle so that she could fly off to her place in the desert, where, far from the serpent, she could be taken care of for two and half years more. The serpent, however, spewed a torrent of water out of his mouth to search out the woman and sweep her away. The earth then came to the woman's rescue by opening its mouth and swallowing the flood which the dragon spewed out of his mouth. Enraged at her escape, the dragon went off to wage war with her offspring, on those who keep God's commandments and give witness to Jesus. He took up position at the shore of the sea."   Rev. 12:1-17

As the Holy Mother of Jesus' pastoral flock, the "New Israel," God foreordained the Blessed Virgin Mary, the "Woman" referred to in Genesis 3:15 and Revelation 12:1-17, to be the Queen of Heaven and Protectress of the One True Church of Jesus Christ—the Roman Catholic Church.[1] Therefore, from the above passages in Revelation 12:1-17 that allude to this, we can reasonably assume that's why Satan hates Mary so much: he became tremendously enraged when he learned that a lowly woman would receive from God power and authority over him, Lucifer, the brightest and most powerful seraphim in heaven.

Eons ago, after God created the earth, he revealed to the heavenly angels his future plans to create a woman who would give birth to an extraordinary male child, a holy son who would receive from the Father absolute dominion over heaven and earth. This child, the Father announced, would be crowned the King of Heaven and Earth, the Son of God, and would inherit from the Father all that he had. This startling revelation caused quite a stir in heaven: many angels felt it beneath their dignity to worship a human being made out of mud. Envious of God's decision to beget Jesus the God-Man, Lucifer, the head of the angels, tried to dethrone God and put himself in God's place, but he was overpowered by Michael the Archangel and cast down to earth, where, now as Satan,[2] he and his demons are condemned to everlasting hellfire for their unforgivable treason against Almighty God.

The Bible recounts the story of Lucifer's lightning fall from grace in the Book of Isaiah:

> "How you have fallen from the heavens, O morning star, son of the dawn! How are you cut down to the ground, you who mowed down the nations! You said in your heart: 'I will scale the heavens; above the stars of God I will set my throne; I will take my seat on the Mount of Assembly, in the recesses of the North. I will ascend above the tops of the clouds; I will be like the Most High!' Yet down to the nether world you go to the recesses of the pit."[3]

In Revelation 12, the chapter on the Woman and the Dragon, the seven heads of the Dragon metaphorically depict the seven deadly sins of Lucifer that caused him and a third of the angels (stars) to lose their place in heaven: pride, envy, anger, greed, indolence, excess, and lust (which, in the case of Lucifer and his cohorts, was a lust for power and glory rather than a lust for flesh). Satan, the "red dragon," has all seven deadly sins within himself, but in his new kingdom, hell, he has put in charge a different devil for each of the seven sins and has given them his full power and authority (symbolized by the "ten horns" on the "seven heads"). Therein lies the clue to the mysterious identities of the first and second Beasts of Revelation 13 (more on them in chapter 9).

After he realized he had fallen from heaven for all eternity, Satan's only recourse was to cause the downfall of mankind, so he seduced Eve, in the Garden of Eden, into disobeying God. Eve's refusal to obey God's wishes, which caused the introduction of evil into the world and the barring of man from heaven, was, centuries later, counteracted by Mary's unselfish, "I will serve." Two millennia ago, when the archangel Gabriel appeared to the Virgin Mary and informed her of God's wishes for her to conceive the long-awaited Messiah, the Redeemer of Mankind, Mary's immediate reply to God's request was—unlike Eve's—obedient and humble:

> *"Behold, I am the handmaid of the Lord. May it be done to me according to your word."*[4]

Because of Mary's humble *"Yes,"* salvation was granted to the fallen world. Thus, Mary played a vital role in the redemption of the human race. That's why she can rightly be called the Co-Redeemer and Co-Mediatrix of man, and that's why she has been assigned by God to assume the highly exalted role of Queen of Heaven and Protectress of the Catholic Church.

As God's Protectress of the Roman Catholic Church, Mary has faithfully stood by and defended the church against the schemes of the devil ever since its inception on Pentecost day, seven Sundays after Easter. Whenever any grave danger threatens the lives of the faithful or the survival of the Catholic Church, Mary appears on earth with prophetic warnings, messages, and pleas for repentance. To help lead her children back onto the road of salvation, Mary has worked many miracles as a testimony to God's favor for the church and a sign of his presence with her. Therefore, it is not wrong to say that besides her son, Jesus Christ, the Blessed Mother is the single greatest advocate of the One True Church.

Judith and Esther: Archetypes of Mary

Mary's vital role as defender of the Catholic Church was foreshadowed in the Old Testament books of Judith and Esther.[5] In these two inspirational and exemplary biblical narratives that presage the future coming of a victorious, holy woman like Mary, God delivers his people through courageous, God-fearing, and beautiful young Jewish women. In the Book of Judith, which chronicles the period of time around the sixth century B.C., the heroine, Judith, the pious young widow of Manasseh, saves Israel from complete annihilation by the Assyrian army when she single-handedly slays the evil Assyrian general, Holofernes, as he lay in a drunken stupor inside his tent. Dressed in her finest attire, Judith, whose Hebrew name means "Jewess," gallantly walked into the Assyrian camp pretending to hand her people over to Holofernes. Fascinated by her striking beauty and words of wisdom, Holofernes planned to ravish Judith in the privacy of his bedchamber after a night of sumptuous eating and drinking. On the night of the banquet, after dismissing all of his servants and guests except for Judith, the inebriated Holofernes passed out on his bed. Seizing the moment given to her by God, Judith drew Holofernes's sword, and with two mighty blows, cut off his head and slipped away from the Assyrian camp, with Holofernes's head stuffed in her maid's food pouch. The next morning, when the Assyrians discovered that their invincible commander-in-chief had been slain by a mere woman, they fled in terror and were routed by the Israeli army in hot pursuit.

The Book of Esther is another inspirational prefigurement of the coming of the victorious Blessed Virgin Mary. In this time-honored classic, Esther, the beautiful young Jewish niece and adopted daughter of Mordecai, faithful Jewish servant to King Xerxes (Ahasuerus) of Persia (486-465 B.C.), is chosen out of all the young virgins of Persia to become the king's new bride. Esther's selection by the Persian king proved to be providential because it occurred at the same time Haman the Agagite,[6] the evil vizier of King Xerxes, concocted a nefarious plot to exterminate the entire Jewish race.

As the chronicler of Esther recounts, Haman was insulted that the king's servant, Mordecai, would not bow down to Haman, so he coerced the king into ordering a decree of extermination against all the Jewish people in Persia. When Mordecai learned of the king's decree, he tore his clothes and pleaded with his niece Esther to intercede to the king on their behalf, knowing that if she failed, the entire Jewish race would be annihilated. So at the risk of her own life, Esther approached King Xerxes without being summoned (an act that carried a penalty of death). But instead of being angered, the king was delighted with the unexpected appearance of his favorite wife. Granting her anything her heart desired, Esther requested that King Xerxes and Haman attend a banquet she was hosting the following day. At the banquet, King Xerxes was so taken by Esther's beauty that he again vowed to grant her anything she desired, up to half his kingdom. Esther merely requested that the king and Haman attend a second banquet of hers, the following day. On the night before the second banquet, King Xerxes couldn't sleep, so he reviewed his court records and discovered that the condemned Mordecai had once informed him about a plot to assassinate the king, which the king had already suspected probably involved Haman. Remembering the loyalty of Mordecai and the devious ambitiousness of Haman, King Xerxes resolved to honor Mordecai and shame Haman. The next day, just prior to the banquet and before Haman was about to ask the king to hang Mordecai on a gibbet he had just built, King Xerxes asked Haman how the king should honor his most faithful servant (which Haman thought, of course, was him). Haman replied to the king that he should be given the highest public honor; whereupon, King Xerxes immediately announced that Mordecai should be so honored. Shamed and red-faced, Haman was stunned. That night, during the second banquet, which was again attended by Haman and the king, Xerxes once more promised Esther anything she desired, up to half of his kingdom. This time Esther requested that she and the Jewish people be spared from the king's decree of extermination. Shocked to find out that his favorite queen was Jewish and therefore was included in the decree of extermination suggested to him by Haman, King Xerxes immediately hanged Haman on the same gibbet Haman had just erected for Mordecai. Since a royal decree was irrevocable, the king's only recourse to save the Jews was to allow them to defend themselves against their attackers—which they did. In the end, all those who conspired to kill the Jews were themselves killed, including Haman's ten sons, who were hanged on the same gibbet as their wicked father. Mordecai then took over Haman's position as the king's second in command.

The Jewish people can thank Esther for their salvation because if it wasn't for her courage and intercession with the Persian king, they would have perished as a people; exactly what Satan wanted because he knew that the future Savior had to be a Jew. Esther's salvation of the Jews is celebrated annually on the Feast of Purim, on the single day that Haman planned to eradicate the Jews, a date for which he had cast lots (the *pur*).

As you've probably figured out by now, the biblical characters of Holofernes and Haman are allegorical representations of Satan, and Judith and Esther's struggles against the two foreshadow Mary's future battle with the devil. Analyzing these two biblical stories more closely, you can see that Esther's intercession with the powerful king of the Persians is analogous to the special, intercessory relationship Mary has with Almighty God, and Judith's striking at the head of Holofernes symbolizes Mary striking at the head of the serpent, who has been battling against the church for the last two thousand years.

Although it may not seem like it now, in the end, Satan is destined to lose the war he is currently waging against Mary's offspring, the Catholic Church. The beginning of the end for Satan started with the birth of Christ, which Satan tried so hard to prevent. Knowing the approximate time that God would come down from heaven and take on human flesh, Satan, through King Herod the Great, tried to search out and destroy Christ by murdering all male children two years and under who were living in Bethlehem and its vicinity.[7] Herod's demonic scheme to murder Christ, however, was thwarted by the angel Gabriel, who warned Joseph in a dream to flee Bethlehem with Jesus and Mary for the deserts of Egypt.[8]

Several years later, when King Herod finally died, the Holy Family was told by Gabriel to return to Palestine and to live in the small village of Nazareth in Galilee, where Jesus grew up and completed his mission as the savior of the world. Enraged at Christ's escape, Satan, the Dragon, went off to wage war on the offspring of Mary.[9]

Now, as the end-times draw nearer, a tremendous battle is being fought between the spiritual forces of light, headed by Jesus Christ, the Blessed Virgin Mary, and St. Michael the Archangel, and the evil forces of darkness, led by Satan and his two demonic beasts. As Christ's special emissary to earth, Mary is playing the pivotal role in this decisive battle for the hearts and souls of countless multitudes. Within the last few centuries, Mary, The Prophetess of Our Times, has appeared on earth many times, imploring humanity to turn back to God before it's too late. Knowing Mary's powerful intercessory role with God, faithful Catholics pray for God's special protection in the old prayer, the "Memorare":

> Remember, O gracious Virgin Mary
> That never was it known
> That anyone who fled to thy protection,
> Implored thy help,
> Or sought thy intercession was left unaided.
> Inspired by this confidence I fly unto thee,
> O Virgin of Virgins My Mother.
> To thee I come,
> Before thee I stand, sinful and sorrowful.
> O Mother of the Word Incarnate, despise not my petition
> But in thy mercy hear and answer me. Amen.

And why shouldn't Christians pray to Mary for help? As Mother of the Word Incarnate, Mary is The Sign for Our Times, The Great Sign Appearing in the Sky, The Woman Clothed with the Sun [Son],[10] with the moon under her feet, and crowned with twelve stars. Unquestionably, the "Woman" of Revelation chapter 12 is Mary, not Israel or the church (although the metaphor of the church is not totally absent from this passage). As Queen of the Apostles, Mary's crown of "twelve stars" symbolizes the twelve tribes of Israel and the twelve apostles of the church. The "moon under her feet" represents Mary's Queenship over heaven and earth, over angels and men—a Catholic doctrine proclaimed by Pope Pius XII on October 11, 1954, in the encyclical *Ad Caeli Reginam*, which is celebrated each year on August 22.

Understandably, many people confuse the "Woman" of Revelation 12 with the nation Israel, but Pope Paul VI, in his encyclical *Signum Magnum,* put an end to this mistake when he correctly identified the "Woman Clothed with the Sun" as Mary. Pope Paul was right: an entire nation like Israel did not "flee into the desert" after "giving birth to a son." It was the Virgin Mary who fled into the desert with Joseph and baby Jesus, because Israel was trying to kill Jesus—and eventually it did, as John the Apostle recorded in his gospel:

"He came to what was his own, but his own people did not accept him."[11]

The gentiles, however, accepted Christ, and for a thousand years the church flourished. The triumph of the Catholic Church wouldn't last forever: the end of the first millennium marked the ascendancy of anti-Christianity and the beginning of the decline of the influence of the Roman Catholic Church. First came the violent rise of Islam in Asia Minor in the seventh century; then the 1054 schism of the Catholic Church into the Western Church at Rome and the Eastern Church at Constantinople, then the decline of the Roman papacy from the "Babylonian Captivity" and the "Great Western Schism" in the fourteenth and fifteenth centuries, then Luther's Protestant rebellion against the church in 1517, followed by the rise of rationalism and anti-Catholic freemasonry in 1717, and the rise of Russian communism in 1917; Nazi fascism in 1933, and anti-Christian materialism in the last half of the twentieth century.

By far, the most destructive satanic attack leveled against the Catholic Church in the last two millennia has been the evil and cunning spirit of rationalism. Born in the eighteenth century out of man's pride in his scientific discoveries, rationalism is a philosophical rejection of the divine revelation of Jesus Christ in favor of human reason and experience alone, and was fathered by the ideologies of humanism, classicism, freemasonry, republicanism (anti-monarchism), and scientism (science worship).

The many evil offspring of rationalism have been ruinous on mankind: the French Revolution in 1789, Darwin's theory of evolution in 1859, Bolshevism in 1917, Naziism in 1933, immoral rebellion and sexual liberation in the 1960s, materialism and greed in the 1970s and 1980s, and post-modernism, feminism, liberalism, and homosexuality within the church in the 1990s.

Although the church has been devastated by the terrible satanic onslaughts wrought by rationalism, the Blessed Virgin Mary has faithfully stood by the Mystical Body of Christ, as she did at the foot of the cross on Golgotha Hill two millennia ago. Mary's first major documented appearance in defense of the Roman Catholic Church occurred in Mexico in 1531. The following chapter explains the history of the events that led up to the Marian apparitions of Guadalupe.

Chapter Two

The Dragon Attacks the Church

"They shall go out and see the corpses of the men who rebelled against me; Their worm shall not die, nor their fire be extinguished; and they shall be abhorrent to all mankind."

Isa. 66:24

The One True Church

The True Church of Jesus Christ—the Catholic Church—was born on Pentecost day, seven Sundays after the first Easter with the descent of the Holy Spirit upon Mary and the apostles gathered together in Jerusalem.[1] Established in the year A.D. 33, this fledgling Christian sect began to be known as the "Catholic Church" early in the second century, as historians have documented from the writings of St. John's disciple, St. Ignatius of Antioch, to the Smyrnaeans (c. 107):

"Wheresoever the bishop shall appear, there let the people be, even as where Jesus is, there is the Catholic Church."[2]

The term "Catholic" comes from the Greek word *katholikos*, which means "universal," and is a name which suitably describes the Catholic Church because its one billion members come from every nation, language, and tribe on earth, making it one of the largest religions in the world (one in every six people are Catholic). Around the middle of the sixteenth century, the Catholic Church began to be called the "Roman Catholic Church" to distinguish itself from members of the Anglican Church in England which broke away from Rome in 1534, yet still considered itself to be "catholic."

The Roman Catholic Church is the One True Church which God intended to be his repository of divine truth, under which the community of believers would unite in one faith, profess one doctrine, share seven sacraments, and be governed by one head, the vicar of Christ on earth. The following facts prove that the Roman Catholic Church is the One True Church:

- Christianity is the only faith, besides Judaism, that was instituted directly by God: all the rest (Buddhism, Islam, Hinduism, Zoroastrianism, Shintoism, etc.) were initiated by man. Any religion founded by a mere man, or an angel, does not come from God. Only God himself can establish the true faith and only Roman Catholicism can trace its roots directly back to its founder, Jesus Christ, the Son of God made man, who made a new covenant with Jew and gentile alike.

- Catholicism is one of the largest religions in the world, if not the largest, and you would expect that from an omnipotent, loving God who wants to save all the children he created. God is not a minimalist; he wants all people of all beliefs to come to know him and be saved.

- No other religion has gained as many converts through missionary activity as the Roman Catholic Church. It was no coincidence that Catholic Spain and Portugal were at the heights of their maritime powers when the New World was discovered, and that the vast majority of navigators and explorers to the New World, Africa, India, and the Far East were Catholic, enabling Catholic missionaries to introduce the One True Faith to these remote, uncivilized areas.

- The True God is a god of love, and his Universal Church is built on brotherly love and charity. No other religion has as many colleges, universities, parochial schools, protective institutions, hospitals, dispensaries, homeless shelters, child welfare centers, nurseries, special care centers, missionary centers, social service centers, and nursing homes as the Roman Catholic Church. No one gives as much money and aid to the poor and underprivileged as the Catholic Church.

- Nearly every country that has been economically blessed and/or made great strides in civilization and learning has been a Christian nation, and can thank Roman Catholicism for its Christian heritage. Countries that have prospered economically, like Japan, South Korea and Taiwan, while not being Christian nations themselves, have, nonetheless, patterned themselves after democratic Christian nations in the West.

- Roman Catholicism is the oldest geopolitical institution in the world and has survived all the emperors, kings, governors, and dictators who have tried to destroy it—Nero, Muhammed, Saladin, Suleiman I, Napoleon, King Henry VIII, Queen Elizabeth I, Hitler, Mussolini, Lenin,

Stalin, and all the rest who waged war on the Catholic Church are long gone, but the Universal Church lives on. As Jesus Christ promised, the gates of hell shall not destroy his church.

• No other religion has had as many verbal attacks for its steadfast dogmas and doctrines as the Roman Catholic Church. Liberals, modernists, feminists, homosexuals, Hollywood, the media, and secular governments and institutions have all attacked the Catholic Church for its uncompromising stance against abortion, artificial contraception, euthanasia, and homosexuality. Find the religion the world hates and you have found the true religion. Darkness hates the light.

• No other religion has had as many miracles, fulfilled prophesies, and apparitions from heaven as the Roman Catholic Church. The tremendous number of authenticated apparitions from Jesus and Mary to Catholics point to which religion is the true religion.

• Satan, of course, knows which one is the real church, and he mocks it with his black masses and satanic rituals that mimic Catholic rituals in an evil, perverted way.

• When psychologists and psychiatrists diagnose cases of demonic possession, which, whether you believe in them or not, still occur in the modern world, whom do they turn to for help? The Catholic Church. Crucifixes, holy water, consecrated hosts, blessed objects, Catholic priests, and the rite of exorcism spell terror for demons who don't want to be sent back to the arid wastes by the true representatives of God.

Peter the Rock

Knowing that he would not be around much longer to lead his fledgling church, Christ ordained Simon Peter in Caesarea Philippi to be the Catholic Church's spiritual representative in his absence. To test his faith, Jesus asked Simon who he was, and Simon immediately replied, "You are the Messiah, the Son of the Living God."
Then Jesus said unto Simon:

> *"Blest are you, Simon son of Jonah! No mere man has revealed this to you, but my heavenly Father. I for my part declare to you, thou art 'Rock,' and on this rock I will build my church, and the jaws of death shall not prevail against it. I will entrust you the keys of the kingdom of heaven. Whatever you declare bound on earth shall be bound in heaven; whatever you declare loosed on earth shall be loosed in heaven."*[3]

To symbolically confirm Simon bar Jonah as the solid foundation of the

Catholic Church, Jesus renamed his chief apostle "Peter," which means "Rock."[4]

In matters pertaining to faith, morals, and jurisdiction, Simon Peter's divinely-appointed headship over the Catholic Church was recognized by all the apostles and early disciples, including the apostle Paul. There was no question of Peter's authority over the church after Christ ascended into heaven. Whenever a council was convened by the apostles, Peter was always acknowledged as its head, even though differences of opinion, as in the matter of Jewish practices, existed in the early church.

After the Council of Jerusalem in 51, in which Simon Peter served as chairman, he established a bishopric in Antioch, and then traveled west to Rome where he established his permanent See. There, in Rome, Peter was crucified upside down in the Roman Circus by Emperor Nero around 64-66. Peter's establishment of his Holy See in Rome and his martyrdom there is not mentioned in the Bible, but we know it to be true from the writings of the early church fathers Tertullian, Ignatius of Antioch, Irenaeus, Clement of Alexandria, and Eusebius of Caesarea.[5]

Why did Simon Peter establish his Holy See in Rome and not in Jerusalem? There are two reasons: First, Christ specifically wanted the vicar of his church to be in Rome, the geopolitical center of the world, because Rome ruled the world and was the "New Babylon," the throne of the Beast. If Christianity was to defeat Satan it had to defeat him from within the devil's capitol and nowhere else, and, second, the capitol of the Christian Church couldn't remain in Jerusalem because the Christian community knew Christ's prophecy of the coming destruction of Jerusalem and had fled across the Jordan to Pella by the time Emperor Titus sacked that city in A.D. 70.[6] Any Jew who hadn't yet fled Jerusalem was put to the sword or sold into slavery. The remainder of the Jews in Palestine were routed by Emperor Hadrian between the years A.D. 132-135, and were dispersed throughout the world (the *diaspora*). Their descendants wouldn't return to Palestine until 1948, nineteen centuries later.

Since Peter was the Bishop of Rome and established his Holy See there, Peter's successors had to have their episcopates in Rome as well. Peter's first three successors in Rome are known from the writings of St. Irenaeus, the great theologian and Bishop of Lyons, who wrote in *Adversus Haereses*[7] (c. 180) that Linus was named as Peter's first successor, and after him was Anacletus (Cletus), and after Cletus was Clement of Rome. The rest of Peter's successors are too well documented by other contemporary historians to be refuted.

In the year 375, after the Roman Empire had converted to Christianity, the title of "Supreme Pontiff" was given to the Bishop of Rome by Emperor Gratian. The pope then became known as the *Pontifex Maximus*, or the supreme "bridgemaker" between heaven and earth; an honorary title previously reserved only for the Roman emperor. Before long Christians started referring to the Roman pontiff as the "pope"; a familiar, loving term derived from the Latin words, *pater paternis* ("papa" for short), which means "father of fathers." This is how the pope has come to be known as the "Holy Father."

Throughout the years, many other titles have been given to the pope to designate his multiple roles and offices: the "Successor of St. Peter," the "Prince of the Apostles," "Primate of Italy," "Archbishop and Metropolitan of the Roman Province," "Sovereign of the State of Vatican City," "Servant of the Servants of God," "Head of the College of Bishops," "Pastor of the Universal Church," and "Patriarch of the West"[8] to name a few.

Heresies Attack the Early Church

Christ promised to St. Peter and the rest of his apostles that the gates of hell would not prevail against the Catholic Church, and for two thousand years, Christ has kept his promise. Although many have tried, no one has been able to destroy the Roman Catholic Church. It is the oldest geopolitical institution on earth, having outlasted every empire, kingdom, government, dictatorship, tyranny, persecution, and heresy that the devil could throw at it—especially the latter.

From the beginning, Satan's favorite method of assailing the Catholic Church has been to attack it from within with heretical doctrines; hoping, of course, to divide the offspring of the Woman—those who keep God's commandments and give witness to Jesus. The number of early heresies is long and tedious but important to note because of how they've been repackaged into today's post-modernistic, anti-Catholic world view. As the Bible says, nothing new is under the sun, including the popular "New Age" movement that is drawing so many millions into heresy:

> "What has been, that will be; what has been done, that will be done. Nothing is new under the sun. Even the thing of which we say, 'See, this is new!' has already existed in the ages that preceded us."[9]

Toward the end of the first century, *Ebionite* heretics denied the divinity of Christ, rejected all the New Testament except St. Matthew, and claimed that part of mankind was created by good angels and the rest by bad angels. *Simonian* heretics, on the other hand, were followers of Simon Magus, a Samaritan sorcerer who believed he was God and who denied the humanity of Christ and man's free will, and who believed in reincarnation. *Cerinthian* heretics denied that God was the creator of the world, insisted that the law of Moses was necessary for salvation, and denied the divinity of Christ.

At the beginning of the second century, *Basilidian* heretics rejected the revelation of scripture, claimed that the God of the Jews was an angel and that the world was created by angels, denied the humanity of Christ, repudiated his miracles, denied the resurrection of the body, and denied Jesus' Passion and Crucifixion. *Gnostics*, on the other hand, were followers of an apostate named Carpocratian, who believed that secret knowledge, or *gnosis*, was to be experienced by only a select few, and that their Gnosticism provided a deeper insight into Christian doctrine than Catholic revelation and faith. Gnostics denied the divinity of Christ, believed that Christ was a ghost and not real flesh and blood, denied Christ's atonement for sins and the resurrection of the body, rejected the Ten Commandments and the God of the Old Testament, believed that all matter like the body was evil, and that an equally powerful bad god created the material world. Some Gnostic sects promoted sensual immorality as a means of union with God and believed in the existence of two souls and reincarnation.

Two other heretical groups, the *Docetists* and *Phantasianists,* denied Christ's humanity (calling it mere appearance), while the *Valentinians* claimed that Mary was not the Mother of God, that salvation is through justification by faith alone (like Protestants), that there is no free will, that people are predestined to be good or bad, and that there is no resurrection of the body. *Marcionites* believed, like the Gnostics did, that there was a good god who created the spiritual realm and an evil god who created the material world. In addition, Marcionites denied the incarnation, rejected the Old Testament, said that the Canon of the Bible consisted only of parts of St. Luke's Gospel and ten letters of St. Paul, and contended that only Jesus the man suffered, not Jesus the Lord. *Cerdonians* believed in two gods (one good and the other evil), denied the resurrection of the body, prohibited marriage, and rejected the Old Testament.

Never seeming to run out of lies, toward the latter half of the second century, Satan concocted a form of religious extremism called *Montanism,* which became popular among many church dissidents. Montanists believed in a rigorous morality, the imminent second coming of Christ, denied the divine nature of the church and its power to forgive sins, and believed that second marriages were adulterous. Another band of late-second-century heretics known as the *Encratites* believed, like the Gnostics, that all matter was evil (as did their breakaway group, the *Severians,* who also believed like the Darwinists of today that matter is eternal and uncreated). *Monarchian* heretics, in turn, denied the doctrine of the Trinity (one God in three persons) and promulgated the heresy that God the Father, God the Son, and God the Holy Spirit were the same person.

Unfortunately, some of the most respected members of the early Catholic Church became heretics. In the first half of the third century, the Christian writer and theologian Tertullian fell under the evil spell of the Montanists, and defected to their side around the year 213. His heretical followers were called *Tertullianists,* and they had bizarre notions, such as that it was unlawful to flee from the persecutions of the Roman emperors. Another group of heretics known as *Origenists* were named after Origen, a well-known Christian theologian turned heretical writer who contended that from the beginning, all human creatures were pure spirits. Origenists believed in a universal restoration following the second coming of Christ, where even those suffering damnation in hell would become pure spirits (but saints could be kicked out of heaven for committing transgressions there). *Novatianists* were followers of a scurrilous priest named Novatian, who set himself up as an anti-pope when he failed to be nominated Bishop of Rome. Novatianists were the introducers of another oppressive heresy called "rigorism," which had a rigoristic attitude towards those who had left the church and returned, or who had lapsed from the faith and repented. To Novatianists, no sin was to be forgiven after baptism, and second marriages were absolutely forbidden.

A particularly loathsome second-century heresy named *Manichaeanism* would reappear in the twelfth and thirteenth century as the heresies of *Albigensianism* and *Catharism.* Manichaean heretics were followers of Mani the Persian, who wandered aimlessly for forty years proclaiming himself to be the "Last Messenger of the True God," and the "Paraclete" that Jesus had promised to send. Manichaeans believed that Satan was an eternally evil god and was the equally powerful rival of the good god. Manichaeans believed Satan came forth from the darkness and wasn't a heavenly angel. They also believed that the devil created matter, which is evil, rejected the Old Testament, claimed that there was two good gods (one of the Old Testament and one of the New), alleged that Christ was pure spirit, espoused reincarnation, and held that human souls had been cast down to earth into material bodies because they had sinned in heaven. Manichaeans rejected the sacraments and the authority of the Catholic Church and state, and adhered to a rigorous moral code. Furthermore, Manichaeans viewed the supreme objection of mankind to be the liberation from matter, like Eastern religions believe.

Around the middle of the third century, *Neoplatonism* drew many members away from the church, especially educators and intellectuals who had studied the writings of the ancient Greek philosophers. Introduced between A.D. 200-250 by the philosophers Saccas, Plotinus, and Porphyry, Neoplatonism encouraged a breakaway from orthodox Christianity and a return to the classical philosophies of Plato and Aristotle. Neoplatonists believed in a magical, mystical interrelationship of sympathies and antipathies between heaven and earth, and a union between "the One" and "the soul" through ecstatic trances. The European rediscovery of the writings of ancient Greek and Roman philosophers from Arab libraries during the later Middle Ages (1200s-1400s) led to the popular revival of Neoplatonism in Italy and the rest of Europe during the Renaissance (1400-1600), and the subsequent development of the ruinous, man-centered philosophies of humanism and rationalism.

Towards the later half of the third century, *Sabellianism* contended that the Father, Son, and Holy Ghost are not three distinct persons in one Godhead, but are three different modes of being and self-manifestations of one God. Another late-third-century heresy called *Donatism* declared that baptism administered by heretics is invalid, that sanctity was a requirement for church membership, and that re-baptism was necessary for belonging to their sect.

As harmful as all these early heresies were to the early Catholic Church, none damaged its unity quite like *Arianism*.

The Arian Heresy

In 311, Emperor Galerius issued an edict of toleration of all Christians in the Western Roman Empire. Two years later, Constantine the Great issued his famous "Edict of Milan," which, for the first time in history, officially recognized Christianity as a lawful religion within the Western Roman Empire. The year before, Constantine had won a great battle for the control of the Western Roman Empire against the pagan tyrant Maxentius. As legend goes, Constantine marched into Rome at midday and saw a cross of light surrounded by the words, *"In hoc signo vinces"* ("In this sign thou shalt conquer"). The following night, Christ appeared to Constantine in a dream, telling him to adopt the Christian Cross as his standard rather than the Roman Eagle. Constantine ordered the monogram of Christ (the Chi-Rho) to be painted on the shields of his soldiers and a standard, fashioned after the cross, to be born by him in battle. Having followed Christ's instructions to the letter, on the day of battle Constantine defeated Maxentius at the Milvian Bridge near the river Tiber, just north of Rome. Maxentius and thousands of his men perished in the waters of the Tiber.

The consequences of Constantine's victory over Maxentius were enormous: the God of the Christians defeated the pagan gods of Maxentius, and Rome, now under the benevolent leadership of Emperor Constantine I, was much more inclined towards Christianity than paganism.

When Constantine defeated the Eastern Roman Emperor Licinius in 324, and became the sole ruler over both the Western and Eastern Roman Empires, he built magnificent Catholic churches and endowed them with lavish gifts and landed property. It was during this period that Constantine began to take a much more active role in ecclesiastical affairs of the Catholic Church and strengthened the power and influence of the Roman Catholic bishops. The sacrifice to pagan gods was discouraged as Constantine openly proclaimed his desire for the conversion of his subjects to Christianity.

A new heresy called *Arianism* began to surface during the reign of Constantine I, which would become a serious threat to Catholic unity. Arianism was named after Arius (256-336), a native of Libya who studied at the theological school of Lucian of Antioch. In 319, following his ordination as a Catholic priest in Alexandria, Arius became involved in a heated controversy with his bishop concerning the divinity of Christ, claiming that Christ was a creature like all other creatures and was not divinely eternal in substance and nature with the Father, and only became part of the divine nature of God in compensation for his death on the cross. Causing a huge rift to develop within the Catholic Church regarding the true nature of Christ, Arius set up his own hierarchy of schismatic Arian bishops and churches, especially within the Eastern Roman Empire. Seeing the havoc that Arianism was wreaking upon Christian unity, Emperor Constantine the Great convened the Council of Nicaea in 325 to resolve the matter. During the assembly, the Catholic Council of Nicaea condemned Arianism as heretical, and, in the context of their Nicene Creed, proclaimed the official position of the church that Christ was begotten, not made, remaining consubstantial (one in being) with the Father. Following the condemnation of Arianism and shortly after the close of the Nicene Council, Arius and his followers were banished to Illyria.

The Council of Nicaea, however, failed to eradicate Arianism altogether. In fact, Arianism was poised for a stunning comeback. This is how Arianism nearly destroyed Christian unity.

Constantinia, the sister of Constantine, was herself a fanatical Arianist, and had as her spiritual advisor the infamous Arian Bishop Eusebius of Nicomedia, who, like Arius, was exiled to Illyria after the Council of Nicaea. The priest who took Bishop Eusebius's place as Constantinia's spiritual advisor was, as fate would have it, another Arian heretic. History records that when Constantinia was about to die, she recommended this new Arian priest to the care of her brother, and before long he convinced Emperor Constantine that Arius was not a heretic after all. Consequently, Constantine recalled Bishop Eusebius and the other Arians back from exile in 334 and reinstated Arius to his former position in the priesthood. To make matters worse for the Catholic Church, Constantine's last act before he died in 337 was to be baptized by the Arian bishop Eusebius.

As a result of Constantine's espousal of Arianism, the terrible rift between Arians and Catholics was renewed again for another forty years, with the proponents of Arianism, especially in the East under the persecutory leadership of Constantius II, himself an avowed Arianist, seemingly on the verge of victory over the orthodox Catholics.

But true to his promise that the gates of hell would never prevail against his church, Jesus Christ raised up champions of the orthodox Catholic faith in the persons of St. Athanasius, St. Basil, St. Gregory of Nyssa, and St. Gregory of Nazianzus. As a result of their heroic efforts in defense of the one true faith against Arianism, on the 28th of February, A.D. 380, Emperor Gratian in the West and Theodosius in the East issued an edict of uniformity, that abolished all toleration of Arianism and paganism, marking the complete reunion of eastern and western churches under the orthodox Catholic faith. A year later, the first Council of Constance condemned Arianism and reaffirmed the Nicene Creed. Likewise, pagan sacrifices were henceforth forbidden and all pagan temples were ordered closed forever. In their places great houses of Catholic worship sprang up, and the last stronghold of paganism, the philosophical school of Athens, was finally closed by Justinian the Great in 529.

For all practical purposes, by the end of the fourth century Arianism and paganism were defeated in the Roman Empire. The fifth century, however, saw the resurgence of newer satanic heresies. The Ecumenical Council of Ephesus in 431 condemned the new heresy of *Nestorianism*, which denied the unity of the divine and human natures in the person of Jesus Christ. Nestorians maintained that Jesus was not God, that God only dwelt in him as a temple, and that Mary was not the Mother of God. The Council of Ephesus also condemned the heresy of *Pelagianism*, which said that man, by his own natural powers and free will, could be sinless and become like a son of God, that Adam's sin was purely personal and didn't pass the stain of original sin on to all humanity, that we are born free of sin like Adam and Eve, that man can do anything God can do, that we don't need a redeemer because the Mosaic Law is sufficient to save us, that there were men who were sinless before Christ, that we don't need God's grace for salvation, and that Peter had no authority over the other apostles.

Another new heresy called *Monophysitism* was condemned by the Council of Chalcedon in 451. It denied the humanity of Christ by claiming that he had a divine nature but no human nature. Out of Monophysitism rose yet another new heresy called *Monothelitism*, which proposed that since Christ is one person, he only has one will rather than two wills (the divine and human). Monothelitism was condemned as a heresy by the Council of Constantinople in 680, which reaffirmed that Christ has two wills corresponding to both his divine and human natures.

The Violent Rise of Islam

Despite the incredible number of heresies that Satan threw at the early church, by the beginning of the seventh century Catholicism had spread throughout most of Europe, North Africa, and Asia Minor, and was promising to convert the whole world to Christ. Unable to stop the spread of Catholicism with heretical doctrines and ten imperial persecutions of Christians by pagan Roman emperors,[10] Satan decided the time had come for a brand new religion to challenge Christianity. This new religion, founded by him, a fallen archangel, would subtly mix the truth with lies, and would be given to the descendants of Abraham's illegitimate son Ishmael, whom the Bible called "a wild ass of a man."[11]

Masquerading as an angel of light, Satan appeared to the Arab Muhammed and announced that both Judaism and Christianity were in error, that Jesus was not divine, that there was no Trinity, and that Allah wanted to give him, Muhammed, the true gospel (which was later assembled from Muhammed's oral teachings and called the "Koran," or "the reading"). The name of this heretical new religion is, of course, Islam, which means "submission to the will of Allah," and its followers are called "Muslims," which means "those who submit."

With incredible foresight, St. Paul had warned the Christians at Corinth in the first century to be on guard against such false apostles preaching "a different gospel" or "another Jesus," because the devil can disguise himself as an "angel of light":

> "For if someone comes and preaches another Jesus than the one we preached, or if you receive a different spirit than the one you received or a different gospel than the one you accepted, you put up with it well enough . . . For such people are false apostles, deceitful workers, who masquerade as apostles of Christ. And no wonder, for even Satan masquerades as an angel of light. So it is not strange that his ministers also masquerade as ministers of righteousness. Their end will correspond to their deeds."[12]

Muhammed's religion of the angel spread like a plague throughout the Middle East and North Africa, gaining its new converts not by love, but by the point of a sword. Vowing to overthrow Judeo-Christianity and convert the world to Islam, as many still do today, fanatical Arab hordes declared a *jihad* ("holy war") on the historic centers of Christian civilization such as Jerusalem, Antioch, Alexandria, and Carthage.[13] Christianity on the European continent was in danger of annihilation, too, as Muslim invaders captured Spain in 714, and then besieged France in 732. But one thing the invading Arabs hadn't taken into account was Christ's promise that his church would never be conquered. Christian forces in Europe defeated the invading Muslims at Poitiers, France, in 732; in Spain in 1212; at Vienna, Austria, in 1529; in the Mediterranean Sea at the Battle of Lepanto in 1571; at Vienna again in 1683; at Belgrade in 1717; and finally in the Balkans in 1912.[14] Notwithstanding their repeated attempts, the Muslims failed to conquer Christianity.

Islam failed to conquer the Roman Catholic Church but had much better success against the Eastern Orthodox Church, capturing most of its lands and greatly reducing its power and influence. The Eastern Orthodox Church of the Byzantine Roman Empire, headquartered in what is now Turkey, had split from the Roman Catholic Church in 1054 over disagreements with papal authority. Relations between eastern and western patriarchies had been growing worse over the centuries, especially since the introduction of the eighth-century eastern heresy of *Iconoclasm* (which maintained that religious statues and painting, so prevalent in the Catholic Church, were idolatrous), and the ninth-century eastern heresy of *Photianism* (which claimed that the Holy Spirit proceeded from the Father, but not the Son). The Greek Schism from the Roman Catholic Church in 1054, and again in 1281, proved disastrous for the Eastern Orthodox Church: the Byzantine capitol of Constantinople, the center of the Eastern Orthodox Church, fell to the Turks in 1453, and has remained in the hands of the Muslims ever since, while the Vatican in Rome, the capitol of Western Christendom, remains to this day in the hands of Christians. History has proven time and time again that God protects his One True Church.

More Heresies in the Second Millennium

The Roman Catholic Church was triumphant over every new heresy in the first millennium, but newer heresies would continue to plague it in the second. *Berengarianism,* a callow heresy which denied the Real Presence in the Holy Eucharist, disrupted the Catholic Church in the middle of the eleventh century, but the eighth-century Miracle of Lanciano, in which a consecrated host turned into real flesh and the consecrated wine into real blood during a doubting priest's celebration of mass, had already disproved that heresy. Numerous other Eucharistic miracles have occurred since Lanciano, the most recent being on December 8, 1991, (the Solemnity of the Immaculate Conception) in Betania, Venezuela, where during an outside mass, the host, at the moment of consecration, bled in front of hundreds of eyewitnesses. The Eucharistic miracle of Betania was captured on video and has been shown in a recent documentary film about a Marian visionary from that area named Maria Esperanza.

With the eleventh-century heresy of Berengarianism defeated by the Miracle of Lanciano, the third-century heresy of Manichaeanism resurfaced again in the eleventh century as *Albigensianism.* Centered in the southern French town of Albi, Albigensians (or Cathars, as they were also known) denied the Trinity, the human birth and resurrection of Christ, believed in a New Testament good god and an Old Testament evil god, believed that the evil god of the Old Testament or Satan created matter which was evil, rejected the sacraments, disdained marriage, adopted sexual promiscuity and vegetarianism, condemned infant baptism and the forgiveness of the fallen away, denied the Holy Spirit's inspiration in the New Testament, repudiated the right of the state to punish criminals, and discarded the role of the clergy. Pope Innocent III (who served as pope from 1198-1216) sanctioned new preaching missions to convert the Cathars to Catholicism until one of his representatives in the region, Peter of Castelnau, was assassinated by them in 1208. Innocent thereupon authorized the weapons of the Crusade as a means of fighting the Cathar heretics, and, by the end of the fourteenth century, the Catholic Church had successfully eradicated Albigensianism from Europe.

In the twelfth century, adherents of the new heresy of *Waldensianism* rejected purgatory and devotion to the saints, protested against Catholic icons, refused to swear oaths, denied the sacraments of penance, holy orders, marriage, extreme unction and confirmation, and denounced indulgences, fasts, and ceremonies. Waldensianism was started by the Frenchman Peter Valdes (incorrectly named "Waldo"), a rich merchant of Lyon and vehement opponent of France's comfortable ecclesiastical establishment. Waldo and his followers, known as the "Poor Men of Lyon," gave away their possessions and preached against the worldliness and materialism of the clergy and the invalidity of the sacraments administered by them. Henceforth, the Catholic archbishop of Lyon forbade the Waldenses to preach in his jurisdiction. The Waldenses were later excommunicated in 1184 by the Council of Verona and persecuted along with the Albigensians in southern France.[15]

In the fourteenth and fifteenth centuries, another new heresy known as *humanism* surfaced amongst the European nobility and the ecclesiastical hierarchy of the Catholic Church following the recent discovery of the ancient writings of the classical Greek philosophers from the libraries of the Arabs during the time of the Crusades (1095-1270), and from the influx of Greek scholars fleeing from the Muslim Turks who were besieging Constantinople in the fifteenth century. Advocating the return to the classical teachings and values of the ancient Greek and Roman philosophers for their own sake rather then their relevance to Christianity, Humanists in the church and state espoused a critical, man-centered individualism and discarded the God-centered Scholasticism being taught in the Catholic universities since the eleventh century. Italian Humanists like Dante, Boccaccio, Petrarch, Pico della Mirandola, Marsilino Ficino, and Cosimo de Medici, the founder of the Platonic Academy of Florence, aspired to "humanize" the virtues of the ancient pagan philosophers and thereby generate a scholarly, religiously neutral approach to civilization. Humanists of the European Renaissance (1400-1600) sought to move away from Jesus Christ as the center of man's interest back to man himself, and many Humanists used this new philosophy to justify their lavish, decadent self-indulgences. Consequently, humanism revived the age-old conflicts between opulent Greek and Roman paganism and self-denying Christianity, which, in turn, headed Western civilization down the slippery slope of disunity and secularization.

The man-centered humanism of the Renaissance provoked a conservative backlash by anti-Catholics who were appalled at the decadence and laxity that had entered the church during the Renaissance, thereby ushering in the most destructive heresy yet—*Protestantism,* which officially began in 1517 with the coming of Martin Luther, was, in reality, a re-synthesis of the age-old heresies of Valentinianism, Nestorianism, Pelagianism, Iconoclasm, Berengarianism, Albigensianism, and Waldensianism.[16] Like the Bible says, "Nothing new is under the sun."

Martin Luther

"Nothing can be more poisonous, harmful or devilish than a man in rebellion."
                                                                    Martin Luther

"There are certain passages in (Paul's letter's) hard to understand. The ignorant and the unstable distort them (just as they do the rest of scripture) to their own ruin."[2]
                                                                    Pet. 3:16

The Catholic Church, when taken as an institution, is holy and perfect like its founder, Jesus Christ, but when taken as a group of people it involves all the faults and weaknesses characteristic of human beings. The church has never claimed that all its members have been saints. In fact, it openly admits that many of its members have been downright scoundrels. Having had many undesirable elements within its hierarchy, however, doesn't mean that the church itself is flawed, or that it should be overthrown. The United States wouldn't abolish the office of the president because it's had several wayward chief executives, so we shouldn't expect the Catholic Church to eliminate its papacy or ecclesiastical hierarchy because of the bad actions of its more notorious members.

Notwithstanding Christ's promise of divine protection for the Catholic Church, throughout history numerous anti-Catholics have regularly cited real and/or imagined abuses within the papacy and priestly hierarchy as justification for their rebellion against church authority and church doctrine. Such is the case with the two most notable forerunners of the Protestant rebellion, John Wycliff and Jan Hus.

In the later half of the fourteenth century, an English philosopher and theologian from Oxford named John Wycliff, dubbed the "Morningstar of the Protestant Reformation," set off a firestorm of controversy when he publicly castigated the hierarchy of the Catholic Church in England for being power mad and materialistic. Wycliff used these charges, which had some merit, as a vehicle to attack the Catholic Church's teachings. Denouncing as unscriptural many of the beliefs and practices of the established church, Wycliff denied the divinely-commissioned authority of the pope and the bishops, dismissed the doctrine of transubstantiation, and rejected the sacrament of penance and the practice of selling indulgences. Arguing that the Bible alone is sufficient for faith, Wycliff favored a more direct relationship with God without the necessity of popes, prelates, or priests as mediators.

Wycliff's attacks on the papacy and church hierarchy couldn't have come at a worse time because the church was already embroiled in a terribly factious split called the "Great Western Schism of 1378-1417." During this darkest period in church history, three rivals for the papacy in Avignon, Rome, and Pisa simultaneously claimed to be the one true pope of the Catholic Church. Needless to say, having three people claim to be pope terribly undermined the authority and prestige of the papacy, and it wasn't until the Council of Constance in 1415, which reunited the church again under one pope, that the reputation of the papacy was restored to its former good standing.

The Great Western Schism had followed another tumultuous period in Catholic Church history known as the "Babylonian Captivity of 1309-1377," in which the papal court was moved to Avignon, France, for the reign of seven French popes over a period of seventy years. Factionalism of French and Italian churchmen, power struggles over the interests of church and state, political, and ecclesiastical turmoil in Italy—all were significant factors contributing to the "Babylonian Captivity" of the papacy, which finally ended when Pope Gregory XI moved the papacy back to Rome in 1377 at the petition of the great Italian mystic, Saint Catherine of Siena.

The heretic John Wycliff surreptitiously used the Babylonian Captivity and Great Western Schism as justification for his own dissension against church teaching and authority, which earned him an international reputation as a provocateur. The most dissident English priest of the Great Western Schism, Wycliff first got his reputation as an agitator in 1374 during a dispute between King Edward III of England and Pope Gregory XI over England's reluctance to pay papal tributes to Rome. Both the English king and English parliament were unwilling to pay papal levies, so Wycliff wrote several pamphlets refuting the pope's authority in England and upholding the right of the English parliament to limit church control in their country. Two years later, Wycliff formulated his doctrine of "dominion as founded in grace," which said that all temporal and spiritual authority is conferred directly by the grace of God and is consequently forfeited when the wielder of that authority, such as the pope and church hierarchy, is guilty of mortal sin. Wycliff did not explicitly say that he considered the Catholic Church to be sinful and worldly, but his insinuation was unequivocal.

Because of his heretical pamphlets supporting the English government's position against Rome, Wycliff was called before the Bishop of London, William Courtenay, on February 19, 1377, to give an account of his doctrines.

The inquisition abruptly ended, though, when John of Gaunt, who had escorted Wycliff, became involved in a fracas with the bishop and his staff. Consequently, on May 22, 1377, Pope Gregory XI issued several bulls accusing Wycliff of heresy, and in May of the following year, Courtenay, now the Archbishop of Canterbury, convened an ecclesiastical court that condemned Wycliff as a heretic and brought about his expulsion from Oxford. Retired to his parish of Lutterworth, the condemned Wycliff died in 1382 before the authorities could carry out his sentence of execution.[17] Unable to carry out sentencing, the Council of Constance (1414-1418) ordered Wycliff's writings burned and his interred remains removed from holy ground and incinerated as a symbolic gesture of his damnation in hell as a heretic, which seems very disrespectful on the part of the church to us today.

Wycliff's followers, the "Lollards," were disbanded at the beginning of the fifteenth century, but not before they had influenced another dissident priest, Jan Hus (1369-1415), to denounce the Catholic Church. Hus, a Bohemian preacher from Prague, was captivated by the schismatic rhetoric of John Wycliff, and like Wycliff before him, publicly criticized the papacy and church hierarchy for their abuses of power and authority. Going against church teachings, Hus believed in the predestination of souls, regarded the Bible as the ultimate religious authority, and held that Jesus Christ, rather than the corrupt ecclesiastical hierarchy, is the true head of the Christian community. Oral tradition, the teaching Magisterium of the church, the divinely-appointed vicarship of Peter, and the ordination of the clergy were irrelevant to Hus because of the prevalent abuses he perceived existed within the church.

Hus's heretical teachings and his demand for radical reforms in the church hierarchy eventually led to his denunciation in 1407, his banning from preaching in 1408, and the burning of his books in 1409. Excommunicated first in 1410, and again in 1412, Hus was called before the Council of Constance in 1414 to defend himself against charges of heresy. Immediately upon his arrival at Constance, Hus was taken prisoner by his enemies. When brought before the Council of Constance, church authorities ordered Hus to recant his heretical teachings and to stop preaching. Refusing to do either, Jan Hus was burned at the stake on July 6, 1415.

Following the deaths of the dissidents John Wycliff and Jan Hus, the perfect vehicle for spreading rebellion against the church finally arrived in 1455, the year Johann Gutenberg invented the movable metal-type printing press in Germany. With the invention of the Gutenberg press, the Bible no longer had to be painstakingly hand-written by monks in monasteries and sold at prohibitive prices to theologians and educators; now it could be cheaply printed in large quantities and easily distributed to the masses. With the Bible now in the hands of commoners, who were free to interpret it however they wished, the Catholic Church's divinely-appointed authority was made more vulnerable to attack. All that was needed was someone brazen enough to come forward and challenge the church by using the Bible as his sole authority. That someone was Martin Luther.

Martin Luther, the founding father of Protestantism, was born on November 10, 1483, and christened "Martin" on November 11 in honor of St. Martin's Day. Young Martin grew up in a strict household with an abusive father, John Luder, who was a rough coal-miner and was said to have once killed a man with his horse bridle during an argument.[18] Perhaps because Martin disliked his cruel father so much, or disliked what his father's last name meant (Luder, in German, means carrion, beast, wretch, debauched, vulgar, lure, bait, whore, or low scoundrel), in 1512 he changed his last name to Luther. Since Martin like playing the lute, a stringed instrument similar to a guitar, Martin "Luter" or "Luther" sounded much more agreeable to him than Martin Luder.

In 1505, Martin Luther enrolled at the University of Erfurt to study law. That July, during a sudden thunderstorm, a bolt of lightning threw Luther and his riding companion from their horses, instantly killing his friend. Overcome with fear, Luther cried out to St. Anne for mercy: "Help me, St. Anne; I will become a monk!"[19] The lightning bolt that killed his friend and nearly killed him had Luther so scared that he vowed to quit law school and enter a monastery. Against the wishes of his family and friends, Luther joined the Augustinian Eremites in Erfurt on July 17, 1505.

On April 3, 1507, Martin Luther was ordained a priest at the Cathedral of Mary in Erfurt. During the solemn celebration of his first mass, Luther froze at the moment of the consecration of the Eucharist, and was unable to speak or move for several minutes (Luther later said it was because he couldn't fathom holding God in his hands). Whatever the real cause of his panic attack, as a monk, Luther was a nervous wreck—no amount of penance could overcome his fear of being damned for all eternity. Luther would spend hours examining his conscience and an equal amount of time in the confessional pouring over his sins in the greatest of detail, much to the annoyance of his confessors. No matter how many works of piety or mortifications of the flesh he performed, Luther couldn't rid himself of the thoughts that kept resounding over and over in his mind that he was going to hell. Luther was so obsessed with his sins that his fellow monks thought him mad. Years later, as an ex-monk, Luther wrote about his excessive scrupulosity and punctiliousness at the Erfurt monastery: "From misplaced reliance on my righteousness my heart became full of distrust, doubt, fear, hatred, and blasphemy of God. I was such an enemy of Christ that whenever I saw an image or a picture of Him hanging on His Cross, I loathed the sight and shut my eyes and felt that I would have rather seen the devil. My spirit was completely broken and I was always in a state of melancholy; for, do what I would, my 'righteousness' and my 'good works' brought me no help or consolation."[20]

Of course, Luther found no solace in trying to keep the rigid monastic vows of poverty, chastity, and obedience because he entered the monastery out of fear of being damned and not out of love for God or the religious life. No matter how hard he tried Luther just couldn't observe the strict rules of monasticism, especially chastity. As a virile young man, Luther longed to satisfy the constant cravings of the flesh. "I am inflamed with carnal desire" he wrote, "while I ought to be fervent in the spirit. I am on fire with the great flame of my unbridled flesh and sit here in leisure and laziness neglecting prayer."[21]

To rid his guilty conscience over his lustful desires, Luther fabricated a whole new theology of salvation; a salvation without obedience to the Ten Commandments; one that would justify carnality and wantonness without the fear of damnation. While sitting in the *cloaca* (toilet) one day,[22] Luther was suddenly struck by St. Paul's passage in Hebrews that said " . . . the just shall live by faith,"[23] to which Luther added one key word not found in the original text, a word which significantly altered the meaning of that passage. The key word that Luther affixed was *alone*. Now, instead of " . . . the just shall live by faith," it became " . . . the just shall live by faith alone." With Luther's insertion of a single word another new heresy was born—the Protestant heresy of *sola fide* or "faith alone." No longer were good works, obedience to the Ten Commandments, or mortifications of the flesh necessary for salvation—faith alone in Jesus Christ assured your entrance into heaven.

Believing that he had rediscovered the true way to heaven, Luther prepared himself mentally to challenge the Catholic Church regarding their doctrine of salvation through faith and good works. He went to work immediately.

On the eve of All Saints' Day, October 31, 1517, more commonly known as Halloween, Martin Luther, age 33, the same age as Christ when he was nailed to the cross, nailed a list of 95 theses to the church door of Wittenberg Castle demanding that Archbishop Albrecht of Mainz put an end to the sale of indulgences (tithes given to remit temporal punishment or get people out of purgatory), which were being sold by the Dominican monk, Johannes Tetzel, in the Brandenburg territories near Wittenberg for the construction of St. Peter's Basilica in Rome. Insisting that salvation for souls came only through *sola fide*, Luther vehemently objected to what he thought was Tetzel's overzealous ways of selling salvation for a price.

Luther was convinced that the pope would support his 95 theses, but when he found out that the pope had interpreted his theses as an attack on papal authority and had sided with Tetzel and Archbishop Albrecht, he knew that he was in danger of being condemned a heretic. Martin Luther was quickly summoned before his superiors to give an accounting for his actions. In defending his 95 theses before his superiors, Luther, like Wycliff before him, argued that the Bible's authority superceded the authority of the pope and the church councils. Scripture, Luther contended, is the ultimate authority; not the priests, bishops, cardinals, church fathers, doctors, teaching magisterium, ecumenical councils, or popes.[24]

Calling his heretical belief *sola scriptura,* "scripture alone," Luther used it to defend *sola fide* by contending that the apostle Paul had made it clear in Hebrews and Romans that justification comes from "faith alone" through unmerited "grace alone" *(sola gratia).* According to Luther's exegesis of Paul's writings, good works and good will were no longer necessary for salvation; all people had to do was accept Jesus Christ as their Lord and personal Savior and wait to be taken to heaven. Once you've accepted Christ, Luther maintained, nothing you could do or sin you could commit could take away your eternal salvation. Gaining rewards and merits though charity, obedience, suffering, self-denial, contrition, piety, sacrifice, and mortifications of the flesh wasn't necessary for salvation anymore. Besides, Luther declared, man can do no good anyway. Because of original sin, Luther maintained, human beings are totally corrupt. The devil enslaves our wills. We are no better than "dung."[25]

Luther's *sole fide,* like the second-century heresy of Valentinianism, was a whole lot easier than the Catholic belief in faith and good works. With *sola fide* no one had to keep the Ten Commandments anymore. The fear of eternal punishments for sins had been taken away. The only mortal sin, according to Luther, was the sin of unbelief in Jesus Christ. So confident was Luther of *sola fide* that he goaded the sinner to "boast of his sinfulness."[26] "Be a sinner and sin stoutly," Luther asserted, "but trust in Christ much more firmly . . . even should you practice whoredom a thousand times a day or deal just as many death-dealing blows."[27] Luther even went so far as to equate keeping the Ten Commandments with hating God: "The [Mosaic] Law," Luther said, "brings forth hatred of God."[28] According to Luther, Moses, the one who brought us the Law, was, "worse than the pope and the devil."[29] Evidently, Luther had forgotten what the apostle Paul said about sinning and the just laws given to Moses from God:

> "What, then, are we to say? 'Let us continue in sin that grace may abound?' Certainly not! How can we who died to sin go on living in it?"[30]

> "What follows from what I have said? That the [Mosaic] law is the same as sin? Certainly not!. . . Yet the law is holy and the commandment is holy and just and good."[31]

A lot of Christians were coming to believe in Luther's heretical doctrine of easy salvation through cheap grace, so the Catholic Church had to do something about Luther and do it fast. After the Diet of Augsburg, around the middle of October in 1518, Luther was summoned to appear before Cardinal Cajetan for questioning about his heretical teachings. At the hearing, Luther refused to recant his beliefs, so on June 15, 1520, Pope Leo X issued a papal bull, *Exsurge Domine*, condemning 41 statements from Luther's writings and threatening him with excommunication. Leo X's papal bull arrived in Wittenberg on October 10, 1520, and Luther defiantly burned the bull and canon law at the Elster Gate on December 10. Now having no choice but to carry out his threat, Pope Leo X excommunicated Martin Luther from the Catholic Church in his papal bull, *Decet Romanum Pontificum,* on January 3, 1521.

Following his excommunication, Luther was called before the Diet of Worms on April 17-18, 1521, to answer the Holy Roman Emperor's charges of heresy. Wasting no time, the Diet's inquisitor got right to the point with Luther: "Do you, Martin Luther, recognize the books published under your name as your own?" "Yes," said Luther. "Are you prepared to recant what you have written in these books?" Luther requested from the Diet time to think and was granted 24 hours. The following day, the question was asked of Luther again. Luther took a deep breath and announced to the inquisitor: "Unless I am convinced by the testimony of the Holy Scriptures or by evident reason—for I can believe neither pope nor councils alone, as it is clear that they have erred repeatedly and contradicted themselves—I consider myself convicted by the testimony of the Holy Scripture, which is my basis; my conscience is captive to the word of God. Thus I cannot and will not recant, because acting against one's conscience is neither safe nor sound. God help me. Amen."[32] The following day the Holy Roman Emperor, Charles V, ordered Luther's books burned and his followers condemned as heretics.

Despite his censure by the Holy Roman Emperor, many of the German princes supported Luther because a wave of nationalistic sentiment was sweeping the German lands as German princes wanted to be free from the political and spiritual dominance of Rome (Protestantism, by the way, got its name from the German princes who "protested" against Rome).[33] Since Lutheranism allied itself well with the German princes' political agenda of autonomy from Rome, they weren't about to let Luther burn at the stake. He was much too valuable for their political cause, so a plan was formulated to save Luther's life. On his way home from the Diet of Worms, Luther was kidnapped and taken into protective custody near Eisenach by his sovereign prince, where he hid out for a year at Wartburg Castle as Junker Jorg.

Meanwhile, the rebellious fever of Protestantism spread quickly through-out Germany and northern Europe, stirring the German peasants to revolt against both church and state. Published in 1525, Luther's inciteful book, *Temporal Authority: To What Extent it Should be Obeyed,* provoked the German peasants to rise up against their princes and to attack and plunder the

Catholic monasteries. The ensuing Peasants' War of 1525, which Luther later admitted he was primarily responsible for starting, ended with the slaughter of thousands of German peasants. At the start of the insurrection, Luther betrayed the peasants and sided with the German princes, condemning the peasants' revolt in his book *Against the Robbing and Murdering Hordes of Peasants.* Luther recommended the German princes act mercilessly towards the peasants: "Such strange times are these that a prince can be more deserving of Heaven by shedding blood than others by praying."[34] "Have mercy on the poor, stab, slay, strangle here wherever you can."[35] Later criticized for fomenting the Peasants' War of 1525 and then turning on the peasants, Luther tried shifting the blame on God: "I, Martin Luther, have slain all the peasants at the time of their rebellion, for I commanded them to be killed; their blood is upon me. But I cast it upon our Lord God; He commanded me to speak as I did."[36]

As he grew older and his heart turned colder, Luther's scathing diatribes against Catholics and Jews worsened. In 1545, Luther wrote a mean-spirited, denigrating book called *Against the Roman Papacy, an Institution of the Devil,* in which he claimed that the Catholic Church was a "synagogue of Satan," its pope the "Antichrist," and warned that "the papacy must be destroyed."[37] Two years prior, Luther had written a hateful, anti-Semitic book entitled *Of the Jews and their Lies,* in which he blamed the Jews for practically everything wrong in society, and recommended horrible cruelties against them as punishment. Luther's fanatical hatred for the Jews continued until the day he died. Three days before his death, on February 18, 1547, his last sermon, "Admonition against the Jews," was a vicious, scathing attack in which he referred to the Jews as Germany's "public enemy."[38]

Martin Luther, the founding father of Protestantism, died on February 18, 1546. Shortly before he died, Luther joked to his close friends, "When I get home to Wittenberg again, I will lie down in my coffin and give the worms a fat doctor to feast on."[39] Luther's self-denigrating wisecrack about himself turned out to be remarkably prophetic because in just a few days time he died, and really did become the diet of worms.

King Henry VIII

As mentioned, the decline of the papacy by the Babylonian Captivity and the Great Western Schism engendered anti-papal sentiments in England, especially within the English government and the English Church. The imposition of papal taxes on the English, papal appointments of foreign prelates in England, and the pope's frequent diversions of England's revenues for Roman purposes all contributed to growing resentment within England towards the pope. Other historical events in England like the Black Plague of the mid-fourteenth century, the Hundred Years' War (1337-1453), the War of the Roses (1455-1485), and the introduction of humanism and Protestantism into England further contributed to England's desire for separation from Rome.

At the beginning of the sixteenth century, the time was ripe for an English rebellion against the Catholic Church; all England needed was someone arrogant enough to step forward and challenge the authority of the pope. That someone was King Henry VIII (1491-1547), one of the most vile and wicked characters in all of history.

In 1509, the relationship between England and Rome was relatively peaceful because the pope had just allowed King Henry VIII to marry his deceased brother's widow, Catherine of Aragon, the Catholic princess of Spain and aunt to the Holy Roman Emperor, Charles V. Henry VIII was a loyal Catholic and had staunchly defended the Catholic Church in England against the onslaught of Lutheranism. In fact, the pope even awarded Henry VIII the distinguished title of "Defender of the Faith" in 1521 for his staunch defense of the seven sacraments in his *Assertio Septem Sacramentorum.*

The amiable relationship between Henry VIII and the pope, however, was short-lived. When Henry's wife Catherine failed to provide the king with a legitimate male successor (Catherine had six children and only one daughter, Mary, survived), the king thought it time to divorce Catherine and marry a much younger wife who could provide him a male heir. Henry had in mind his wife's Protestant handmaid, eighteen-year-old Anne Boleyn, who, rumor had it, was Henry's illegitimate daughter from an affair he had with Anne's mother, Lady Elizabeth Boleyn.[40] Lady Boleyn is said to have warned King Henry before he married her daughter, "Sir, for the reverence of God, take heed what you do in marrying my daughter, for, if you record your own conscience well, she is your own daughter as well as mine." Henry arrogantly responded back, "Whose daughter soever she is, she shall be my wife."[41]

Since Catherine of Aragon's first husband, Arthur, was the king's deceased brother, Henry's Lord Chancellor, Thomas Cardinal Wolsey, appealed to Rome in 1527 to have the king's marriage to Catherine annulled on the grounds that it was an illegitimate marriage, which the pope shouldn't have allowed in the first place. But when Cardinal Wolsey failed to secure an annulment from Pope Clement VII, who declared Henry's marriage to Catherine legitimate, the irate king sacked Wolsey in 1529 and replaced him with Thomas Cromwell.

On Easter Sunday 1532, Friar William Peto preached a sermon attended by Henry and Anne at Greenwich, in which he warned the king that if he divorced Catherine and married the young woman sitting next to him, God would punish him as he did the wicked King Ahab, and the dogs would lick up his blood, too. Red-faced with anger, Henry got up and walked out of the church with Anne Boleyn in tow, and Friar Peto was subsequently banished from England for having insulted the king.[42]

The new Lord Chancellor, Thomas Cromwell, hastily arranged for a secret marriage between Henry VIII and Anne Boleyn in January of 1533 because Anne was pregnant with Henry's child. In a direct challenge to Rome's authority, on June 1, 1533, another of Henry's lackeys, the Archbishop of Canterbury, Thomas Cranmer, declared Henry's first marriage to Catherine invalid, and the second marriage to Anne Boleyn legitimate. Anyone who criticized Henry's new marriage to Anne Boleyn risked the chopping block, so the English parliament had no choice but to declare Anne Boleyn the new queen. A few brave souls in the English Church, however, condemned Henry's bigamous marriage and became martyrs for their belief. On April 20, 1534, the mystic Elizabeth Barton, the "Nun of Kent," was put to death for denouncing Henry's divorce, along with four priests.[43]

When word of Henry's second marriage to Anne Boleyn reached the pope, Clement VII excommunicated Henry from the Roman Catholic Church in September of 1533. The Catholic Church in England then countered the king's excommunication by severing all ties with Rome. On March 30, 1534, a Parliamentary Act of Succession established the Anglican Church in England, and a subsequent Act of Supremacy on November 3, 1534, made Henry VIII its Supreme Head. The Anglican Church was placed under Henry's total control and all English subjects were compelled, under threat of death, to renounce the pope and swear a new oath of allegiance to Henry, the Supreme Head of the Anglican Church. Sir Thomas More, the well-respected Lord Chancellor of England, refused to swear the new oath to Henry, and for his loyalty to the pope, was beheaded on July 6, 1535, shortly after Bishop John Fisher's beheading on June 22, 1535. King Henry had the two martyrs' heads impaled on pikes and displayed on the London Bridge as a warning to all those who thought about challenging his authority.

The only hindrance to King Henry VIII's total control over the Church in England were the Catholic monasteries, so Henry ordered his chief minister, Thomas Cromwell, to report on the condition of the English monasteries, and to find charges against them so that he would have cause to seize them—some of which dated back nine hundred years. As expected, a year later, in 1536, Cromwell reported back to Henry that the monasteries were overrun with drunkards, homosexuals, gluttons, prostitutes, and lazy, ignorant sloths.[44] Feigning to be shocked at their wanton depravity, Cromwell claimed that these historic religious communities were full of "profound bawdry, drunken knaves, and whores in feather beds."[45] With Cromwell's report in hand, England's parliament passed a law that same year which allowed for the king's confiscation of England's monasteries and all their real and personal property, including all their jeweled ornaments, gold and silver chalices, plates, crucifixes, censors, candlesticks, altars, vestments, statues, paintings, books, Bibles, and even the gold wedding rings off the nuns' fingers and their earrings and silver thimbles. Between 1536 and 1540, Henry VIII plundered and seized a total of 645 Catholic monasteries, 90 Catholic colleges, 110 Catholic hospitals, and 2,374 chantries and free chapels.[46] Monasteries, priories, abbeys, convents, farms, granges, lands, estates, tenements, hereditaments, houses, stock, goods, chattels—everything of value was seized by the king's army.

The spoils of the monasteries were divided between the king and the English nobility, who were in complicity with the king's plunder, and family fortunes in England were founded on the Catholic Church's stolen property. One man in particular who helped administer the seized properties, the appropriately-named Sir Richard Rich, acquired for himself 59 church manors, 31 rectories, and 28 vicarages.[47] Thomas Cromwell, the Protestant vicar-general of the Anglican Church who orchestrated the seizures, kept for himself about 30 estates, while King Henry used his share of the enormous booty for erecting elaborate buildings and making ships and armaments to wage war with his Catholic enemies.[48]

By 1540, the king's sale of church properties soared to around £90,000 a year—a tremendous amount of money back then.[49] Heartlessly, the poor peasants who had lived on the church's properties, paying modest rents, were suddenly thrown out onto the streets to beg. Likewise, the lame and the sick were thrown out of Catholic hospitals to fend for themselves or die. The forced ejection of the poor and needy during the reign of Henry VIII greatly increased England's poverty and pauperism well into the next century.[50]

The king's seizure of church property did meet with some resistance, however. Catholic priests, monks, and friars desperately tried to protect their monasteries from confiscation, but their heroic efforts were in vain. Many were killed in battle and about 200 of them were captured and executed by Cromwell. The Abbot of Glastonbury, Richard Whiting, was drawn and quartered, and his head and limbs were hung on the entrance to his abbey. John Houghton, the prior of a convent of Carthusian monks in London, was also drawn and quartered, and one of his arms was nailed over the entrance to his monastery.[51] The Abbots of Reading and Colchester were also executed. (On October 25, 1970, Pope Paul VI canonized forty persons from England and Wales who were martyred in the Protestant persecutions from 1535 to 1671.)[52]

King Henry VIII's extreme brutality towards the Catholic laity who resisted his dissolution of the monasteries was appalling. On October 23, 1536, thirty to forty thousand armed protesters from the northern counties marched in what was called the "Revolt of the Pilgrimage of Grace." The march, however, was brutally subdued by the king's army, and two hundred sixteen of the pilgrims were executed by Thomas Cromwell on July 12, 1537.[53]

Queen Anne Boleyn failed to produce a male heir for Henry, so he had her beheaded on June 19, 1536, on the trumped-up charges of arrogance, treason, adultery, and incest with her brother. Since Anne had given Henry one daughter, Elizabeth I, but no sons, Henry determined that his marriage with Anne was damned from the start. Thereupon, the Protestant Archbishop, Thomas Cranmer, declared Henry's second marriage to Anne Boleyn null and void, and certified Henry's two daughters, Mary and Elizabeth, as bastards.

The day after Anne was beheaded, Henry married Jane Seymour. Seymour succeeded in giving Henry a son, Edward VI, but she died after Edward's difficult delivery.[54] The frail and sickly Edward VI lived only 16 years. He died on July 6, 1553, the same day St. Thomas More was murdered by his father (July 6, 1535), and the same day the heretic Jan Hus was burned at the stake (July 6, 1415).

After the death of Jane Seymour, Henry arranged for a fourth marriage with the German Anne of Cleves in 1539, but was displeased when she arrived in England because he thought her too ugly. Henry was reported to have said of Anne: "I liked her before I met her. Now I like her less." After only six months of marriage, Henry divorced Anne of Cleves on July 9, 1540, but didn't behead her because it would have started a war with the Germans.

King Henry VIII married his fifth wife, the youthful Catherine Howard, on July 23, 1540, but beheaded her on February 13, 1542, for her "unchaste behavior" with her lover.

In 1543, Henry married his sixth and last wife, Catherine Parr, but by then the wife-murdering, church-robbing, incestuous king had become a fat, impotent, gluttonous whale of a man. Tormented for years by smelly, ulcerating sores on his leg, which historians think were caused by syphilitic spirochetes (worms), Henry VIII died a horribly painful death on January 28, 1547, at the age of 56. During the carriage ride to the ruined chapel of Synod Abbey, where King Henry was to lie in state, his coffin was jostled and burst open. The next morning, when workmen came to repair it, a plumber's dog was seen licking up the putrefied blood and ooze of Henry's bloated corpse that had leaked out onto the floor—exactly as Friar Peto had predicted would happen in 1532 if Henry divorced Catherine of Aragon for Anne Boleyn.[55] Those who witnessed the sickening scene were visibly shaken,[56] for they remembered Friar Peto's prophecy about Henry's fate in regards to the biblical story of wicked King Ahab's blood being licked up by dogs for his murdering and stealing from God:

> "This is what you shall tell him [Ahab], 'The Lord says: After murdering, do you also take possession? For this, the Lord says: In the place where the dogs licked up the blood of Naboth, the dogs shall lick up your blood, too.'"[57]

As for Thomas Cromwell, the architect of the plundering of the Catholic monasteries in England and Henry's vicar of the Anglican Church, he was beheaded by Henry VIII on July 23, 1540, after he fell from the king's grace and was branded a traitor. And as for the Protestant Archbishop of Canterbury, Thomas Cranmer, who joyfully persecuted Catholics during the reign of Henry VIII, he was burnt at the stake on March 21, 1556, by Queen Mary I, "Bloody Mary," Catherine of Aragon's Catholic daughter, who succeeded the throne after the Protestant Lady Jane Grey was executed for usurping Mary's rightful position to the throne. Vicious religious persecutions and retaliations in England and Ireland would continue for many years, all because of King Henry VIII's insistence upon having a son.

Chapter Three

Our Lady of Guadalupe:
Mexico 1531

"I will set a sign among them; from them I will send fugitives to the nations . . . to the distant coast lands that have never heard of my fame, or seen my glory; and they shall proclaim my glory among the nations."

Isa. 66:19

The Church Replenished through Mary

On December 9, 1531, fourteen years after the beginning of Martin Luther's Protestant rebellion and three years before King Henry VIII's Anglican insurrection—both of which swept into heresy over five million members of the Roman Catholic Church, and for the next two centuries devastated both Protestants and Catholics with innumerable inquisitions, tortures, murders, uprisings, The Thirty Years War, and extreme poverty and misery—Our Lady appeared in the New World to a poor Indian peasant named Juan Diego on a mountain top outside of Mexico City. As a result of Mary's appearance to Juan Diego, eight million Mexican Indians converted to Roman Catholicism, which was more than enough to make up for the devastating losses to Protestantism in Europe. Never in the history of the world have so many people converted from one religious belief to another in such a short period of time as in Mexico. The following is an historical account of the events leading up to Mary's appearance there.

Looking for a western route to the East Indies, Christopher Columbus landed on the island of San Salvador in 1492, and was soon followed by a swarm of Catholic missionaries and explorers from Spain and Portugal, the "first of the world powers." In 1504, a nineteen-year-old Spanish conquistador named Hernando Cortés (1485-1547) sailed for the New World and arrived on the island of Hispaniola. Under his commander, Diego Velázquez, Cortés fought in the conquest of Cuba in 1511, and for his part in the victory, became mayor of Santiago. Cortés's reputation and loyalty persuaded his commander, now the governor of Cuba, to select him to head an expeditionary force of Spanish soldiers to the mainland in 1519 to look for gold and riches to send back to the Spanish crown. At the time of Cortés's departure, however, Velázquez suspected him of disloyalty and attempted to appoint a replacement to head the expedition. Refusing to step down, Cortés eluded Velázquez and arrived on the shores of what is now Vera Cruz, Mexico, with 600 of his loyal Spanish soldiers. That day was April 22, Good Friday.

Upon landing in Mexico, Cortés befriended the neighboring Indian tribes and established a town on the Yucátan coast in preparation for his conquest of the mainland. Setting out towards the Aztec capitol of Tenochtitlán (now Mexico City), Cortés engaged the Tlaxcatec Indians in battle. Although the Tlaxcatecs fought valiantly, their primitive weapons were no match for the muskets, steel swords, and terrible-sounding cannons of Cortés's soldiers. Particularly frightening to the Tlaxcatecs were the huge, armor-clad horses the Spaniards were riding. They had never seen horses before and thought that they were centaurs (half horse, half man). Resigning in defeat, the Tlaxcatecs elected to join forces with Cortés to take on their most hated enemy, the mighty Aztec Indians, rulers of Mexico.

In 1519, the Aztec empire was divided into 38 provinces and was populated by ten million Aztecans and their conquered Indian slaves. Compared to other primitive Indian nations in the Western Hemisphere, the Aztecs were more accomplished in mathematics, astronomy, architecture, medicine, philosophy, artistry, and handicrafts. They worshiped about 1,600 gods, which included gods of the sun, moon, rain, wind, fire, corn, and maguey plant. Their mightiest gods were Quetzelcoatl, the feathered stone serpent god, and Huitzilopochtli, the god of war and "Lover of Hearts and Drinker of Blood." The Aztecs believed that their gods demanded a constant supply of human blood to appease their wrath, so they performed at least 50,000 human sacrifices each year, primarily on Indian prisoners of war, which included women and children (one out of every five Indian children was sacrificed).[1] Aztec sacrifices were extremely gory and usually involved the high priest ripping out the victim's still-beating heart while the victim was being held over a sacrificial stone atop a huge Aztec pyramid. After the human sacrifice, which was really Satan's way of mocking Christ's sacrifice on the cross, the hapless victim's body was flung down the pyramid's steep steps to be chopped up and eaten by cannibals waiting on the ground. Other, more horrendous methods of human sacrifice and cannibalism, such as skinning or eating victims alive, or being fed to wild beasts, were common practices with the bloodthirsty Aztecs. The blood lust of the Aztec sacrifices often reached a state of frenzy, with tens of thousands of victims slaughtered in a single day. In 1487, at the inauguration of the Great Temple of Tenochtitlán dedicated to the Aztec war and sun god Huitzilopochtli, 20,000 captured Indian rebels from northern Oaxaca were sacrificed in a single day on order of the Aztec emperor Ahuitzotl.[2] (This notorious temple was rediscovered on February 21, 1978, right next to the Catholic Cathedral in Mexico City.)[3]

On his way towards the Aztec capitol of Tenochtitlán, Cortés was met by friendly Aztec envoys sent by their emperor, Montezuma II. Montezuma was unsure whether the newly-arrived white men with black beards were humans or gods because Aztec legend maintained that the feathered serpent god, Quetzelcoatl, sailed to sea one day, vowing to return to the Aztec empire around the year 1519; so Montezuma thought maybe Cortés was the returning Quetzelcoatl. Just a few years before the arrival of Cortés, Montezuma had been warned by Aztec soothsayers that someday his empire would be overthrown by white men from across the ocean who would bring with them knowledge of the true god. Their prophecy was based on a dream by Montezuma's sister, Princess Papantzin, in 1509, in which a luminous being led her to the shore of the ocean and showed her huge ships arriving from afar with black crosses on their sails and on the sailors' foreheads (helmets). The white men, the princess was told in her dream, would conquer the Aztec Empire and bring knowledge of the One True God. Other omens coinciding with the arrival of Cortés, such as strange lights in the sky, fires in the temples, and the sudden appearance of deformed animals and men, convinced Montezuma that superior supernatural forces were at work, so he had better treat Cortés hospitably.[4]

Cortés and his men were cordially welcomed and housed in Montezuma's palace, and were free to move about Tenochtitlán as they pleased. Cortés feared, however, that this unusual hospitality was a trap, so he took Montezuma prisoner just in case. To prove that he meant the Spaniards no harm, Montezuma allowed Cortés to loot the Aztec treasury of its gold and precious works of art. But Cortés wasn't satisfied with just robbing the Aztecs of their wealth, he wanted to make them Spanish subjects and convert them to Christianity, so he assembled the Aztec nobles and demanded that they become Spanish subjects. Weeping, Montezuma agreed. With the Aztecs offering little resistance, Cortés converted the sacrificial Aztec temple into a church, destroyed the Aztec pagan idols, and halted their sacrificial rituals.

Meanwhile, 900 Spanish soldiers from Cuba under the leadership of the conquistador Narváez arrived in Mexico to arrest Cortés. When Cortés got word of Narváez's arrival he left Tenochtitlán to engage him in battle. Meanwhile,

while Cortés was away, the garrison he left behind in Tenochtitlán killed 600 Aztec nobles who were assembled at an Aztec religious ceremony. Shocked out of their passivity, the Aztecs vowed revenge on the Spaniards, but waited for the return of Cortés before they launched their surprise counterattack.

Cortés met Narváez in battle and was able to defeat him because many of Narváez's men came over to Cortés's side when he told them of the riches awaiting them in Tenochtitlán, and how the Aztecs were offering little resistance to their plundering. Upon Cortés's triumphant return to Tenochtitlán, the angry Aztecs, under the leadership of Montezuma's brother, Cuitlahuac, stormed the Spaniards' palace. Emperor Montezuma was put on the palace roof to try to quell the revolt, but was stoned to death by his own people. A full scale Indian uprising followed. Cortés and his men narrowly escaped Tenochtitlán under cover of darkness, but vowed to return with a stronger army and take the city back.

With the Spaniards chased off, another enemy far more deadly entered Tenochtitlán—smallpox. The deadly virus, previously unknown to that part of the world, decimated Tenochtitlán, killing Emperor Cuitlahuac and allowing the regrouped Cortés an opportunity to take back the capitol. Eight hundred and fifty Spanish soldiers and their 60,000 Indian allies besieged the Aztec capitol for four months, cutting off their food and water supplies.

Escaping Indian slaves that were being held captive by the Aztecs joined forces with the Spanish soldiers. In heavy fighting (Cortés lost three quarters of his men), the Aztec capitol of Tenochtitlán fell to the Spaniards on June 10, 1521, nearly a year after Cortés was forced to flee the city. In the end, the Aztec Empire was overthrown, just as Princess Papantzin had dreamed. Tenochtitlán was leveled and Mexico City was built in its place.

Neither the Spanish nor the Aztecs were innocent of horrible crimes. It's unfair for Indians to accuse the Spanish of crimes against humanity by conquering the Aztecs without remembering the atrocities the Aztecs committed against their fellow Indians, as well as against captured Spanish soldiers. Diseases brought in from Europe, such as smallpox, measles, and the plague, killed far more Indians (nine in ten) than Spanish swords and muskets. The Indians, on the other hand, gave the conquistadors syphilis, which ravaged Europe when infected Spanish and Portuguese sailors returned home and spread the deadly spirochete to their lovers.

Without question, God had led the explorers into the New World for a very important reason: to replenish the Roman Catholic Church from the decimation of Protestantism. But where Christ goes, Satan always follows. Exploitation and cruelty towards the Indians was perpetrated by many, but not all of the European conquistadors and colonizers. Much of the brutality levied against the Indians was falsely justified by the mistaken belief that the Indians had no souls. Many high-ranking Spaniards like Queen Isabella, however, believed that Indians did have a soul. The Catholic Church ended the heated debate in 1537 when Pope Paul III promulgated the brief *Cardinali Toletano* and the papal bull *Sublimi Deus,* both of which upheld the human dignity and rights of the Indians, proclaiming them to be *veri homines* (real men and women with souls).[5] In addition, in 1537, Pope Paul III excommunicated all Catholics who were slave traders (although relatively few Portuguese and Spanish traders actually quit the trade for fear of excommunication).[6] In 1542, the "New Laws" were passed in Burgos, Spain, giving protection against enslavement to the American Indians. Former colonist turned Dominican missionary, Bartolomé de las Casas, championed the New Laws and the cause of Indian rights, which won him the Bishopric of Chiapas, Mexico, in 1545, but also the hostility of many of the greedy colonists.[7]

One particular Spanish colonist named Juan Ginés de Sepúlveda justified the brutality of Spanish troops by citing the biblical text, "Go out to the highways and hedgerows and compel them to come in that my home may be filled."[8] Because of this kind of twisted logic, the New Laws safeguarding Indian rights were repealed in 1546. The newly-founded Jesuit Order, however, went out of its way to defend the Indians in the New World, especially in Brazil, which brought the wrath of the colonists down upon both the Jesuits and the Indians. Sadly, more Indians in Brazil converted to Christianity at the point of a colonist's sword than through the kindness and generosity of the Jesuit missionaries.

The Aztec Empire disintegrated after the fall of Tenochtitlán in 1521, and was incorporated into the Spanish crown. Blood-stained temples where hundreds of thousands of human sacrifices were offered in propitiation to bloodthirsty pagan deities were demolished and replaced by Catholic churches.[9]

Having fulfilled his mission of conquering Mexico for Spain, in 1526, Hernando Cortés was succeeded by five Spanish administrators, known as the First Audience, who, unfortunately, were led by the cruel and vindictive Don Nune de Guzmán. When Prior Juan Zumárraga of the Franciscan monastery was chosen First Bishop of the New World in 1528, he immediately voiced his opposition to Spain regarding the cruelty of Don Nune de Guzmán towards the Indians, who were stubbornly resisting conversion to Christianity. Don Nune de Guzmán, in turn, retaliated against Zumárraga's friars and threatened to do physical harm to Zumárraga, who then appealed to his king for immediate help. When Charles V, the King of Spain and Emperor of the Holy Roman Empire, found out about the cruelty and vindictiveness of Don Nune de Guzmán, he replaced the entire First Audience with a Second Audience in 1530, headed by Bishop Don Sebastian Ramirez y Fuenleal.

Before the arrival of Bishop Don Sebastian Ramirez y Fuenleal from Europe, the Aztec Indians were threatening to retaliate with force against Don

Nune de Guzmán. Prior Juan Zumárraga prayed to the Blessed Mother to prevent another Aztec uprising like had happened against Cortés in 1520, and to send him Spanish Castilian roses (foreign to Mexican soil) as a sign that God had answered his prayer. This is a true account of what happened.

Juan Diego

On the morning of December 9, 1531, a poor Aztec Indian peasant named Juan Diego was visited by sounds of heavenly music and a vision of the Blessed Virgin Mary as he walked across Tepeyac Hill on his way to mass in Mexico City. Calling him in the diminutive, "Juanito . . . Juan Dieguito," the Virgin Mary instructed Juan to go to Bishop Zumárraga and request that a church be built in her honor on Tepeyac Hill:

> *"Know for certain, dearest of my sons, that I am the perfect and perpetual Virgin Mary, Mother of the True God, through whom everything lives, the Lord of all things, who is Master of Heaven and Earth. I ardently desire a teocalli [temple] be built here for me where I will show and offer all my love, my compassion, my help and protection to the people. I am your merciful Mother, the Mother of all who live united in this land, and of all of mankind, of all those who love me, of those who cry to me, of those who have confidence in me. Here I will hear their weeping and their sorrows, and will remedy and alleviate their sufferings, necessities and misfortunes.*
>
> *"Therefore, in order to realize my intentions, go to the Bishop of Mexico City and tell him that I sent you and that it is my desire to have a teocalli built here. Tell him all that you have seen and heard. Be assured that I shall be very grateful and will reward you for doing diligently what I have asked of you. Now that you have heard my words, my son go and do everything as best you can."*[10]

Juan did as Mary instructed and went to see the bishop. The bishop received Juan graciously into his hacienda but didn't believe his story, and Juan left dejected. Walking back in the direction of Tepeyac Hill, Juan met the Blessed Virgin again. He apologized to Mary and begged forgiveness for not convincing the bishop, and asked that she give her request to someone of higher standing so that it may be believed. Mary smiled reassuringly and told Juan that her request had to be delivered by him alone. She sent Juan back again the next day, but again the bishop was incredulous and told Juan that he needed a sign from the vision in order to believe. Juan left the hacienda and trekked back up Tepeyac Hill, and the Blessed Virgin appeared to him once more. Juan related his failure to Mary and tearfully begged her to give the bishop a sign so that he would believe. Mary smiled and told Juan to return here the next day and he would have his sign. That same day, Juan's uncle, whom he had been caring for, fell deathly ill (some accounts say the uncle had been shot with an arrow, some say it was the plague), so Juan stayed home to care for him. On December 12, the future feast day of Our Lady of Guadalupe, Juan rose early to fetch a priest to hear his dying uncle's confession and to administer the last rites. In his haste, Juan tried to skirt around the other side of Tepeyac Hill to avoid Mary, but she intercepted him along the way. Relaying his immediate concern for his uncle and requesting the Virgin Mary to please come back tomorrow, Mary tenderly answered back:

> *"Do not be troubled or weighed down with grief. Do not fear any illness or vexation, anxiety or pain. Am I not here who is your Mother? Are you not under my shadow and protection? Am I not your fountain of life? Are you not in the folds of my mantle? In the crossing of my arms? Is there anything else you need? Do not let the illness of your uncle worry you because he is not going to die of his sickness. At this very moment, he is cured."*[11]

Mary then instructed Juan to climb back up the hill where she had appeared to him three days earlier, and carefully gather the flowers growing there in abundance and bring them back to her. Up the hill, Juan found beautiful and fragrant Castilian roses growing in the rocky frozen soil (Tepeyac's altitude is 7,000 feet, and in December, it gets very cold. The chances for roses growing there is zero. Furthermore, Castilian roses are not native to Mexico and could never grow in the harsh, rugged, high altitude desert terrain of primarily rocks, cactus, mesquite, and thistles). Juan joyfully gathered the roses in his *tilma*, a simple peasant's cape made of maguey fibers, and presented them to the Blessed Mother. Mary rearranged them carefully in the *tilma* and told Juan to take them directly to the bishop as proof of her appearance, and not to open them until he was in the presence of the bishop. At the bishop's hacienda, Juan was brought before a gathering of important dignitaries, which included Bishop Zumárraga and Bishop Don Sebastian Ramirez y Fuenleal, the governor of Mexico. Juan related Mary's instructions to him and then opened his *tilma* to show the flowers. As the roses fell to the floor, the skeptical audience was dumbstruck: a magnificent portrait of the "Woman Clothed with the Sun, with the Moon Under Her Feet" appeared on Juan's *tilma*. The Spanish dignitaries immediately fell to their knees, making the sign of the cross on their way down. The bishop and his visiting dignitaries had their sign from heaven.

The next day, the entire group made their way back to Tepeyac Hill to the same spot of Juan's apparitions. Afterwards, a triumphal procession was made to the Cathedral of Mexico City, with the *tilma* paraded around for all to see. By now, Juan's uncle had fully recovered and had told his nephew and the bishops that, at the moment of his recovery, Mary had appeared to him requesting in his native language, Nahautl, that she be remembered as *Coatlaxopeuh*("She who crushes the serpent"). Historians generally agree that Bishop Zumárraga's interpreter probably mistook *Coatlaxopeuh* for "Guadalupe," which is phonetically similar. Guadalupe, which means "wolf river," was a famous Marian shrine in Estramaudra, Spain. That's what the Spanish had thought Mary wanted to be remembered by—Our Lady of Guadalupe.

Mary's appearance to Juan Diego at the former site of the temple of Tonantzin, the pagan mother goddess, on Tepeyac Hill, and the miracle of the roses and the *tilma,* were very meaningful to the Aztec Indians. They now believed that Mary was the real Mother of God and that Christ, her son, was God in the flesh. Mexican Indians flocked by the thousands to visit the shrine of Our Lady of Guadalupe that was put up in a matter of days.[12]

By 1539, eight million Mexican Indians had accepted the Catholic faith because of the appearance of Our Lady of Guadalupe; more than enough to replace the 5 million Europeans who defected from Catholicism during the Protestant rebellion. Today, over 93% of Mexico's 100 million citizens are Roman Catholics, and 46% of the world's Catholics live in Latin America.[13]

The true miracle of Guadalupe wasn't the roses or the *tilma,* but the flood of conversions to Roman Catholicism. There's no doubt that Juan Diego's retelling of the miraculous events at the Tepeyac shrine in his native language to Indian pilgrims was far more effective than a million Spanish missionaries. Other conversions were inspired by the reports of miracles coming from petitions to Our Lady. In one particular case, an Indian accidentally killed by an arrow at the celebration of the procession of the *tilma* to the Tepeyac shrine was brought back to life when the whole community prayed on his behalf. The Indian served for the remainder of his life as an assistant to Juan Diego, who was chosen by Bishop Zumárraga to be permanent caretaker of the Tepeyac shrine. (A painting of the "Miracle of the Dead Indian" by three artists done around 1533 was rediscovered behind the altar of the old 1622 church when it was restored in 1960.)[14]

In 1570, the Archbishop of Mexico ordered an exact replica of Our Lady of Guadalupe painted and sent to King Philip II of Spain. King Philip then gave the painting to Admiral Andrea Doria, where it was placed in his cabin during the Battle of Lepanto on October 7, 1571.[15] The Battle of Lepanto was a major naval victory that safeguarded Christian Europe from the invading Turkish fleet, and was the biggest naval engagement since the Battle of Actium in 32 B.C. In the battle, which was led by Don John of Austria, the invading Turkish fleet of Selim II, the Ottoman Sultan, was utterly destroyed by ships of a Holy League composed of the Papal States, Spain, and Venice. (After the battle it was discovered that Selim's fleet was rowed by 15,000 chained Christians slaves, all of whom were released by the victors.)[16] The image of Our Lady of Guadalupe, prayed to before the battle, was credited by the Christian naval commanders with the victory. Since 1811, this replica of the *tilma* has been kept at the shrine of Our Lady of Guadalupe at San Stefano d'Aveto, Italy.

The *Tilma*

Our Lady's appearance in Mexico has been officially confirmed by the Catholic Church as worthy of belief. The first official recognition came from the Archbishop of Mexico, who canonically established the validity of the Tepeyac apparitions in 1557, nine years after the deaths of Juan Diego and Archbishop Zumárraga (Archbishop Zumárraga died just three days after Juan Diego).[17] In 1754, Pope Benedict XIV issued a papal bull approving Our Lady of Guadalupe as Patroness of Mexico, with the Sacred Congregation of Rites issuing a decree approving an office and mass in her honor. In 1910, Pope Pius X proclaimed Our Lady of Guadalupe the Patroness of Latin America, and in 1979 Pope John Paul II became the first pontiff in history to visit the shrine of Our Lady of Guadalupe in Mexico.

Juan Diego's *tilma* has been thoroughly investigated by science and proven to be an authentic miracle. Despite exposure to the harsh Mexican climate, the handling and touching by thousands of admirers and investigators, the smoke of incense and countless votive candles, a disastrous flood in 1629, nitric acid accidentally spilled on it in 1791, and a bomb explosion on November 14, 1921 by anti-government terrorists attempting to destroy it, the *tilma* has miraculously held together, without sizing or varnish, for over 450 years.[18] (Maguey cactus fibers have an approximate life span of only twenty years before decomposing.)[19]

A painters' commission under the Viceroy, the Marquis of Mancera, commissioned in 1663 to study the sacred image, testified under oath that "it is impossible, humanly, for an artificer to paint or produce a thing so excellent on a cloth as coarse as is the *tilma* or *ayate* on which appears the divine picture." The commission added, "The imprinting of the said Picture of Our Lady of Guadalupe on the *ayate* or *tilma* of the said Juan Diego, was, and must be understood and be declared to have been, a supernatural work and a secret reserved to the Divine Majesty."[20] A special committee of three professors from the Royal University examining the image also declared, "The continuance through so many years of the Holy Picture's freshness of form and color, in the presence of such opposing elements, cannot have a natural cause. Its sole principle is He who alone is able to produce miraculous effects above all the forces of nature."[21] In 1756, celebrated painter Miguel Cabrera and other artists declared that the colors, style, and detail of the sacred image would be impossible to reproduce: "The plan of this Holy Picture," Cabrera said, " is so singular, so perfectly accomplished, and so manifestly marvelous, that we hold it for certain that anyone who has any knowledge whatever of our art must, on seeing it, at once declare it to be a miraculous portrait."[22]

The miraculous image of Our Lady of Guadalupe on Juan Diego's *tilma* serves as a constant visual reminder that Mary is the "Woman Clothed with the Sun." As Patroness of Latin America, Mary continues to watch over her children in the West with the love of a mother's heart, calling her children to take refuge under her generous mantle. Each year between 15-20 million pilgrims visit the shrine of Guadalupe in Mexico City, which is the most visited shrine in the world. In fact, the Feast Day of Our Lady of Guadalupe (December 12) is the most celebrated feast day in existence, besides Christmas and Easter.[23]

Chapter Four

Our Lady of the Miraculous Medal: Paris, France, 1830

"You, O Deists, profess yourselves the Enemies of Christianity, and you are so: you are also the enemies of the Human Race and of Universal Nature... Deism is the Worship of the God of this world by means of what you call Natural Religion and Natural Philosophy, and of Natural Morality or self-righteousness, the selfish virtues of the Natural Heart."

William Blake, *Preface to Jerusalem*, 1820

Rationalism, Deism, Freemasonry, and the Enlightenment

The Protestant revolt from the Catholic Church in the sixteenth century was followed in the seventeenth and eighteenth centuries by the wholesale repudiation of Christianity itself. The divisive principles upon which Protestantism was founded—the rejection of 1,500 years of apostolic tradition, the teaching authority of the Catholic magisterium, and the primacy of the pope for a more subjective, individualistic interpretation of the Bible— soon led to the complete rejection of Christianity itself. Age-old Christian dogmas and doctrines concerning God, the universe, and the true meaning of life were replaced by deities called Human Knowledge, Reason, and Nature.

During this idolatrous period in history, which secular historians have paradoxically called "The Enlightenment," rationalism became the new religion of the clever and the learned who believed that human reason and experience alone were the only credible sources of true knowledge and understanding, and that all previously held beliefs, such as Catholicism, should be questioned, if not totally discarded. The world, according to rationalists, runs on a predetermined set of impersonal, mechanical, physical, and mathematical laws subject to direct observation and quantification by the experimental methods of human science, so any ecclesiastical claims of divinely-revealed supernatural truths not amenable to scientific testing and observation are to be doubted. In other words, if you can't see it, smell it, hear it, taste it, or feel it, it doesn't exist.

Most of the universities' intellectuals and scholars during this "Age of Reason" were rationalists and put their faith in human science instead of religion, which they cynically looked upon as a superstitious anachronism from the Middle Ages. To rationalists, it would be modern science, not religion, that would finally put an end to all human misery and suffering, and bring about the perfectibility of the human race. One such overly-optimistic rationalist with a religious-sounding name, Joseph Priestley (1733-1804), proudly predicted that modern science would " . . . overturn in a moment . . . the old building of error and superstition [religion]."[1] Priestley and other rationalists like him believed that, by discovering the working mechanisms of the material universe, man, through his inherent goodness, could take charge of his own destiny and turn earth into heaven. Human science and technology, they claimed, would become the twin engines that would drive civilization towards a new utopia, and with them man could have his happiness right now. There was no need of postponing pleasures in this life for the hope of a spiritual reward in an afterlife for earthly mortifications.

To many rationalists in the eighteenth century, God, if he existed at all, existed not as the stern and vengeful God of the Christian Bible, but as some kind of natural, cosmic force: an impersonal "cosmic-watchmaker," not responding to human prayer or need, separate from a universe made to run on its own. This neo-pagan, "Nature is God" heresy became known as *Deism.* Deism, at its core, is anti-clerical, anti-Christian, and deeply suspicious of organized religions—especially Roman Catholicism. In fact, many Deists were clandestine Freemasons—members of a super-secret, anti-Catholic, anti-monarchial, international fraternity founded in London in 1717 for the express purpose of spreading rationalism, anti-Catholicism, and political revolution throughout the world.[2] Deists and Masons conspired together to promote the overthrow of the European monarchs and the Catholic Church, believing that church and state should be separate from each other by law, and that organized religion should only be tolerated if it is practiced privately. Republics, Deists said, should only be interested in the material welfare and protection of their citizens' liberty, not the eternal salvation of their souls.[3]

The Enlightenment's new heresy of rationalism spread like wildfire throughout Europe and the New World during the late-eighteenth century because rebellious man wanted to be free from both the spiritual authority of the Roman Catholic Church and the temporal authority of the European monarchs. As a result of rationalism and freemasonry, which was condemned by Pope Clement XII in 1738, the Catholic Church, the privileged nobility class, and the ruling monarchs of Europe, especially in France, came under increasingly vicious verbal attacks. Under freemasonry's seductive banner of "liberty, fraternity, and equality," kings and popes were publicly castigated as instruments of repression and exploitation of the common masses (the same charge later used by Karl Marx and the Communist Party).

Rationalism's most vociferous champion, François-Marie Arouet de Voltaire (1694-1778), cheered on the common man in France to rise up and "crush the infamous thing," meaning, of course, the Roman Catholic Church.[4] A well-known French playwright, novelist, deist, freemason, and a populizer of human science and philosophy, Voltaire was an extremely prolific writer, writing over a thousand separate works, many of which were extremely anti-Catholic and anti-monarchial. An outspoken cynic and skeptic, Voltaire was obsessed with individual freedom of conscience and reason, and hated the authoritarianism of Catholicism and monarchism. He and the other French *philosophes,* like Helvétius, Diderot, Baron d'Holbach, Rousseau, and Montesquieu, did everything in their power to propagate the spread of the two demons named Rationalism and Revolution, which were poised to strike a deadly blow to France.[5]

The French Revolution

France, the "eldest daughter of the Roman Catholic Church," was, during the eighteenth century, the center of European civilization and commerce, with one in five Europeans living and working in that country. The high cost of the French and English colonial wars, however, and the terrible mismanagement of the government and economy by King Louis XVI and Queen Marie Antoinette, had caused the French national debt to skyrocket. Subsequently, the poor peasants of France, many living on the feudal manors of the frequently absent privileged nobility, were forced to pay higher and higher taxes to the king to fund the growing national debt, in addition to the fees and privileges already paid to their landlords. The Catholic Church in France, on the other hand, enjoyed a tax-exempt status on all its properties (the church avoided paying taxes by payment of periodic "free gifts" to the monarchy). Because of this perceived injustice towards the common man, hatred of the Catholic Church and the French monarchy grew amongst the middle and lower classes in France during the late-eighteenth century, egged on by the popular writings of left-wing rationalists and revolutionaries like Voltaire. At the beginning of 1789, a violent revolution in France against the monarchy and Catholic Church was looming on the horizon. Here is how it started.

In 1789, the French realm consisted of three estates: the nobility, the Catholic Church, and the commoner. The commoners included the better-off urban middle classes—lawyers, merchants, manufacturers, bankers, doctors, financiers, traders, craftsmen, and entrepreneurs, who rose in affluence, class consciousness, and numbers during the eighteenth century but had no real voice in politics, which made them very angry and resentful towards the French nobility and Catholic Church. On June 17, 1789, the first stage of the French Revolution began when the majority of the Third Estate delegation to the Estates General (the commoners) were joined by some of the lower-ranking clergy and nobles in declaring themselves the National Constituent Assembly—the new primary spokesmen for France. Locked out of their Versailles meeting place on orders from the outraged king, the National Constituent Assembly convened in a nearby tennis court three days later. On June 20, 1789, members of the National Constituent Assembly took the famous "Tennis Court Oath," pledging not to disband until they drafted a new French constitution.

In retaliation against their defiance, an angered King Louis XVI called out the troops to "defend Paris from unrest," a move the Third Estate, which represented 96 percent of the French population, interpreted as an act of civil war against them.[6] Subsequently, on July 14, 1789, a Parisian mob stormed the Invalides and Bastille prisons looking for arms to defend themselves against the king's soldiers. As this was happening, rural peasants—fearing a counter-revolution by those loyal to the king—ran amok, setting fire to manor houses, destroying Catholic monasteries and the bishops' residences, and murdering some of the nobles who resisted.

In an effort to appease the "Great Fear" being spread throughout France by rioting peasants, on August 4, 1789, the National Constituent Assembly abolished the feudalism, venality, and privilege of the monarchy and the nobles—the so-called "Ancient Regime." On August 27, the Declaration of the Rights of Man and of the Citizen was approved by the National Assembly, which guaranteed (for men only) freedom of speech, freedom of the press, due process of law, the sovereignty of the people over the monarchy, and religious toleration (except for the Catholic Church, of course). To prove their deep-seated anti-Catholic bias, within several months the National Constituent Assembly began confiscating the church's property. Her treasures of art were pillaged, her sacred vessels stolen, her institutions of charity and learning suppressed, and her feudal lands confiscated. Now deprived of her principal source of income, the Catholic Church in France went broke and was forced to become a ward of the state. On July 22, 1790, the French king enacted the Civil Constitution of the Clergy, which placed all Catholic Church property under the control of the state. Monasteries, convents, and religious houses were abolished, priests were now employed as civil servants of the state, and the number of dioceses was cut from 154 to 83.[7] Bishops and pastors were now chosen by French citizens instead of the church, ecclesiastical offices were abolished, and priests and bishops were required to swear an oath of allegiance to the new revolutionary constitution. Any cleric who refused to swear an oath was thrown out of his office and banished to French Guiana in South America.[8] Many brave French priests died as a result of their deportation to these disease-infested hellholes. Thousands more emigrated to the United States, England, and Germany to escape certain death.

The new French revolutionary constitution, finished in 1791, gave the French monarchy a limited role in government, with the majority of political power invested in the well-to-do middle class. The National Assembly, dominated by the middle class, sold off church property and public lands, abolished trade unions and guilds, and then only allowed well-off people to vote—moves seen by the now terribly disillusioned lower classes as benefiting only the upper-middle class. A rebellion by the poor peasants of France against the National Assembly was fomented.

The second stage of the French Revolution began in the summer of 1792, when the moderate-upper-middle-class leaders (Girondists) of the National Constituent Assembly were confronted by the more radical middle-middle-class Republicans (Jacobins).[9] On August 9, 1792, peasant mobs led by Georges Jacques Danton and his brigand band of Jacobins stormed the Tuileries, took King Louis XVI prisoner, and set up a National Convention to govern France. Danton and his extremists had the support of the lower classes because they promised to fix rising prices and support the peasants economically. Little did the peasants realize that their support of the radical Jacobins would open Pandora's box.

During the "September Massacres" that followed the storming of the Tuileries, rioters in Paris, members of the Parisian mob known as the *sans-culottes*,[10] went on a three-day orgy of blood when they broke into Parisian prisons on September 2, 1792, and hacked to death more than 1,100 nobles, clergy, and ordinary criminals who had not yet been guillotined by the National Assembly. The murderous *sans-culottes* then attacked an almshouse containing prostitutes, insane women, and young orphaned girls, butchering everyone inside. A friend of the queen was beheaded and her head stuck on a pike and paraded before the Temple where the royal couple was imprisoned. On September 21, 1792, the French monarchy was formally abolished by the Jacobins and the First Republic of France proclaimed at the first session of the National Convention in Paris. Committing the terrible sin of regicide, the First Republic of France beheaded King Louis XVI on January 21, 1793, followed by his wife, Marie Antoinette, on October 16, 1793.

The radical and murderous Jacobin faction rose in power on April 6, 1793, as the National Convention created the Committee of Public Safety, made up of twelve extremist Jacobin leaders. The three most notorious leaders—Jean Paul Marat, Georges Jacques Danton, and Maximilien Robespierre—were all hardened disciples of one of the Enlightenment's most disreputable *philosophes,* Jean-Jacques Rousseau.[11] As the primary leader of the Jacobins, the nefarious Robespierre instituted France's bloody "Reign of Terror" from June 1793 to July 1794, in which at least 20,000 French citizens were murdered, including 215 priests and a number of bishops.[12]

Imitating what the future Antichrist will do, on November 24, 1794, Robespierre and his Jacobins changed the Gregorian calendar into a "natural" calendar, with the first year beginning at the start of the French Revolution. The twelve months were divided up into thirty days each and renamed after climatic changes. Weeks lasted ten days instead of the usual seven. Sundays and religious holidays, including Christmas and Easter, were abolished. Days of the week were renamed, and feast days of saints were renamed after plants, tools, and animals.[13] The practice of Christianity was strictly forbidden by the Jacobins.

On November 10, 1793, Martin Luther's birthday, Jacobins put a woman of ill repute on the altar of the Catholic Cathedral of Notre Dame and mockingly worshiped her as the "Goddess of Reason."[14] Deism was then proclaimed the official religion of France, with the celebration of the "Feast of the Supreme Being and Nature" established on June 8, 1794.

The apparent triumph of Deism in France over Catholicism was short-lived though, for, like the Bible says in Rev. 13:10, "If one is destined to be slain by the sword, by the sword he will be slain." In July of 1794, the three leaders of the murderous Jacobin Party died violent deaths themselves. Marat was stabbed to death in his bathtub on July 13, 1793, by a fanatical, young female Girondist; Danton and his followers were guillotined by Robespierre on April 5, 1794; and Robespierre and his followers were themselves guillotined on July 28, 1794, by a conspiracy of Convention deputies.

Robespierre's bloody "Reign of Terror" had finally come to an end by August of 1794 because public sympathy in France had turned against the flagrant terrorism of the Jacobins and their Committee of Public Safety. The moderate-upper-middle class Republicans regained control of the government and the radical Jacobins were forced to flee for their lives. Political prisoners were released, conscription for France's revolutionary wars against Europe was ended, freedom of worship was restored, the Catholic Church was separated from the state, priests, royalists, and émigrés returned to France, a new constitution was drafted, and the executive branch was reorganized into a Directory of Five Republican leaders. New elections were held in France that brought the return of many peace-seeking pro-monarchists.[15]

But peace wouldn't last long in France; she still had to pay dearly for the rebellious crimes committed during the French Revolution. Fearing the re-establishment of the French monarchy by the returning pro-monarchists, the

Directory of Five Republican leaders called on General Napoleon Bonaparte to keep them in power, which Bonaparte did, but at a tremendous cost to France. If the French Revolution spilled the blood of tens of thousands of Frenchman, Napoleon would spill the blood of hundreds of thousands. What other fate would you expect to befall a nation that had murdered its king and queen and then tried to "crush" its Catholic Church?

Napoleon Bonaparte

In a 1799 coup d'état, with the approval of the majority of Frenchmen, the popular military leader from the island of Corsica, Napoleon Bonaparte, seized absolute power in France. Tired of wars, revolution, and anarchy, France was ready for a strong leader. On August 2, 1802, the French people proclaimed Napoleon Bonaparte France's Consul for Life, and then on December 2, 1804, Napoleon crowned himself Emperor of France. After twelve years of being without a king, the Republic of France now had an emperor, who, like Alexander the Great, was itching to conquer the world for his own personal glory.

Napoleon Bonaparte, the vainglorious little warmonger from Corsica who dreamed of the glory days of France and of ruling the world, expanded the French Revolutionary Wars in Europe by attacking Austria, Britain, the Netherlands, Sweden, Italy, Sicily, Piedmont-Sardinia, Tuscany, Naples, Malta, Prussia, Spain, Portugal, Switzerland, Russia, Egypt, Palestine, and Syria. After conquering Rome and the Papal States, Napoleon captured Pope Pius VI in 1798 and imprisoned him in France, where he died in Valence in 1799. Convincing themselves that Pius VI would be the last pope, the enemies of the Catholic Church rejoiced in his capture and death. But the pope's enemies were wrong: they had forgotten the promise Christ made to Peter nineteen centuries before. The combined armies of Italy, Austria, and Russia regrouped and drove Bonaparte out of Italy in 1799, and the College of Cardinals elected Pope Pius VII the 251st pope. Napoleon subsequently negotiated a *Concordat* with the new pope in 1801, allowing Catholicism, still the majority religion in France, to be practiced and taught without state interference. But Napoleon's concession to Rome didn't mean that he was now a friend of the Catholic Church—he restored Catholicism in France strictly for political purposes. Elsewhere in Europe Napoleon ordered church property confiscated, ecclesiastical offices abolished, lands and buildings seized, and religious houses suppressed.

Napoleon's empire reached its zenith by 1809, with most of Europe controlled by the Bonaparte family. France's revolutionary slogans of "liberty, equality, and fraternity" turned into subjugation and repression of the worst kind, especially against the Catholic Church. Napoleon broke off relations with the new pope on February 13, 1806, after Pius VII expressed reservations about Napoleon's own "imperial catechism," which proclaimed Napoleon as "God's minister on earth." Three years later, on July 6, 1809, Napoleon arrested Pope Pius VII and imprisoned him after Pius excommunicated Napoleon from the Catholic Church for annexing the Papal States to the French empire. (Pius VII remained imprisoned at Fontainebleau, France, until the European Allies liberated him in 1814.)

Following his excommunication, Napoleon's demise came swiftly—like Hitler's, it came after he turned traitor and declared war on his former ally, Russia. Napoleon invaded Russia on June 24, 1812, but found everything of value burned by the retreating Russians. After besieging the burned-out city of Moscow, Napoleon's retreating Grand Army suffered tremendous losses from famine, the horrible Russian winter, and pursuing Russian soldiers. Then on October 19, 1813, Napoleon was defeated at the Battle of Leipzig by the European Allies (Russia, Prussia, Austria, and Britain). The following April, in 1814, Napoleon's "Grand Army" was defeated and the European Allies entered Paris victorious. Costing the lives of hundreds of thousands of Frenchmen in his quest to rule the world, Napoleon was forced to abdicate to France's new king, Louis XVIII, on April 6, 1814, and was exiled to the island of Elba.

But as some of the Allies had feared, on March 20, 1815, Napoleon returned from Elba with a force of 1,500 men, marched on Paris, and regained power. Assembling another army, Napoleon won a couple of quick victories against the Allies, but at the Battle of Waterloo on June 18, 1815, was defeated for good by Britain's Duke of Wellington. Napoleon was thereby banished forever to the island of St. Helena in the far-off South Atlantic, where he died in boredom and despair on May 5, 1821. Louis XVIII, the brother of King Louis XVI, was reinstalled on the French throne by the European Allies and reigned until his death in 1824.

The French Revolutionary and Napoleonic Wars between 1789 and 1815 caused tremendous suffering in France, Europe, Russia, and the Middle East. Casualties numbered in the millions; the European economy was left in tatters; horrible counter-revolutionary reprisals known as the "White Terror" by pro-monarchists and pro-Catholics ravaged western France[16]; and the Catholic Church in Europe was plundered of much of its property. France was right back where it was before the start of the French Revolution: the monarchy that was deposed in 1792 was back in power, and virtually all the lands that France had captured under Napoleon were given back to their rightful owners.

The July Revolution

The new political stability in France that had begun in 1815 after the exile of

Napoleon, lasted only 15 years. On July 25, 1830, King Charles X of France, brother of King Louis XVI and Louis XVIII, illegally suspended the constitution in order to abrogate recent parliamentary elections, which had resulted in an increase in radicals and pro-revolutionaries in office. Open insurrection in the streets of Paris by militant Republicans threatened to tear France apart again. The July Revolution of 1830 forced King Charles X, who had tried to restore the earlier authority of the Catholic Church, to abdicate on August 2. On August 9, the Duke of Orléans, Louis-Philippe, the "Citizen King," was crowned king by the radical liberals. Only by divine intervention was France spared a repeat of the horrible atrocities that followed the French Revolution in 1789.

Rue de Bac

A week before the onset of the July Revolution in Paris the Blessed Virgin Mary appeared to twenty-four-year-old Catherine Labouré at the Mother house of the Sisters of Charity, at 140 Rue de Bac in Paris. Catherine, whose pet name was Zoë, was the daughter of a yeoman-farmer from Fain-les-Moutiers in the Côte d'Or. She was the ninth of eleven children and worked on the family farm without any formal schooling. Catherine's mother, whom she loved dearly, died when she was only nine; thereupon, Catherine asked the Blessed Mother to be her new mother. At age 19, sensing God's call to the religious life, Catherine felt an inner urge to join the Sisters of Charity like her elder sister Louisa had. But Catherine's hard-headed father needed her help on the farm and wouldn't consent. One day Catherine had a dream of an old priest celebrating mass who beckoned her to come to him. In her dream, Catherine panicked and fled, coming to the room of a bed-ridden sick person where the same old priest now stood beside her and said, "My child, it is good to care for the sick. You run away from me now, but one day you will be glad to come to me. God has his designs on you! Do not forget it."

Catherine's father was totally against his daughter joining a convent, so he sent Catherine to Paris in 1828 to stay with her brother who owned a restaurant, hoping that the Parisian nightlife and the company of men would lure her away from her dream of becoming a nun. But Catherine grew tired of the debauchery of Paris, so she went to stay with her Aunt Jeanne, who worked at a girl's finishing school in Châtillon. Catherine hated the frivolity of Châtillon's high society as much as she hated the debauchery of Paris.[17] Aunt Jeanne finally convinced Catherine's father to let her join the Sisters of Charity in Châtillon after Catherine visited the sister's house and saw a portrait of the same old priest in her dream—St. Vincent de Paul, founder of the Congregation of the Mission (Lazarists) and the Sisters of Charity.

Zoë Labouré became a postulant of the Sisters of Charity on January 22,

1830, taking her birth name Catherine as her religious name. After her three-month postulancy in Châtillon, she was sent to Paris to the convent of the Sisters of Charity in the Rue de Bac to begin her novitiate—just four days before the translation of the relics of St. Vincent de Paul from Notre Dame to the Lazarist church in the Rue de Sèvres.

On the night of the festivities of the translation, Catherine began to have visions of the heart of St. Vincent, followed by visions of Christ the King a couple of months later. The vision of Christ was followed by Christ the King's symbols falling to the ground, which Catherine understood to mean that the King of France would soon be overthrown. The first of three apparitions of Our Lady of the Miraculous Medal began a month later. On the night of July 18, 1830, just hours away from the Feast of St. Vincent, Catherine was awakened in her sleep by the voice of a "shining child," about five years old, standing beside her bed.

"Sister, Sister, Sister! Come to the Chapel. The Blessed Virgin is waiting for you."

The startled and sleepy-eyed Catherine replied, "But how can I cross the dormitory? I will be heard."

"Be calm," the little angel replied back. "It's half past eleven. Everyone is asleep. Come, I am waiting for you."

As Catherine quietly entered the chapel that was somehow all aglow with the light of votive candles, the little boy angel announced suddenly:

"Here is the Blessed Virgin; here she is."

With the sound of rustling silk, Mary, so young and beautiful, appeared sitting on the director's chair beside the altar. Catherine, in awe at what was happening, at first didn't believe her eyes. This time Catherine's guardian angel sternly admonished her in a grownup's voice:

"This is the Blessed Virgin!"

Now convinced that the apparition was real, she knelt on the floor and tenderly hugged Mary's knees and put her hands in Mary's lap. Mary conversed with Catherine at length on the proper conduct of a sister and then tearfully confided in her prophetic secrets, some of which have been revealed and some that remain mysteries. What we do know that was said is as follows:

"Our dear Lord loves you very much. He wishes to give you a mission. It will be the cause of much suffering to you, but you will overcome it, knowing that what you do is for the glory of God. You will be contradicted, but you will have the grace to bear it. Don't be afraid.

"You will see certain things. You must report them. You will be given the words through prayer.

"The times are very evil. Misfortunes will fall upon France. The entire world will

be overcome by evils of all kind. But come to the foot of the altar. Here, great graces will be poured out upon all those who ask for them in confidence and fervor. They will be bestowed on the great and the small . . .

"The moment will come when the danger will be extreme. It will seem that all is lost. At that time, I will be with you. Have confidence. You will recognize my coming and the protection of God over the community, the protection of St. Vincent over both communities. Have confidence; do not be discouraged; I will be with you then.

"But it will not be the same for other [religious] communities—there will be victims—among the clergy of Paris there will be victims—Monseigneur the Archbishop.

"My child, the cross will be treated with contempt; they will hurl it upon the ground. Blood will flow; they will open up again the side of Our Lord. The streets will run with blood. Monseigneur the Archbishop will be stripped of his garments. My child, the whole world will be in sadness."[18]

Catherine understood in her heart that this prophecy would take place within forty years' time.[19]

Mary then left as quickly as she came. The little angel escorted Catherine back to her cell and then he vanished, too. Within a week the Blessed Mother's prediction about King Charles X's downfall came true. Once again, anarchy reigned in the streets of Paris during the "Glorious Three Days" of the July Revolution of 1830. The streets of Paris became a bloodbath and King Charles X was forced to flee for his life. Fierce persecutions against Catholic priests and religious organizations were started by the revolutionaries and Archbishop de Quelen had to flee for his life twice. The Sisters of Charity on Rue de Bac, however, were left unharmed—just as Mary had predicted.

When the puppet-king, Louis-Philippe, took the throne on the first of August in 1830, the French revolutionaries were, for now, satisfied that they had won a victory: Louis-Philippe was a figurehead with virtually no real power in government.

The February Revolution

Eighteen years later, in the same year that Karl Marx's *Communist Manifesto* was published, revolution once again threatened to destroy the peace of France and Europe. France's February Revolution of 1848 broke out after Prime Minister Guizot made it illegal to hold political meetings without government permits. When young radicals began holding dinner banquets with the secret intention of discussing politics, the government then tried outlawing dinner banquets. One such banquet that was banned in Paris set off one of the most bloody urban street riots ever seen in that city. King Louis-Philippe fled to London and a Second French Republic was proclaimed by radical left-wingers and workers demanding political and economic reforms.

In June of that same year, the radicals of the February Revolution who had promised welfare and employment for all were brutally crushed by the Minister of War, General Louis Cavaignac. The workshops that had been created by the government to reduce unemployment were being used by radical militants to recruit another revolutionary army. In response, the French government shut them down, putting many Frenchmen out of work. When the government of France then decreed that all unemployed single men between 17 and 25 be conscripted for military service, and all other unemployed or striking workers be transported to labor in the countryside, the French people revolted. Thousands died in four days of street fighting in Paris and three thousand more were later executed. Many of those not killed were deported. In the midst of the fighting, the Catholic Church was viciously attacked again and the Archbishop of Paris, Denis-Auguste Affre, was mortally wounded by a stray bullet at barricades in Paris while attempting to persuade insurgents to submit to governmental authority. Mary's prophecy to Sister Catherine Labouré regarding the victimization of the Archbishop of Paris had been fulfilled for the second time in France's February Revolution of 1848.

France's February Revolution spread to Italy, Germany, Austria, and Hungary, threatening the stability of the European monarchies. Pope Pius IX was forced to flee the Vatican in November of 1848, as a new leftist Republic was declared in Rome. In France, Prince Louis Napoleon, the nephew of Napoleon Bonaparte, was elected president of the Second Republic in December of 1848, with egomaniacal plans of his own—he intended to become another French dictator like his uncle. On December 2, 1852, Louis Napoleon was crowned Emperor Napoleon III, the second emperor of France. By that time, Mary had already appeared to two farm children in La Salette, France, in 1846, to warn the French people to be on guard against the evils of Napoleon III (I write more on the prophecies of La Salette in the next chapter).

The French Communards

On July 19, 1870, the short but terrible Franco-Prussian War between Napoleon III and Otto von Bismarck began. In no time at all, France was soundly defeated at Sedan and Emperor Napoleon III overthrown.

With the ouster of Emperor Napoleon III, France became a Republic for the third time on September 4, 1870. Beset by a terrible famine, Paris was captured by the advancing Prussian army on January 28, 1871, and the beleaguered French army conceded victory to the Prussians on May 10. As a result of the Franco-Prussian War, a united Germany now became the strongest nation in the world, and we now know the danger that posed to world peace.

France, on the other hand, was humiliated and has never regained her stature as a world power—something that the proud French people have never been able to live down.

Fearing the institution of another French monarchy, the radical Commune of Paris (the communards), led by left-wing writers, artists, socialists, intellectuals, idealists, rowdies, and the French National Guard, took over a Paris hotel on March 28, 1871, shouting "Vive la Commune." After taking over the city, an all-out battle for Paris began on May 21. The conservative marshal of France's army, Comte de MacMahon, entered Paris with his Versailles troops and retook control of the city on May 28, boulevard by boulevard, barricade by barricade, body by body. Befittingly, the left-wing, anti-Catholic communards made their last stand in a cemetery. There they were totally annihilated by MacMahon.

An estimated 20,000 communards died in defending Paris during the communard uprising or were executed in retaliation for the killing of hostages, which included Archbishop Georges Darboy of Paris. Mary's 1830 prophecies to Sister Catherine Labouré about the misfortunes of France and the sufferings of the Archbishop of Paris had come true for the third time in forty years: first in 1830, then in 1848, and then in 1870-71.

The Miraculous Medal

After the apparition of July 18, 1830, Mary visited Catherine Labouré again on November 27, 1830, in the chapel at the convent on Rue de Bac at 5:30 P.M., during the novices' evening prayers. Seen only by Catherine, Mary suddenly appeared in a white silken robe and long, flowing veil, standing on a green serpent coiled over a white globe. Mary held in her outstretched hand a golden globe surmounted by a cross. With her gaze directed towards heaven, the golden globe suddenly disappeared. With her hands extended towards heaven, each finger exhibited rings with beautifully colored gems, from which rays of light were cast downward from some of the precious jewels upon the white globe beneath her feet. Mary explained to Catherine the meaning of the vision:

> "The globe you see represents the whole world, especially France, and each person in particular. They [the rays] are the symbols of the graces I shed upon those who ask for them. The gems from which rays do not fall are the graces for which souls forget to ask."

As she was talking, the apparition of Mary was framed in a semi-circle with the words *"O Mary, conceived without sin, pray for us who have recourse to thee."* Mary's hands then went down to her sides with the palms facing forward. The frame of Mary then turned 180 degrees. On the backside of the frame was a large "M" intersected by a bar surmounted by a cross. Under the "M" were the sacred hearts of Jesus and Mary—his crowned with thorns and hers pierced by a sword. Mary then gave Catherine these instructions:

> *"Have a Medal struck after this model. All who wear it will receive great graces; they should wear it around their neck. Graces will abound for those who wear it in confidence."*[20]

Catherine told no one except her confessor, Father Aladel, what she had seen. Understandably, the Father, at first, was quite skeptical and unwilling to take Catherine's request seriously. But as time went on practically everything that Catherine had predicted had come true. Afraid of displeasing Mary and God for his unbelief, Fr. Aladel convinced himself that Catherine was telling the truth. With Fr. Aladel's testimony, the Medal of the Immaculate Conception, as it was first called, was finally struck in 1832 by order of Archbishop de Quelen of Paris.

Mary's medal became an overnight sensation, as reports of miraculous healings and conversions began circulating by those who wore it. So many, in fact, that the people began calling it the "Miraculous Medal."

The most famous miracle associated with the Miraculous Medal is the conversion of a bigoted Jew, Alphonse Ratisbonne, to Catholicism after a friend, Baron Bussiere, had convinced him to wear the Miraculous Medal in a dare. Taking the dare, Ratisbonne, who hated Catholics, went to the Church of St. Andrea's with Bussiere one day to make arrangements for the funeral of a recently deceased mutual friend, Comte de la Ferronays, who had prayed for Ratisbonne's conversion right before he died. Ratisbonne was alone in the church, when suddenly Mary appeared to him in a side chapel, looking exactly like she did on the Miraculous Medal. So profoundly shaken was Ratisbonne that he immediately converted to Catholicism and later went on to became a priest, taking the name Marie Alphonse Ratisbonne.[21]

Sister Catherine, meanwhile, transferred to Enghein Hospital near Paris where she would care for the poor, the elderly, and the infirm for the next 45 years. At the order of her confessor, Catherine wrote down everything relating to her apparitions for church records, including a request by Mary to have a statue sculpted in her honor. Mary's last request was finally fulfilled when a statue of the "Gracious Virgin" was sculpted and placed on the altar of the Chapel of the Miraculous Medal in Paris twenty years after Catherine's death (December 31, 1876).

On May 28, 1933, Catherine Labouré was beatified in St. Peter's Basilica in Rome, and on July 27, 1947, she was canonized. Her incorruptible body remains on display in the Chapel of the Miraculous Medal in Paris for all the world to see, more youthful-looking now than when she died. Sister

Catherine's incorruptible body serves as a testimony to her saintliness and the validity of the apparitions in Rue de Bac. And thanks to Catherine's special mission from God, the hundreds of millions of medals that have been struck since 1832 have given inspiration and hope to countless multitudes.

Chapter Five

Our Lady in Tears:
La Salette, France, 1846

"Nation will rise against nation, and kingdom against kingdom; there will be famines and earthquakes from place to place."

Matt. 24:7

Famine in Europe

By the 1840s, more than half of the 8.5 million people living in Ireland were surviving solely on potatoes. For nearly a century there had been over twenty large-scale failures of the Irish potato crop, but the potato blight of 1845 was without precedent.[1] The extremely wet, foggy weather in the summer of 1845 caused the potatoes to putrefy within a few days of lifting from the soil. When the potato blight reappeared in 1846 and 1847, famine and death spread rapidly across Ireland. By 1851, nearly one million Irish had starved to death and another million were forced to emigrate to the United States or England.

France, too, was hit hard by famine in 1846, as its wheat, potato, walnut, and grape crops were stricken with disease. France's failed agricultural harvests, ensuing economic depression, and famine of 1847 were some of the main precipitating factors of the European Revolution of 1848. During the four bloody "June Days" revolution in Paris in 1848, 1,500 French revolutionaries were killed by France's General Cavaignac and 3,000 more hunted down and executed. The ruthless routing of the rebels in Paris by General Cavaignac triggered rebellions in other capitals throughout Europe in the bloody summer of 1848.

Two years prior, on September 19, 1846, the Blessed Virgin Mary had appeared to two young cattle herders from Corps, France, named Mélanie Mathieu (Calvat) and Maximin Giraud, on a mountainside in the parish of La Salette near Grenoble, in Southeastern France. Mélanie, 14, and Maximin, 11, had just gotten up from their afternoon nap in a sunny pasture and were trying to round up their two employers' cattle when all of a sudden a brilliant ball of light appeared down in a ravine. As the startled children looked on in amazement, the radiant figure of a woman began to emerge from inside the ball. She was an extraordinarily beautiful young lady, dressed in a heavenly fabric bursting with light and wearing a luminous crown. She appeared to be sitting down and bent forward at the waist with her hands covering her face as if she were trying to conceal her crying. Slowly, the tearful young woman stood up and crossed her arms against her chest. Speaking on Jesus' behalf, she addressed the two children in a serious tone of voice:

> *"Come to me, my children. Do not be afraid. I am here to tell you something of the greatest importance.*
>
> *"If my people will not obey, I shall be compelled to loose my Son's arm. It is so heavy, so pressing that I can no longer restrain it.*
>
> *"How long I have suffered for you! If my Son is not to cast you off, I am obliged to entreat Him without ceasing. But you take no least notice of that. No matter how well you pray in future, no matter how well you act, you will never be able to make up to me what I have endured for your sake.*
>
> *"'I have appointed for you six days for working. The seventh I have reserved for myself. And no one will give it to me.' This is what causes the weight of my Son's arm to be so crushing.*
>
> *"The cart drivers cannot swear without bringing in my Son's name.*
>
> *"These are two things that make my Son's arm so burdensome. If the harvest is spoiled it is your fault. I warned you last year [1845] by means of the potatoes. You paid no heed. Quite the reverse, when you discovered that the potatoes had rotted, you swore, you abused my Son's name. They will continue to rot and by Christmas this year there will be none left.*
>
> *"If you have grain, it will do you no good to sow it, for what you sow the beasts will devour, and any part of it that springs up will crumble into dust when you thresh it. A great famine is coming. But before that happens, the children under seven years of age will be seized with trembling and die in their parents' arms. The grownups will pay for their sins by hunger. The grapes will rot and the walnuts will turn bad . . . "*

The lady then turned to Mélanie and gave her a secret that only she could hear. She did likewise for Maximin. Then she continued speaking out loud:

> *"If people are converted, the rocks will become piles of wheat, and it will be found that the potatoes have sown themselves. . . .*
>
> *"Only a few rather old women go to Mass in the summer. All the rest work every Sunday throughout the summer. And in winter, when they don't know what to do with themselves, they go to Mass only to poke fun at religion.*

"During Lent they flock to the butcher shops, like dogs. . . . My children, you will make this known to all my people."[2]

As Mary rose in the air and faded from view, Mélanie guessed that perhaps the heavenly visitor was a great saint. Returning to Ablandins, the little mountain village where their employers lived, Maximin told Pierre Selme, one of the owners of the livestock that they'd been tending, everything that happened. Maximin then told Baptiste Pra, Mélanie's employer, the same story. When Mélanie was later quizzed about the apparition, she corroborated Maximin's testimony to what they saw.

The village of Ablandins was soon buzzing with excitement over the apparition. In the days that followed, the mayor, the town councilor, the police, and the parish priest thoroughly cross-examined the pair, but were unable to trip them up. They threatened them with jail, ridiculed them, offered them bribes, called them liars, but still the children refused to recant or alter their stories.

When examining the site of the apparition, one of the investigators broke off a piece of rock where the lady had been sitting, which was known to be a source of water during the heavy rains and spring snow melt. To his amazement, water came gushing forth, which was very unusual for the dry summertime. He bottled some of it and brought it back to a seriously ill woman who lived in town. The sick woman made a novena to Our Lady of La Salette for nine days and each day drank some of the spring water. On the ninth day her health was miraculously restored.

Pilgrimages to La Salette occurred spontaneously, as reports of miracles circulated throughout France. Hundreds of thousands were drawn by an irresistible force to make a sojourn there. People began going to confession again, attending mass reverently, and receiving communion. Working on Sundays ceased, and religious holy days were celebrated with reverence for God, and people stopped using the Lord's name in vain. Many conversions took place in France because of La Salette, and a true spiritual revival swept the land.

A bishop's delegation, headed by Father Rousselot and Father Orcel, affirmed "the extraordinary event at La Salette," and five years later, on November 16, 1851, Cardinal Lambruschini approved the findings. A new community of priests began functioning nearby (the Missionaries of La Salette), which spread to many other parts of the world. A shrine to Our Lady of La Salette was erected and a basilica finished in 1879. Today, millions of pilgrims continue to visit La Salette each year, and it is one of the most visited shrines in the world.

As adults, the two young visionaries of La Salette led rather unremarkable lives. Maximin tried to become a priest but decided that wasn't his calling. He went through several career changes before dying at age forty in 1875. Mélanie, a lifelong mystic, became a nun (Sister Mary of the Cross), but went from convent to convent looking for the contentment that she never found. She had a hard time adjusting to the solitude and discipline of consecrated living and craved too much the public affection and notoriety that she received as a young visionary. After countless sufferings, which included the stigmata of Christ and the contradiction of unbelievers, especially within the church, Mélanie died while getting ready for mass on December 15, 1904.

The Secret of La Salette was written down by Maximin and Mélanie in 1851 and delivered in a sealed envelope to Pope Pius IX, who was given permission to make Mélanie's secrets known in 1858. Maximin's secret was more of a benign, personal nature, while Mélanie's was meant to be a detailed prophetic warning to the world, for the near term and future. The most explicit, lengthy, and prophetic message to date, the Secret of La Salette, foresees the coming of wars and revolution; Satan's release from hell with all his minions in 1864 for the end-times battle against the church; the coming of false prophets and false wonders; satanic miracles; the erroneous belief in reincarnation, occultism, channeling, spirit guides, near-death experiences that preach another gospel; the profanation of the sacred, religious hypocrisy and apostasy; unbelief; pick-and-choose Catholicism; carnality within the ranks of the religious; the suppression and persecution of the Catholic Church; government-sponsored secularism and anti-Christianity; revolution; civil wars; the rise of communist and fascist dictators (the forerunners of the Antichrist); the coming of Word War I; the rise of Hitler and the Second World War; natural disasters, severe storms, floods, fires, plagues, earthquakes, altered seasons, famines; an increase in violent crime; general rebellion against all authority; a time of false peace; the two assassination attempts on Pope John Paul II's life, his physical and spiritual suffering; the three-day chastisement of the world; the triumph of the Catholic Church after the chastisement; the short period of peace that follows; the incarnation of the Antichrist from Rome; Satan's final battle against the church; the destruction of Rome; and the end of the world. Whew! What a secret!

The Secret of La Salette

The Secret of La Salette has been substantiated with incredible accuracy by historical events and reaffirmed, in part, by twentieth-century visionaries. Nothing in the secret contradicts sacred scripture or the teachings of the Catholic Church. La Salette's message, in its entirety, taken from Fr. Gouin's book, *Sister Mary of the Cross: Shepherdess of La Salette,* is as follows:

"The priests, the ministers of my Son, the priests by their wicked lives, by their irreverence and their impiety in the celebration of the holy mysteries, by their love of money, their love of honors and pleasures, the priests have become cesspools of impurity. Yes, the priests are asking for vengeance, and vengeance is hanging over their heads. Woe to the priests and those dedicated to God who by their infidelity and their wicked lives are crucifying My Son again! The sins of those consecrated to God cry out towards heaven and call for vengeance, and now vengeance is at their door, for there is no one left to beg mercy and forgiveness for the people. There are more generous souls, there is no one left worthy of offering a spotless sacrifice to the Eternal on behalf of the world.

"God will strike in an unprecedented way.

"Woe to the inhabitants of the earth! God will exhaust his wrath upon them, and no one will be able to escape so many afflictions altogether.

"The chiefs, the leaders of the people of God have neglected prayer and penance, and the devil has bedimmed their intelligence. They have become wandering stars which the old devil will drag along with his tail to make them perish. God will allow the old serpent to cause divisions among those who reign, in every society and every family. Physical and moral agonies will be suffered. God will abandon mankind to itself and will send punishments which will follow one after the other for more than thirty-five years.

"The society of men is on the eve of the most terrible scourges and the gravest events. Mankind must expect to be ruled with an iron rod and to drink from the chalice of wrath from God.

"May the vicar of my Son, Pope Pius IX never leave Rome again after 1859; may he, however, be steadfast and noble, may he fight with his weapons of faith and love. I will be at his side. May he be on his guard against Napoleon [III]; he is two-faced, and when he wishes to make himself Pope as well as Emperor, soon God will draw back from him. He is the eagle who, always wanting to rise higher, will fall on the sword he wished to use to force his people to be raised up.

"Italy will be punished for her ambition in wanting to shake off the yoke of the Lord of Lords. And so she will be left to fight a war; blood will flow on all sides. Churches will be locked up or desecrated. Priests and religious orders will be hunted down, and made to die a cruel death. Several will abandon the Faith and a great number of priests and members of religious orders will break away from the true religion; among these people there will even be bishops.

"May the Pope guard against the performers of miracles. For the time has come when the most astonishing wonders will take place in the earth and in the air.

"In the year 1864, Lucifer together with a large numbers of demons will be unloosed from hell; they will put an end to faith little by little, even in those dedicated to God. They will blind them in such a way, that unless they are blessed with a special grace, these people will take on the spirit of these angels in hell; several religious institutes will lose all faith and lose many souls.

"Evil books will be abundant on earth, and the spirit of darkness will spread everywhere a universal slackening in all that concerns the service of God. They will have great power over Nature; there will be churches built to serve these spirits. People

will be transported [spiritually] from one place to another by these evil spirits, even priests, for they will not have been guided by the good spirit of the gospel which is the spirit of humility, charity and zeal for the glory of God. On occasion, the dead and the righteous will be brought back to life.

('That is to say that these dead will take on the form of righteous souls which have lived on earth, in order to lead men further astray; these so-called resurrected dead, who will be nothing but the devil in this form, will preach another Gospel contrary to that of the true Jesus Christ, denying the existence of Heaven; that is to say, the souls of the damned. All these souls will appear as if united with their bodies.')

"In all places there will be extraordinary wonders, because true faith has died and a false light shines on the world. Woe to the Princes of the Church whose only occupation will be to heap wealth upon more wealth, and to preserve their authority and proud domination!

"The vicar of my Son will have much to suffer, as, for a time, the Church will be the victim of great persecution: this will be a time of darkness. The Church will suffer a terrible crisis.

"As the holy Faith of God is forgotten, every individual will wish to be his own guide and superior to his fellow men. Civil and ecclesiastical authority will be abolished. All order and justice will be trampled underfoot. Nothing will be seen but murder, hatred jealousy, falsehood and discord without love for the mother country or the family. The Holy Father will suffer greatly. I will be by His side to the end in order to receive his sacrifice. The wicked will make several attempts on his life, but they cannot harm Him. But neither he nor his successor will live to see the triumph of the Church of God.

"All the civil governments will have one and the same plan, which will be to abolish and do away with every religious principle, to make way for materialism, atheism, spiritualism and vices of all kinds.

"In the year 1865, there will be desecration of holy places.[3] *In convents, the flower of the Church will decompose and the devil will make himself like the King of all hearts. May those in charge of religious communities be on guard against the people they must receive, for the devil will resort to all his evil tricks to induce sinners into religious orders, for disorder and the love of carnal pleasures will be spread all over the earth.*

"France, Italy, Spain and England will be at war. Blood will flow in the streets. Frenchmen will fight Frenchmen, Italian will fight Italian. A general war will follow which will be appalling. For a time, God will cease to remember France and Italy because the Gospel of Jesus Christ has been forgotten. The wicked will make use of all their evil ways. Men will kill each other, massacre each other even in their homes.

"At the first blow of His thundering sword, the mountains and all of Nature will tremble in terror, for the disorders and crimes of men have pierced the vault of the heavens. Paris will burn and Marseilles will be engulfed. People will believe that all is lost. Nothing will be seen but murder, nothing will be heard but the clash of arms and blasphemy.

"The righteous will suffer greatly. Their prayers, their penance and their tears

will rise up to Heaven, and all of God's people will beg for forgiveness and mercy and will plead for my help and intercession. And then Jesus Christ, in an act of His justice and His great mercy will command His Angels to have all His enemies put to death. Suddenly, the persecutors of the Church of Jesus Christ and all those given over to sin will perish and the earth will be desert-like. And then peace will be made, and man will be reconciled with God. Jesus Christ will be served, worshiped and glorified. Charity will flourish everywhere. The new kings will be the right arm of the Holy Church, which will be strong, humble, pious in its poor but fervent imitations of Jesus Christ. The Gospel will be preached everywhere and mankind will make great progress in its Faith, for their will be unity among the workers of Jesus Christ and man will live in fear of God.

"This peace among men will be short-lived. Twenty-five years of plentiful harvest will make them forget that the sins of men are the cause of all the troubles on this earth.

"A forerunner of the Antichrist, with his troops gathered from several nations, will fight against the true Christ, the only Savior of the world. He will shed much blood and will want to annihilate the worship of God to make himself be looked upon as a God.

"The earth will be struck by calamities of all kinds (in addition to plague and famine which will be widespread). There will be a series of wars until the last war, which will then be fought by the ten kings of the Antichrist, all of whom will have one and the same plan and will be the only rulers of the world. Before this comes to pass, there will be a kind of false peace in the world. People will think of nothing but amusement. The wicked will give themselves over to all kinds of sin. But the children of the Holy Church, the children of the Faith, my true followers, they will grow in their love for God and in all the virtues most precious to Me. Blessed are the souls humbly guided by the Holy Spirit! I will fight on their side until they reach a fullness of years.

"Nature is asking for vengeance because of man, and she trembles with dread at what must happen to the earth stained with crime. Tremble, earth, and you who proclaim yourselves as serving Jesus Christ and who, on the inside only adore yourselves, tremble, for God will hand you over to His enemy, because the holy places are in a state of corruption. Many convents are no longer houses of God, but the grazing ground of Asmodeus and his like. It will be during this time that the Antichrist will be born of a Hebrew nun, a false virgin who will communicate with the old serpent, the master of impurity, his father will be a Bishop. At birth he will spew out blasphemy; he will have teeth, in a word, he will be the devil incarnate. He will scream horribly, he will perform wonders, he will feed on nothing but impurity. He will have brothers who, although not devils incarnate like him, will be children of evil. At the age of twelve they will draw attention to themselves by the gallant victories they have won; soon they will lead armies aided by the legions of hell.

"The seasons will be altered, the earth will produce nothing but bad fruit, the stars will lose their regular motion, the moon will reflect only a faint reddish glow. Water and fire will give the earth's globe convulsions and terrible earthquakes which will swallow up mountains, cities, etc. . . .

"*Rome will lose the Faith and become the seat of the Antichrist.*

"*The demons of the air together with the Antichrist will perform great wonders on earth and in the atmosphere, and men will become more and more perverted. God will take care of his faithful servants and men of good will. The Gospel will be preached everywhere, and people of all nations will get to know the truth.*

"*I make an urgent appeal to the earth. I call on the true disciples of the living God who reigns in Heaven; I call on My children, the true faithful, those who have given themselves to Me so that I may lead them to My Divine Son, those whom I carry in My arms, so to speak, those who have lived according to My spirit. Finally I call on the Apostles of the last Days, the faithful disciples of Jesus Christ who have lived in scorn for the world and for themselves, in poverty and humility, in scorn and in silence, in prayer and mortification, in chastity and in union with God, in suffering and unknown to the world. It is time they came out and filled the world with light. Go and reveal yourselves as My cherished children. I am on your side and within you, provided that your faith is the light which shines upon you in these unhappy days. May your zeal make you hungry for the glory and the honor of Jesus Christ. Fight children of light, you, the few who can see. For now is the time of all times, the end of all ends.*

"*The Church will be in eclipse, the world will be in dismay. But now Enoch and Elijah will come, filled with the spirit of God. They will preach with the might of God, and men of goodwill will believe in God, and many souls will be comforted. They will make great strides forward through the virtue of the Holy Spirit, and will condemn the diabolic errors of the Antichrist. Woe to the inhabitants of the earth! There will be bloody wars and famines, plagues and infectious diseases. It will rain with a fearful hail of animals. There will be thunderstorms which will shake cities, earthquakes which will swallow up countries. Voices will be heard in the air. Men will beat their heads against walls, call for death, and on the other hand death will be their torment. Blood will flow on all sides. Who will be the victor if God does not shorten the duration of the test? At the blood, the tears and the prayers of the righteous, God will relent. Enoch and Elijah will be put to death. Pagan Rome will disappear. The fire of Heaven will fall and consume three cities. All the universe will be struck with terror and many will let themselves be led astray because they have not worshiped the true Christ who lives among them. It is time; the sun is darkening; only faith will survive.*

"*Now is the time, the abyss is opening. Here is the king of kings of darkness, here is the Beast with his subjects, calling himself the Savior of the world. He will rise proudly in the air to go to Heaven. He will be smothered by the breath of the Archangel Saint Michael. He will fall, and the earth, which will have been in a continual series of evolutions for three days, will open up its fiery bowels; and he will be plunged for eternity with all his followers into the everlasting chasms of hell. And then water and fire will purge the earth and consume all the work's of men's pride and all will be renewed. God will be served and glorified.*"[4]

La Salette was the first of the Marian apparitions prophesying the terrible world wars to come, as well as an imminent chastisement on unrepentant man. God chose to give these warnings to two young children because of their lack of knowledge of eschatology and theology, their faithfulness to the message, and their credibility against skeptics and nay-sayers. For as the passage in scripture says:

> "Out of the mouth of babes and infants you have drawn a defense against your foes, to silence enemy and avenger."[5]

Chapter Six

Our Lady of Lourdes:
France, 1858

"Darwinian Man, though well-behaved, at best is only a monkey shaved!"

W. S. Gilbert, *Princess Ida*

The Doctrine of the Immaculate Conception

On December 8, 1854, in his encyclical *Ineffabilis Deus,* Pope Pius IX defined the doctrine of the Immaculate Conception, which commemorated Mary's preservation from original sin from the first moment of her conception:

"The doctrine which holds that the most Blessed Virgin Mary was preserved from all stain of original sin in the first instant of her conception by a singular grace and privilege from Almighty God . . . has been revealed by God and must therefore be firmly and constantly believed by all the faithful."

By making this proclamation, Pope Pius IX ratified the long-held Catholic tradition of the Immaculate Conception, and instituted its solemnity as a holy day of obligation to be celebrated each year on December 8.[1]

The Cynicism and Unbelief of Science

As expected, most intellectuals and scholars of the mid-nineteenth century ridiculed Pope Pius IX's dogmatic proclamation of Mary as the Immaculate Conception because, for one reason, the English naturalist Charles Darwin had supposedly just proven, in an essay he had written in 1844, that mankind had evolved from monkeys through the random, impersonal processes of natural selection, and hadn't been purposely created by an intelligent God in his own likeness to be given dominion over the earth and an eternal inheritance in heaven as Christians claim.[2] To the unbelieving secular scientists, *Darwinian Evolution,* the inherent progeny of godless rationalism, proved that there was no Adam and Eve, no original sin, no fall from grace, no Redeemer, and no Immaculate Woman Full of Grace.

Long ago rejecting the religion of their ancestors, most intellectuals of the nineteenth century believed in Darwinian evolution and the other popular atheistic philosophies of human science like *Positivism,* which states that theology and metaphysics are earlier, imperfect modes of knowledge, and that true, "positive" knowledge is based on natural phenomenon and their properties and relations verified only by the empirical sciences. If you couldn't see it, smell it, touch it, or taste it, it didn't exist. Another popular atheistic philosophy in the nineteenth century was the *Mechanistic* theory, which maintains that all physical processes, such as life, are mechanically determined and capable of complete explanation by chemistry and physics. The mechanistic philosophy, which asserts that everything is a machine, is itself closely related to yet another nineteenth-century atheistic philosophy called *Materialism,* which says that everything in the universe is made of matter only.[3] Materialism, in turn, is closely akin to an earlier atheistic philosophy called *Naturalism,* the popular, cynical philosophy of the Enlightenment which maintains that everything there is belongs to nature, and the apparent exceptions, like miracles and visions, can be explained away by science. The vast majority of today's scientists and intellectuals still ascribe to one or more of these popular atheistic philosophies.

Rationalists, Darwinists, Positivists, Mechanists, Materialists, and Naturalists, by their own definitions, are either atheists or agnostics,[4] and believe that Catholic dogmas like the Immaculate Conception are for the poor, ignorant, and easily led masses of the Catholic Church—not the clever and learned elite of the esteemed universities like themselves.

But once again, God proved all the clever and learned wrong when he sent the Blessed Virgin Mary to Lourdes, France, in 1858 to testify to the truthfulness of Pope Pius IX's doctrine of the Immaculate Conception. Unfortunately, a year after Our Lady appeared in Lourdes, Darwin's infamous book, *On the Origin of the Species by Means of Natural Selection; or, the Preservation of Favored Races in the Struggle for Life,*[5] the so-called "book that shocked the world," was published in England in 1859. It would go down in history as the book most responsible for destroying the faith of hundreds of millions, if not billions, of Christians. Not surprisingly, Darwin's atheistic theories are still being taught in the majority of our public schools and universities as scientific fact, not theory.[6]

The following is a brief account of the apparitions of Our Lady of Lourdes to Bernadette Soubirous and the validation of the dogma of the Immaculate Conception by the Virgin Mary herself, both of which disprove Darwin's degrading axiom that human beings are nothing more than walking, talking monkeys.[7]

Bernadette Soubirous

Bernadette Soubirous was a poor little peasant girl who lived with her family in a cold, drafty little room about the size of a bedroom, in a section of an old building that used to be a prison. Bernadette's family became impoverished when debt forced her father to lose his mill, which also served as their home. Destitute and out of work, Bernadette's father could only get odd jobs, which barely paid enough to feed his family.

The eldest of six children, fourteen-year-old Bernadette was a sickly girl who frequently suffered from asthma and other ailments. The draftiness of the little room where her family lived only worsened her condition. Although sickly, Bernadette was a good, obedient, and kind little girl, but not very well educated—especially on matters concerning Catholic doctrines and traditions. On February 11, 1858, Bernadette's mother sent Bernadette, her sister, Toinette, and a neighbor girl out to gather firewood at the grotto of Massabielle near the River Gave. Alone near the grotto while the other two girls were off gathering wood, Bernadette noticed something strange:

"I had just begun to take off my first stocking [to cross the canal in front of the grotto] when suddenly I heard a great noise like the sound of a storm. I looked to the right, to the left, under the trees of the river, but nothing moved; I thought I was mistaken. I went on taking off my shoes and stockings; then I heard a fresh noise like the first. I was frightened and stood straight up. I lost all power of speech and thought when, turning my head toward the grotto, I saw at one of the openings of the grotto a rosebush, one only, moving as if it were very windy. Almost at the same time there came out of the interior of the grotto a golden-colored cloud, and soon after a lady, young and beautiful, exceedingly beautiful, the like of whom I had never seen, came and placed herself at the entrance of the opening above the rosebush. She looked at me immediately, smiled at me and signed me to advance, as if she had been my mother. All fear had left me but I seemed to know no longer where I was. I rubbed my eyes, I shut them, I opened them; but the lady was still there continuing to smile at me and making me understand that I was not mistaken. Without thinking of what I was doing, I took my Rosary in my hands and went on my knees. The lady made a sign of approval with her head and herself took into her hands a Rosary which hung on her right arm. When I attempted to begin the Rosary and tried to lift my hand to my forehead, my arm remained paralyzed, and it was only after the lady had signed herself that I could do the same. The lady left me to pray all alone; she passed the beads of her Rosary between her fingers but she said nothing; only at the end of each decade did she say the 'Gloria' with me. When the recitation of the Rosary was finished the lady returned to the interior of the rock and the golden cloud disappeared with her."[8]

Bernadette explained what happened on the way home to the other two girls who saw nothing, and asked her sister to keep it a secret; but, of course, she couldn't. When her mother found out what Bernadette had seen, she scolded Bernadette and told her to drive those silly illusions out of her head. But Bernadette knew in her heart they were real. She went on to explain the lady's appearance:

> "She had the appearance of a young girl of about sixteen or seventeen. She is dressed in a white robe, girdled at the waist with a blue ribbon which flows down all around the neck; the sleeves are long and tight-fitting. She wears upon her head a veil which is also white; this veil gives just a glimpse of her hair and then falls down at the back below her waist. Her feet are bare but covered by the last folds of her robe except at a point where a yellow rose shines upon each of them. She holds on her right arm a Rosary of white beads with a chain of gold shining like the two roses on her feet."[9]

The three girls went back to the grotto three days later, this time armed with holy water to test the spirit. Mary reappeared once again, but only Bernadette could see her. When Bernadette poured some of the holy water on the ground, Our Lady only smiled. Bernadette was now convinced that this wasn't some trick of the devil.

By now the whole village was well aware of what was going on at Massabielle. When Bernadette returned to the grotto with some of the townsfolk for the third time on February 18, the lady appeared with the request that Bernadette return fifteen more times at regular intervals. In the course of this apparition, Mary told Bernadette that she couldn't promise her happiness in this world, but that happiness would be waiting for her in heaven.

A physician accompanied Bernadette on her next trip and concluded that he could find nothing abnormal in her physical condition during her ecstasy. It was February 21, Bernadette's sixth apparition, when the lady told Bernadette to:

> "*Pray for sinners.*"

Great crowds were now following Bernadette to the grotto of Massabielle, alarming the public officials that someone might get hurt or fall off the steep ledges surrounding the grotto opening. So the Procureur Impérial, M. Dutour, told Bernadette not to go down to the grotto any more. But Bernadette refused on account of her promise to the lady to return. Taken aback by her determination, the Procureur said he would have to think it over. However, the police commissioner, Dominique Jacomet, was more determined to put a stop to what he thought was a charade. The commissioner, however, found no inconsistencies in Bernadette's story upon interrogation, so he only threatened her with imprisonment if she ever went back to the grotto.

Bernadette's father came to the police station to take her home, and the commissioner gave them both a stern warning not to go back to the grotto. Defying police orders, on her way home, Bernadette turned around and went back to the grotto. Shadowed by the police and a mob that followed her, Bernadette had no apparition that day, but had to endure the cruel taunts of hecklers and unbelievers.

Two days later, on February 23, Bernadette returned to the grotto and was graced by another apparition of Mary, who implored:

> *"Penitence!"*

The following day Mary told Bernadette to:

> *"Drink from the fountain and bathe in it."*

Puzzled because there was no fountain at the grotto of Massabielle, Bernadette began scooping frantically at the ground, generating laughter and mocking remarks from those in the crowd who were thinking she had gone mad. But to the crowd's astonishment, moisture began to seep from the ground where she'd been digging, and Bernadette took some of the water, drank it, and smeared some of the mud on her face.

Within a couple days the small trickle of water turned into a stream. On February 26, Our Lady told Bernadette to:

> *" . . . kiss the ground on behalf of sinners."*

The next day Bernadette was instructed by Mary to tell the clergy to build a chapel at the grotto of Massabielle. On March 2, Mary told Bernadette that people should come to the grotto in processional form, but Abbé Peyramale quite rudely told Bernadette that he was not accustomed to taking orders from strange apparitions, and that if the lady wanted a chapel and processions at the grotto she must first identify herself. At the request of Abbé Peyramale, on March 25, the Solemnity of the Annunciation of Mary and Bernadette's sixteenth apparition, the lady finally identified herself to Bernadette:

> *"Que soy era Immaculado Councepciou!"* (*"I am the Immaculate Conception."*)

Bernadette, a simple girl of little education, had no idea what "Immaculate Conception" meant, but relayed the message to Abbé Peyramale anyway. At the sound of Bernadette's words, the Abbé's heart jumped in his chest. He knew then that the lady was the Blessed Virgin Mary and that she'd come to affirm Pope Pius IX's proclamation of the dogma of her Immaculate Conception.

A shrine was soon built at the grotto of Massabielle, and its spring water quickly gained a reputation for its healing power. On January 18, 1862, Bishop Lawrence, the Bishop of Tarbes, the diocese in which Lourdes belongs to, issued a letter recognizing the apparitions of Lourdes as worthy of belief:

> "We are convinced that the Apparition is supernatural and comes from God. . . . "[10]

Sister Marie-Bernarde

Bernadette had her eighteenth and last apparition on July 16, 1858, the Feast of Our Lady of Mount Carmel. Afterward, she entered the convent of the Sisters of Charity and Christian instruction in Nevers, France, at the age of 22, and lived there until she died at age 35 on April 16, 1879. Sister Marie-Bernarde (Bernadette's religious name) was infirm much of the time in her convent, suffering from tuberculosis, bone disease, tumors, asthma, and general ill health. The coldness, severity, and jealousy directed towards her by her Mother Superior, Marie-Thérèse Vauzou, and others in the convent greatly exacerbated Bernadette's suffering.

When Sister Marie-Bernarde's body was exhumed thirty years later on September 30, 1909, as part of an ecclesiastical investigation leading up to beatification and canonization, it was found to be incorrupt. No decay, no odor, no trace of corruption—although her skin was parched and had darkened after being washed, so a wax cast of her face and hands were made to hide the discoloration.[11] On her last exhumation, April 18, 1925, Bernadette's body still showed no sign of decomposition. Today, it remains on display in a crystal reliquary in the chapel of her convent, St. Gildard, in Nevers, France, as testimony to Our Lady of Lourdes.

Bernadette Soubirous was canonized a saint on December 8, 1933—the Solemnity of the Immaculate Conception. Tens of millions continue to come every year to worship at Lourdes' three basilicas and visit the grotto of Massabielle to partake in its healing spring waters, which have cured untold numbers of physical and spiritual maladies. One of the most famous cures was the restoring of Louis Bouriette's eyesight. Bouriette was a local stonemason, blind in one eye, who helped build the original basin around the spring that Bernadette had uncovered. When he rubbed some of the mud on his blind eye and prayed to Our Lady, his sight was miraculously restored.[12] By 1986, sixty-three other miracles had been authenticated by independent medical examination as worthy of belief.[13]

Chapter Seven

Our Lady of Hope:
Pontmain, France, 1871

"May he [Pope Pius IX] be on his guard against Napoleon [III]; he is two-faced, and when he wishes to make himself Pope as well as Emperor, soon God will draw back from him. He is the eagle who, always wanting to rise higher, will fall on the sword he wished to use to force his people to be raised up... Paris will burn and Marseilles will be engulfed. People will believe that all is lost. Nothing will be seen but murder, nothing will be heard but the clash of arms and blasphemy."

Our Lady of La Salette, 1846

The Franco-Prussian War

The Franco-Prussian War erupted on July 19, 1870 when the second emperor of France, Napoleon III, declared war on Germany. Napoleon III was pressured by Prussia's Prince Otto von Bismarck into attacking Prussia when Bismarck pushed for the candidacy of Prince Leopold von Hohenzollern-Sigmaringen for the Spanish throne, recently vacated by Queen Isabella II in 1868. Napoleon III, who wanted to maintain French military dominance in Europe, was adamantly opposed to Leopold becoming the Spanish monarch and sent the French ambassador, Comte Vincente Benedetti, to Ems, a spa in northwestern Germany being visited by King William I of Prussia, with instructions to demand that the Prussian monarch order Prince Leopold to withdraw his candidacy for the Spanish throne. William I, head of the Hohenzollern family, was angered by Napoleon's demands, but gave Benedetti permission to communicate directly with Leopold by telegraph. Leopold could not be

99

reached, but his father, Prince Charles Anthony, wired a retraction of the candidacy in the name of his son.

Not satisfied with Leopold's retraction, the vainglorious Napoleon III was determined to humiliate Prussia at all costs, even at the cost of war. Antoine Agénor Alfred, duc de Gramont, the French foreign minister, demanded that William I submit a personal letter of apology to Napoleon III and a guarantee that Leopold's candidacy would never be revived. But in an interview with Benedetti at Ems, Kaiser William rejected Napoleon's demands. That same day, Otto von Bismarck obtained King William's authorization to publish the humiliating French demands. Bismarck, however, purposely revised the Ems telegram in such a way as to whip up the anger and hatred of the French and German people towards each other. Bismarck intended to provoke a war with France that would rally the German people behind Prussia, thereby unifying the divided German states into a more powerful German empire—the Second Reich, as Hitler called it.

Knowing that a war with Prussia was inescapable, the militarily ill-prepared Napoleon III declared war on Prussia on July 19, 1870. The southern German states, in fulfillment of their treaties with Prussia, immediately joined Kaiser William in a common front against France. The French were able to mobilize about 200,000 troops; the Germans, however, quickly organized an army of about 400,000. In the major battles at Weissenburg (August 4), at Woerth (August 6), and at Spichern (August 6), the French Army under Marie Edme Patrice Maurice, comte de MacMahon, was defeated. The wounded MacMahon was ordered by Napoleon to fall back on Châlons, and Marshal Achille Bazaine, in command of all French troops east of Metz, was directed to maintain his positions. Metz was to be held at all costs.

Napoleon's orders to hold Metz at all costs split the French forces in two, and they were never able to reunite. On August 12, Napoleon handed the supreme command over to Bazaine, who was badly beaten in the great battles of Vionville (August 15) and Gravelotte (August 18), and was thereby forced into Metz where he was besieged by two German armies. Napoleon ordered MacMahon to relieve Metz, but on August 30, the Germans surprised and defeated MacMahon's leading corps at Beaumont; whereupon Napoleon decided to withdraw his French army to Sedan.

On September 2, 1870, Napoleon's army suffered a terrible defeat at the battle of Sedan: Napoleon III and his top military commanders were captured, along with 100,000 French soldiers. Upon receiving word that Napoleon had been captured in Sedan, Paris rose in revolt: the Legislative Assembly was dissolved and France was proclaimed a republic for the third time in one hundred years. With the Prussian army pounding on the doors of Paris, on October 7, the minister of the new French Republic, Léon Gambetta, made a dramatic escape from Paris by balloon, and with his chief assistant, Charles Louis de Saulces de Freycinet, carried on from Tours the organization and equipment of 36 military divisions. Their efforts were futile, however, and Gambetta's army was at length driven into Switzerland, where it was disarmed and disbanded.

On October 27, 1870, Marshal Bazaine's forces surrendered at Metz with 173,000 men. Paris, meanwhile, was subjected to a horrible siege and unrelenting bombardment by the Germans. With Paris cut off from re-supply, starving Parisians consumed every last scrap of food in the city, including horses, dogs, cats, rats, and wild animals in the zoos. The last of the beautiful old trees in the Bois de Boulogne and the Champs Élysées had to be chopped down for fuel. Engulfed in flames, Paris finally fell to the Prussians on January 28, 1871. As the Blessed Virgin Mary had prophesied would happen in La Salette, Paris burned.

The moderate liberal, Louis Adolphe Thiers, who was elected president of the Third Republic of France on February 17, 1871, negotiated a peace settlement with the Prussians. The final treaty, signed on May 10, 1871, at Frankfurt am Main, provided that the French province of Alsace (except Belfort) and part of Lorraine, including Metz, were to be ceded to the German Empire, and that France was to pay a war indemnity of 5 billion francs, with German troops occupying the Alsace-Lorraine until that amount was paid in full.

The Communard Uprising

The short but terrible Franco-Prussian War devastated France politically, economically, and militarily, but unified Germany into the most powerful nation on earth, which the proud French people in Paris found too humiliating to accept.

After the war, the political instability in Paris came to loggerheads. Seizing the opportunity after the Prussian defeat of the French Army, armed left-wing French communards took control of Paris on March 18, 1871. Shouting *"Vive la Commune,"* while marching down the boulevards of Paris, the Parisian communards—composed primarily of radical Republicans, National Guardsmen, writers, artists, bohemians, socialists, communists, anti-Catholics, and anarchists—set fire to public buildings (including the Tuileries palace and the Palais Royal), and murdered hundreds of innocent hostages, which included the Archbishop of Paris, Georges Darboy.[1]

Arriving from his stronghold of Versailles, Louis Thiers' troops, under the leadership of Marshal MacMahon, surrounded the communards on May 28, and before their insurrection was crushed, at least 20,000 communards were killed in battle or executed without trial during what has come to be known as France's "Bloody Week" (May 21-28).

As for the defeated Charles Louis Napoleon Bonaparte III, the former president and emperor of France who yearned for personal greatness and glory like his uncle, Napoleon Bonaparte, he died in disgrace two years later in England on January 9, 1873. Everything Mary predicted in La Salette about Napoleon III's rise and fall and the burning of Paris and Marseilles had come true.

Mary Appears in Pontmain

On January 18, 1871, King William I of Prussia was proclaimed emperor of the new German Empire—the Second Reich. Just the night before, on January 17, the Blessed Virgin Mary had appeared to four young children in a small rural village called Pontmain, on the border between the Normandy and Brittany sections of France. Eugène Barbadette, 12, and his brother Joseph, 10, were finishing their chores on that snowy January evening when Eugène noticed something unusual above his neighbor's house. It was a beautiful lady suspended in air, smiling and looking straight at him. The snow had suddenly stopped and Eugène could easily make out her features. She was dressed in dark blue, appearing to be in her late teens. She wore a long blue dress with golden stars that covered her arms and legs completely. On her collar was a band of gold and on her head was a black veil, topped by a gold cap resembling a crown. A thin red band ran across her cap. On her feet were blue slippers tied with gold ribbons. Eugène called his father and brother over to see the lady, but only young Joseph could see her. Bierot Barbadette ordered the boys back inside and told them not to say anything about what they saw. But when they finished their chores, the two boys raced back outside to see if the apparition was sill there. Sure enough, the young lady was there, smiling ever so sweetly.

Perplexed by his sons' insistence that they saw a lady, the father called for his wife to come and look. But she couldn't see anything either, except for three bright stars forming a triangle above the barn, which the boys said wear framing the lady's head and shoulders. When the mother went to get Sister Vitaline at the convent, the sister admitted that she couldn't see the lady either. Remembering the stories of the apparitions at La Salette and Lourdes, in which Mary was seen only by children, Sister Vitaline and the mother went to the schoolhouse and brought back three more children. As they walked towards the barn, one of the children named François Richer, age 11, pointed to the sky and shouted that there was something bright over Monsieur Guidecoq's house. As they got closer, another girl named Jean-Marie Labosse, age 9, cried out, "Oh, the beautiful lady, with the blue dress and the golden stars." They had seen exactly what the two brothers had seen. A third child from the convent schoolhouse, however, saw nothing.

As a crowd began to gather around the four visionaries, Abbé Guerin, the parish priest, began to recite the Rosary. As the onlookers joined in, the lady began to get bigger and her golden stars more numerous. A large blue oval appeared around her and a red cross formed on her left side. When the Rosary was said, the Abbé had the people recite the Magnificat. At that moment a large white banner unrolled below the lady's feet with the message:

"But pray, my children."

When the crowd began the litany of Loretto, a second message materialized, one letter at a time:

"God will hear you in a little while."

Many of the townsfolk began to weep as they remembered their sons, who were off fighting against the advancing Prussian army—the eldest son of Bierot Barbadette being one of those soldiers. As the people began to pray more ardently for peace, the message on the banner continued:

"My Son allows himself to be touched."

Hope now filled their hearts about the war's end.

As they began to sing the hymn "My Sweet Jesus," the lady's expression turned to sorrow and a large red crucifix appeared in her hands. As they sang, one of the stars from outside the oval moved inside it to light four candles surrounding the lady: two at the level of the lady's shoulders and two at the level of her knees. The parishioners immediately took this as a sign that Jesus was pleased with their custom of lighting four candles before each mass in remembrance of their soldiers.

The villagers in Pontmain learned the next day that General Schmidt of the Prussian Army had received orders to stop his planned attack of Laval, the area in which Pontmain was located. Within eleven days all Prussian troops surrounding Laval were evacuated, and the Treaty of Frankfurt was signed three months later on May 10, 1871, effectively ending the Franco-Prussian War.

The apparition of Mary at Pontmain was authenticated by the local bishop on February 2, 1872. Eugène and Joseph Barbadette went on to become priests and Jean-Marie Lebosse joined the Sisters of Holy Family in Bordeaux. Each year, hundreds of thousands of pilgrims continue to visit the basilica of Our Lady of Hope in Pontmain.[2]

Chapter Eight

Our Lady of Silence:
Knock, Ireland, 1879

"A time to rent, a time to sew; a time to be silent, a time to speak."

Eccles. 3:7

Ireland Retains the Faith

The conversion of pagan Ireland to Catholicism is traditionally credited to St. Patrick of Caerwenr in the fifth century, but, in fact, there were Catholic missionaries, like Bishop Palladius of Wicklow, in Ireland ahead of Patrick. Although he wasn't the first Christian to arrive in Ireland, St. Patrick founded so many churches, ordained so many priests and bishops, and won so many hearts to Christ, that he can justly be credited with the conversion of Ireland to Catholicism.[1]

In the fifth, sixth, and seventh centuries, Catholic monasteries in Ireland became powerful centers of religious, intellectual, and cultural life. Abbots from Irish monasteries sent hundreds of missionaries into mainland Europe to educate and convert the pagan Europeans to Christianity. The most notable among the great Irish missionaries were St. Columba, St. Columban, St. Gall, St. Killian, St. Aidan, and St. Finan of Lindisfarne.

As a stronghold of Christianity after the fall of the Western Roman Empire, Ireland enjoyed relative peace and prosperity for many centuries until the Vikings attacked it in 795. For the next couple of centuries, Ireland was besieged by Scandinavian marauders who captured Dublin in 838, Waterford in 914, and Limerick in 920. Brian, the king of Ireland, defeated the Vikings at Clontarf in 1014, and drove them out of Ireland, but not before the pagan Vikings had been converted to Christianity.

The next to invade Ireland were the Normans (descendants of Norwegians) who landed in Ireland around 1160 and tried to carve out feudal domains for themselves and impose their Norman rule over part of the native population.

With the arrival of the Normans, Ireland was torn by internal strife as several rival kings, both native and Norman, lay claim to Brian's vacated throne. Diarmait, the Norman king of Leinster, left Ireland and sailed to England (which had a sizeable population of Normans) to enlist the aid of King Henry II against the native Irish. Henry agreed to Diarmait's request for support in 1170 by sending him Richard de Clare, the Norman Earl of Pembroke ("Strongbow"), who joined with Diarmait to capture the Irish strongholds of Waterford and Dublin. King Henry II himself then crossed over into Ireland in 1171, and asserted his Anglo authority within the Pale (the area surrounding Dublin). Pope Adrian IV, the only Englishman ever to become pope, then granted all of Ireland to Henry II, using as justification the forged *Donation of Constantine*, which was thought at that time to be an authentic document made out by the Roman emperor Constantine I, giving all the Western Roman Empire over to the pope to do as he pleased. (The facts of the matter are uncertain, but the papal bull *Laudabiliter* attributed to Adrian may have been a forgery.[2]) With the arrival of the English, Ireland, in effect, was politically divided between the majority, i.e. the native Irish, and the Anglo-Irish of Norman descent.

Despite the numerous expeditions by English kings into Ireland during the next several hundred years, English influence in Ireland remained negligible. But when King Henry VIII inherited the English throne at the beginning of the sixteenth century, the vicious persecutions of native Irish Catholics began anew.

As previously mentioned, King Henry VIII broke away from the Roman Catholic Church in 1534 because of the pope's refusal to allow him to divorce his first wife, Catherine of Aragon, for the much younger Anne Boleyn. In defiance of the pope, Henry made himself the Supreme Head of the Church in England (Anglican Church) and forced all Englishmen to renounce the pope under threat of death.

Between 1536-1540, King Henry VIII seized all the Catholic monasteries in England and imposed harsh Anglican reforms on Irish Catholics. Crowning himself "King of Ireland" on January 23, 1542, Henry confiscated Catholic Church property in Ireland and tried to turn Ireland into a Protestant colony by sending Protestant colonizers from England and Scotland into the northern Ulster province. The Protestant colonization of Ulster, in turn, sparked a revolt by Irish Catholics, which was ruthlessly put down by the king's army.

After King Henry VIII died in 1547, his son, Edward VI, became king at the young age of nine. Young Edward continued in his father's bloodthirsty footsteps by viciously persecuting the Catholic Church in England and Ireland. He enlisted German mercenaries to rout Catholics from England and set up English plantations on confiscated Irish land.

When King Edward VI died in 1553 at age sixteen, Henry's Protestant granddaughter, Lady Jane Grey, whom the Protestants in parliament wanted to become queen of England to protect their necks from Catholic reprisals, tried to usurp the throne from the rightful heir, Mary Tudor, Henry's Catholic daughter from his first marriage with Catherine of Aragon.[3] Lady Jane Grey was queen for only nine days before she was captured and beheaded by Catholic forces loyal to Mary Tudor.

When Mary became queen, she instituted severe reprisals on the Protestant ringleaders in parliament who had persecuted Catholics during the infamous reigns of Henry VIII and Edward VI. "Bloody Mary," as she was dubbed by her Protestant enemies, burned at the stake at least three hundred Protestants, including Henry VIII's lackey Archbishop, Thomas Cranmer, and a handful of other Protestant bishops, committing murder like her father.

After reinstating Catholicism as the official religion of England, Queen Mary wed Philip II of Spain on July 25, 1554, causing English Protestants to suspect an imminent Catholic invasion from Spain, which never happened. After only five years of being queen, Mary died on November 17, 1558, at the relatively young age of 42. Mary's half-sister, Elizabeth I, daughter of Henry VIII by Anne Boleyn, succeeded her as queen of England. A Catholic in name only, Queen Elizabeth immediately converted back to Protestantism after her coronation, and like her Protestant father and half-brother Edward before her, forced the Catholic English and Irish to convert to Anglicanism.

"Good Queen Bess," the "Supreme Governor of the Church of England," instituted many, many more reprisals against Catholics than Mary did against Protestants. Elizabeth made it a crime to attend Catholic services in England and imprisoned priests who dared to say mass—all Catholic priests were ordered to leave England or be regarded as traitors.[4] Anyone suspected of being a Catholic was subject to surprise searches of their homes and risked exorbitant recusancy fines, seizure of their property, imprisonment, and even torture and execution.[5] Over in Ireland, dozens of priests were murdered on orders of Queen Elizabeth I, and many Catholic-owned lands were confiscated and turned into English plantations by the queen.[6]

The so-called "Virgin Queen," as Elizabeth I was dubbed because she never married, not because she was a virgin like the Virgin Mary, was known to have her fair share of lovers. One of her favorite lovers was Sir Walter Raleigh, an English Protestant explorer whose expedition landed in Roanoke Island (in present-day North Carolina). Raleigh named the entire area "Virginia" in honor of Elizabeth, who gave Raleigh 40,000 acres of prime, confiscated Irish land around Youghal.[7]

Never one to hide her disdain for Catholics, Queen Elizabeth even stooped so low as to have her Catholic cousin and rival to the English throne, Mary Stuart, Queen of Scots, beheaded in 1587, after offering her asylum from her Protestant enemies in Scotland and then imprisoning her for 19 years in Carlisle.[8] For betraying her cousin, Pope Pius V excommunicated Queen Elizabeth I in 1570, in his bull *Regnans in Excelsis.*

Queen Elizabeth I died on March, 23, 1603, after forty-five years on the English throne. During her long, infamous reign, Elizabeth drained the English economy in years of supporting Protestant rebellions in Ireland, France, Spain, and the Netherlands, and had thousands of Catholics burnt at the stake, hanged, drawn and quartered, beheaded, gibbeted, stretched on the rack, or thrown into dungeons to rot.[9]

Succeeding Elizabeth I, James VI, the Protestant king of Scotland and son of Mary, Queen of Scots, was crowned King James I of Great Britain on July 25, 1603. In 1605, Catholic zealots in England conspired to blow up parliament and James I by using 20 barrels of gunpowder, but the plot was uncovered and the ringleaders, Guy Fawkes and his conspirators, were all either executed or killed in fighting.

As bad as the clashes were between English Catholics and Protestants, the greatest religious conflict in England at the beginning of the seventeenth century was between the Anglicans and an upstart radical Protestant sect known as the Puritans (so-called because they wanted to "purify" the Anglican Church, which they felt was still too papist). Led by Oliver Cromwell, Puritans in the House of Commons feared that the new Protestant king, Charles I, the son of King James I, who died in 1625, was becoming too "absolutist," so they refused to legislate any more taxes for King Charles' foreign wars. In retaliation for their defiance, Charles I dissolved the Puritan-led parliament on March 2, 1629, and ruled without one until 1640.

In 1640, a civil war in England was about to break out between the militant Puritans in parliament and the "royalists" forces of King Charles I. Taking full advantage of the Protestant divisions in England, Catholics in Ireland formed a rebel parliament in Kilkenny, called the Catholic Confederacy, and allied themselves with the English royalists. The new Catholic Confederacy in Ireland then demanded from the Puritan-dominated English parliament freedom of conscience and worship, government by Catholic officials, and restitution of seized Catholic property. The Catholic Confederacy, however, was divided in its demands: Anglo-Irish Catholics sought mainly to preserve their Catholic faith, while "Old" Irish Catholics wanted to recover their confiscated property and preserve their Gaelic language and way of life. Opting for violence over negotiation, in October of 1641 the Old Gaelic Catholic Irish rebelled against Protestant colonizers in Ulster, massacring 10,000 English and Scottish settlers and successfully driving them from their province. The Old Irish felt that they had suffered far too long from the indignities of losing their lands, their religion, their language and culture, and their voice in government to the English.

As expected, a civil war erupted in England in 1642 between Puritan forces led by Oliver Cromwell and royalists forces led by the king. Cromwell's "Model Army," as it was called, was made up mostly of the lower English classes and Puritans in parliament, and believed it was fighting "God's fight" against a tyrannical, pro-Catholic king. Unfortunately, for both England and Ireland, Cromwell routed the royalist forces at Naseby in 1645, and on January 30, 1649, beheaded King Charles I at Whitehall Palace, committing the horrific sin of regicide. Charles II, the king's son, was immediately proclaimed the new king of England by Scotland and Ireland, but not before the Puritans in parliament had whisked him away to the Hague, Netherlands, to keep him from succeeding to the English throne.

On May 29, 1649, the Puritan-dominated parliament abolished the English monarchy and made Oliver Cromwell the de facto ruler over Great Britain. Now in total charge of the English army, Cromwell called for immediate revenge on the Irish Catholics who had supported the defeated Charles I during the English Civil War, so he invaded Dublin on August 15, 1649 (the Solemnity of the Assumption of Mary). From 1649-50, Cromwell, the so-called "Lord Protector" of Great Britain, massacred 1,500 Old Irish civilians, Anglo-Irish royalists, and Catholic priests at Drogheda and Wexford. Then, when he ordered the execution of all Irish freedom fighters continuing to resist, panic gripped the remaining Catholic Irish garrisons and they surrendered, hoping for clemency—many were executed anyway. Those fortunate enough to escape execution had their lands confiscated and were banished to western Ireland.

Cromwell compensated his Puritan soldiers with huge tracts of prime Irish land, justifying it as "the righteous judgment of God." Those Catholic Irish who had fought back lost two-thirds of their property, while those who didn't fight, but simply failed to show proper regard for Cromwell, lost only one-third. Not content to just steal their lands, 20,000 Catholic Irishmen were sold into slavery by Cromwell in the West Indies.[10] Catholic priests in Ireland were banned and hunted down—a reward of £5 was given to anyone bringing in the head of a wolf or a Catholic bishop.[11]

In his zealous quest to turn Great Britain into a "Bible-believing," Puritan nation free of decadent Catholics and Anglicans, Cromwell ordered all theaters, pubs, and whorehouses shut down. In spite of Cromwell's puritanical intentions of forcibly bringing morality back to England, English society deteriorated into moral degeneracy. Three radical sects sprang up after the English Civil War that helped bring about the downfall of Puritanism. The "Levelers" advocated leveling all social class and privilege, the "Diggers" believed that land belonged to the commoners and only those who dug in the ground should be allowed to eat, and the most radical sect of them all, the "Ranters," made up of bawdry whoremongers and drunkards, believed that they were forever saved and beyond sin, and could do as they damn-well pleased.

Having committed the unpardonable sins of regicide and war against the One True Church, Oliver Cromwell and the Puritans brought upon England the curse of social, political, and religious anarchy, which God would soon avenge. After Oliver Cromwell died on September 3, 1658, the English parliament decided it had had enough of the anarchy wrought by Puritanism, so it restored Charles II to the English throne as a constitutional monarch in May of 1660 and brought back the Anglican Church as the official Church of England. Under King Charles II, some redress was made to Catholics who had been unjustly persecuted by the Puritans under Cromwell, but that would not stop God's avenging the spilling of so much innocent blood in the name of religion.

In the year 1665, London was struck by her worst plague in two centuries—75,000 Londoners, both Catholic and Protestant, died and the streets leading out of the city were choked by people fleeing for their lives from the deadly pestilence. Households who were hit hardest by the plague painted red crosses on their doors, accompanied with the plea, "Lord have mercy on us."[12] And if that wasn't punishment enough, the following year, on September 5, 1666, a tremendous firestorm broke out in London which lasted four days and nights, razing 400 acres with 87 English churches and 13,000 houses completely destroyed. The Old St. Paul's Cathedral, whose spire had already been destroyed by two direct lightening strikes, was now totally destroyed. London's fire started on a Sunday night in a baking house on Pudding Lane. The parish watchman saw the fire when it first broke out and went to warn the lord mayor of London, Sir Thomas Bloodworth, but he was totally unconcerned: "Pish! A woman might piss it out," he is reported to have said. But the following morning, when Bloodworth witnessed firsthand the terrible destruction the fire had wrought on his city, he cried like a fainting woman: "Lord, what can I do? I am spent."[13] Londoners found out too late that innocent blood is worth a lot to God and he will avenge it.

Despite the horrible losses in London to the 1665 plague and fire of 1666, religious persecution continued unabated in England. In 1673, England's Protestant parliament passed the infamous Test Act, which was drafted to bar Roman Catholics from holding political office. Five years later, in 1678, two anti-Catholic rumor mongers, Israel Tonge and Titus Oates, falsely testified before parliament that Jesuit priests were plotting to assassinate the ailing King Charles II and put James II (Charles's Catholic brother and Duke of

York) on the English throne in order to massacre Protestants. Believing the lie of a great Jesuit conspiracy, hysteria gripped Protestant England, and once again, innocent Catholics became the target of unjustified persecutions.[14]

In 1685, King James II, a convert to Catholicism, acceded to the English throne when his Protestant brother, Charles II, died without issue. Before Charles II died, Protestants had been accusing him of being a Catholic at heart, and planning to bring in French troops to restore Catholicism in England. Whether this was true or not, his successor, King James II, wanted to end the many years of religious fighting in England, so he issued a Declaration of Indulgence in April of 1687, which granted political and religious toleration to Catholics. (This royal declaration was issued only after King James II failed to persuade the English parliament to repeal the discriminatory, anti-Catholic Test Act.)

Fearing that King James II was trying to reinstate Catholicism in England, the following year Protestants started the "Glorious Revolution" of 1688, which forced King James II to flee for his life to France. King James II's vacated throne was then taken over by the Dutch Protestants William III (Prince of Orange) and Mary II in 1689. That same year, with the approval of William and Mary, the English parliament passed a Bill of Rights, which insured a constitutional monarchy free from Catholic succession: no Catholics could ever sit on the English throne again, and until this day, they haven't. A Toleration Act was also passed that year, which allowed religious freedom of expression for Protestants only, because anti-Catholic persecutions were renewed again during the reign of William and Mary.[15]

The Protestant Penal Laws

The deposed King James II enlisted the support of Irish Catholics in 1690 to help him win his rightful throne back, but was defeated by King William of Orange at the Battle of the Boyne in Ireland,[16] which left the Irish Protestant minority in firm control of most of Ireland (only one-seventh of Ireland remained in the hands of Irish Catholics after the battle).[17] With the minority Protestant Irish now controlling the majority of Irish land, a wide range of burdensome social and political restrictions known as the "Penal Laws" were enacted by the Protestant Irish parliament in 1695 and thereafter for the next two centuries, and placed upon the shoulders of the Irish Catholics. Here are twenty of the worst laws: (1) Catholic schools were prohibited and Catholics couldn't teach or send their children abroad for education. (2) All Catholic clergy were required to be registered with the Protestant parliament; rewards were given for discovering those priests who hadn't. (3) Under penalty of imprisonment, any two justices of the peace could force a Catholic to tell where he attended mass, who was there, who was the priest, and where he lived. (4) No Catholic could purchase any manors, or lease one for more than thirty-one years. (5) Any Protestant suspecting someone of holding property in trust for a Catholic, or of being concerned on any sale, lease, mortgage, or any contract for a Catholic, could file a bill against the accused trustee and confiscate his estate or property. (6) Any Protestant seeing a Catholic tenant of a farm, the produce of which farm exceeded one-third of the rent, could expel the Catholic and enter in on the lease in his stead. (7) Any Protestant seeing a Catholic with a horse worth more than £5 could take his horse immediately upon tendering him £5 for it. (8) No Catholics were allowed to be jurors. (9) Catholics were required to pay double amounts to the militia, which could seize their horses at will. (10) Catholics could be forced into military service against a Catholic prince, and levies were imposed on them for the recompense of any Protestant relative, even if a Catholic was the first in line as heir. (12) Protestants with estates in Ireland weren't allowed to marry Catholics in or out of Ireland. (13) All marriages between Protestants and Catholics were annulled, even if children were born. (14) Any Catholic priest caught performing a marriage between a Protestant and Catholic, or two Protestants, was hanged. (15) A Catholic father could loose his child to a Protestant relative if that child showed signs of becoming a Protestant. (16) If any child of a Catholic became Protestant, the parent was to be instantly summoned by the Chancery and made to swear under oath the full value of his possessions, which the Chancery would distribute as it saw fit. (17) If any of the sons of a Catholic father became Protestant, this son was to possess all that the father had, and the father could not sell, could not mortgage, and could not leave legacies or portions of his estate to his remaining Catholic sons. (18) If there were no Protestant heir, the estate of a deceased Catholic was divided equally amongst all Catholic relatives, regardless of the wishes of the deceased. (19) If the wife of a Catholic turned Protestant, the husband's will was set aside and she was made a participant of all his possessions, no matter how good or bad a wife she was. (20) Any Catholic priest who renounced his faith was to be paid £30 a year for life by the Protestant Church of Ireland.[18]

Because of these intentionally burdensome laws, many Catholic Irish lost everything they had and were forced into begging to survive. Those who could left Ireland for other parts of Europe and America, but the majority stayed behind, even though they were powerless to change the laws because they had no say in government.

In 1793, when war broke out between Britain and France, a Catholic Relief Act was passed by the English parliament to appease the anger of Irish Catholics, so that they wouldn't ally themselves with France and become the back door to a Catholic invasion of England. Parliament's Catholic Relief Act of 1793 allowed Irish Catholics to bear arms, sit on juries, vote if they were forty shilling freeholders, take degrees at Trinity College in Dublin, and become officers in the military below the rank of general, but not hold government office or seats in parliament.[19]

These concessions granted in the Relief act, however, could not contain the growing number of Catholic dissenters. After two centuries of persecution in the hands of the Protestants, Irish Catholics decided they had had enough. On June 21, 1798, a revolt at Vinegar Hill in Wexford sprang up, but was quelled by superior British forces, and a planned invasion of Ireland by French Revolutionary forces coming to Ireland's aid had to be called off. Another Catholic uprising broke out on July 23, 1803, after the forced union of Ireland with Great Britain in 1800, and two more failed Catholic uprisings occurred in Ireland in 1848 and 1867.

The Irish Potato Famine

The champion of Irish Catholic causes, Daniel O'Connell, the Irish Barrister, campaigned for Catholic civil rights in 1823 by forming a mass movement of Irish priests, Catholics, and moderate Irish Protestants. In an attempt to curb this growing Catholic unrest in Ireland, on May 9, 1828, the infamous Test Act of 1673, which forbade Roman Catholics and non-conforming Protestants from holding public office, was repealed by the British parliament under pressure from the Duke of Wellington, the Prime Minister of Great Britain. A year later, on April 23, 1829, the Catholic Emancipation Act was passed, which allowed Irish Catholics to again hold public office and seats in England's parliament.

But just as the social and political climate in Ireland began to improve, a famine set in. A terrible potato blight (fungus) started in 1845 and didn't stop until 1848. Half of Ireland's potatoes rotted in 1845, all rotted in 1846, most went bad in 1847, and again in 1848. And if the potato blight wasn't bad enough, the winter of 1846-47 was the longest and coldest in recorded history.[20] Cold weather combined with the potato famine caused diseases like typhus, relapsing fever, dysentery, dropsy, and cholera to spread out of control, killing the Irish en masse.

The sight of cartloads of prime Irish grain being shipped to the tables of the well-fed English by the starving, homeless Irish as they were being evicted from their land and one-room hovels by heartless Anglo-Irish landlords engendered within the Irish an extreme hatred for the English. The English Whig government under Lord John Russell was ultimately to blame for fomenting Ireland's anger and resentment. It refused to allow the English government to buy enough food for the starving Irish peasants, all the while importing the cream of the Irish grain crops to fatten England's bellies and granaries. England had ample resources to come to Ireland's rescue but chose not to, which was nothing less than a pre-planned genocide. Lord Russell's permanent secretary to the Treasury, Charles Trevelyan, had even gone on record as saying that in his view, the Irish potato famine had reflected the wishes of an all-wise Providence.[21] Ethnic cleansing is not new to the twentieth century.

Ireland was the only country in Europe where the population actually fell in the nineteenth century—by about half. By 1850, the population of Ireland had shrunk from 8.5 million to 6.5 million. One million Irishmen had lost their lives from starvation or disease and another million had emigrated to the United States, Europe, or England. On the long and hazardous voyage to America, one in six Irish immigrants died in their cramped, unsanitary quarters, which caused the Irish refugee ships to be nicknamed "coffin ships."

The huge influx of Irish Catholic immigrants into American cities during the mid-nineteenth century was a major cause of alarm for the residing descendants of Anglo-American Protestant colonists, who feared losing their majority status and cultural and religious uniformity. Beginning in the 1830s, anti-Catholic and anti-immigrant Nativist parties sprang up in many American cities, and by 1854 became a major political force in the United States with the formation of the American Party or "Know Nothing" Party, so-called because when questioned, members would always reply they "knew nothing." By 1855, Protestants in the Know Nothing Party controlled all but one New England state, and won in Maryland, Delaware, Kentucky, New Jersey, Pennsylvania, California, and nearly every southern state. The following year the Know Nothing Party nearly won the presidential election by calling for the exclusion of Catholics and foreigners from voting and holding office, and requiring a mandatory 21-year waiting period for citizenship.

With no political representation and no money of their own, newly-arrived Irish-Catholic immigrants were forced to accept the most menial and degrading work and to live in filthy, disease-ridden urban slums. When looking for better work the Irish were often turned away by placards on factory and shop doors bearing the inscription "NINA," which meant, "No Irish Need Apply." Still, the disillusionment and hard living conditions the Irish encountered in America was better than starving to death in Ireland.[22]

For the Catholic survivors of the Irish potato famine who elected to stay behind in Ireland, their refusal to give up was soon rewarded. In July of 1869, the liberal Prime Minister of England, William Gladstone, severed the Protestant Church of Ireland's link with the Irish state, and by 1871, the dominance of the Protestant Church over Catholicism in Ireland was finally disestablished—a major victory for the beleaguered Irish Catholic Church, which had suffered over three centuries of persecution at the hands of Protestants.[23]

Apparitions in Knock

Another poor potato harvest hit Ireland hard in 1879, the third in three years, but heaven was about to offer a ray of hope for the Irish Catholics who had suffered so much in the last three centuries. On August 21, 1879, the Blessed Virgin Mary appeared outside a little Irish church in the village of Knock, located in the County of Mayo. Here is the true story of her apparition.

Margaret Beirne was locking up the church on that stormy night when she noticed a bright light coming from the south end of the church. At first glance she thought she saw statues of Mary, Joseph, and St. John the Evangelist standing next to a new altar, on top of which was a lamb and a cross. Margaret didn't think too much about it because the little church had lost two of its statues the previous year in a storm, so she thought these statues were their replacements. Archdeacon Cavanagh's housekeeper, Mary McLoughlin, noticed them too but, like Margaret, thought they were new statues that the pastor had picked up in Dublin. They both thought it was odd, though, that the pastor had left them out in the rain.

Mary McLoughlin left the church and then went over to Margaret Beirne's house. When Mary decided it was time to leave, Mary Beirne, Margaret's older sister, volunteered to walk Mary McLoughlin home. On their way home, the two Mary's walked by the church in the pouring rain and noticed the statues still standing there. Mary Beirne, being the more inquisitive of the two, decided to take a closer look. As she approached, she jumped back with a start:

> "They're not statues. They're moving. It's the Blessed Virgin Mary!"

Mary Beirne immediately ran home to get her mother and brother who went to the church to see the apparition. While still there, word of the apparition spread quickly and at least 22 people witnessed them that night. This is how the apparition appeared.

The entire back wall of the church was bathed in a bright light, which was capable of being seen from quite a distance, as attested to by a farmer named Patrick Walsh. The figures were raised about two feet off the ground. The altar, with the lamb and cross, was surrounded by angels hovering above. Mary, the largest of the figures, wore a white cloak and sash, with a long veil flowing from the back of her head to her feet. On the top of her veiled head was a gold crown. Between the crown and the edge of the veil was a golden rose. Her hands were raised to the level of her shoulders as she looked up towards heaven in prayer. St. Joseph was standing to Mary's right, head bowed and hands folded in prayer. St. John the Evangelist, wearing a bishop's miter, was standing to Mary's left, with his right hand raised and his left arm cradling what looked like the Holy Bible.

The three figures stood silent, a few feet away from the church wall. Although the rain was falling and the wind was blowing hard, the ground beneath the figures and the back wall of the church remained completely dry. One of the visionaries, a teenager named Patrick Hill, walked up to touch the figures. As he reached out they moved back, not allowing themselves to be handled. Patrick later testified to authorities that they were real, three-dimensional people, not just projections on a wall. He could make out their eyes, their hair color, their skin texture, everything. The angels' wings appeared to be fluttering, too. The book on St. John's arm was open and Patrick could see the writing on the pages.

As the small crowd knelt before the apparition in prayer, the heavenly visitors remained silent. Not a word was spoken. After several hours the figures then suddenly disappeared.

An ecclesiastical commission was set up several months later to investigate the apparition in Knock. Some members on the committee were skeptical at first and suspected a Protestant hoax, so the head of the committee, the Archbishop of Tuam, Dr. McHale, made no official statement one way or the other. Unofficially though, he sided with Archdeacon Cavanagh, who believed his parishioners' stories. As the case in previous Marian apparitions, some members of the clergy and members of religious institutes were jealous that Mary had appeared to commoners and not to them. But not Reverend Cavanagh—he was convinced that the apparition of Knock was meant for the common people of Ireland, not for the clergy.

Since the Catholic Church at that time made no official pronouncement concerning the authenticity of the apparition at Knock, Catholics were free to let their conscience be their guide. Many pilgrimages were formed by the Irish archbishops in the years that followed, as the faithful felt an inward call to visit Knock. A shrine was built and a basilica was erected in honor of Our Lady of Knock. The greatest endorsement of Knock came when Pope John Paul II celebrated mass at the basilica in 1979 during the centennial anniversary of the apparition. At the ceremony, Pope John Paul presented the national shrine with a gold rose, in memory of the golden rose worn by Mary during her apparition.

The Silent Message of Knock

The apparition in Knock stood silent and appeared to give no message, but, in fact, it did. Silence, sometimes, speaks louder than words. Let's look again at the apparition to uncover its silent message.

Mary appeared with her foster husband, St. Joseph, and her adopted son, St. John the Evangelist, wearing the gold crown of the Queen of Heaven; so there's no mistaking who she was or who they were. The lamb on the altar was, of course, Jesus Christ, the spotless sacrificial Lamb mentioned in the Book of the Revelation. John, the Beloved Apostle and the author of the Gospel according to John, the three Epistles of John, and the Book of Revelation, is shown in the apparition with an open book resting on his left arm. Since we are now in the days of which the angel of the apocalypse warned, John's Bible was probably opened to the Book of Revelation. John's right hand is raised in the apparition as if swearing an oath to the truth of this book. Nineteen hundred years ago Jesus appeared to John to testify about the events in the Book of Revelation. John said:

> "I myself give witness to all who hear the prophetic words of this book."[24]

And,

> "Happy is the man who reads this prophetic message, and happy are those who hear it and heed it, for the appointed time is near."[25]

Thus, John's appearance in Knock with the Book of Revelation on his arm indicates that we are now in the period of the end times.

The little holy village of Knock, therefore, is a reminder of Christ's invitation to us in the Book of Revelation.[26]

> "Behold, I stand at the door and knock. If anyone hears me calling and opens the door, I will enter his house and have supper with him."[27]

And in the Gospel of Luke:

> "Ask and you will receive, seek and you shall find, knock and the door will be opened to you"[28]

Although our time is running out, Christ is still knocking on the doors of our hearts to let him in. Just where we are in relation to the chronological sequence of events symbolized in the Book of Revelation is anybody's guess. The events in the Book of Revelation weren't meant to take place overnight: they occur over a period of years, perhaps several centuries or more. But from the spiritual "signs of the times," the increased frequency and intensity of the "earth's pangs," and the unprecedented number of Marian apparitions and warnings in the twentieth century, the Catholic Church knows for certain that we are getting closer and closer to that appointed time.

Chapter Nine

Our Lady of the Rosary: Fátima, Portugal 1917

"There will be signs in the sun, the moon, and the stars . . . "

Luke 21:25

The Cova da Iria

The most important Marian apparitions of the twentieth century, perhaps of all time, were given to three young shepherd children in a remote location called the Cova da Iria (Cove of Irene) near Fátima, Portugal, between May 13 and October 13, 1917. These apparitions in Fátima were important not so much because of the stupendous Miracle of the Sun performed by the Virgin Mary on October 13 in front of 70,000 eye witnesses, but because of the prophecies made by Mary of what horrible things would afflict the world if mankind didn't heed God's warnings and convert. Knowing that God's call to conversion wouldn't be respected, Mary foretold in advance at Fátima the rise and fall of Russian communism, the coming of the Second World War, the approaching chastisement for the punishment of humanity's sins, and much more.

The Fátima prophesies have been a real stumbling block for atheists and scoffers who deny the existence of Marian apparitions. Everything has been so well documented by historians that no one of any academic standing and reputation can denounce the prophecies of Fátima as false, without looking uninformed on the facts. Fátima remains today a living testimony of God's deep

117

concern for our salvation and proof that he always warns the world ahead of time before he punishes it:

> "Indeed, the Lord God does nothing without revealing his plans to his servants, the prophets."[1]

Fátima and Islam

To truly appreciate the messages of Fátima, one must first know a little about the history of Portugal. Fátima actually begins in 1188 with the legend of the origin of the Arabic name of the town of Fátima, Portugal. During the time of the European Crusades against the Moorish invaders of Spain and Portugal, the daughter of the powerful Muslim prince of Alcacer do Sal, whose name just happened to be Fátima, was captured by a Christian knight named Don Gonçalo Hermingues. After he converted her to Christianity, the knight married the beautiful princess, baptizing her under the new Christian name of Oureana (from which the Portuguese village of Ourem takes its name). Tragically, Oureana died soon afterwards, and her broken-hearted husband, Don Gonçalo, devoted the rest of his life to God by joining the Cistercian abbey of Alcobaça. The Cistercians founded a small priory in the neighboring mountains where Brother Gonçalo was sent, and taking along the remains of the wife he loved so much, Brother Gonçalo named the place "Fátima" in honor of her Muslim name. [2]

When the Moors invaded the Iberian Peninsula of Spain in 711 and threatened the whole of Western Christendom in Europe, it looked as if the onward march of Islam was unstoppable: the territory Islam had conquered was larger than that conquered by the ancient Roman Empire. Here is how Islam spread so fast.

Since about the year 610, an orphaned Arab named Muhammed (whose daughter's name was also Fátima) had been preaching in Mecca that an "angel of light"[3] had appeared to him announcing the "true word of God." This angel supposedly had revealed to Muhammed that Judaism and Christianity had "misinterpreted" the word of God and that Jesus Christ was only a wise prophet, not the Son of God as Christians maintained. This mysterious angel then told Muhammed that he, not Jesus, was God's "truest prophet," and that he, Muhammed, was greater than Jesus. As mentioned in chapter two, the appearance of a deceiving angel had been foretold by the Apostle Paul when he cautioned the Corinthians to be on guard against such false apostles preaching "another Gospel" or "another Jesus," because the devil can disguise himself as an "angel of light."[4]

After his visitation by the deceiving angel, Muhammed was obsessed with converting the polytheistic Arab tribes to the monotheistic religion of Islam. At first, Muhammed encountered stiff resistance by the Arabs of Mecca, but in his flight from Mecca to Medina he was welcomed by most of the Arabs in Medina as a true prophet. Those in Medina who didn't accept Muhammedism were brutally crushed by Muhammed in three successive battles. After the first two battles, Muhammed expelled the recalcitrant Jews living in Medina, and after the third battle he massacred the males of the only remaining Jewish tribe for collaborating with his Arab enemies in Mecca.

By 630, Muhammed had defeated the Arab opposition in Mecca, and by the time of his death in 632, six centuries after the death of Christ, Islam had overtaken Western Arabia. Within the next thirty years Islam had conquered Arabia, Syria, Jerusalem, Mesopotamia, Egypt, Persia, Afghanistan, Libya, North Africa, and was pounding on the doors of Southern Europe and the Byzantine Empire.

Islam's lightning conquests were extremely violent—just the opposite of the peaceful, non-violent spread of Christianity by the apostles and their disciples. Satan's objective for Islam was to halt the spread of Christianity by force and replace it with a fanatical new religion of his own that would lead men away from their savior, Jesus Christ. Hence, he gave it his full power.

In the ensuing power struggles over the leadership of Islam between the minority Shi'ite Muslim sects, who claimed direct lineage from Muhammed through Fátima, and the Sunni Muslim sect of the majority, Islam's leaders resorted to murders, assassinations, robberies, political intrigues, and constant factional infighting to maintain their hold on power. Here are just a few examples of their atrocities: Muhammed's son-in-law, Ali, the Shi'ite husband of Fátima, was assassinated by a poisoned sword in 661, after choosing to negotiate with the Sunnis rather than fight;[5] in 680, Muhammed's grandson, al-Husayn, was killed in a battle with the Sunnis when he refused to recognize his rival's claim as caliph;[6] in 744, the Umayyad caliph, al-Walid II, was murdered in Syria by his own family for his extravagant and pleasure-seeking lifestyle; [7] in 750, the Abbasid Shi'ites, descendants of Muhammed's uncle, al-Abbas, and rulers over Mesopotamia, invited their Sunni rivals to a peaceful dinner, then after massacring them, dined over their dead bodies;[8] Abu'l-Abbas, the brutal caliph of the Abbasids and whose nickname was *al-Saffah,* "Shedder of Blood," was known to have dug up the bodies of his Sunni rivals and publicly flog their remains;[9] in 786, Harun al-Rashid was suspected of murdering his brother, the Abbasid caliph al-Hadi, to gain control of the Abbassid dynasty in Baghdad;[10] in 791, the Shi'ite Imam, Idris of Morocco, was murdered by a poisoned toothpick sent by Harun al-Rashid of Baghdad for Idris' part in a failed revolt against al-Rashid;[11] in 1021, the notorious caliph al-Hakim, head of the Fatimid Shi'ite sect that conquered Egypt (named Fatimid because they claimed they descended from Muhammed's daughter Fátima), was allegedly killed by his sister, Sitt al-Mulk, because of his capricious cruelty, which included whimsical executions and the ordering of the demolition of Christianity's holiest shrine, the Church of the Holy Sepulcher in Jerusalem.[12] Caliph al-Hakim's attack on the Holy Sepulcher shrine was the main reason that Pope Urban II ordered the First Crusade to the Holy Land in 1095; to make it safe again for Christian pilgrims.

As you can see, numerous are the accounts of violence and intrigue in Islam—that's how it spread and that's how it conquered the Holy Land. One of Islam's main objectives was, and still is, to overthrow Judaism and Christianity, the religions of "infidels."[13] Very early on, Muslims conspired to conquer Christian Europe and the rest of the world for Allah. In 711, an Arab expeditionary force in North Africa, seeking to expand Islam's territories, crossed the Straits of Gibraltar and landed on the Iberian Peninsula of Spain. By 714, all but the northernmost region of Spain had been conquered by Muslims. The seemingly unstoppable Arab hordes, whose battle cry from the Koran was "Paradise lies in the shadow of the sword," threatened the whole of Europe with annihilation. In 732, on the one-hundredth anniversary of Muhammed's death, Muslim armies led by Abd al-Rahman sacked Bordeaux and Poitiers in France, and advanced on Tours and the Catholic monastery of St. Martin, Christendom's finest monastery. Coming to Christian Europe's rescue, the Frankish general, Charles Martel, "The Hammer," rode south to engage the Arabs in a decisive six-day battle at Poitiers. On the seventh day the Christians defeated the Muslims and Abd al-Rahman lay dead on the battlefield. Europe was saved from Islam, except for the Arab Emirate of Cordoba on the Iberian Peninsula of Spain.

In the extreme northwest of the Iberian Peninsula, a number of Christian kingdoms (Asturias and León) managed to hold their own against the Muslim invaders and became the point of departure for the Reconquista—the reconquest of the peninsula. In 1085, King Alphonso VI of León and Castile, Spain's most powerful Christian monarch, retook Toledo from the Arabs. In 1094, the Spanish knight "El Cid Campeador" (Lord Champion) reconquered Valencia, which was being threatened by North African Berbers (Almoravids) called in to help the besieged Arab Muslims. On October 28, 1147, Moorish rule in Spain finally ended when Muslim forces in Lisbon surrendered to an allied Portuguese-French force under Alfonso Henriques. The Iberian Peninsula was, once again, Catholic.

Catholic Portugal

Still under Spanish rule, Portugal's boundaries were drawn up in a treaty with Castile in 1297, and Mary the Mother of God was proclaimed Portugal's Protectress. With the help of divine providence, the Portuguese won their independence from Spain on August 15, 1385, the Solemnity of the

Assumption of Mary. John of Portugal's heavily outnumbered Portuguese army beat the better-equipped Spanish army in the Battle of Aljubarrota near Fátima. Everyone, including Pope Boniface IX, called it a miracle. In gratitude, King John of Portugal built the beautiful Dominican church and monastery of Bathala a few miles from Fátima, appropriately calling it "Our Lady of Victory."

For the next two centuries, Portugal's economy and missionary activities flourished. Ship building, great maritime discoveries, foreign trade (which, unfortunately, included slave trading), and colonial expansion turned Portugal into the richest nation in Europe by 1521—thanks to such intrepid Portuguese navigators and explorers as Prince Henry the Navigator, Vasco da Gama, Pedro Álvares Cabral, Bartholomew Dias, Alfonso de Albuquerque, and Ferdinand Magellan. Accompanying Portuguese explorers were Jesuits missionaries, who introduced the Gospel of Jesus Christ into Africa, the East Indies, Asia, Japan, the Philippines, and South America. Roman Catholicism owes Portugal a debt of gratitude for its worldwide growth.

Portugal's golden era, however, lasted but two centuries. In 1578, King Sebastian's campaign against Muslim North Africa bankrupted the Portuguese economy: eight thousand Portuguese soldiers were killed and Sebastian and most of his nobility lay dead on the battlefield of Alcázar-el-Kebir in Morocco. Predictably, King Philip II of Spain took advantage of Portugal's disaster in Morocco by annexing the weakened Portugal to Spain in 1580.

Portugal, however, regained its independence from Spain in 1641, when the Catalans rose up against Madrid and the duke of Braganza entered Lisbon and declared himself King John IV. Fighting between Spain and Portugal would last for another twenty-eight years, with the outnumbered Portuguese winning battle after battle. In 1688, the year of England's "Glorious Revolution," Spain officially recognized Portugal's independence.

The battle for Catholic Portugal would continue though, as another enemy far more deadly than the Spanish or Moors was eager to conquer it. That enemy was freemasonry.

Freemasonry Infiltrates Portugal

Not all was well after Portugal regained her independence from Spain. In the middle of the eighteenth century, the twin specters of European rationalism and anti-Catholic freemasonry crept into the doorway of Portuguese politics in the person of Sebastião José de Carvalho e Mello, the Marquês of Pombal and a notorious Freemason and anti-Catholic. Elected in 1750, this all-powerful chief minister of King Joseph Emanuel persuaded the king in

1759 to sign an edict expelling the Jesuits from all Portuguese lands. One hundred eighty-six priests and 300 scholastics were rounded up and dumped on the shores of the Papal States. Elsewhere, dozens of Jesuit missionaries in Asia, India, Africa, and South America were forcibly removed from their missions and left to rot in the dank dungeons of Balem and Fort St. Julian. At least 270 Portuguese missionaries died as a result of their banishment by King Joseph.[14]

Portugal's first Masonic lodge, joined to the Grand Lodge of London, was founded in 1727. Like all other Masonic lodges, its secret agenda was to overthrow all monarchies and to crush the Catholic Church. In their places, the Masons conspired to establish a godless, humanistic republic totally subservient to the anti-Catholic ideals of the Masonic elite. By 1755, Masonic ideology had so infiltrated the Portuguese government and the universities of Lisbon that both the rightful authority of the monarchy and the influence of the Catholic Church in secular affairs were in serious jeopardy—especially the Society of Jesus, Masonry's most vocal critic.

With anti-Catholic Masonry growing in power in Portugal and the influence of the Catholic Church waning, a divine warning was sent to that once holy country. On Sunday, November 1, 1755, All Saints Day, while most of the townspeople were in church, a terrible earthquake rocked Lisbon's foundation, killing 10,000 people and reducing the city of 500,000 to rubble. A huge flood by the river Tagus, backed up and come roaring back into Lisbon, and was followed by six days of uncontrollable fires.

The terrible Lisbon earthquake was a prelude to Portugal's impending tribulations. First, the expulsion of the Jesuits in 1759. Then, at the beginning of the nineteenth century, the soldiers of Imperial France under Napoleon Bonaparte invaded Portugal three times between 1807 and 1810, forcing the Portuguese resistance into an undesirable alliance with Protestant Britain, who then sent occupation troops into Portugal. The occupation of Portugal in 1808 by Protestant British forces eventually forced King João VI and the Portuguese royal family into exile in Brazil, which allowed freemasonry to get an even stronger foothold in Portugal.

In 1820, a Masonic revolt broke out in Lisbon, plunging Portugal into a civil war that lasted eight years. A liberal constitutional monarchy was set up and the pro-Masonic monarch, Dom Pedro I, was recalled from exile in Brazil and placed on the Portuguese throne in 1826; whereupon, Masonic persecutions of the Catholic Church were vigorously renewed. (Masonic persecutions of the Catholic Church temporarily eased up, however, in 1842 when Portuguese minister Costa Cabral re-established diplomatic relations with Rome and reconstituted some of the disbanded religious orders.)

Following the French Communard revolution in 1871, a group of radical Portuguese Freemasons organized a violently anticlerical Republican party of their own, modeled after the notorious Italian Carbonari. On February 1, 1908, two Republican members assassinated Portugal's King Carlos I and his son, Luis Filipe. The king's youngest son, Manuel II, who was more sympathetic to the causes of the radical Republicans and Masons, became Portugal's new king at age eighteen.

On October 5, 1910, a Masonic Republican revolt led by Portuguese army and navy officers overthrew the constitutional monarchy of Manuel II, and he was forced to flee for his life. The deposed royal family fled to Gibraltar and a provisional government, composed of anti-Catholics, liberals, intellectuals, artists, Carbonari, and Masons was instituted under Portugal's new leader, Teófilo Braga. Braga's provisional government immediately went to work drafting anticlerical legislation: churches were sacked, church property confiscated, seminaries controlled, convents closed, monasteries and religious institutions suppressed, the celebrating of mass and wearing of clerical garb forbidden, Jesuits were denied citizenship, holy days were downplayed, and the ringing of church bells was severely restricted.

On April 20, 1911, the notorious *Law of Separation of Church and State* went into effect in Portugal, much to the delight of the Freemasons. Divorce laws were relaxed, Catholic weddings were outlawed, cremation was allowed, illegitimacy was recognized, cemeteries were secularized, religious oaths were abolished, and religious instruction in school was prohibited.[15] Alfonso Costa, the main architect of these new anti-Catholic laws, proudly boasted to his Masonic friends:

> "Thanks to this law of separation, in two generations Catholicism will be completely eliminated in Portugal."[16]

But Costa was wrong: he hadn't counted on the pope's swift and certain counterattack. On May 24, 1911, Pope Pius X, in his encyclical *Jamdudum in Lusitania,* declared "null and void" Portugal's Law of Separation of Church and State. The Republican government of Portugal immediately responded to the papal encyclical by banishing the Catholic hierarchy from Portugal. Among those exiled were the Patriarch of Lisbon, the Archbishops of Braga and Évora, the bishops of Porto and Viseu, and numerous other bishops and priests.[17]

The Republican banishment of the Catholic hierarchy triggered two coup attempts by Catholic loyalists—one in 1912 and one in 1915. Both, however, failed. At the time of the second failed coup, Europe was embroiled in World War I, and it looked as if Portugal would probably be drawn into the fray (Germany, in fact, declared war on Portugal on March 9, 1916). Hopes for reinstating a pro-Catholic monarchy would have to wait until the war was over. For the time being, Masonry still ruled Portugal.

Heaven, however, had its own agenda. The Blessed Mother was on her way to save Portugal from the Masons and to warn the sinful world about its dire future.

Our Lady of the Rosary

In the summer of 1915, eight-year-old Lucia dos Santos and her younger cousins, Jacinta and Francisco Marto, were tending sheep on the hill of Cabeco, not far from Fátima, Portugal. Around midday, right after lunch, they began to pray the Rosary, like they did most every day. Suddenly, an angelic figure appeared before their eyes. Not knowing what to do, the children continued praying, but kept their eyes transfixed on the mysterious figure poised in the air in front of the trees. As soon as they were done saying the Rosary, the angel from heaven disappeared, not having said a word.

The same angelic figure appeared to the children three more times—in the spring, summer, and fall of 1916. When he returned to the shepherd children in the spring of 1916, the angel spoke for the first time to Lucia and Jacinta. Francisco couldn't hear what was said, but he could see the angel talking:

> *"Do not be afraid! I am the Angel of Peace. Pray with me."*

As the angel bowed down, touching his forehead to the ground, he began to pray:

> *"My God, I believe, I adore, I hope and I love You! I ask pardon of You for those who do not believe, do not adore, do not hope and do not love You!"*

Having repeated the prayer three times, the angel rose and said:

> *"Pray thus. The Hearts of Jesus and Mary are attentive to the voice of your supplications."*

The angel then left. When the angel returned in the summer of 1916 and found the three taking a siesta in the shade of a large tree, he startled them with an abrupt voice:

> *"What are you doing? Pray, pray very much! The Holy Hearts of Jesus and Mary have designs of mercy on you. Offer prayers and sacrifices constantly to the Most High. Make of everything you can a sacrifice and offer it to God as an act of reparation for the sins which He is offended, and in supplication for the conversion of sinners. You will thus draw down peace upon your country. I am its Angel Guardian, the Angel of Portugal. Above all, accept and bear with submission the suffering which the Lord will send you."*

In the fall of 1916, the angel reappeared holding a chalice and the Holy Eucharist, which was dripping blood into the cup. Kneeling down beside the children, he had them repeat three times a prayer that confirmed the

Catholic doctrine of Transubstantiation—the True Presence of Jesus in the Eucharist:

> *"Most Holy Trinity, Father, Son and Holy Spirit, I offer You the most precious Body, Blood, Soul and Divinity of Jesus Christ, present in all the tabernacles of the world, in reparation for the sacrileges, outrages and indifference by which He Himself is offended. And through the infinite merits of his most Sacred Heart, and the Immaculate Heart of Mary, I beg of You the conversion of poor sinners."*

Upon rising, the angel gave the communion wafer to Lucia and the blood from the chalice to Francisco and Jacinta, saying as he did:

> *"Take and drink the Body and Blood of Jesus Christ, horribly outraged by ungrateful men! Make reparations for their crimes and console your God."*

The angel repeated the Most Holy Trinity prayer three more times and then disappeared. Afterwards, Lucia and her two cousins felt exhausted and were incapable of working. Upon returning home, feeling an inner command to keep quiet, they told no one about the apparition of Portugal's guardian angel and his giving to Jacinta and Francisco their first communion. They had already been ridiculed enough the year before when little Jacinta told her parents she'd seen an angel at the Cova da Iria.

On May 13, 1917, the three little shepherds (Lucia, now 10, Francisco, 9, and Jacinta, 7) were tending sheep in the Cova da Iria when a flash of light like a bolt of lightning suddenly lit up the sky. Lucia rounded up the sheep and headed for home, thinking that a thunderstorm was on its way. Halfway down the slope they saw another flash. The children had gone only a few steps further when a woman more brilliant than the sun, dressed in white with hands folded in prayer and a Rosary made of beautiful pearls hanging over them, with a brilliant golden globe suspended by a gold chain around her neck, appeared to them standing on a small holm oak tree. As with the angel, only Lucia and Jacinta could hear the lady speak. Addressing Lucia, the lady said:

> *"Do not be afraid. I will do you no harm. I am of Heaven. I have come to ask you to come here for six months in succession, on the 13th day, at this same hour. Later on, I will tell you who I am and what I want. Afterwards, I will return here yet a seventh time."*

Lucia asked if they would go to heaven and the lady answered Lucia that, yes, she and her cousins would go to heaven, but that Francisco would have to say many rosaries. When Lucia asked about two of her teenage girlfriends who had just recently died, the lady said that one was in heaven and the other was in purgatory until the end of the world (it is thought that she had violated her chastity). The lady then asked the two girls:

> *"Are you willing to offer yourselves to God and bear all the sufferings He wills to send you, as an act of reparation for the sins by which He is offended, and of supplication for the conversion of sinners?"*

"Yes, we are willing," the girls answered.

"Then you are going to have much to suffer, but the grace of God will be your comfort."

After a few moments the lady then said:

"Pray the Rosary every day, in order to obtain peace for the world, and the end of the war."

Lucia then asked the lady when the war would end.

"I cannot tell you that yet, because I have not yet said what I want."

At that moment, rays of light emanating from the lady's hands penetrated their hearts and communicated to their young souls reflections of themselves as God sees them; something predicted to happen to everyone before the chastisement. When the children knelt down in prayer the lady told them to pray the Rosary everyday, in order to obtain peace for the world and the end of the war. After that, she ascended back towards the east and was taken up into the sky.[18]

As the lady had forewarned, the three children began to suffer almost immediately. Father Ferreira, the parish priest, didn't believe they saw a lady from heaven; he thought their story was just a childish ruse to gain attention—or something worse, a clever deception by the devil. Siding with Father Ferreira, Lucia's mother, Maria Rosa, and Lucia's sisters treated Lucia with scorn and contempt, threatening her with severe punishments if she didn't admit that she fabricated the whole thing. But Lucia and her two cousins didn't give in to these threats: they knew what they had seen and weren't about to deny the truth.

Word spread quickly throughout Portugal that three young peasant children from the tiny hamlet of Aljustrel near Fátima had witnessed an apparition of the Virgin Mary at the Cova da Iria, and that the Blessed Mother had promised to reappear on the 13th of each month for six consecutive months. A sizeable crowd gathered at the Cova da Iria on June 13 in eager anticipation of the second apparition. Like the previous month, around midday, the flash of light was seen by the children, followed by the appearance of the lady on the holm oak tree. The crowd of onlookers saw neither the flash of lightning nor the lady, but some said they heard a soft murmur when Lucia was listening to the lady speak, while others said they noticed the shoots of the holm oak bending as if something were pressing them down. The children saw in front of the lady's right palm a heart encircled and pierced by thorns. After a moment, the lady began to speak to Lucia:

"I wish you to come here on the 13th of the next month, to pray the Rosary each day, and to learn how to read. Later, I will tell you what I want."

When the lady was done speaking, Lucia asked her for the cure of a sick person.

"If he is converted, he will be healed during the year."

She then asked that they be taken to heaven.

"Yes, I will take Jacinta and Francisco [to heaven] soon. But you are to stay here some time longer. Jesus wishes to make use of you to make me known and loved. He wants to establish in the world devotion to My Immaculate Heart. To whoever embraces this devotion I promise salvation; these souls shall be dear to God as flowers placed by me to adorn his throne."

Saddened by the news that Francisco and Jacinta would be leaving without her, Lucia asked if she would have to stay here all alone.

"No, My daughter. Do you suffer a great deal? Don't lose heart. I will never forsake you. My Immaculate Heart will be your refuge and the way that will lead you to God."

The following month, on July 13, the lady returned as promised and began to speak:

"I want you to come here on the 13th of next month, and continue praying the Rosary everyday in honor of Our Lady of the Rosary, in order to obtain peace for the world and the end of the war [WWI], because only She [Our Lady of the Rosary] can help you.

"Continue to come here every month. In October, I will tell you who I am and what I want, and I will perform a miracle for all to see and believe.

"Sacrifice yourselves for sinners, and say many times, especially when you make some sacrifice: O Jesus, it is love of You, for the conversion of sinners, and in reparation for the sins committed against the Immaculate Heart of Mary."

At that moment, the lady opened her hands and rays of light penetrated the earth, opening up the abyss of hell with its oceans of fire. Lucia later described the seen in horror:

"Plunged in the fire were demons and souls in human form, like transparent burning embers, all blackened or burnished bronze, floating about in the conflagration, now raised into the air by the flames that issued from within themselves together with great clouds of smoke, now falling back on every side like sparks in huge fires, without weight or equilibrium, amid shrieks and groans of pain and despair, which horrified us and made us tremble with fear. The demons could be distinguished by their terrifying and repellent likeness to frightful and unknown animals, black and transparent like burning coals."[19] (Lucy would later say that the vision lasted only a moment and that if Mary had not first promised to take them to heaven on May 13, she would have died of fright.). Looking up as if pleading for mercy, Lucia heard the lady say:

"You have seen hell, where the souls of poor sinners go. To save them, God wishes to establish in the world devotion to My Immaculate Heart. If what I say to you is done, many souls will be saved and their will be peace. The war [WWI] is going to end, but if people do not cease offending God, a worse one [WWII] will break out in the reign of Pius XI. When you see a night illumined by an unknown light, know

that this is the great sign given you by God that He is about to punish the world for its crimes, by means of war, famine and persecutions of the Church and the Holy Father.

"To prevent this, I shall come to ask for the consecration of Russia to My Immaculate Heart, and the Communion of Reparation on the First Saturdays. If My requests are heeded, Russia will be converted and there will be peace; if not, she will spread her errors throughout the world, causing wars and persecutions of the Church. The good will be martyred, the Holy Father [the Pope] will have much to suffer, various nations will be annihilated.

"In the end, My Immaculate Heart will triumph. The Holy Father will consecrate Russia to Me, and she will be converted, and a certain period of peace will be granted the world.

"In Portugal, the dogma of the Faith will always be preserved . . . When you say the Rosary, say after each mystery: O my Jesus, forgive us our sins, save us from the fires of hell. Lead all souls to heaven, especially those in most need."

In her message of July 13, Mary made it clear that God wants the faithful to pray the Rosary daily, consecrate Russia to the Immaculate Heart, make the Communion of Reparation on the First Saturdays, and establish world devotion to the Immaculate Heart of Mary. God is giving us Our Lady of the Rosary as our only hope for peace and our last chance for salvation. To reject her is to reject his salvation.

Yet despite God's warning, there are still too many people in this world who blaspheme the Holy Spirit by ridiculing the Mother of God. Some even make fortunes publishing and broadcasting terrible lies about the Virgin Mary and the Catholic Church, going so far as to lead others to believe that Mary is the "Whore of Babylon" mentioned in the 17th chapter of the Book of Revelation.[20]

The Third Secret of Fátima

On the same day that the children saw a vision of hell, Lucia was given a special secret known as the Third Secret of Fátima, that she was to deliver to the pope in a sealed envelope, who was supposed to reveal its contents by 1960.[21] Pope John XXIII opened the sealed envelope in 1959, but declined to make its contents known. When asked why not, his only remark was "It doesn't concern my pontificate." The Third Secret would remain a mystery for the next forty years until pope John Paul II decided to release it to the public in 2000, when its contents made more sense. More on that later.

Fátima Prophecies

Our Lady's public revelations of July 13, 1917 were the most important revelations in history because they correctly predicted, with one hundred per cent accuracy:

The coming of a much worse war (World War II) in the reign of Pope Pius XI (1922-39): Remember that Mary had predicted the coming of World War I, which she called the "general war," back in 1846 in La Salette, France.

The preceding of World War II with an unknown light illuminating the sky: This actually happened on January 25-26, 1938, when an aurora borealis set the skies of the northern hemisphere ablaze with a glowing red fire.

The spread of Russia's "errors" (communism): At the time of Fátima, Russia was governed by the provisional government of Alexander Kerensky. The Bolsheviks (communists) didn't seize power until November 7, 1917. At the time of Mary's appearance in Fátima, Russia was still a Christian nation. It wasn't until February 5, 1918 that Lenin began communism's war against religion.

Russian (Soviet) provoked wars and persecutions of the church: the Spanish Civil War, the Korean War, the wars in Indo-China, Angola, Mozambique, Afghanistan, and Nicaragua; and persecutions of the church in the Soviet Union, Spain, Eastern Europe, the Baltic, the Balkans, Asia, Africa, Latin America, and Portugal.

The good will be martyred: Tens of thousands of priests and religious, including bishops, were executed by communists. Fifty to sixty thousand priests and religious were murdered within the Soviet Union alone.

Various nations annihilated: Ukraine during the time of Stalin's famine (1929-34), Poland during WWII, Eastern European countries behind the Iron Curtain.

The suffering of the Holy Father: Pope John Paul II's assassination attempt by the Islamic terrorist, Mehmet Ali Agca (hired by Bulgarian communists working for the Soviet Union), on May 13, 1981, the 64th anniversary of Fátima; then on May 12, 1982, Pope John Paul II was unharmed when a man with a knife was overpowered by guards in Fátima, Portugal; and another assassination attempt in the Philippines during World Youth Day in January of 1995 by the Islamic terrorists Ramzi Yousef, Abdul Hakim Murad, and Wali Khan Amin Shah; in addition to numerous other health problems (dislocated shoulder, fractured femur, hip replacement, removal of a colon tumor, gall bladder removal, an appendectomy, and Parkinson's disease). In Fátima, Mary was only repeating what she had said in La Salette: *"The Holy Father will suffer greatly. I will be by His side to the end in order to receive his sacrifice. The wicked will make several attempts on his life, but they cannot harm Him."*

The conversion of Russia in the end: The totalitarian, atheistic regime of the Soviet Union fell on Christmas Day, December 25, 1991. On that day, Russia went back to being a Christian nation after throwing off the atheistic yoke of communism—all without bloodshed.

A certain period of peace granted to the world after the conversion of Russia: We are in that period now.

Portugal would retain the Faith: The Masonic Republic of Portugal finally fell in 1926. Portugal remains a Catholic nation to this day.

Freemasonry Fights Fátima

By August of 1917, Mary's appearances at Fátima were beginning to unite Catholics all over Portugal. Thousands upon thousands of Portuguese faithful were making pilgrimages to the Cova da Iria on the 13th of each month in eager anticipation of Our Lady's reappearance. Naturally, this huge gathering of Catholics was seen by the atheistic government of Portugal as a threat to their political power. The Freemasons feared that Fátima would encourage the Portuguese people to rise up and support the ousted pro-Catholic monarchists, so they conspired to halt the Cova da Iria gatherings by force. Artur de Oliveira Santos, the Administrator of the district of Vila Nova de Ourem and the founder-president of the Masonic Lodge of Vila Nova de Ourem, summoned the three children and their fathers to appear before him on August 11 at the town hall of Vila Nova; but of the three children, only Lucia went. When Lucia arrived, the Administrator ordered her to reveal the contents of the Third Secret and promise never to return to the Cova da Iria. She, of course, refused. Having failed to intimidate Lucia, the Administrator dismissed her and her father, but promised he would get what he wanted—even if it meant killing the three children.

On August 13, before they were to go to the Cova da Iria, Santos kidnapped the three children and took them to the prison in Ourem. Santos was confident that they would crack under pressure and confess to him that the apparitions at the Cova were a "clerical conspiracy" designed to bring back the monarchy. First he tried bribing them with money and expensive gifts, but that didn't work. Then he threatened to throw them into a cauldron of boiling oil; leading Francisco and Jacinta away one at a time, leaving poor Lucia to believe that they'd been killed and that she would be next. The cruel Administrator's coercion failed to get the children to recant their stories, so reluctantly Santos let them go.

Even though the children had been abducted on the day that the lady was to appear again, she appeared at the Cova da Iria at midday on August 13, just as she said she would. Hundreds of people witnessed the clap of thunder, the flash of light, the appearance of the little cloud over the holm oak, and the strange rainbow of colors that covered the Cova when Mary appeared.

Since Lucia, Jacinta, and Francisco were physically prevented from going to the Cova da Iria on August 13, the lady inwardly compelled the children to go to the pastures of Valinhos, where she appeared to them on August 19. This was the content of her message:

> "I want you to continue going to the Cova da Iria on the 13th, and to continue praying the Rosary every day. In the last month, I will work a miracle so that all may believe. If you have not been taken away to the City, the miracle would have been even greater. Saint Joseph will come with the Child Jesus, to give peace to the

world. Our Lord will come to bless the people. Our Lady of the Rosary and Our Lady of Sorrows will also come."

Lucia then asked the lady what she wanted to have done with the money left at the Cova da Iria.

"Have two litters made. One is to be carried by you and Jacinta and two other girls dressed in white; the other is to be carried by Francisco and three other boys. The money from the litters is for the feast of Our Lady of the Rosary, and what is left over will help towards the construction of a chapel that is to be built here."

Lucia then asked for the lady to cure some sick persons.

"Yes, I will cure some of them during the year. Pray, pray very much for sinners; for many souls go to hell because there are none to sacrifice themselves and pray for them."

On September 13, the crowd assembled for the apparition, estimated to be about 30,000, was treated to a heavenly show. At midday people began shouting as a luminous globe, moving from east to west, glided slowly and effortless through the cloudless skies as it descended towards the holm oak tree where it came to rest. During the apparition, flower petals fell from the skies and puffs of clouds were seen rising up from the arch around the tree, as though someone with an invisible thurifer was incensing the apparition with smoke. After the apparition, the globe rose up to the east and disappeared in the sun. But not everyone saw the globe; only those who were granted the privilege by heaven.

The September 13 message from the lady was this:

"Continue to say the Rosary to obtain the end of the war. In October Our Lord will come, as well as Our Lady of Sorrows and Our Lady of Mount Carmel. Saint Joseph will appear with the Child Jesus to bless the world."

Again, Lucia asked for the cure of some sick persons.

"Yes, I will cure some, but not others, because Our Lord does not trust them."

Lucia then said that the people would like to have a chapel here.

"With half the money make litters to be carried in procession on the feast of Our Lady of the Rosary; the other half is for the chapel."

Lucia then offered to give the lady two letters and some perfumed water to take with her.

"Those are not needed in heaven."

Then the lady said:

"In October I will perform a miracle so that all may believe."

The Miracle of Fátima

On the 13th of October, the day that the lady promised to perform a miracle, a persistent rain fell in Fátima; muddying roads and fields and making travel darn near impossible. Despite the awful weather conditions, between fifty to seventy thousand people showed up—the largest crowd yet. Everyone was anxious for the miracle, including the skeptical press, who was there to disprove it. The majority of the press, of course, was positive that nothing would happen: this was their one big chance to expose Fátima as a hoax.

At about one o'clock in the afternoon, midday by solar position, Lucia, moved by an inner voice, instructed the crowd to close their umbrellas despite the rain and say the Rosary. As they were saying the Rosary, a column of bluish smoke rose three times in the air around the children, and then the rain suddenly stopped. At about one thirty, Lucia announced the lady's arrival. The lady, as everyone expected, formally identified herself to the children as the Blessed Virgin Mary. This is what she told Lucia:

> *"I want a chapel to be built hear in My honor. I am Our Lady of the Rosary. Continue to say the Rosary every day. The war will end soon and the soldiers will return to their homes."*

Lucia asked for the cure of some sick and the conversion of some sinners.

> *"Some, yes; others no. People must amend their lives and ask pardon for their sins. They must not offend Our Lord anymore for He is already too much offended."*

Nothing more was said. As the Blessed Mother ascended back into the sky, the clouds parted and the sun came out. Lucia then shouted, "Look at the sun! Look at the sun!" The sun, a silvery disc, was capable of being looked at without hurting the eyes. Suddenly, it began to dance and spin and throw off a multitude of colors like a rainbow. In unison, the crowd shouted, "Miracle! Miracle!"

But the crowd's joy turned to terror when the sun suddenly appeared to race towards the earth at blinding speed. "We shall all be killed!" they screamed. Believers and non-believers alike fell on their knees begging for God's forgiveness. In the blink of an eye, the sun reversed its descent and returned to its normal zenith, and amazingly, the crowd noticed that everything was dry—their clothes, the ground, everything!

During Fátima's "Dance of the Sun," which lasted about ten minutes, the three children saw visions of the Holy Family, Our Lady of Sorrows, and Our Lady of Mount Carmel—just as Mary had promised on August 19 and September 13.

The miracle of the sun was seen as far away as twenty-five miles. At Sao Pedro de Muel, the poet Alfonso Lopes Vieira witnessed the spectacle in the sky from his veranda. His nearby relatives saw it too. In the little village of

Alburitel where the three seers lived, the entire population witnessed the miracle of the sun.[22]

The purpose of the "Dance of the Sun" was twofold: First, the Blessed Virgin Mary had intentionally used the sun to perform a miracle so that people would know that she is the "Woman Clothed with the Sun." Second, the annunciation of a miracle three months in advance so that critics of Fátima could be on hand, and then its happening on the exact day and hour that it was foretold, was proof of Fátima's authenticity. Now even the most cynical critic couldn't deny that something inexplicable had happened in Fátima.

Lucia's mother and the parish priest, Father Ferreira, both unbelievers at first, were now convinced that Fátima was from God and not from the devil. Many atheists came to believe too. The Editor in Chief for the secular Masonic newspaper *O Seculo,* Avelino de Almeida, witnessed first hand what had happened and reported that the miracle "defied all laws of the cosmos."[23] Defending himself two weeks later before the anticlerical press, Almeida backed up his story in *Illustracao Portuguesa* with a dozen photographs showing the crowd in a state of ecstasy. Here is his report:

> "What did I see at Fátima that was even stranger? The rain, at an hour announced in advance, ceased falling; the thick mass of clouds dissolved; and the sun—a dull silver disc—came into view at is zenith, and began to dance in a violent and convulsive movement, which a great number of witnesses compared to a serpentine dance, because the colors taken on by the surface of the sun were so beautiful and gleaming . . . Miracle, as the people shouted? A natural phenomenon, as the learned would say? For the moment, I do not trouble myself with finding out, but only with affirming *what I saw* . . . The rest is a matter between Science and the Church."[24]

There were too many witnesses in Fátima on October 13 to deny what happened, so unbelievers tried explaining it away as some sort of collective hallucination—an autosuggested mass hysteria. They insisted that the sun would have destroyed the earth had it moved that close to the earth's orbit, so the miracle couldn't have really happened. But they were wrong: the sun "danced" in Fátima through an optical vision sent from God to all who were present, both atheist and believer alike, which was still a miracle.

Jacinta and Francisco

On June 13, 1917, the Virgin Mary said that she would soon come to take Jacinta and Francisco to heaven, and sure enough she did. Towards the end of October, 1918, Jacinta and Francisco contracted the Spanish flu that went on to kill twenty million people worldwide. Both had a brief recovery period where they appeared to be getting better, but then suffered a severe relapse on December 23. The Blessed Virgin Mary visited them both in the hospital and said that she would take Francisco sooner than Jacinta. Francisco died on April 4, 1919.[25]

In December of 1919, Our Lady visited Jacinta again and told her that she would be transferred to a Lisbon hospital where she would die all alone. And as Mary said, Jacinta was transferred to Lisbon and died all alone, without family or friends, on February 20, 1920. Jacinta had told the doctor in Lisbon beforehand that she would die that day, but he didn't believe she was that ill. He should have listened to her.

Jacinta had several visions of the future before she died. In one vision she saw the pope in a big house, with his head buried in his hands, weeping. Outside were many people—some throwing stones, some cursing. In another vision she saw multitudes of people on a highway, crying with hunger and nothing to eat, like the Kosovo refugees of 1999. The Holy Father was in a church praying before the Immaculate Heart of Mary and many people were praying with him.[26]

Revelations to Sister Lucy

Not long after Jacinta died, Lucia entered the convent of the Daughters of Mary on August 26, 1923. Two years later she transferred to a Carmelite institute in Pontevedra, the Dorothean Sisters, on October 25, 1925. On December 10, 1925, while in her cell, Lucia had an apparition of Mary and the Child Jesus. In her hand the Blessed Mother held out her Immaculate Heart, encircled by thorns. Then the Child Jesus spoke to Lucia:

> *"Have compassion on the Heart of your Most Holy Mother, covered with thorns, with which ungrateful men pierce It at every moment, and there is no one to make an act of reparation to remove them."*

Mary then said:

> *"Look My daughter, at My Heart, surrounded by thorns with which ungrateful men pierce Me at every moment by their blasphemies and ingratitude. You at least try to console Me and announce in My name that I promise to assist at the moment of death, with all the graces necessary for salvation, all those who, on the First Saturday of five consecutive months shall confess, receive Holy Communion, recite five decades of the Rosary, and keep me company for fifteen minutes while meditating on the mysteries of the Rosary, with the intention of making reparation to Me."[27]*

On July 16, 1926, Lucia left Pontevedra to enter the novitiate of the Dorothean Sisters at Tuy in Spanish Galacia. On June 13, 1929, Sister Lucia had a spectacular apparition of the Holy Trinity in the chapel of Tuy during holy hour. Jesus appeared to Lucia on a luminous cross, with God the Father and the Holy Spirit (in the form of a dove) on top of the cross. Jesus was bleeding from his right rib cage and the blood flowed onto a Communion Host and collected into a chalice at his side. Under the left arm of the cross were the words "Mercy" and "Grace." Our Lady of Fátima was at the foot of the cross with her Immaculate Heart, crowned with thorns, in her left hand. Mary said to Lucia that the time had come to make known her Fátima directives of July 13, 1917:

> *"The moment has come when God asks the Holy Father [Pius XI] to make, in union with all the bishops of the world, the consecration of Russia to My Immaculate Heart, promising to save it by this means."*

> *"So numerous are the souls which the justice of God condemns for sins committed against Me, that I come to ask reparation. Sacrifice yourself for this intention and pray."*

On May 29, 1930, Lucia had a revelation from Jesus in the chapel at Tuy while she was contemplating the apparition of December 10, 1925, asking herself why only five first Saturdays and not more. This is what Our Lord said to Lucy:

> *"My Daughter, the reason is simple. There are five types of offenses and blasphemies committed against the Immaculate Heart of Mary:*

> *1. Blasphemies against the Immaculate Conception.*
> *2. Blasphemies against Her Virginity.*
> *3. Blasphemies against Her Divine Maternity, in refusing at the same time to recognize Her as the Mother of Men.*
> *4. The Blasphemies of those who publicly seek to sow in the hearts of children indifference or scorn or even hatred of this Immaculate Mother.*
> *5. The offenses of those who outrage Her directly in Her holy images.*

> *"Here, My daughter, is the reason why the Immaculate Heart of Mary inspired Me to ask for this little reparation, and in consideration of it, to move My mercy to pardon souls who have the misfortune of offending Her. As for you, always seek by your prayers and sacrifices to move My mercy to pity for those poor souls."*[28]

Jesus made it perfectly clear to Lucia: if you blaspheme the Mother of God you risk the fires of hell. Simple as that. Critics of Mary should heed this warning, especially those who claim that Mary, in her authenticated apparitions, is really the devil in disguise. These people should remember what Christ said to the Pharisees when they accused him of casting out demons by the power of Beelzebub, the prince of demons: *"On judgment day you will be held accountable for ever unguarded word spoken. By your words you will be acquitted, and by your words you will be condemned."*[29] The Pharisees blasphemed the Holy Spirit by committing the unforgivable sin of accusing Christ of being in league with demons. Blaspheming Christ's Mother is no different than blaspheming Christ himself.

The church was too slow in consecrating Russia to the Immaculate Heart of Mary so the Soviet Union continued to spread her errors. Jesus complained to Lucia in August of 1931 about the church's indecision under Pope Pius XI to follow through on his specific requests in Fátima:

> *"They did not want to heed My request! . . . Like the King of France [Louis XIV] they will repent and do it [consecrate Russia to the Immaculate Heart], but it will be late. Russia will have already spread its errors throughout the world, provoking wars and persecutions against the Church: the Holy Father will have much to suffer."*[30]

King Louis XIV reneged on spreading devotion to the Sacred Heart of Jesus, requested by Our Lord through St. Margaret-Mary Alacoque at the Visitation convent in Paray-le-Monial on June 17, 1689. A hundred years to the very day of Jesus' unfulfilled request, the French Revolution began on June 17, 1789, eventually leading to the guillotining of King Louis XVI and the overthrow of the French monarchy. Like the King of France, Pope Pius XI died in 1939 without having carried out God's request to consecrate Russia to the Immaculate Heart of Mary in communion with the bishops of the world.

Portugal Keeps the Faith

The anti-Catholic Masonic authorities of Portugal suffered a great blow by the appearance of Mary in Fátima. In the elections that followed, the Democratic, Republican, and Evolutionist parties all lost votes, which they blamed on Fátima. An evil Masonic conspiracy was then launched to put an end to the Fátima pilgrimages. On October 22, 1917, at the instigation of the prefect of the district of Santarém, José António dos Reis, the chapel at the Cova da Iria was dynamited, which caused a tremendous public outcry for the overthrow of the Masonic government.

On December 8, 1917, the Solemnity of the Immaculate Conception, the Minister of State, Sidonio Pais, a moderate Republican and former Freemason, launched a successful coup against the anti-Catholic Masonic government and declared the dissolution of parliament. Nominating himself dictatorial president, Pais immediately lifted the restrictions against the Catholic Church, re-established diplomatic relations with the Vatican, reopened the churches, and restored the rights of the Jesuits.

Ousted Masons tried to get back in power by killing Pais. After an unsuccessful assassination attempt on December 6, 1918, Pais was gunned down on December 14. For the moment, freemasonry was back in power in Portugal, and, predictably, anarchy returned to the government. Fearing mass demonstrations again and another coup, this time the Masons elected not to reinstate anticlerical legislation.

Despite Masonry's violent attempts to keep visitors away from Fátima, which included the demolition again of the sanctuary on March 6, 1922, pilgrims continued to come in the hundreds of thousands. On May 13, 1924, their faith and courage was rewarded when a mysterious shower of flowers fell from heaven on two hundred thousand pilgrims gathered together at Fátima for the seventh anniversary of Our Lady's first appearance there. Among those present was the newly elected Bishop da Silva of Leiria, who publicly testified to the miraculous occurrence of the flowers.

As it happened, two years later the Portuguese Freemasons were ousted from government for the last time. Fearing a Soviet-backed communist attempt to seize power in Portugal, the army under General António Carmona took control of the government on May 28, 1926. Carmona, a staunch pro-Catholic, became president of Portugal until 1951. António de Oliveira Salazar, another loyal supporter of the Catholic Church, then took over after Carmona left and governed Portugal until 1968.

After its defeat of Masonry, Portugal recovered its economic, political, and moral stability, and a true Catholic renaissance was born: millions were converted and vocations to the priesthood and religious institutes skyrocketed in Portugal. Portugal retained the faith as Mary promised in Fátima, but converting Russia would prove much more difficult.

Lenin's Campaign Against God

Savage, inhuman capitalism in the 19th and 20th centuries gave rise to communism's only kernel of truth: the rich industrialist classes exploited the poor, working masses to their advantage. So, behind the altruistic facade of social and economic justice, the evil founders of Russian communism inculcated their true, arcane objectives: world-wide revolution and the forceful overthrow of all capitalistic governments; the establish of a core ruling elite from Russia that would hold the reigns to all economic and political power; and the elimination of all religions that believed in an afterlife reward instead of communism's scientifically-manufactured earthly utopia (before it was called communism it was called "scientific socialism" because it was based, in large part, upon the atheistic teachings of social Darwinism).

The ensuing Marxist-Leninist war on Christianity, which has been called the most vicious anti-Christian tyranny since the days of the Roman Emperor Diocletian, created more martyrs in its first decades of existence than in all the previous centuries combined. In the Russian Orthodox Church alone fifty thousand priests, monks, and nuns were martyred by the Soviets between the 1920s and the 1930s. Some estimates put the number of martyred clergy and religious of all Christian denominations as high as 140,000.[31]

The brutal Soviet campaign against religion officially began on February 5, 1918, the day Vladimir Ilyich Lenin, a former lawyer and freemason living in Switzerland before the war and now a fully-committed revolutionary, ordered a decree which ended all state support for the Russian Orthodox Church, denied all churches and synagogues in Russia the legal right to own property, and prohibited all religious instruction in any school where non-religious courses were taught.[32] Desecrations of Russian churches, monasteries, synagogues and shrines followed soon afterwards, encouraged by the atheistic hatred in Lenin's words:

"Every religious idea, every idea of any divinity is the most inexpressible vileness."[33]

On February 24, 1922, Lenin ordered the meltdown of all sacred vessels made of precious metals kept in Russian, Ukrainian, and Belorussian churches. To silence the protests, Lenin arrested the Orthodox archbishop of Moscow and thirteen Catholic priests in Petrograd. On April 26, fifty-four people, including priests and deacons, were tried for inciting opposition to the government seizures. A month later, four Orthodox priests and one Orthodox deacon were executed.[34] Charged with the same offenses, Russian Orthodox Archbishop Benjamin of Petrograd was convicted on August 6 (the Feast of the Transfiguration) and secretly executed sometime afterwards.[35]

Four months later, on December 5, 1922, the Soviet government closed all of Petrograd's Catholic churches, and within months Catholic priests were taken to Moscow for trial.[36] On March 10, 1923, all the defendants were found guilty of disobeying Lenin's decree. Archbishop Cieplak and Monsignor Constantine Budkiewicz were sentenced to death, but on Holy Thursday, Archbishop Cieplak's death sentence was commuted to ten years in solitary confinement. Monsignor Budkiewicz wasn't as lucky: he was executed on Easter morning, 1923, becoming the first Catholic priest martyred by the Soviet Union.[37]

Faced with certain execution, Patriarch Tikhon of the Russian Orthodox Church cracked under the relentless Soviet pressure. In June of 1922, he shamefully signed a conciliatory statement approving Soviet communism: "I have completely adopted the Soviet platform, and consider that the church must be non-political."[38] From then on the Russian Orthodox Church became the spineless political vassal of Lenin's communist state.

After only six years in power, Lenin, whose Slavic name Vladimir means "Lord" or "Ruler," died at home on January 21, 1924, supposedly from a stroke.[39] Believed by many historians to have been murdered by his enemy and successor, Joseph Stalin, Lenin left a legacy full of the blood of God's saints, murdering at least 1,200 priests and 28 bishops in five years time. Befitting the bloodthirsty color of his god, the Red Dragon, Lenin's lifeless body was wrapped in a blood-red blanket and placed in a scarlet-colored coffin, and put on display inside a red mausoleum in Red Square. Lenin's red tomb contained all the violent, satanic symbols of the Soviet Union: the hammer, the sickle, and the red satanic pentagram.[40]

Ten months before he died, on the day before the aforementioned Catholic priests arrived in Moscow for trial and execution, Lenin suffered a severe stroke, his second, on March 9, 1923, after which he flew into a blind rage at Stalin. Temporarily losing his speech and becoming paralyzed on his right side, Russian doctors recorded Lenin's panicked utterances about the devil coming to get him:

"Help-oh . . . the devil . . . devil . . . evi helped, if it . . . evi . . . ."[41]

The terrified look on Lenin's face after his second stroke said it all: Lenin knew the devil was coming for him soon and he was powerless to escape.

The Man Of Steel

After Lenin died on January 21, 1924, religious persecutions against Jews and Christians were resumed with a vengeance in the spring of 1929 by the Soviet Union's new leader, Josef Vissarionovich Djugashvili, who haughty nick-named himself "Stalin" (The Man of Steel). Stalin took up where Lenin left off, passing a law containing 17 church-control statutes, which specifically forbade any religious activities outside of church services, including charity. Religious instruction to children, except by parents in the home, was strictly forbidden.

By law, Soviet citizens were required to worship Stalin and the founders of communism in place of Jesus Christ. Oaths of allegiance were sworn by the Soviet people to Stalin under penalty of death. Proclaiming himself to be the Soviet Union's new messiah, Stalin was glorified by the Russian people as the "Coryphaeus of Science and Technology," the "Sun of Our Planet," "Leader and Teacher," and the "Greatest Genius of All Times and All Nations." In his honor, huge murals and images of Stalin, Lenin, Marx, and Engels were hung on buildings, in schools, in hospitals, in auditoriums, and even in confiscated churches (the abomination of desolation). In order to eliminate the Christian worship of God on Sundays, Stalin, like the Antichrist to come, changed the days of the week to a four-day workweek followed by a day of rest.[42]

Working fast, by 1930 Stalin had closed half of the churches in Moscow and all the monasteries in Ukraine. Great numbers of religious icons were burned, Sundays were suppressed, factory workers were forced to sign a declaration of formal apostasy and hatred against God or else forfeit their ration cards, clothing, and lodging. Clergy were denied public housing, demonstrations against churches were held on holy days—especially Christmas and Easter. (On one Christmas, a procession of tanks manned by ruffians dressed in sacred vestments spat on the cross, while armored vehicles transported huge Christmas trees from which marionettes representing Catholic and Orthodox bishops were hung in effigy.)[43] All sorts of sacrileges against Christ were encouraged by Stalin.

Trying his best to outdo the persecutions of Lenin, in May of 1932 Stalin proudly announced his "anti-religion five-year plan"; boasting to the Soviet people that by 1937:

> " . . . not a single house of prayer will be needed any longer in any terri-
> tory of the Soviet Union, and the very notion of God will be expunged as
> a survival of the Middle Ages and an instrument for holding down the
> masses."[44]

Soviet citizens who refused to go along with Stalin's five-year plan and renounce their Christian faith were sent on Stalin's orders to the Solovetsky Islands labor camp in the White Sea area of the Arctic Circle. Opened in 1923, the Soviet prison camp had been a collection of monasteries and churches built during the fifteenth-century: the monastery of the Trinity; the monastery of Savvatyevsky; the cathedrals of the Assumption and the Transfiguration; the Church of the Beheading on Sekirnaya Hill; and the Golgotha-Crucifixion Monastery on the island of Anzer where the Blessed Virgin Mary is believed to have appeared to a monk named Job during an all-night vigil at the bottom of a hill, requesting that a church and monastery be built there dedicated to the Crucifixion and that the hill be renamed after Golgotha, because, Mary prophesied, this site " . . . *will be white by the suffering of countless multitudes.* "[45] Mary's prophecy to Job of the suffering of countless multitudes came true during the horrifying times of Stalin's famine (1929-1934) and Stalin's purges (1934-1939), when tens of millions of people disappeared forever in the frozen Soviet gulags (forced labor camps) of Solovetsky, Orotukan, and Belomor Canal. It's estimated that between 1935-41, more than 19 million Soviet citizens were arrested by Stalin. With less than half of them shot, the majority perished in the frozen gulags of Siberia.[46]

Like Lenin and Hitler, Joseph Stalin was another forerunner of the Antichrist to come. Born in Russian Georgia to a drunken cobbler on December 6, 1878, the third and only son to have survived through infancy, baby Joseph's left arm was deformed and shorter than his right, his eyes were yellow, and the toes on his left foot webbed. Stalin's great-grandfather called Joseph's deformed foot "the devil's hoof."[47]

Christened on December 17 at the Orthodox Cathedral of the Assumption of Mary at Gori in Russian Georgia, Stalin's mother dedicated him to God and vowed to make him a priest because she was so thankful to God for letting one of her sons live through infancy.[48] Like Hitler and the coming Antichrist, Stalin grew up in the church before rebelling against it.

An illness at age six left Joseph Stalin's face terribly pockmarked, which only added to his existing deformities and bad temperament. Stalin was rude and arrogant, with a quick-temper and an extreme hatred for Jews and authority figures. Like Luther before him, he hated his abusive father, who frequently got drunk and beat him and his mother, until he abandoned them to fare for themselves. At the insistence of his mother, because of her vow she made to God when he was born, Joseph attended to Gori Church School in 1888, and then entered Tiflis Seminary in 1894 to become a priest. At Tiflis, the insubordinate young Joseph, who didn't want to be there in the first place, was first introduced to the revolutionary socialist ideals of Mikhail Bakunin, the father of Russian anarchism, when he was given a copy of Sergei Nechaev's *Revolutionary's Catechism.*

In the late-nineteenth century, Russian schools and seminaries were inundated with Marxists and revolutionaries, so after reading Nechaev's *Revolutionary's Catechism,* Stalin decided to become one too. Convinced that Darwin had disproved the existence of God, Stalin handed a fellow seminarian a book by Darwin one day and said: "There is no God, they are deceiving us."[49]

Kicked out of Tiflis seminary in 1899 for his irreligious views and troublesome behavior, Stalin joined the revolutionary underground movement (Stalin's revolutionary code name was "Koba," the hero in his favorite book, *The Parricide [Father Killer],* by Georgian author Kazbegi).[50] Inciting antigovernment demonstrations wherever he could, Stalin was always on the run, was arrested numerous times, and was finally exiled to Siberia.[51] Escaping from Siberia on January 5, 1904, Stalin joined Lenin's Congress of the Russian Social Democratic Workers' Party, the fledgling Communist Party, and became one of its most feared leaders; excelling in assassinations, bombings, robbery, extortion, terrorism, and general anarchy.

Stalin was placed on the Communist Party Central Committee by Lenin, whom he idolized, and was made one of the first four Politburo members. In April of 1922, the Communist Party Central Committee promoted Stalin to General Secretary of the Party.[52] Through sheer ruthlessness and terror, Stalin positioned himself to become Lenin's successor upon his death. Lenin, however, was adamantly opposed to Stalin's takeover of the Party because he was so barbarous. In fact, just before he died, Lenin wrote a "testament" letter addressed to the Communist Central Committee warning them not to keep Stalin as General Secretary of the Communist Party because he was too wicked. But that letter was never made public to the whole Party Congress and Stalin became the unchallenged head of the Soviet Union anyway.

Stalin's sadistic legacy as the second head of the Soviet Union is well documented: he was personally responsible for the deaths of tens of millions of Soviet citizens and *kulaks* through famines, purges, pogroms, deportations, executions, assassinations, murders, tortures, and banishments to slave labor camps. (The bear devours its own.) What is not well known is that just before he died on March 5, 1953, Stalin was planning the roundup of Soviet Jews to send to Siberian gulags, and had already arrested nine Jewish doctors on trumped up charges of conspiracy to kill Soviet leaders with lethal doses of medicine. Stalin was also planning to provoke a military confrontation with the United States because of his recent development of nuclear weapons, and had begun ringing Moscow with anti-ballistic missiles in case of a U.S. nuclear counterattack.

Fortunately for the world, on March 1, 1953, Stalin suffered a severe stroke that left him in terrible agony and near death. Stalin's daughter, Svetlana, described her father's long death agony in all its gruesome justice:

> "Father's death was slow and difficult . . . His face was discolored and different . . . his features were becoming unrecognizable . . . The death agony was terrible. It choked him slowly as we watched. At the last minute he opened his eyes. It was a terrible look—either mad or angry and full of the fear of death . . . Suddenly he raised his left hand and seemed either to be pointing upward somewhere or threatening us all . . . then, the next moment, his spirit after one last effort tore itself from his body."[53]

Joseph Stalin died on March 5, 1953, the same day he was to begin rounding up Soviet Jews for deportation to Siberia concentration camps. Stalin's remains were put on display next to Lenin's with great pomp and ceremony, but eight years later, on October 31, 1961 (Halloween), Soviet leader Nikita Khrushchev, who in 1956 had publicly denounced Stalin's purges and pogroms, quietly took Stalin's body from the sacred mausoleum and buried it near the Kremlin wall. Half of the Soviet population, once victims of Stalin's fiendish barbarities, rejoiced in The Man of Steel's posthumous fall from grace.

A Second, Worse War

Because of the consecration of Portugal to the Immaculate Heart of Mary by the Portuguese prelates on May 13, 1931, Portugal remained at peace for the next forty years: Portuguese freemasonry was dissolved in 1935; the civil war that ravaged Spain between 1936-1939 stayed out of Portugal; and miraculously, Portugal managed to stay out of WWII.

An omen that WWII was about to ravage the earth was seen in 1938. On the night of January 25-26, 1938, a tremendous light like a distant forest fire burning in the dark, illuminated the skies over Scandinavia, Western Europe, Northern Africa, and North America; triggering numerous reports of a gigantic conflagration burning somewhere beyond the horizon.[54] Civil authorities told callers not to worry, that it was only an aurora borealis (northern lights).

Sister Lucia, however, recognized the red glow for what it really was—the divine warning that a worse war was about to ignite the world in flames, foretold to Lucia by Mary on July 13, 1917:

> *"When you see a night illumined by an unknown light, know that it is the great sign given you by God that He is about to punish the world for its crimes, by means of war, famine, and persecutions against the Church and the Holy Father . . . "*

The Second World War began two months after the unknown light when Hitler invaded Austria on March 12, 1938. By war's end in August of 1945, fifty million people had been killed, including 6 million Jews and 5 million gentiles who were beaten, starved, worked to death, or murdered in Nazi concentration camps.[55] This death toll, however, doesn't include the sixty million Soviets killed during the times of Lenin's famine (1921-1922), Stalin's famine (1929-1934), and Stalin's purges (1934-1939). If you combine the mortality figures of Lenin and Stalin to WWII's death toll, between 100-150 million people died in wars, famines, and politico-religious persecutions in just the first half of the twentieth century. No wonder God sent the Blessed Virgin Mary to Fátima to warn the world that it was about to be punished.

After the Second World War, the Allies wanted nothing more than to put an end to war, so they intentionally ignored intelligence reports of the horrible religious persecutions going on within the Soviet Union.[56] Stalin had duped Roosevelt, Churchill, and the rest of the West into thinking that the communists had finally ended their persecutions of religion when he temporarily reopened some of the churches and synagogues during WWII to boost Russian morale. But once the war was over and the Nazis were defeated, religious persecutions started anew in the Soviet Union, something the Vatican was well aware of it.

The Fátima messages regarding the spread of "Russia's errors" were perceived by the Western Allies as too confrontational, so extreme pressure was put on the new pope, Pius XII, to ease up on the anti-communist rhetoric.[57] Reluctantly, Pius XII agreed and instituted a new Vatican policy of Ostpolitik—negotiation, dialogue, diplomacy, foreign aid, and peaceful coexistence, rather than direct, ideological confrontation.

Russia Spreads Her Errors

The lack of a strong, unified voice against the Soviet Union at the end of WWII only encouraged Stalin to demand more concessions from the Allies. At the Yalta conference in February of 1945, the Allies shamefully handed over Eastern Europe and the Far East to the communists, sealing the fate of 2.8 million refugees: 800,000 were immediately executed and 1.5 million more were deported to Siberian gulags.[58] Sovereign countries that had existed in

Eastern Europe and elsewhere before WWII were now annihilated, as predicted would happen in Fátima.

A Cold War developed between the two remaining superpowers that would last for 45 years, with legitimate fears that communists were infiltrating into the highest levels of Western governments, and that the Soviets were planning to conquer the world for Marxism by overthrowing democratic countries one by one. The spiritual stakes were tremendous in the Cold War: if the Soviets succeeded in conquering the world, religion would be outlawed or severely curtailed, as it was in the Soviet Union and China. It was paramount, therefore, that the Catholic Church properly consecrate Russia to the Immaculate Heart of Mary.

Sister Mary Lucy (Lucia), at the Carmelite convent at Coimbra since 1948, had a conversation with a Mexican priest named Father Fuentes, the Postulator of the beatification causes of Jacinta and Francisco, on December 26, 1957. In that meeting, she told Father Fuentes that a diabolic wave was sweeping the earth and a decisive battle was being waged between the Woman (Mary) and the Red Dragon (Satan), in which only one side would emerge victorious. Sister Lucy told Father Fuentes that the devil had declared all out war on the Catholic Church, especially its pastors and consecrated souls, because he knows that if you strike the shepherds of the church, the flock will scatter. The devil, Lucia said, planned to lead as many souls away from God as he could, before he is chained up for "a thousand years." Sister Lucy also told Father Fuentes that unless Russia was converted that country would be God's instrument of chastisement for the world. To prevent this God has given us two remedies: the Holy Rosary and devotion to the Immaculate Heart of Mary. Sister Lucy said:

> "Father, the most Holy Virgin is very sad because no one has paid any attention to Her [Fátima] message, neither the good nor the bad. The good continue on their way, but without giving any importance to Her message. The bad, not seeing the punishment of God actually falling upon them, continue their life of sin without ever caring about the message. But believe me, Father, God is going to chastise the world and it will be in a terrible manner. The celestial chastisement is imminent . . .
>
> "Tell them, Father, that many times the Most Holy Virgin told my cousins as well as myself, that Russia would be the instrument of chastisement chosen by Heaven to punish the whole world if we do not beforehand obtain the conversion of that poor nation . . .
>
> "Father the devil is about to wage a decisive battle with the Blessed Virgin, as he knows what it is that offends God the most, and which in a short space of time will gain him the greatest number of souls. Thus, the devil does everything to overcome souls consecrated to God, because in this way he will succeed in leaving the souls of the faithful abandoned by their leaders, thereby the more easily will he seize them . . .

"Father, the Most Holy Virgin did not tell me that we are in the last times of the world, but She made me understand this for three reasons. The first reason is as follows: She told me that the devil is about to wage a decisive battle against the Blessed Virgin, and a decisive battle is the final battle where one side will be victorious and the other side will suffer defeat. Also, from now on we must choose sides. Either we are for God or we are for the devil; there is no in-between.

"The second reason is as follows: She said to my cousins as well as myself, that God is giving two last remedies to the world: the Holy Rosary and the devotion to the Immaculate Heart of Mary. These are the last two remedies that signify that there will be no others.

"The third reason is as follows: In the plans of Divine Providence, God always, before He is about to chastise the world, exhausts all the other remedies. Now, when He sees that the world has not heeded any of them, then as we say in our imperfect manner of speaking, He offers us with a certain trepidation, the last means of salvation, His Most Holy Mother. Indeed if we despise and reject this last means, we will not have any more forgiveness from Heaven, because we will have committed what the Gospel calls the sin against the Holy Ghost. This sin consists of openly rejecting, with full knowledge and consent, the salvation, which He offers. Let us remember that Jesus Christ is a very good Son and that He does not permit that we offend and despise His Most Holy Mother . . . "[59]

Following the Second World War, the new Vatican policy of Ostpolitik, dialogue and peaceful coexistence with the Soviets instead of denouncement and condemnation, resulted in half-hearted, partial consecrations of Russia to the Immaculate Heart of Mary by Pius XII on October 31, 1942 and July 7, 1952, and by Pope Paul VI on November 21, 1964. Thus, without the total consecration of Russia to the Immaculate Heart of Mary, Russia continued to spread her errors throughout the world, and religion, especially Catholicism, was its primary target.

Martyrdom Behind the Iron Curtain

"From Stettin in the Baltic to Trieste in the Adriatic an iron curtain has descended across the continent."

Sir Winston Churchill, Fulton, MO
March 5, 1946

The Soviet crackdown on religion in Eastern Europe began during the Second World War when the Soviet Army occupation of Eastern Poland, Lithuania, and Latvia brought about the closure of Catholic publishing houses, schools, hospitals, seminaries, and churches. As in The Soviet Union, priests were arrested, religious holidays were abolished, Vatican representatives were expelled, Catholic marriage ceremonies were outlawed, and millions of Catholics were deported to die in Soviet gulags.[60] By the end of WWII, communists had become firmly entrenched in Albania, Czechoslovakia, Romania, Bulgaria, Yugoslavia, Hungary, Estonia, Latvia, Lithuania, and Poland. Soviet forces occupied all of these countries except for Yugoslavia, where Josip Tito somehow managed to maintain sole control over that region.

Tito's persecutions of the church in Yugoslavia began as soon as he came to power when he closed forty-nine seminaries, along with numerous Catholic schools, hospitals, nursing homes, and orphanages. By September of 1945, 243 Yugoslav priests and religious had been killed by Tito, 169 imprisoned or forced into slave labor camps, and 89 officially listed as missing. Archbishop Aloysius Stepanic of Zagreb, Croatia (the Yugoslav Catholic primate) was arrested and tried for complicity with the Nazis and the Croatian *Ustashis* and sentenced to sixteen years hard labor.[61] Orthodox bishops Simrak, Carevich, and Garich were executed, while bishops Sarich and Rozman were exiled.

In Czechoslovakia, the Greek Catholic bishop of Mukacevo, Bishop Romzha, was murdered in a hospital in 1947 after his car was hit by a Soviet police bus. Three years later, Father Josef Toufer died from torture in 1950 after the secret police staged a phony miracle in his church and then accused him of staging it. And a decade later, Czechoslovakia's main Greek Catholic leader, Bishop Gojdic of Presov, died in prison in 1960.

In Romania, the communist regime sent 12 bishops to prison and killed, jailed, or deported 650 priests. Bishops Ioan Suciu of Blaj, Valeriu Frentiu of Oradea, and Vasile Aftenie of Bucharist died in Sighet prison; Bishop Aftenie of Bucharist was murdered in the city's interior-ministry building in 1950 or 1951; Bishop Rusu of Maramures perished in Gherl prison; and Bishop Balan of Lugoj and Cardinal Hossa of Cluj both died while interned at the Orthodox monastery.

In Hungary, on Good Friday in 1945, Bishop Vilmos Apor of Gyor was machine-gunned in his doorway by a drunken soldier after trying to protect several dozen girls who had taken refuge inside. Bishop Anton Durcovici of Iasi starved to death in prison, and Bishop Aaron Marton of Alba Julia was arrested in 1949 after refusing to delete a clause about the pope's supremacy and for challenging the Party's say in choosing ecclesiastic offices.[62]

In Bulgaria, Passionist Bishop Eugene Bossilkoff was executed along with three Catholic priests in 1952 on charges of spying for the Vatican.

In the Ukraine, the Ukrainian Eastern-rite Roman Catholic Church was completely eradicated in 1946, and replaced by the state-controlled Russian Orthodox Church (Stalin had virtually wiped out the Ukrainian Orthodox Church in the 1930s, replacing it with the more subservient Russian Orthodox Church, forcing faithful Catholics in the Ukraine to celebrate mass underground). Cardinal Josyf Slipyj, head of the Ukrainian Eastern-Rite Church, was arrested on April 11, 1945, along with all his bishops—eleven of whom died in prison. By 1946, 800 Ukrainian priests had been imprisoned. By 1950, 4,119 Ukrainian Catholic churches had been destroyed or confiscated and given over to the Russian Orthodox.[63]

Freedom fighters in Catholic Lithuania, some 100,000 strong, were organized in 1946 as the United Movement for Democratic Resistance. With the support of the Lithuanian Catholic Church, they put up fierce resistance against the Soviets for several years before finally being crushed. Moscow responded by removing every Lithuanian bishop from his diocese. Bishop Borisevicus of Telsiai was shot in prison in 1947. Archbishop Teofilis Matulionis of Kaisiadorys, formerly a Russian priest who already spent thirteen years in Stalin's jails, was arrested on December 18, 1946, and sentenced to seven years in Siberia, where he joined Archbishop Reinys of Vilnius, who later died in Russia's Vladimir prison in 1953. From 1946 to 1948, 357 Lithuanian priests were exiled to slave labor camps in Russia and Siberia—one third of all Lithuanian priests.[64]

In Hungary, a law passed in June of 1949 by the Hungarian communists closed 3,148 Catholic schools and 1,500 Protestant. Cardinal Mindszenty was arrested on the day after Christmas for denouncing the Hungarian law and promptly taken to the headquarters of the secret police where he was drugged, stripped naked, and whipped with a rubber truncheon until he finally broke; whereby, he signed a false confession and was tried and found guilty in a show trial.[65] He died in exile in Austria, after sixteen years. The primate of Czechoslovakia, Archbishop Beran, had likewise been imprisoned in 1949 for voicing his opposition to his country's ecclesiastical restrictions.[66]

Between 1948 and 1953, 700 Polish Catholic priests along with Polish cardinal Stefan Wyszynski had been deposed and imprisoned by the communists.[67] Polish bishop Czeslaw Kaczmarek was arrested in 1953, and like Cardinal Mindszenty, broke under two and a half years of imprisonment and torture.[68]

By 1952, the Hungarian Communist Party had closed all Hungary's junior seminaries and half of the senior seminaries. All Catholic schools and hospitals were taken over by the government, all religious orders banned, all Catholic associations dissolved, and all Catholic publishing houses and newspapers and periodicals severely curtailed. Over 400 Hungarian priests and 3,000 religious were imprisoned. Two archbishops were jailed, four more were under house arrest, and two more, as well as five auxiliary bishops and the Abbot General of the Benedictine Monastery in Pannonhalma, were not recognized by the communist government. In Poland the very same year, four bishops were imprisoned awaiting trial, ten percent of Polish priests were in jail, and numerous others exiled. Poland's Catholic press was entirely shut down in 1953. In Czechoslovakia, by 1951, 3,000 priests were imprisoned, seven Czech and three Slovak bishops were sentenced to die, and the rest got imprisonment. By 1955, 13 Czechoslovakian bishops were removed from office with eight other bishops missing.[69] In Yugoslavia, bishops and priests were physically beaten, and by 1953, two bishops had died in prison with a third missing.[70]

The Khrushchev Era

In the power vacuum left by the death of Stalin in 1953, Nikita Khrushchev became the *de facto* third head of the Soviet Union as First Secretary of the Communist Party's Central Committee when Soviet Premier Malenkov was forced out of office by Khrushchev on February 8, 1955 and replaced with Nikolai Bulganin. Malenkov, a hard-line Stalinist who unsuccessfully tried to overthrow Khrushchev in a coup on July 3, 1957, was later exiled to Siberia in November of 1961.

Once Khrushchev established his full authority, the revisionist head of the Soviet Union immediately began plans for de-Stalinization by denouncing in a 50-page speech to the Twentieth Congress of the Communist Party on June 5, 1956, Stalin's "cult of personality" as a brutal, psychologically deranged torturer and mass murderer. But when it came to cracking down on anti-Russian dissidents in European satellite states, Khrushchev could be just as ruthless as Stalin. Khrushchev's tanks crushed an anti-communist uprising in East Berlin on June 21, 1953, resulting in the construction of the Berlin Wall on August 31, 1961 to circumvent the mass exodus of East Berliners to free West Berlin. Berlin had previously been the site of the first Cold War confrontation between East and West when Stalin closed all access to the city on June 24, 1948, trying to starve the German people into submission. (In "Operation Vittles," the U.S. and Britain responded with an unprecedented airlift that saved the lives of literally hundreds of thousands of East Berliners.)

On October 30, 1956, an anti-Soviet uprising by Hungarians in Budapest was answered by Khrushchev with the might of four Soviet armored divisions, turning into a full-scale war with 25,000 Hungarians killed. The communist crackdown started when a large crowd poured down Stalin Boulevard and toppled the 25-foot bronze statue of Stalin that had been erected on the site of the razed Regnum Marianum church.

Between 1958-1964, Khrushchev stepped up persecutions against the church in the Soviet Union and Eastern Europe, which had been eased some-what during WWII to boost morale (for propaganda purposes, Stalin had allowed the Russian Orthodox Church to stay alive during WWII as long as it was subservient to him). In the late fifties and early sixties, Khrushchev actively began closing more Russian Orthodox churches and seminaries. Between 1955 and 1962, the number of active Russian Orthodox priests was reduced from 35,000 to 14,500. Half of the churches were closed or used for something other than worship. Of the 48,000 Orthodox churches, all but 6,800 had been demolished or put to secular use. All religious instructions by priests were outlawed by Khrushchev and religious instruction in the home severely curtailed.[71]

The Ukrainian Eastern-rite Catholic Church was banned under Stalin in 1946, and remained that way under Khrushchev. In Lithuania, Catholic Bishop Matulionis, having returned to his country after exile in a Soviet concentration camp, was exiled again after consecrating his successor without the permission of the Kremlin. In 1958, Bishop Julijonas Steponavicius of Vilna was likewise exiled for refusing to order his diocesan priests to stop teaching children the Catholic faith. Although Khrushchev allowed a remnant of the Lithuanian Catholic Church to exist, he exerted strict control over it. The number of men allowed in the Lithuanian seminaries by Khrushchev was cut by fifty per cent. Khrushchev also banned Lithuanian priests from visiting parishioners during holy days and from conducting retreats for laymen.[72]

The Brezhnev Doctrine

For being too reform-minded, Khrushchev was ousted from power in October of 1964 and replaced with hardliner Leonid Brezhnev, a cunning survivor of Stalin's purges who abolished most of the administrative reforms made under Khrushchev. Like Khrushchev, Brezhnev wasn't afraid to use force on any Warsaw Pact government who strayed too far from Soviet ideology. In what has come to be known as the "Prague Spring," Brezhnev ordered 200,000 Soviet soldiers with tanks into Prague, Czechoslovakia in August of 1968 to force the liberal government leader Alexander Dubcek to abandon his experiments in free speech and free assembly. The Soviet invasion of Prague gave rise to the "Brezhnev Doctrine," which claimed that the Soviet Union had the right to intervene militarily in any communist state threatened by "counterrevolution."

Under the protective mantle of the "Brezhnev Doctrine" and the cowardly capitulation of the United Nations, the diabolic forces of communism advanced into Southeast Asia. Ho Chi Minh's Soviet-supplied Viet Cong and North Vietnamese Army forces invaded South Vietnam, a stronghold of Catholicism, defeating the hapless South Vietnamese and United States military forces in 1975.

For Southeast Asia in 1975, things were looking pretty grim. Pathet Lao communist forces had overtaken Laos in 1975, and the Khmer Rouge communists under Pol Pot captured the Cambodian capital of Phnom Penh on April 17, 1975, evacuating three million inhabitants to countryside villages and forced labor camps in a single day. Tens of thousands of Cambodians died from exhaustion and executions along the way in Pol Pot's "purification campaign" of Cambodia. It was one of the most tragic events in human history. By the time the invading Vietnamese Army finally overtook the genocidal Khmer Rouge regime of Pol Pot in 1979 and installed a puppet government of their own, disease, torture, executions, starvation, and war had killed an estimated two million Cambodians—half of Cambodia's (Kampuchea's) population.

Everywhere you looked in the 1970s—Asia, Africa, the Middle East, Latin America, and Western Europe—communism was on the march. Over in Catholic Portugal, the communists were threatening to seize power in the country Mary had promised in Fátima to protect. On March 5, 1974, 200 Portuguese military officers convened in Cascais to discuss Portugal's continued fighting in colonial Angola and Mozambique against African rebels seeking independence from Portugal. The result was the formation of the pro-communist Armed Forces Movement (MFA) and the ouster of Portuguese ruler Marcelo Caetano in a coup on April 25. A provisional coalition government with strong ties to the Soviet Union was setup by the MFA and the Portuguese Communist Party, with exiled Portuguese communist Alvaro Cunhal returning from Prague, Czechoslovakia as a principal minister of the new pro-communist government. Infiltrating the media, Cunhal's Communist Party immediately launched a campaign of sweeping political and social reforms. Seeing the bad direction his country was headed in, conservative General Antonio Spinola, the leader of the junta that expelled Caetano, called for a demonstration rally of "the silent majority of Portuguese" on September 28. But Cunhal's government and the MFA were able to stop the anti-communist rally from taking place.[73] General Spinola then resigned in September of 1975 and was replaced by General Fransico de Costa Gomes.

A bungled attempt at a counter-coup by General Spinola took place on March 11, 1975, resulting in the formation of the Council of the Revolution, which answered only to the MFA. The Council immediately began nationalizing banks and insurance companies, controlled labor unions, closed down private newspapers and formed workers' committees. These events brought the provisional government of Portugal into direct confrontation with the Catholic Church, which, with the exception of Portuguese bishops, had remained silent up until now. Joining with the Portuguese primate, Archbishop Francisco Maria da Silva of Braga, the Vatican vehemently appealed to Portuguese Catholics to halt the advance of communism in their country, reminding them of the Blessed Virgin Mary's warning to three young children in Fátima, Portugal on July 13, 1917:

> *"I will come to ask for the conversion of Russia to My Immaculate Heart and the Communion of Reparations on the First Saturdays. If they comply with my requests,*

Russia will be converted and there will be peace. If not, Russia will spread her errors throughout the world . . . provoking wars and persecutions of the Church; the good will be martyred; the Holy Father will have much to suffer; various nations will be annihilated.

"In the end, My Immaculate Heart will triumph; the Holy Father will consecrate Russia to me and she will be converted, and a certain period of peace will be granted to the world. In Portugal, the dogma of the faith will always be preserved."[74]

The Portuguese Catholics responded to the church's appeal by organizing one of the largest pilgrimages in history to Fátima, over one million people, on May 13, 1975—the fifty-eighth anniversary of Mary's first appearance to the three children. A workers' committee responded to the pilgrimage by seizing the Catholic radio station, Radio Renaissance, on May 27. With the MFA revealing their hidden agenda to turn Portugal into a "revolutionary worker's state," loyal Catholics mobilized for action. On July 13, 1975, the anniversary date of Mary's warning to little Lucia Santos in Fátima, ten thousand Catholics gathered in Aveiro to demonstrate against the radio station seizure, while Catholic farmers gathering in Rio Maior destroyed the headquarters of the local Communist Party. In town after town, with the army too reluctant to interfere, communist buildings were destroyed by angry Catholic demonstrators. Twenty-two communist headquarters were destroyed in the first nine days alone. After a month, virtually every communist headquarter in northern Portugal was demolished and every hammer and sickle flag was torn from its mast and ripped to shreds. By April of 1976 it was all over. Free elections were once again held in Portugal and the anti-Catholic communists were ousted from power. Mario Soares, a moderate Socialist, became Premier and Colonel Eanes became President.[75] Once again, the Catholic faith had been preserved in Portugal—exactly as Mary prophesied would happen.

The Paw of the Bear

In 1977, a Marxist-Leninist revolutionary group in Nicaragua known as the Sandinist National Liberation Front (Sandinistas) began its attacks on Nicaragua's government, demanding the ouster of its leader, President Anastasio Somoza, after he declared martial law in 1974 because the Sandinista guerrillas had kidnapped Nicaraguan officials. After a bitter civil war, the Sandinistas, backed by Fidel Castro and the Soviet Union, overthrew Somoza's regime on July 17, 1979; whereupon, Somoza resigned and went into exile. A five-man communist junta led by Daniel Ortega was installed by the Sandinistas in Somoza's place. What followed was typical of newly installed Marxist governments: mass murder of political prisoners, censorship of the media, persecution of religious groups (especially the Catholic Church), and nationalization of private businesses. President Ronald Reagan lobbied hard for congressional aid to support Nicaragua's freedom fighters (the Contras), but the House voted the aid down in 1985. The "Iran-Contra" scandal (money derived from the illegal sale of weapons to Iran funneled back to the Contras) grew out of Reagan's frustration to halt the spread of communism in Central America. Understandably, Reagan feared that unless the United States, the world's strongest superpower, backed the pro-Western Latin America governments militarily, Nicaragua and the rest of the Western Hemisphere nations would fall like dominoes to the advancing communists. But Reagan was wrong: in a surprising upset, Violeta Barrios de Chamorro defeated Daniel Ortega in national elections on February 25, 1990, effectively ending the Sandinista's hold on power in Nicaragua.

Half a world away in Afghanistan, Islamic President Muhammed Daud was killed in a coup by rebel troops on April 28, 1978 and replaced with pro-communist civilian Nur Muhammed Taraki, who immediately began to turn Afghanistan into a communist satellite of the Soviet Union. Organized resistance by Islamic fundamentalists to Taraki's moves began in less than a year. Taraki's Prime Minister, Hafizalluh Amin, was singled out as the scapegoat and was targeted for elimination by Tariki. The plot failed and Amin got away. Taraki then stepped down from power and was soon eliminated himself. The supposed failure of the communist Afghans to govern themselves was the justification the Soviets used for the invasion of Afghanistan on Christmas Day in 1979.[76] As soon as they invaded Afghanistan the Soviets shot Hafizalluh Amin and replaced him with puppet leader Babruk Karmal. A long and bitter battle ensued between the Soviets and the Afghan freedom fighters that didn't end until the Soviet forces pulled out of Afghanistan on February 15, 1989. When it was all over, the Kremlin reported that more than 15,000 Soviet troops had been killed (probably closer to 40,000-50,000), and the U.S. Army Foreign Military Studies Office reported that over 2 million Afghans were killed and half of the Afghan population made refugees (now over half the world's refugees are Afghan).[77]

John Paul II-The Pope of Fátima

Although the onward march of Russian communism looked unstoppable in the late 1970s, time was running out for the Soviet Union. Just as the early Christians defeated the pagan Roman Empire with nothing but the weapons of love, so God's love was about to halt the worldwide spread of communism. It all began with one man of God, Karol Cardinal Wojtyla, the Archbishop of Cracow—a shrewd survivor of the dual tyrannies of Stalinism and Naziism, and the first non-Italian to be elected pope in 455 years.

Pope John Paul II, the only Slav ever to be elected pope and the first pope to come from a communist country, was born on May 18, 1920, in Wadowice, Poland, a small village of about 15,000 located just 25 miles from the infamous Nazi concentration camps of Auschwitz and Birkenau, where 1.5 million lives were sacrificed—150,000 of them Catholic. On the day of Karol Wojtyla's birth, three years after Fátima, there was a solar eclipse that many historians believe confirmed an ancient Catholic prophecy that said that the 264th pope would be born under the sign of *labor solis*.[78]

As a young man, Karol Wojtyla majored in linguistics at the Jagiellonian University in Cracow until the Nazis came and shut the school down; whereupon, the future pope spent the rest of WW II working in a stone quarry and a chemical factory while secretly studying for the priesthood in an underground seminary. Risking almost certain execution if he was caught, Karol Wojtyla courageously helped save the lives of many of his Jewish friends by providing false identities and hiding places, as well as organizing and acting in underground theaters to help boost the morale of Polish resistance fighters.[79]

Ordained after the war in 1946, Karol Wojtyla spent two years in Rome at the Pontifical Angelicum University working on his doctorate in philosophy. Returning to Poland as a parish priest and student chaplain, Wojtyla spent the next two years studying ethics in Cracow, and was appointed to a chair in moral theology. In 1954, he began teaching at the Catholic University of Lublin and soon became head of the department of ethics. In 1958, Father Karol Wojtyla became a bishop, choosing a golden M on his coat of arms and the Latin motto *Totus Tuus sum Maria* (all yours, Maria) in honor of Mary, the Patroness of Poland. At just 42 years of age, Bishop Wojtyla became Archbishop of Cracow in 1962, and in 1967, he became Karol Cardinal Wojtyla.

As the spiritual leader of a nation of 35 million Poles, ninety-five per cent of whom are Catholic, Karol Cardinal Wojtyla was the perfect candidate for the 263rd successorship of the Chair of St. Peter. He was fluent in seven languages, an expert in philosophy and phenomenology, a prolific reader, writer of four books and more than 500 assays and articles, a poet, playwright, guitar player, lover of music, an athlete, skier, and mountain climber. (It was absolutely necessary for this pope to be an athlete because of the tremendous physical and spiritual suffering he was about to endure.) As a young, strong, charismatic, intellectual cardinal and outspoken critic of communism, Karol Cardinal Wojtyla was just what the Church needed at that time: a strong, stouthearted leader to fight for the rights of those long oppressed by tyranny and injustice.

It was no coincidence that the Holy Spirit selected a Pole to be pope at the close of the second millennium because Catholic Poland had undergone so many persecutions in its 1000 year history, and it was fitting that the spark that ignited the flame against communism would come from Poland. Here is a brief history of that holy land.

Poland became a Catholic nation with the baptism of its fifth Piast sovereign, Mieszko I, in A.D. 966. King Mieszko married a Roman Catholic, Princess Dubrovka, from Catholic Bohemia in 965, and in 990, by the solemn Piast Pact, he gave the entire nation and state of Poland over to the ownership of the Holy See of Peter in Rome, in the person of Pope John XV.[80] In 1025, Boleslav the Brave, having the blessing of Pope John XIX, became the first king of Poland independent from the Holy Roman Empire. Two centuries later, in 1264, the Piast king Boleslav Pobozny granted Jews the General Charter of Jewish Liberties, which guaranteed for them a self-governing Jewish nation within Poland.[81] In the fourteenth century, King Casimir III of Poland encouraged the immigration of Jews to serve as tax-collectors and bankers, and by 1939, forty per cent of the world's Jews lived in Poland.[82] No other nation on earth welcomed the Jews as much as Poland did, which is a great tribute to the true spirit of Catholicism.

As a nation totally devoted to Christ, Catholic Poland was governed first by the Piast Dynasty, then an elected monarchy, then a constitutional monarchy, and finally a republic in 1795. When no legal head of government was seated, such in the case of a sudden death of the Polish leader, the Primate Bishop of Poland, the *Interrex,* would temporarily rule the government. To the Poles, the Western ideal of separation of church and state was unthinkable. The Catholic Church was inseparable from the Polish government and the Polish people.

Up until the middle of the seventeenth century, Poland was a major European power that had successfully withstood attacks from the Swedes, Mongols, Tartars, German Teutonic Knights, Ukrainians, Russians, Cossacks, and Ottoman Turks. But starting in 1648, the Unitary Republic of Poland was suddenly attacked on all sides by Ukrainian Cossacks, Russians, Swedes, Prussians, Hungarians, and Turks, and for the first time in her history was in danger of being completely annihilated. At one point, only the Pauline Monastery on Jasna Gora—the Bright Mountain—overlooking the town of Czestochowa, was all that was left of free Poland. Preserved in that monastery was the famous Black Madonna, a sacred Polish icon said to have been painted by St. Luke himself from a plank of a table belonging to the Holy Family in Nazareth. While under siege from the Swedes, Czestochowa's priests prayed to the icon for divine protection, and the monastery fortress of Jasna Gora held. After forty days the besieging Swedish army retired. In gratitude, Polish King Jan Kazimierz proclaimed the Blessed Virgin Mary, Queen of Poland.

Although saved as a nation at Jasna Gora, the incessant wars, political intrigues within the Polish parliament (*Sejm*) over monetary issues and the constitution,[83] bubonic plagues, slave raids, and mass murders had put an end to Poland's golden era as a major European power. Half of her population and many of her towns were destroyed, and she was a severely weakened nation.

By 1683, Poland was the only major Catholic power preventing a Northern European hegemony of the major Protestant powers of Prussia, Sweden, Saxony, Denmark and Hungary (Transylvania). Hence, a joint Protestant/Russian Orthodox plan for the total dissolution of Catholic Poland was put into effect by Frederick the Great of Prussia and Catherine the Great of Russia. Their two-fold plan was for the subversion of Poland from within by anti-Catholic Freemasons infiltrating into the government, and disruption of foreign commerce and military attacks from without by the Swedes, Germans, Hungarians, and Russians. The joint Prussian/Russian plan for Poland's annihilation succeeded: Poland could no longer defend itself militarily, and was thereafter partitioned three separate times by Prussia, Russia, and Austria; first in 1772, then again in 1793, and finally in 1795. From then on Catholic Poland no longer existed as a free nation, except briefly between 1807-14 when Napoleon Bonaparte neutralized Russia and Prussia, and again when Germany and her defeated allies signed the Armistice agreement in November of 1918, which ended WW I and gave Poland back her independence.

During the tripartite occupation of Poland, a campaign of "Russification" was implemented by Russia to force the Poles into adopting their Russian language and culture. Only the Catholic Church kept Polish language and culture alive, and served as the main bastion of Polish nationalism. Patriotic uprisings against forced Russification broke out in 1794, 1831, 1848, and 1863, but they were of no avail: the Russian forces were just too strong for the Poles.

Polish poet Juliusz Slowacki, the author of *King-Spirit*, a play about the martyrdom of Poland's most venerated saint, Bishop Stanislaw, wrote a poem in 1848 about the trepidation of the Italian pope, Pius IX, after the pope refused to support the Poles in their uprising against Russia occupation. Slowacki's poem, written in the same year that Marx and Engels wrote their *Communist Manifesto,* proved Slowacki an incredible prophet because he predicted the future election of a Polish pope and his subsequent victory over Russian tyranny:

> Amid discord God strikes
> At a bell immense,
> For the Slavic Pope,
> Open is the Throne.
> This one will not flee the sword,
> Like the Italian.
> Like God, He will bravely face the sword,
> For Him, world is dust . . .
> So behold, here comes the Slavic Pope,
> A brother of the people.[84]

In 1919, Lenin's Bolshevik army invaded Poland with 800,000 men, but was repelled on August 15, 1920 by the Polish Army, which had rededicated their nation to Mary.[85] Poland's victory against Lenin's Bolsheviks will always be remembered by faithful Poles as the "Miracle of the Vistula." Peace in Poland lasted only 19 years, however. On September 1, 1939, Hitler, in his hellish pact with Joseph Stalin to annihilate Catholic Poland once and for all, blitzkrieged into western Poland with six armored divisions, eight motorized divisions, and 1.25 million German soldiers, triggering the start of World War II when Britain and France immediately declared war on Germany. While Hitler was attacking from the west, Stalin simultaneously sent his Red Army in to occupy eastern Poland. Poland was annihilated and the Roman Catholic Church was targeted by the Nazis and the communists, along with Jews, politicians, professors, teachers, writers, intellectuals, and military officers.[86] By 1942, over 7,500 Polish priests had been deported to the concentration camps of Sachsenhausen-Oranienburg, Buchenwald, Radogoszcz and Opausa, and by war's end, 4 Polish bishops, 1,932 priests, 850 monks, and 289 nuns had been murdered.[87] As one of the forerunners of the Antichrist to come, Adolph Hitler built 8,500 concentration camps in Poland. Eighteen million Europeans (mostly Jews and Catholics) were imprisoned in these camps, and 11 million died—3.5 million from Poland alone. By the end of the war, 6 million Polish citizens had been killed, including 644,000 in combat and a million in Siberian labor camps.[88] At least 4,000 Polish army officers had also been murdered by Stalin and buried in the Katyn Forest in 1940.[89]

On September 7, 1944—Black Sunday—German squads preparing to evacuate in the face of the advancing Soviet Army rounded up all adults for deportation to Germany, which, more than likely, meant certain death for those chosen. Karol Wojtyla's name was on the Nazi's list but somehow he evaded capture and survived.[90] After the war, Father Karol Wojtyla was sent to Rome for his doctorate. The rest is history: by the power of the Holy Spirit, Karol Cardinal Wojtyla was elected the 264th pope on October 16, 1978.

Dedicating himself to Mary to fight the tyranny and injustice he had miraculously survived during the Second World War, Pope John Paul II must have known that the only way to defeat the enslavement of Soviet communism was to start the destabilization process from within the Eastern bloc nations themselves. Therefore, immediately after he was elected pope he began calling for freedom of speech, freedom of assembly, freedom of worship, democratic representation, self-determination, just wages, adequate housing, and better living and working conditions for all countries, especially those behind the Iron Curtain. Wasting no time in voicing his adamant opposition to heartless capitalism and repressive communism, John Paul II published his first encyclical, *Redemptor Hominis,* in March of 1979, castigating Western materialism and Marxist economic determinism; both of which lauded secular materialism over the spirit and dignity of the human being. In an implicit reference to the repressive communist regime in Poland, John Paul said "It is difficult to accept . . . a position that gives only atheism the right of citizenship in public and social life, while believers are . . . barely tolerated or . . . deprived of the rights of citizenship."

Following the publication of *Redemptor Hominis,* John Paul II embarked on the most ambitious evangelical traveling itinerary since the days of St. Paul the Apostle. By design, the pope's first two stop-offs were Mexico and Poland, counties with populations that were predominantly Roman Catholic that had suffered tremendous persecution under repressive, dictatorial regimes. Landing in a Mexico City airport on the first leg of a February 1979 journey to Latin America (home of 42% of the world's Catholics), the pope was preceded by an ominous 6.3-magnitude earthquake that shook the city's populace just hours before his arrival. The Mexican government, with no formal ties to the Vatican and whose constitution still prohibited the Catholic Church from operating schools and priests from wearing clerical garb in public or saying anything against the Mexican government, was no friend of the Catholic Church. Mexican President Jose Lopez Portillo reluctantly greeted John Paul at the airport with a cordial handshake in front of a cheering crowd estimated to be in the millions, but you could tell on his face that he wasn't pleased about the pope's visit. The pope was there to attend the third Latin American Bishops' Conference dealing with the controversial topic of "liberation theology"—an often violent Marxist movement that cropped up in the late 1960s after the reforms of Vatican II amongst liberal priests and religious in Latin America in response to the oppressive, dictatorial regimes in Central and South American. Liberation theologians tried portraying Christ as an economic reformer and a Socialist champion of the working class, which was tantamount to equating Christianity with Marxism. Liberation theology's outspoken leaders at that time, Peru's Father Gustavo Gutierrez, Ecuador's Bishop Leonidas Proano Villalba, and El Salvador's Archbishop Romero, saw in Christ the *Manifesto Messiah*—a revolutionary socio-political activist fighting for the rights of the downtrodden lower-class against the wealthy and oppressive upper-class and tyrannical dictators. But in a speech to the Bishop's conference at Puebla, Pope John Paul II emphatically rejected the fallacy of Christian-Marxism: "This idea of Christ as a political figure, a revolutionary, as the subversive man from Nazareth, does not tally with the church's catechesis." While definitely in favor of a "more just and equitable distribution of goods," the pope urged bishops to first of all, "be priests, not social workers or political leaders or functionaries of a temporal power." Being from a communist country, Pope John Paul II knew all too well what Marxism truly believed in, and it wasn't Christianity.

Following his controversial trip to Mexico, Pope John Paul II triumphantly returned to his homeland of Poland in June of 1979. A worried Leonid

Brezhnev tried to keep the Polish Secretary, Edward Gierek, from hosting the papal trip but failed. In his gleaming white cassock, native son Karol Cardinal Wojtyla triumphantly returned to his communist homeland as Pope John Paul II, kneeling and kissing the ground of Warsaw as he stepped from the plane. "Poland," the pope said to an exuberant crowd of millions, "through the course of history has been linked with the Church of Christ and the See of Rome by a special bond of spiritual unity."

At the close of the ecstatic first day of the papal trip to Poland, an outdoor papal mass for 500,000 people was held at downtown Victory Square. The huge throng of humanity, singing the Polish hymn *Christ Conquers,* burst into a ten-minute ovation when John Paul declared, "Without Christ it is impossible to understand the history of Poland."

John Paul II made three dozen public appearances on his first trip to Poland. At the Jasna Gora Monastery in Czestochowa, where the Black Madonna is enshrined, the pope led half a million pilgrims in an elaborate consecration of Poland and the church to Mary, the *"Krolowa Polski"* (the Queen of Poland). The pope also visited his hometown of Wadowice, his former see of Cracow, the former Nazi concentration camps of Auschwitz and Birkenau, the cell of a beatified Franciscan priest (Maximilian Kolbe) and the town of Gniezno where Polish Christendom's first See was established in the year 1000. On the last day of his visit, an exhausted Pope John Paul celebrated a highly symbolic mass in honor of the 900th anniversary of the slaying of Poland's most venerated martyr, St. Stanislaw, defender of human rights against tyrannical rulers.

It's impossible to deny the tremendous psychological effect that Pope John Paul II's papal visit had on the Polish people, and the worry he caused the communist leadership in Moscow. Following the pope's trip to Poland, the Kremlin ordered a top secret, worldwide campaign against the new pope and his evangelical activities, which Leonid Brezhnev called "dangerous" and "aggressive." On November 13, 1979, the Secretariat of the Communist Party's Central Committee in Moscow approved a six-point "Decision to Work Against the Policies of the Vatican in Relations with the Socialist States." The Kremlin's "Decision" called for the "mobilization" of Lithuanian, Latvian, Ukrainian, and Byelorussian Communist Parties, and of Tass, Soviet television, the Academy of Sciences, "and other organizations . . . of the Soviet State" to commence "propaganda against the policies of the Vatican." The Kremlin instructed the KGB to "publicize in the Western countries that Vatican policies are harmful . . . and above all, to show that the leadership of the new pope . . . is dangerous to the Catholic Church."[91] The Politburo, in fact, was convinced that Polish-born Cardinal Krol of Philadelphia and Zbigniew Brzezinski, President Jimmy Carter's National Security Advisor, had masterminded Wojtyla's election to the papacy in order to undermine communism.

As the Kremlin feared would happen, in August of 1980, just 33 years after the beginning of communist rule in Poland, 16,000 angry Polish workers at the Lenin Shipyard in Gdansk, praying before the portraits of Pope John Paul II and the Blessed Virgin Mary and singing the hymn *Oh God, Who Has Defended Poland,* joined striking workers from 200 other factories and enterprises already on strike for seven weeks in protest of sharp rises in meat prices and shortages of consumer goods after the government lifted artificial price control subsidies to help defray the 19 billion dollars in loans owed to Western banks. Polish strikers in Gdansk threatened to sweep the country and install a non-communist government if their demands for increased wages, lower prices, shorter workweeks, more consumer goods, freer trade unions, the legal right to strike, freedom for all political prisoners, and the abolition of censorship were not met.

The Vatican unequivocally sided with the striking Gdansk workers, as John Paul II, in front of 900 Polish visitors to Rome, recited two traditional prayers for his motherland, assuring them that "We in Rome are united with our fellow countrymen in Poland."

The alliance of the pope with Solidarity was extremely uplifting for the Poles. Just ten years earlier, in December of 1970, violent price riots had left dozens of Polish workers dead after Communist Party leader Wladyslaw Gomulka responded to their price riots with the use of force. But that proved to be a costly political mistake, as shortly afterwards, on December 20, Gomulka was forced to resign. In August of 1980, Edward Gierek, the new Polish Communist Party leader, wanted nothing more than to avoid a repetition of the past labor upheavals of 1956, 1970, and 1976, but within a few weeks half a million workers in 500 factories and enterprises in the northern seacoast area and key industrial centers in the south were on strike, threatening Warsaw with economic paralysis. Seeking to defuse the crisis before the Soviets became involved, Gierek offered strike leader Lech Walesa a pay raise for the Gdansk shipyard workers, but Walesa, a devout Roman Catholic not wanting to betray the other striking workers, refused Gierek's offer. Walesa's defiant attitude spread quickly. New strikes erupted in the neighboring ports of Gydynia and Sopot, then the major shipbuilding center of Szczecin near East Germany, and the industrial city of Elblag only 30 miles from the Soviet Union. Not long after the strikes spread, Party Boss Edward Gierek was replaced for "health reasons" by Stanislaw Kania. When Kania promised to comply with most of the strikers' demands, including their right to form independent labor unions, a relaxation of censorship, the right to strike, and the public broadcasting of Sunday mass (not available since 1947), striking workers at Gdansk agreed to return to work.

At the end of summer in 1980, Gdansk workers and their labor leader Lech Walesa organized the now famous "Solidarity" labor movement—a federation of 50 independent labor unions supported by three quarters of a million Polish communists, claiming representation of 10 million workers throughout

Poland. The moderate leadership in Solidarity, however, which Lech Walesa represented, couldn't put an end to Poland's growing labor unrest and anti-Russian sentiment, and strikes continued to break out during the fall and winter of 1980 after Party Boss Kania failed to keep the promises of reform he made in August. Pope John Paul II met with Lech Walesa and a 13-member delegation from Solidarity in January of 1981 to try to defuse the crisis situation in Poland. Irritating some of Solidarity's more militant members, the Catholic Church was being more conciliatory to the Polish government, siding with Lech Walesa and Solidarity's more moderate factions in negotiations with Polish Party Boss Stanislaw Kania. But John Paul II left no doubt who he backed: "I wish to assure you," he told Walesa, "that during your difficulties I have been with you in a special way, above all through prayer, but also in every way discreetly possible." John Paul reiterated to Walesa that the right to form free unions is "one of the fundamental human rights," and that the formation of Solidarity is "an event of great importance."

The pope's meeting with Lech Walesa and the Solidarity members in the Vatican no doubt fueled the Soviet's suspicion that the pope was the real impetus behind Poland's newfound courage and boisterous demands for more political and economic reforms, and from there on out things got worse.

The impasse between Solidarity and the Polish government in 1980 took a turn for the worse when 3.2 million Polish farmers demanded the right to form "Rural Solidarity," to which Moscow immediately responded with a resounding "Nyet."You see, in the Kremlin's mind, left unchecked the reform-minded Solidarity movement threatened to spill over to other Warsaw Pact nations, which, in turn, might lead to the eventual downfall of the Soviet Union itself. Fearing this, Soviet leader Leonid Brezhnev was in a quandary over what to do about Solidarity and the pope. He was 74 and in poor health, the Soviet military was becoming stuck in a Vietnam-like quagmire in Afghanistan, and John Paul II had threatened to go to Poland if the Soviets invaded his mother country, which would force a potentially embarrassing situation for the Soviets of having to arrest the pope (John Paul II admits that he even considered quitting if the Soviets invaded Poland). Furthermore, Poland was more than 25 billion dollars in debt and desperately in need of additional foreign assistance, which the ailing Soviet economy would have to come up with if they controlled Poland. The AFL-CIO was also threatening to boycott Polish goods if the Soviet's intervened, and President Ronald Reagan warned of the "grave consequences" of Soviet intervention, threatening the "Evil Empire" with economic sanctions and another arms race.

In the fall of 1980, with 55 Soviet divisions poised on the Polish border and ready to strike at a moment's notice, as they did in Hungary in 1956 and Czechoslovakia in 1968, Lech Walesa and Solidarity's moderates reached an agreement with Poland's new prime minister General Wojciech Jaruzelski, avoiding the possibility of a general strike. Moscow had been urging Jaruzelski to declare martial law, but, being the patriot that he was, Jaruzelski adamantly refused; knowing full well that martial law would provoke a nationwide general strike and a retaliatory Soviet invasion. Unable to coax Jaruzelski into declaring martial law, which the Soviets, of course, were hoping to use as a pretext for invasion, Brezhnev convinced hard-line Party members in the Politburo to grant Solidarity a temporary reprieve because he and KGB Chief Yuri Andropov had a secret, diabolic scheme to halt the momentum of Solidarity—hire an assassin to kill John Paul II.

The Soviet Assassination Attempt on the Pope

On May 13, 1981, the 64th anniversary of the Blessed Mother's first appearance in Fátima, Pope John Paul II was shot several times by the Turkish assassin Mehmet Ali Agca, as he was riding around St. Peter's Square in his open-air "popemobile." In the ambulance on the way to Agostino Gemelli Polyclinic, John Paul faintly called out "Madonna, Madonna" to save his life; and she did, as it was later reported that the pope had an apparition of Mary while in the hospital in which she explained to him that she had prepared his life from birth for a "special mission."[92] He was to be the suffering pope of Fátima and La Salette!

By all the doctors' accounts, Pope John Paul II should have died after he was shot: the wound to his abdomen was extremely serious, requiring partial resection of both intestines and a temporary colostomy. But the Virgin Mary herself was watching over her pope. She would save his life:

"The Holy Father will suffer greatly. I will be by His side to the end in order to receive his sacrifice. The wicked will make several attempts on his life, but they cannot harm Him."

". . the Holy Father will have much to suffer . . . "

These prophecies of Mary in La Salette and Fátima regarding a "suffering pope" pertain to John Paul II, who, since becoming pope in 1978, has suffered from bullet wounds, colon cancer, a colostomy, gallstones, gall bladder removal, a dislocated shoulder, a fractured femur, hip replacement, an appendectomy, and Parkinson's disease. Now aware of his destiny as the suffering pope, John Paul II explained to the International Eucharistic Conference in Lourdes in July of 1981after a long and painful convalescence from his shooting that "God has permitted that I myself, in my own body, experience suffering and weakness."

Returning to the Vatican after his convalescence from the gunshot wounds,

Pope John Paul prayed at the tombs of the previous popes and confessed "There could have been another tomb, but the Blessed Virgin . . . has willed otherwise."[93] Gratefully, John Paul acknowledged that "For everything that happened to me on that day, I felt the extraordinary Motherly protection and care, which turned out to be stronger than the bullets."[94] (The bullet that should have killed the pope was placed in the gold crown of Our Lady of Fátima and the pope's sash with a bullet hole was placed in Jasna Gora.)

Pope John Paul's assassin, 23-year-old Mehmet Ali Agca, had been imprisoned in 1979 for the murder of Turkish newspaper editor Abdi Ipekci, but escaped in November of that same year with the aid of a group of neo-fascist Turks from the National Action Party posing as prison guards. Sentenced to death, Agca left behind a note at the maximum-security prison threatening to kill Pope John Paul II, whom he called the "Commander of the Crusades." Three days after his escape, a Turkish newspaper received another letter from Agca demanding the cancellation of the pope's trip to Turkey. "The Russian imperialists fear that Turkey will organize a new power in the Middle East along with brotherly Islamic countries," the letter read. Russia, Agca claimed, was sending "a spiritual leader and commander of crusades, John Paul II." Agca then warned, "I will shoot the Pope if this untimely visit is not canceled." Killing the pope would supposedly be Agca's retribution for the 1979 attack by Islamic radicals on Mecca's Grand Mosque, which he maintained was carried out by the United States and Israel.[95]

Pope John Paul II was to meet with Patriarch Dimitros I, head of the Eastern Orthodox Church, on the feast of St. Andrew in Istanbul Turkey (in the same month that Agca escaped) with the goal of establishing talks on the future reunification of the Roman Catholic and the Eastern Orthodox Church, and it was there that Agca planned to assassinate the pope. The historic meeting took place without incident, however, but it had to have worried Soviet officials who saw spiritual reunification of East and West as a serious threat to their hold over the Russian Orthodox Church, the Ukrainian Eastern-rite Catholics, and Roman Catholics in Latvia, Lithuania, and Byelorussia. The Soviets could ill afford to let Catholics in the Ukraine, Latvia, Lithuania, and Byelorussia do what Catholic workers did in Poland. So, turning up their anti-Catholic propaganda, Pope John Paul II was viciously attacked in the Soviet press for calling the first synod of Ukrainian Uniate Catholic bishops since the Ukrainian Church had been banned by Stalin in 1946. In the Byelorussian journal *Polyma*, communist officials demonized the pope, calling him a "cunning and dangerous ideological enemy . . . a malicious, lowly, perfidious and backward toady of the American militarists."[96] This vitriolic, anti-papal diatribe coming from *Polyma* set the stage for the KGB's planned assassination of the pope, using the Islamic terrorist Mehmet Ali Agca as their cover. (The name Mehmet, by the way, is an Islamic variant of the name "Muhammed"). Here is how "Muhammad" tried to kill "Christ's Vicar."

Mehmet Ali Agca, known by the KGB to have already threatened to kill the pope during his visit to Istanbul, left Turkey for an odyssey that would take him through Iran, Bulgaria, Western Europe, North Africa, possibly the Soviet Union, and finally, Rome. In January of 1981, Agca arrived in Rome and met with right-wing Turks and Bulgarian agents, who had a notorious reputation as hired thugs for the KGB, to discuss plans to assassinate the pope and Lech Walesa, who, as you remember, was in Rome at that time visiting the pope.[97] The KGB plot to kill Walesa and the pope, however, had to be abandoned because of tight security. The assassination of the pope was then hurriedly rescheduled for May because French and Romanian secret services had supposedly uncovered their conspiracy.

The deputy commercial attaché at the Bulgarian embassy in Paris, Iordan Mantarov, second in command of the Bulgarian secret service in Paris before his defection, told *New York Times* reporter Nicholas Gage that he knew that the Soviet KGB had plotted with Bulgarian agents to assassinate the pope because of the threat he posed to communist control.[98] But for obvious political reasons, the pope's killer(s) could not be linked to Bulgarian communists or the Kremlin, so that made well-known Islamic terrorist Ali Agca the perfect candidate for the job because he had already threatened to kill the pontiff once before. Lending credibility to Gage's charge that the KGB was behind the attempted assassination of the pope, German authorities in April of 1981 taped a conversation between Ali Agca in Majorca, Spain and a German-Turkish terrorist, Musar Serder Celebi, with known ties to Bulgaria communist agents. In that conversation, Agca is reported to have said "I have received the money . . . I will go to Rome to finish the job."[99] In case he was captured or killed, Agca intentionally left behind phony notes in his pocket and his rented room that his co-conspirators hoped would convince investigators that Agca was a right-wing political ideologue acting alone. Despite Agca's feeble attempt to protect his communist co-conspirators from discovery, a large amount of circumstantial evidence was gathered by Italian investigators that definitely pointed to a KGB-Bulgarian-Turkish connection, with possibly two Turkish assassins instead of one.

During Ali Agca's trial, prosecutors released evidence of Agca's positive identification of Bulgarian agents from unnamed police photographs and his knowledge of telephone numbers that matched the Bulgarian embassy and a Bulgarian agent's apartment.[100] With Agca's admission that he had been trained as a terrorist by Bulgarian and Czech experts in a camp in Latakia, Syria,[101] and that the KBG had orchestrated the whole plot, Italian investigating magistrate Ilario Martella charged three Bulgarians and five Turks with conspiring to kill the pope, but charges were later dropped for lack of sufficient evidence to convict. The KGB was careful not to leave a paper trail that would indicate their involvement, and the Italian government couldn't get a conviction on the co-conspirators based on Agca's testimony alone because his testimony was often contradictory and he purposely acted up in court like he was a lunatic, yelling and screaming that he was "Jesus Christ."[102]

During what was touted by the Italian press as "the trial of the century," accused assassin Mehmet Ali Agca yelled out several times in the courtroom, "The assault on the Pope is connected to the Third Secret of Fátima." (By the way, Ali Agca's sister is named Fatma or Fátima.[103]) The Third Secret of Fátima was written down by Lucia Santos, and sealed in an envelope before being opened by Pope John XXIII in 1959, who read it but opted not to reveal its contents because, he said, "It did not concern his pontificate." According to Cardinal Joseph Ratzinger, head of the Vatican's doctrinal office, Pope John Paul II read the Third Secret of Fátima while recovering in the hostpital from his shooting, and it was then that he realized he was the suffering pope of Fátima. After his recovery, John Paul II then related its contents to Ali Agca when he visited him in his jail cell, thus explaining Agca's outbursts later on during his trial about the Third Secret of Fátima being connected to his shooting of the pope.

After years of speculation about the Third Secret foretelling everything from a nuclear holocaust to the end of the Roman papacy, its contents, in part, was revealed to the public on May 13, 2000 during the pope's celebration of the beatification of Jacinta and Francisco. This day also marked the eighty-third anniversary of Our Lady's appearance in Fátima and the nineteenth anniversary of the pope's assassination attempt in Rome. While the ceremonies in Fátima were in progress, Vatican Secretary of State Cardinal Angelo Sodano told the world press that part of the Third Secret of Fátima speaks of a "bishop clothed in white" who "falls to the ground, apparently dead under a burst of gunfire," an obvious reference to Pope John Paul II. (The first two secrets of Fátima were already public knowledge and have to do with the revelation of hell to the visionaries and the consecration of Russia to the Immaculate Heart of Mary and the Communion of Reparation on First Saturdays.)

The Third Secret of Fátima Finally Revealed

Pope John XXIII read the Third Secret of Fátima for the first time in August of 1959 in accordance with God's directive that it be read to the public by 1960, when the message would appear "more clear," but decided not to reveal its contents. His only remark was "This does not concern the years of my pontificate."[104] Pope John XXIII's successor, Paul VI, likewise read the Third Secret in 1963 and he, too, decided to keep it unrevealed. Pope Paul's successor, Pope John Paul I, is presumed to have read the Third Secret, but he died only a month after he was elected pontiff in August of 1978, so there is no way to be sure that he read it. Pope John Paul II read the secret while recuperating from his shooting, but he, too, decided not to reveal its contents.

On a solemn pilgrimage to Fátima in May of 1982, commemorating the first anniversary of his surviving an assassination attempt, John Paul II told Sister Lucy that it was "neither necessary nor prudent to reveal the contents of that Secret, seeing that the world would not undestand it."[105] He would only say that "The message of Fátima is, in its fundamental nucleus, the appeal to conversion and penance as in the Gospel . . . "[106] But for reasons known only to him, on June 26, 2000, Pope John Paul II finally released the entire contents of the Third Secret of Fátima as written down by Sister Lucy in 1944, ending years of speculation about its contents. Here is the Third Secret in its entirety as punctuated by Sister Lucy.

> *"The Third part of the secret revealed at the Cova da Iria-Fatima, on 13 July 1917.*
>
> *"I [Sister Lucy] write in obedience to you, my God, who command me to do so through his Excellency the Bishop of Leiria and through your most Holy Mother and mine.*
>
> *"After the two parts which I have already explained, at the left of Our Lady and a little above, we saw an Angel with a flaming sword in his left hand; flashing, it gave out flames that looked as though they would set the world on fire; but they died out in contact with the splendor that Our Lady radiated towards him from her right hand. Pointing to the earth with his right hand, the Angel cried out in a loud voice: 'Penance, Penance, Penance!' And we saw in an immense light that is God: 'something similar to how people appear in a mirror when they pass in front of it' a Bishop dressed in white 'we had the impression that it was the Holy Father'. Other bishops, priests, religious men and women going up a steep mountain, at the top of which there was a big cross of rough-hewn trunks as of a cork-tree with the bark; before reaching there the Holy Father passed through a big city half in ruins and half trembling with halting step, afflicted with pain and sorrow, he prayed for the souls of the corpses he met on his way; having reached the top of the mountain, on his knees at the foot of the big cross he was killed by a group of soldiers who fired bullets and arrows at him, and in the same way there dies one after another the bishops, priests, religious men and women and various lay people of different ranks and positions. Beneath the two arms of the cross there were two angels each with a crystal in his hand, in which they gathered up the blood of the martyrs and which they sprinkled the souls that were making their way to God."*

In reading the contents of the Third Secret, one can clearly see the symbolism of Our Lady of Fátima preventing God's wrath from starting a global thermonuclear war. Aware of Sister Lucy's warnings that God was threatening to use Russia as his instrument of chastisement upon the world unless it was consecrated to the Immaculate Heart of Mary, Pope John Paul II properly consecrated Russia to Mary several times in the early 1980s, the last being in 1985, thereby preventing a nuclear holocaust. Satan tried his hardest to stop the pope from consecrating Russia to Mary's Immaculate Heart by having him shot on May 13, 1981, the sixty-fourth anniversary of Fátima (symbolized in the last half of the Third Secret by the soldiers' shooting the "suffering bishop dressed in white," an obvious reference to the assassination attempt on Pope

John Paul II by Bulgarian agents working for the KGB). Similarly, the symbolism behind the suffering and martyrdom of God's holy people on the mountain leading to the cross in the Third Secret refers, of course, to the tens of thousands of religious martyrs who have died at the hands of communists during their demonic, seventy-year reign in the Soviet Union and its satellites.

The Holy Alliance

With the embarrassment of being implicated by the Italian government in a plot to kill the pope, a charge the Soviet Union vehemently denied and then blamed on the CIA, the Kremlin now felt that a direct Soviet military invasion of Poland would have too many negative political and economic ramifications, such as risking an armed resistance by the Polish army, undermining relations with the West, alarming Third World countries, and draining the already beleaguered Soviet economy. The Soviet Union decided that a military crackdown on Solidarity had to come from within Poland itself, using Polish troops and security forces. Polish General Wojciech Jaruzelski was ordered by the Soviets to act as their proxy.

General Jaruzelski replaced Kania as Communist Party Boss and sole head of the Polish government, and on December 13, 1981, declared martial law and arrested key members of Solidarity. All Solidarity union activities were suspended, public meetings were banned, communication to the outside world was cut off, travel restricted, airports closed, and a strict curfew imposed on the Polish people. Dozens of people were killed in Jaruzelski's crackdown and at least 5,000 arrested, including Solidarity leader Lech Walesa who was taken under house arrest to Warsaw and confined in a remote hunting lodge.[107] In October of 1982, the Polish parliament outlawed Solidarity and the formation of any union not directly supervised by the Polish communist government. Polish workers took to the streets in protest, but with martial law in effect protestors were quickly dispersed by Polish riot police and security units.

Worried about the hard-line crackdown in Poland, President Ronald Reagan, the son of a working-class Irish-Catholic father, and Pope John Paul II met for the first time in the Vatican on June 7, 1982, to discuss ways of keeping the Solidarity labor movement alive while continuing their covert operations within Poland and the Eastern bloc countries. Out of these meetings at the Vatican came what the Western press has called, in annoyance to the pope, the "Holly Alliance." An alliance between the president and the pope was only natural because both were ardent enemies of communism and both had recently been shot by would-be assassins. President Reagan was shot in Washington, D.C., by John W. Hinckley, Jr. on March 30, 1981, just six weeks prior to the assassination attempt of the pope. Satan obviously wanted both of them dead because of the powerful threat they posed to his world-wide communism.

Following their survival of assassins' bullets, Reagan and the pope were in total agreement that the forces of evil that tried to kill them were providentially thwarted because of God's will that they live. (The pope, however, would never publicly agree with the press about the circumstantial evidence showing a Soviet-Bulgarian-Turkish involvement in his assassination attempt, diplomatically preferring to put the blame on the devil only.) According to Pio Cardinal Laghi, the former apostolic delegate to Washington, a close friend of Ronald Reagan's had told him that Reagan once said, "Look how the evil forces were put in our way and how Providence intervened." And according to former National Security Advisor Judge William Clark, both Reagan and John Paul agreed that their not dying was "miraculous."[108]

One factor that probably made the alliance between Reagan and the pope work so well was that most of the key members of the Reagan Administration involved in the covert operations in Poland were Roman Catholics. Among them were CIA chief William Casey, Secretary of State Alexander Haig (whose brother was a priest), National Security Advisers Richard Allen and William Clark, former Deputy Director of the CIA and Ambassador at Large Vernon Walters, and Vatican Ambassador William Wilson. (The pope, in fact, had already been working with President Jimmy Carter through Zbigniew Brzezinski, the Catholic Polish-born National Security Advisor, on matters concerning Poland and the Soviet Union.) In consultation with Pope John Paul II, the decision was made by President Reagan and his staff to funnel food, clothing, money, and communication equipment to underground Solidarity members in hiding through an intricate network of CIA and NSC agents, foreign diplomats, AFL-CIO union members, and Catholic priests, bishops, and cardinals.[109] The smuggled contraband coming through Scandinavia included communications equipment, videocassette recorders, printing presses, photocopiers, and radio transmitters. The radio transmitters were used by Solidarity members to interrupt government broadcasts, such as live coverage of the national soccer championship, with messages of "Solidarity lives!" and "Resist!"

Even before the combined U.S.-Vatican covert operations in Poland, a secret directive was signed by President Ronald Reagan in early 1982, which authorized a wide range of economic, diplomatic, and covert measures to "neutralize efforts of the U.S.S.R." A "five-point strategy" was drawn up by the Reagan administration, which was intended to collapse the Soviet economy by escalating the arms race with Star Wars, encouraging reform movement in Eastern bloc countries, linking foreign aid to the Soviet Union with their human rights record, employing economic sanctions and denying Western technology, increasing psychological pressure through anti-Soviet propaganda on Radio Liberty, Voice of America, and Radio Free Europe.[110]

The economic and political pressures coming from the United States and the Vatican paid off: Lech Walesa was released after eleven months in custody and the pope was allowed to return for his second trip to Poland in July of 1983. As a gesture of goodwill from the Polish government, the enforcement of martial law was relaxed after the pope left and then suspended for good.

Mikhail Gorbachev-The Closet Christian

In an amazing turn of events, one right after the other, three of the top Politburo conspirators who plotted John Paul II's assassination met with their own deaths instead. Hard-line Soviet leader Leonid Brezhnev died on November 10, 1982 and was replaced by KGB Chief Yuri Andropov. Andropov then died on February 9, 1984 and was replaced by Konstantin Chernencko. Chernencko then died on March 10, 1985 and was replaced by the young and healthy Mikhail Sergeyevich Gorbachev.

Mikhail Gorbachev, the seventh and final head of the Soviet Union and presumed by many of his colleagues to be a closet Christian, unknowingly helped the Blessed Virgin Mary bring about the conversion of Russia and the disintegration of the Soviet empire. Here is his story.

Named after St. Michael the Archangel, Mikhail Gorbachev was secretly baptized into the Russian Orthodox Church by his grandparents and mother, Maria Panteleyevna, who remained a faithful churchgoer all of her life. (Each year Gorbachev's mother was said to have baked a birthday cake for her son decorated with the letters "XB!" *Xristos Boskres!* "Christ has Risen!")[111]

Although an avowed Leninist, Gorbachev made frequent references to God and Christ in his public speeches, leading his communist colleagues to suspect that he was a Christian. (At least he didn't try to hide the fact that he'd been baptized or that his grandparents hid icons of Christ and Mary behind portraits of Lenin and Stalin on their walls.)

Gorbachev was born on March 2, 1931, and grew up in Privolnoe, a small village in the steppe lands of southern Russia's Stavropol territory of the North Caucuses and Ukraine: a region where faith in Christ is deeply rooted and communist attempts to destroy belief in God have proven fruitless. Gorbachev became interested in politics in his youth, and like everyone else who planned a political career, joined the Komsomol or Young Communist League. Gorbachev entered law school at Moscow University in 1950, and after successfully obtaining his Juris Doctor, returned to Stavropol in 1955 to obtain a degree in agriculture. As a well-respected member of the Communist Party, Gorbachev quickly worked his way up the higher echelons of political power by implementing pragmatic economic measures and agrarian reforms in the highly inefficient Soviet farm collectives. As a reward for his successes, due in large part to exceptionally good weather, in 1978 he was appointed Secretary of the Central Committee in charge of agriculture.

Publicly critical of the tyrannies of Joseph Stalin, Gorbachev aligned himself during the Brezhnev era with KGB chief Yuri Andropov. The Andropov alliance paid off for Gorbachev in 1980 when he was given full membership to the Communist Party's elite Politburo. With the sudden death of Andropov in 1984, the General Secretary of the Communist Party and Chairman of the Presidium of the Supreme Soviet after the death of Leonid Brezhnev, Gorbachev's power base in the Kremlin congealed. Following the embarrassing death of Andropov's successor, Konstantin Chernencko, just a year later, a youthful, healthy, fifty-four-year-old Mikhail Gorbachev was chosen by the old guard Politburo members to be the next General Secretary of the Communist Party and head of the Soviet Union. That same year, Pope John Paul II, this time with the cooperation of his bishops, officially conse-crated Russia again to the Immaculate Heart of Mary. (The similarities between Gorbachev and Pope John Paul II are striking: both were Slavs, both were baptized Christians, both had charismatic personalities, both were chosen to be leaders after the quick deaths of their predecessors, and both were in their fifties.)

Wanting to improve the faltering and overly-bureaucratic Soviet economy, reverse atheism's moral decay, cut expenditures on armaments, reduce tensions over the crackdown on Solidarity and the Soviet occupation of Afghanistan, Mikhail Gorbachev implemented his new policies of *glasnost* (openness) and *perestroika* (restructuring). Along with glasnost and pere-stroika came Gorbachev's lessening of restrictions against religion, personal property ownership, private enterprise, foreign investment, political dissent, Jewish emigration, and democratic elections.

In the first year of Gorbachev's ascension to power and his implementation of glasnost and perestroika, things seemed to go well for him. The Western world had fallen in love with Gorbachev and opened their arms to embrace his reforms. But early in 1986, the new fruits of glasnost and perestroika began to sour. The spring of 1986 marked the beginning of a catastrophic year for the Soviet Union. On April 26, an accident at the Chernobyl nuclear power plant at Pripyat in the Ukraine released more radiation than all the world's nuclear tests and nuclear bombs combined. And as if Chernobyl wasn't bad enough, in October of that same year a Soviet sub sank in the Atlantic, taking with it two nuclear reactors and 32 nuclear warheads.[112] Three years later, on April 7, 1989, another nuclear-powered Soviet sub sank in the Norwegian sea, killing 42 crew members. Yet a third Soviet sub burst a pipe in its nuclear reactor on June 26, 1989, but made it safely back to port without sinking.

Frustrated with all the negative publicity coming from the West over how bad the Soviets handled the Chernobyl disaster and the slow implementation of his economic reforms within the Soviet Union, Gorbachev lashed out at the Kremlin in 1987 with allegations of stagnation and failure to prevent an economic crisis. In a speech before the Central Committee on January 27, obviously aimed at Kremlin hard-liners trying to thwart his economic and political reforms, Gorbachev denounced his hard-line Stalinist opponents, accusing their hero Stalin of "enormous and unforgivable crimes." Gorbachev praised Khrushchev for his de-Stalinization programs and, as a gesture of his goodwill to the critics of communism, pardoned 140 political prisoners.

In an effort to defuse the Cold War, on December 8, 1987, Reagan and Gorbachev signed their first treaty to reduce the size of their nuclear armaments. Two months later, Gorbachev announced plans to begin pulling Soviet troops out of Afghanistan. But on February 13, 1988, violent strikes and clashes between Muslims Azerbaijans and Christian Armenians broke out in the Nagorno-Karabakh region of Soviet Azerbaijan. Gorbachev unwisely sent Soviet troops to the Armenian capital on March 24 to put down the unrest, triggering renewed criticisms of communist brutality from the West. Compounding the ethnic and religious fighting in Azerbaijan, eight months later, on December 7, an earthquake measuring 6.9 on the Richter scale struck Soviet Armenia, killing 25,000 and leaving half a million Armenians homeless.

As part of his plan to remove restrictions against freedom of worship in the Soviet Union, in 1988 Mikhail Gorbachev allowed the Soviet Union's 50 million Russian Orthodox and 10 million Catholics to begin reopening and refurbishing their churches and monasteries, in commemoration of the 1000th anniversary of the birth of Orthodox Christianity in Russia. Russian church bells were ringing again, Bibles were being allotted, evangelism allowed, worship services televised, religious art openly displayed, religious prisoners released, and arrests of dissidents curtailed. Then, in a move toward a more representative form of government, on July 1, 1988, the Supreme Soviet accepted Gorbachev's proposal to replace the General Secretary of the Communist Party as the Soviet Union's top executive, with the creation of the new post of President. On October 1, 1988, General Secretary Mikhail Gorbachev, after ousting hard-line politburo members Andrei Gromyko and Yegor Ligachev, was elected President of the Soviet Union (while still retaining his position as General Secretary of the Communist Party). On March 26, 1989, the first free elections in the Soviet Union were held. The elections established a new governing body, the Congress of People's Deputies; half of whom were non-communists. Dissident Boris Yeltsin, deposed head of the Communist Party in Moscow, was elected to the Congress and then became Gorbachev's most vocal opponent.

The transfer of the leadership of the Soviet Union away from the

Communist Party and the formation of the Congress of People's Deputies encouraged more ethnic rivalries and nationalistic fervor amongst the 104 nationalities in the Soviet Union's 15 republics. In the spring of 1989, ethnic unrest and rioting broke out in Georgia, Uzbekistan and Kazakhstan, drawing renewed criticisms from the West when Soviet troops were called out once again to restore order in those republics. That spring, the Communist Party carried out a purge of its Central Committee to rid itself of hard-liners resisting Gorbachev's efforts to implement political and economic reforms. In a matter of days, 110 Party officials were removed from office and the Central Committee was reduced from 310 to 251.[113] Speaking before the Council of Europe in Stratsbourg, France in July of 1989, Gorbachev renounced the use of force against Eastern bloc nations and abandoned the infamous "Brezhnev Doctrine," which was used to justify force against any Warsaw Pact nation seeking autonomy from the Soviet Union. Encouraged by Gorbachev's disavowal of the hard-line Brezhnev Doctrine, six Eastern European nations overthrew their own communist governments in 1989: they were Poland, East Germany, Hungary, Czechoslovakia, Bulgaria and Romania.

The Iron Curtain Comes Down

In Poland's first free governmental elections in 44 years, voters sent a wake-up call to communist incumbents by electing predominantly Solidarity-backed, non-communist candidates (Solidarity had been legalized again in 1989). Tadeusz Mazowiecki, a senior Solidarity member, became Poland's first non-communist Christian prime minister since before WWII.

On September 10, 1989, Hungary opened its borders to East Germany and announced it would allow East Germans to emigrate to West Germany via Austria, despite vehement protests from East Germany's hard-line communist leader Erich Honecker. A mass exodus from Hungary ensued. By November 1, 50,000 East Germans—mostly young adults, taking with them highly needed job skills—had entered into West Germany. Honecker was forced to resign and was placed under house arrest. On October 18, the reconstituted government of East Germany allowed its citizens to cross at will into the West through the Berlin Wall. After two days, one million persons a day were crossing over to West Berlin. The Brandenburg Gate, closed since 1961, was ceremonially opened and the Berlin Wall was partially torn down. By the end of December, 340,000 East Germans had permanently relocated to West Germany.

On October 19, 1989, Hungary ended more than 40 years of one-party communist rule when the Hungarian parliament voted to legalize opposition political parties. Over in Czechoslovakia, massive protests forced the resignation of Czechoslovakian Communist Party leaders. Vaclav Havel, the leading

Czech dissident, was elected president on December 29. In a move to reassure Havel's new government, "Prague Spring," the Soviet-led invasion of Czechoslovakia in 1968, was condemned by Gorbachev and the four leaders of the satellites (Bulgaria, East Germany, Hungary and Poland) who had participated.

On November 10, 1989, Bulgarian president and Communist Party Boss, Todur Zhivkov, resigned. Calling for democratic reforms and free elections, Foreign Minister Peter Mladenov, Zhivkov's replacement, proceeded to purge the Bulgarian politburo of hardline communists.

Over in communist Romania, the bloodthirsty tyrants Nicolae Ceausescu and his wife Ilena—hated for their extreme vanity and self-aggrandizement; frequent use of torture and retaliations against political dissidents; zealous persecutions of Eastern-rite Catholics and Transylvanian Lutherans; destruction of Romanian peasant villages and churches; creation of Romania's filthy and inhumane orphanages that warehoused hundreds of malnourished and diseased babies; and for living a lavish, opulent lifestyle while the rest of Romania starved[114]—were overthrown on December 25, 1989. This event followed massive demonstrations in Bucharest, which had spontaneously formed to protest the ruthless crushing of anti-Ceausescu demonstrators in Timisoara's Maria Square by the *Securitate* (security police) on December 15-17. Ceausescu had ordered the army to shoot unarmed demonstrators on sight while he flew off to Iran to place a wreath on the grave of the Ayatollah Khomeini. At first the Romanian army obeyed Ceausescu's orders to open fire on the Timisoara demonstrators. But when the army officers refused to continue to fire on the demonstrators a couple of days later, Ceausescu's dreaded Securitate—the communist equivalent of Caesar's Praetorian Guard and Hitler's SS—was called in and immediately started executing the officers who had countermanded Ceausescu's orders. Following the execution of some of Romania's top military officers, the Romanian security police then turned their machine guns on the unarmed demonstrators. Thousands of men, women, and children were brutally massacred, and their bodies were hauled out in garbage trucks and buried in mass graves in remote sections of Romania's forests. As justification for his brutality against the unarmed demonstrators, Ceausescu falsely blamed the riots on Hungarian Lutherans who had supposedly conspired under the dissident Rev. Laslo Tokes, an outspoken critic of Ceausescu and minister of the Hungarian Reformed Church, to retake Transylvania.[115] Fearing their overthrow, Ceausescu and his wife tried to flee Romania in a helicopter, but in a powerful statement of divine justice, Ceausescu, the despotic "Pig of Romania," and his wife were captured and charged by a Romanian military tribunal with subverting the economy, siphoning off government money into foreign bank accounts, murdering top army officers during the Romanian demonstrators, employing foreign mercenaries to kill Romanian citizens, and with the genocide of 60,000 Romanians. Found guilty of all charges, on Christmas Day, 1989, the unrepentant and obstinate Nicolae Ceausescu and his wife were taken out of the makeshift courtroom and immediately executed by a hastily assembled military firing squad. Their wide-eyed, disbelieving corpses were videotaped lying face down in pools of blood and televised for the whole world to see what fate awaits murderous dictators who hate God and mock him and his people with impunity.

The unrest in Romania and the overthrow of the Ceausescu family was the most violent in the six East European communist countries that fell. By the end of the year, 7,000 Romanians had lost their lives and all the members of the hard-line politburo had been arrested. Ceausescu, who liked to refer to himself as the "Genius of the Carpathians" and the "Danube of Thought," had been warned ahead of time by Gorbachev to abandon his hard-line stance, but vowed that he'd implement reforms in Romania only "when pears grow on poplar trees."

At the same time that communist parties were being toppled one after the other in Eastern Europe, a worried Mikhail Gorbachev was moving to expand diplomatic relations with the Vatican. On April 15, 1989, Gorbachev allowed Pope John Paul II to appoint the first Roman Catholic bishop of the Byelorussian Republic since 1926.[116] On December 1, 1989, Gorbachev, declaring the need for "spiritual values" and the "revolution of the mind," became the first communist leader of the Soviet Union to travel to the Vatican and meet with the pope, whom he greeted as "Your Holiness." The following year, on March 15, 1990, Russia resumed full diplomatic relations with the Vatican after 67 years. Then, on September 26, 1990, the legislature of the Soviet Union approved a new Law on Freedom of Conscience, officially ending all suppression of religion by the Soviet Union.

In Eastern Europe, full diplomatic relations between Poland and the Vatican were resumed in 1989 after a hiatus of 44 years. In Czechoslovakia, the government allowed four new Catholic bishops to be appointed for the first time in several decades. On February 6, 1990, Hungary announced it was removing restrictions on the Roman Catholic Church, which had been in effect for 40 years. Also establishing new diplomatic ties to the Vatican were Czechoslovakia, Rumania, and Bulgaria.

In the first half of 1990, growing ethnic unrest and demonstrations against the Soviet Union within its 15 republics dominated the evening news. A state of emergency was declared on January 15 in the southern Soviet Republic of Azerbaijan. More than 11,000 Soviet troops were brought into that Republic because of an uprising of the Azerbaijan Popular Front against the communist government and because of ethnic clashes between Christian Armenians and Muslim Azerbaijans. Anti-Armenian rioting broke out the following month in Tadzhikistan and in Uzbekistan, and in Kirghizia, rioting between Kirghiz and Uzbeks in June left 148 dead.[117]

In the Baltic region of the Soviet Union, Lithuania declared itself independent on March 11, 1990. An angry Mikhail Gorbachev, calling the Lithuanian declaration of independence "illegitimate and invalid," sent in Soviet forces on March 21 and cut off oil and natural gas supplies in April, forcing Lithuanians to suspend their declaration of independence on June 29. On March 11, Estonians pleaded with the United Nations and the Russian parliament to help free their country from 40 years of Soviet rule. And on May 4, Latvia voted to begin a transition to independence from the Soviet Union, whereupon Gorbachev angrily condemned the Latvians and sent Russian tanks and Black Berets into Riga on May 7 to intimidate the Latvians.

In the Ukraine, the second largest Soviet Republic and home of the world's largest underground religious community (the Eastern-rite Catholics), Ukrainians declared their sovereignty on July 16, 1990, but stopped short of claiming full independence from the Soviet Union. Following Ukraine's lead, Byelorussia declared its sovereignty on July 27, Tadzhikistan on August 24, Georgia on October 29, and Kirghizia on December 12.

In Eastern Europe, the Yugoslav Communist Party voted on January 22, 1990 to give up its monopoly on power in favor of a multiparty system, but ethnic and religious rivalries between the Yugoslav Republics of Serbia, Slovenia, Croatia, and Bosnia-Herzegovina threatened to tear Yugoslavia apart. In Bulgaria, parliament elected a politically independent judge, Dimitar Popov, as prime minister and approved the first multiparty government in December. In Czechoslovakia, the first free elections since 1946 were held in June. On October 3, East Germany and West Germany finally reunited, ending their forty-five-year separation. In Poland, the Communist Party voted to disband on January 29. Polish president Wojciech Jaruzelski announced his resignation on September 19, and after the first free elections in Polish history, was replaced by Solidarity leader Lech Walesa on December 9.

Desperately trying to keep the Soviet Union alive, the Central Committee of the Russian Communist Party on February 7, 1990, acting on a proposal by Mikhail Gorbachev, agreed to give up its monopoly on political power. The Soviet parliament voted in favor of a strong presidency and elected Mikhail Gorbachev president on March 15, and in a Communist Party election on July 10, retained Gorbachev as their leader.

The Death Knell of the Soviet Union

The year 1991 turned out to be the final year of existence for the Soviet Union. The Warsaw Pact, created in 1955 by the Soviet Union and its Eastern

European satellites—Bulgaria, Czechoslovakia, East Germany, Hungary, Poland, and Romania—in response to the formation of NATO, dissolved on March 31. In a last ditch effort to circumvent the death knell of the Soviet Union, a coup led by hard-line Party hacks of the government, the military, and the KGB arrested Mikhail Gorbachev at his summer vacation home in the Crimea and took control of the government on August 19. Coup leaders Gennadi Yanayev, Vladimir Kryuchkov, Dmitri Yazov, and Boris Pugo announced they were forming a State Committee for the state of emergency and banned protests, closed independent newspapers, and moved hundreds of tanks and troops into Moscow. But Boris Yeltsin, who was elected president of the Russian Republic on May 29, 1990, openly defied the coup with military forces loyal to him. Hundreds of thousands of Russians rallied around Yeltsin in open defiance of the communist hard-liners. With the Russian military reluctant to move against Yeltsin and the Moscow demonstrators, the coup leaders lost their nerve and their revolt collapsed on August 22, the Feast of the Queenship of Mary. Remarkably, only three young men died in the failed coup. Resurrected from his Crimean grave after three tense days, Mikhail Gorbachev returned to Moscow and resigned as head of the Communist Party on August 24, banning the Communist Party from any further role in the governing of the Soviet Union. Gorbachev then tried to reach an agreement with the breakaway republics that would somehow keep the Soviet Union alive, but to no avail. Ukraine seceded from the Soviet Union on August 24, Byelorussia on August 25, Moldavia on August 27, Azerbaijan on August 30, Uzbekistan and Kirghizia on August 31, and Turkmenia on October 27.

On December 8, 1991, the Feast of the Immaculate Conception of Mary, the Commonwealth of Independent States was born. The three breakaway republics of Russia, Byelorussia, and Ukraine voided the Union treaty and declared the Soviet Union "dead." On December 21, eleven of the fifteen republics of the rapidly disappearing Soviet Union met in Alma-Ata, Kazakhstan to restore order out of the confusion. On December 24, the Russian Republic took over the permanent seat on the U.N. Security Council. Then, on December 25th, 1991, Christmas Day in the West and exactly 12 years after the Soviets invaded Afghanistan, Mikhail Gorbachev officially resigned as president of the U.S.S.R. The blood-red hammer-and-sickle communist flag atop the Kremlin was replaced that day by the Russian national flag, and the Soviet Empire was no more.

December 25, 1991, the date the Soviet Union died, is extremely symbolic not only because we celebrate Christmas on that day but because the year 1991 was a palindrome year. A palindrome is something that, whether read from the beginning or the end, is the same, like the name Hannah. God, in fact, is a palindrome. He is the same from eternity past to eternity future, and like the year he defeated the Soviet Union, 1991, he is the same from beginning to end.

Remember what Jesus said to John the Evangelist in the last chapter of the Book of Revelation about who he really is—God:

> *"I am the Alpha and the Omega, the First and the Last, the Beginning and the End!"*

When something as magnanimous as the death of the Soviet Union occurs in a palindrome year on Christmas day, know for sure that Jesus is coming soon. By the way, the next palindrome year will occur only eleven years after 1991, in the year 2002. God only knows what will happen then because they have identical calendars!

Russia is Converted

> *"In the end, My Immaculate Heart will triumph. The Holy Father will consecrate Russia to me, and she will be converted, and a certain period of peace will be granted the world"*

Those were the words of the Blessed Virgin Mary on July 13, 1917, foretelling a future pope who would triumph over Russian communism. This pope, under the special protection of Mary, was Karol Cardinal Wojtyla—Pope John Paul II.

During a solemn pilgrimage to Fátima on May 13, 1982 to thank the Blessed Virgin for having saved his life from an assassin's bullet exactly one year before, John Paul II renewed—with a collegial invitation to all the bishops of the Catholic Church—the consecration of the world to the Immaculate Heart of Mary, with "special mention" of the Russian people. (Partial consecrations were previously done by Pius XII on October 31, 1942 and July 7, 1952; and by Pope Paul VI on November 21, 1964.) John Paul II renewed this act of offering and consecration three more times: on October 16, 1983; on March 25, 1984; and finally, on December 8, 1985, the year Gorbachev came to power. As history has shown, Pope John Paul II's proper consecrations of Russia to the Immaculate Heart of Mary finally converted the Soviet Union, which threw off the yoke of communism on Christmas Day, 1991.

The Mortally Wounded Beast

> "Then I saw a wild beast come out of the sea with ten horns and seven heads; on its horns were ten diadems and on its heads blasphemous names. The beast I saw was like a leopard, but it had paws like a bear and the mouth of a lion. The dragon gave it his own power and throne, together with great authority. I noticed that one of the beast's heads

seemed to have been mortally wounded, but the mortal wound was healed. In wonderment, the whole world followed after the beast. Men worshiped the dragon for giving his authority to the beast; they also worshiped the beast and said,

"Who can compare with the beast, or come forward to fight against it?

"The beast was given a mouth for uttering proud boasts and blasphemies, but the authority it received was to last only forty-two months. It began to hurl blasphemies against God, reviling him and the members of his heavenly household as well. The beast was allowed to wage war against God's people and conquer them. It was likewise granted authority over every race and people, language and nation. The beast will be worshiped by all those inhabitants of earth who did not have their names written at the world's beginning in the book of the living, which belongs to the Lamb who was slain. Let him who has ears heed these words! If one is destined for captivity, into captivity he goes! If one is destined to be slain by the sword, by the sword he will be slain! Such is the faithful endurance that distinguishes God's holy people."   Revelation 13:1-10

The First Beast of the Apocalypse—who is like a "leopard" because of his bloodthirstiness and treachery, a "bear" because he savagely kills and devours his own people, and a "lion" because he hungrily roams the earth in search of more prey—is the demonic equivalent to St. Michael the Archangel in that he wields the power of Satan, the seven-headed Dragon of Revelation 12. As a fallen archangel completely subservient to the devil, the First Beast gives human beings power without end or measure to tempt them into worshiping him, "Power of Satan," instead of God. The First Beast can therefore be called "Human Power," or more accurately "Political Power," because he has been granted the authority to raise up earthly kingdoms and governments completely antithetical to the service and worship of the triune God.

As you recall from Scripture, the devil has been given the authority by God to choose the temporal rulers of this earth, and he gives that power to whomever he wishes—even to Jesus Christ if he would've accepted it. Satan tempted Christ in the desert with the glory of all his earthly kingdoms if he would renounce God the Father and bow down before him instead:

"I will give you all this power and glory of these kingdoms; because the power has been given to me, and I give it to whomever I wish. Prostrate yourself in homage before me, and it shall all be yours."

Christ's immediate rebuke of Satan, *"You shall do homage to the Lord your God; him alone shall you adore,"*[118] was meant to be a warning to all those who worship the First Beast—Power and Glory.

Since the beginning of civilization, seven satanic empires symbolized in the Book of Revelation by the seven-headed Beast have persecuted the civilized world, having had the devil's power (represented by the beast's "ten horns" and "ten diadems [crowns]") to conquer and enslave God's people (Jews and

Christians) for a certain period of time. In chronological order these seven satanic empires are: Egypt (3100-665 B.C.), Assyria (725-609 B.C.), Babylon (626-539 B.C.), Medo-Persia (539-330 B.C.), Greece (330-37 B.C.), Rome (37 B.C.-A.D. 400), and the Union of Soviet Socialist Republics (1922-1991), which, like the seven-headed Beast from the Sea, also had seven heads (Lenin, Stalin, Khrushchev, Brezhnev, Andropov, Chernencko, and Gorbachev).

In 1917, the year Mary appeared in Fátima, Russian communism arose suddenly in Petrograd out of the turbulent swells of revolutionaries and anarchists, metaphorically referred to as the "sea" in the Book of Revelation. At the height of its power, the Soviet Union, the last of these seven evil kingdoms, had dominion over a third of the population of the world and occupied one-sixth of the earth's surface (spanning two continents and eleven time zones containing more than 100 ethnic groups and languages). Springing forth from St. Petersburg (Petrograd) on April 3, 1917 (Easter) with the return of the exiled revolutionist Vladimir Ilyich Ulyanov (Lenin) from Switzerland in a sealed boxcar, Russia's surging red tide of communism—humanistic, materialistic, Darwinistic, and atheistic—soon overflowed the entire world, seducing peoples of every race, ethnic group, religion, language, and nationality with its awesome power and boastful, anti-religious propaganda (see Appendix A for some of the Soviet Union's proud boasts and blasphemies).

The Soviet Union was officially created in 1922, and by 1991 virtually every race and people, every language and nation had been adversely affected by it; either by Moscow-sponsored invasions and takeovers, attempted takeovers, establishment of communist parties within non-communist states, infiltration of communist sympathizers and spies within democratic countries, or by strategic alliances, pacts, or trade agreements with the Soviet Union.

Enveloped within the huge communist sphere of the Soviet Union were the following countries: Bulgaria in 1946, Hungary and Poland in 1947, Czechoslovakia and East Germany in 1948, North Vietnam in 1954, Cuba in 1960, South Yemen in 1969, Angola, Laos, and South Vietnam in 1975, Ethiopia and Mozambique in 1977, Afghanistan in 1978, Cambodia in 1979, and Nicaragua in 1981. Other communist countries remaining neutral in their relations with the Soviet Union, but, nonetheless, Marxist-Leninist in ideology, were: Albania, China, North Korea, Romania, and Yugoslavia.

Bent on ruling the world and eliminating the worship of God, the Soviet Union was allowed to wage war on God's people and to conquer them, but only for a short while (70 years) before it was mortally wounded by Mary.

The mortal wounding of the Soviet Union, the seventh head of the Beast from the Sea, is symbolized by Mikhail Gorbachev's port-wine birthmark on the top of his head, which looks exactly like a bleeding mortal head wound. The blow that inflicted that symbolic mortal wound was delivered by the Blessed Virgin Mary through the Pope of Fátima, John Paul II, on December 25, 1991, the day that Gorbachev resigned as the seventh and last head of the Soviet Union.

God even put it into the minds of the secular press to report the demise of the Soviet Union in apocalyptic terminology to proclaim the triumphal conversion of Russia to the Immaculate Heart of Mary and to solve the mystery of the identity of the Mortally Wounded Beast of Revelation 13. Reporting for *Newsweek* magazine on the December 8 agreement between Russia, Byelorussia, and Ukraine to form a Commonwealth of Independent States, Peter McGrath, in his own words, pronounced that the Soviet Union was "mortally wounded," just two days before Gorbachev resigned:

> "If Mikhail Gorbachev didn't already know he was mortally wounded, Sunday's phone call from Minsk should have told him. On the line was Stanislav Shushkevich, chairman of the Byelorussian parliament. The message was straightforward: the union is dead, long live the Commonwealth of Independent States."[119]

Likewise, *Time* magazine reporters John Kohan and Strobe Talbott, who later became the Deputy Secretary of State under President Clinton, reported that in an exclusive interview with Gorbachev, following the Commonwealth's declaration of the Soviet Union's death, that Gorbachev's presidency was, in their own words, "mortally wounded":

> "Gorbachev had clearly decided to use the session to counteract the wide-spread impression that his presidency was mortally wounded by what several of his advisers had earlier in the week called the 'second coup.'"[120]

God intentionally wanted the secular press to announce to the world the miraculous and peaceful triumph of the Immaculate Heart of Mary over the Soviet Union, the seventh head of the First Beast, so the following week, December 30, 1991, the Blessed Virgin Mary's portrait appeared on the cover of *Time* magazine. The cover story, entitled "The Search for Mary," gave special mention to the Catholic Church's recognition of Mary's central role in the recent downfall of the U.S.S.R. Thus, *Time* magazine, owned by Time-Warner and one of the most widely circulated magazines in the world, unknowingly assisted in God's plan to warn us of "the signs of the time" through Mary's miraculous and peaceful triumph over the Soviet Union.

Centuries ago, Mary's future mortal wounding of the Soviet Union, the seventh head of the First Beast, was foreshadowed in the Old Testament biblical story of Judith beheading Holofernes, the wicked Assyrian General besieging Israel:

> "Blessed are you, daughter, by the Most High God, above all the women on the earth; and blessed be the Lord God, creator of heaven and earth who guided your blow at the head of the chief of our enemies."[121]

Remember, Genesis 3:15 foretold where the Woman's offspring would strike the serpent—in the head:

> "I will put enmity between you [serpent] and the woman, and between your offspring and hers; He will strike at your head, while you strike at his heel."

Another Old Testament prefiguration of Mary striking at the serpent's head, which is under her heel, is seen in the Canticle of the prophetess Deborah, (Judges 5:24-27). Deborah praises Jael, the Israeli wife of Heber the Kenite, for slaying Sisera, the evil commander of the Canaanite charioteers besieging the Israelites in 1120 B.C. Inspired by God, Jael courageously slew Sisera with a blow to the head after he fell asleep in her tent while hiding under a rug from the pursuing Israelites who, though inferior in strength, had providentially routed Sisera's forces at the river Kishon:

> "Blessed among women by Jael . . . With her left hand she reached for the peg, with the right for the workmen's mallet. She hammered Sisera, crushed his head; she smashed, stove in his temple. At her feet he sank down, fell, lay still; down at her feet he sank and fell; where he sank down, there, he fell, slain."

The prophetess Deborah promised Barak, the Israelite commander, that Jehovah would deliver Sisera's forces unto him for defeat, but God had told her that Barak would not gain the glory for himself, for the Lord would have Sisera fall into the power of a woman.

Yet another Old Testament prefiguration of Mary crushing the head of the serpent can be seen in the death of the wicked king Abimelech (Judges 9:1-57). Abimelech, the son of a Shechemite concubine, had formed a conspiracy with his mother's family to have his 71 brothers murdered after the death of his father Gideon so that he would be the sole ruler of Shechem. Killing all but one of his brothers (Jotham, who had hid himself), God exacted revenge on Abimelech three years later when a Thebezite woman dropped a piece of a millstone on his head, crushing his skull, just as Abimelech was about to set fire to the door of the tower where the inhabitants of Thebez had fled for their lives from Abimelech's army. Mortally wounded, Abimelech had his aid dispatch him with his sword so that he wouldn't die a humiliating death at the hands of a mere woman.

> Draw your sword and dispatch me, lest they say of me that a woman killed me."

The three preceding Old Testament stories of courageous women striking the wicked enemy in the head foreshadow Mary's future mortal wounding of the Soviet Union, the seventh head of the First Beast.[122] Just as the character of Jesus Christ was prefigured in the Old Testament, so was the character and role of the Blessed Virgin Mary.

As additional proof that the Blessed Virgin Mary and Pope John Paul II were key to the downfall of the godless Soviet Union, three months later, on March 3, 1992, Gorbachev admitted in a major newspaper article that "Pope John Paul II played a major role in the collapse of communism in Eastern Europe," and that the events in Eastern Europe "might not have been possible without the presence of the pope, without the great role—including political—which he knew how to play on the world scene."[123]

It was God's will that Pope John Paul II be the Rock that crushed the Beast from the Sea. If the Slavs were the people who gave rise to communism then a Slav had to be the one to defeat it.

The Revived Roman Empire

Because the spirit of discernment is not with them, many people mistakenly identify the seventh head of the First Beast, the "Revived Roman Empire," with the European Union (EU) or some kind of future United States of Europe (USE). But they are wrong: the seventh head of the beast, the Revived Roman Empire, was the Soviet Union, not the EU or future USE. Similarly, the mortally wounded beast is not the future Antichrist who some people predict gets shot in the head and then rises from the dead—it was the demonic power that resided in the Soviet Union, which will rise again before the end of the world.

The Romanov empire of Russia, named after the Romanov family that ruled Russia from 1613-1917 and which gave rise to the Soviet Union in 1922, often referred to itself as the "Third Roman Empire."[124] Ivan the Great, the prince of Moscow (1462-1505) who began the territorial expansion of Russia that eventually ended in the huge expanse of territory known as the Soviet Union, and who was a distant relative of the first Romanov head, Michael Romanov, likewise referred to Moscow as the "Third Rome."[125] Ivan the Great actually believed he was a direct descendent of the Roman emperor Caesar Augustus. In the fifteenth century, when Ivan married Sophia Paleologus, a niece of the last Byzantine emperor, he claimed for himself the title of "Russian Emperor" and began calling himself a *Czar*, a Slavic contraction of the word *Caesar*. To bolster his claim that Moscow was now the new Rome and that he was the new Roman emperor, Ivan also added the words *Autokrat* (Greek for "absolute ruler") and *Gosudar* ("sovereign") to Czar (*Tsar*), and affixed to the Russian family crest the two-headed eagle that had symbolized the Eastern Roman or Byzantine Empire.

There is ample evidence to suggest that the Soviet Union was the "Revived Roman Empire," the seventh head of the First Beast. Russia's national symbol, the bear, which is alluded to in the metaphorical description of the beast who "was like a leopard but had paws like a bear" in Revelation 13, is a good indication that the mortally-wounded Soviet Union represented the Revived Roman Empire. After the Soviet invasion of Afghanistan on Christmas Day in 1979, the paw of a bear stepping on an Afghanistan bear trap appeared on the cover of the January 28, 1980 issue of *Time* magazine, suggesting that Afghanistan may become the Soviet Union's Vietnam. And it did: the war in Afghanistan drained the Soviet economy and was one of the reasons the Soviet Union fell so soon, unlike the previous six evil empires which lasted much longer.

Another fact that suggests that the Soviet Union was the Revived Roman Empire came from the Chernobyl nuclear power plant explosion in the Ukraine. On April 26, 1986, a freak accident at Chernobyl shocked the world and became the symbolic sign of the careless and criminally negligent treatment of our planet in the end times, as predicted would happen in Revelation 8:10-11:

> "When the third angel blew his trumpet, a huge star burning like a torch crashed down from the sky. It fell on a third of the rivers and the springs. The star's name was "Wormwood" [a bitter plant named Artemisia absinthium] because a third part of all the waters turned to wormwood. Many people died from this polluted water."

The explosion and fire at the Ukrainian nuclear power plant in Chernobyl, which means Wormwood in Ukrainian, released huge amounts of radioactive gases into the environment, contaminating fresh water reservoirs near the plant and forcing the evacuation of over 49,000 people. The power plant explosion carried the radiation two thirds of a mile up and the jet stream winds swept the contamination all the way to Scandinavia and Northern Europe. Twenty countries showed radiation levels higher than normal and hundreds of millions of people were exposed. By June 5, 1986, the death toll from Chernobyl reached 26. Three years later, tests showed dangerously high levels of radiation in villages 200 miles from the plant. Scientists predict that an estimated half a million people will eventually get cancer from Chernobyl because subsequent tests have revealed that the explosion at Chernobyl, before it was sealed up in a concrete "sarcophagus," gave out as much radiation as all the nuclear tests and exploded nuclear bombs combined.

As if to validate the identity of the Soviet Union as the Revived Roman Empire, on April 26, 1987, the first anniversary of the Ukrainian nuclear power plant accident in Chernobyl, the Blessed Virgin Mary appeared to a twelve-year-old peasant girl named Marina Kizyn in Hrushiv, Ukraine, at the chapel of the Blessed Trinity. She told the young girl that Ukraine (the first nation to declare Mary her queen), because of its long history of suffering and faithfulness to Catholicism, had been chosen by God to help lead the godless Soviet Union back to Christ.[126] Unlike Fátima and Lourdes where only children saw Mary, in Hrushiv Mary was subsequently seen by hundreds of thousands of adult witnesses, including Josyp Terelya, a world-famous Catholic activist from Carpathian Ukraine who survived twenty years imprisonment and torture in the Soviet gulags simply because he refused to renounce his Catholic faith.[127] (This was the second time Terelya had seen an apparition of Mary; the first was when she appeared to console and counsel him as the communist authorities were purposely trying to freeze him to death in Cell 21 at Vladimir prison, one of the Soviet Union's most notorious prisons located approximately 100 miles outside of Moscow.[128] On February 12, 1972, Mary appeared to Josyp in a warm, blinding light inside Terelya's cell, which his prison guards noticed.[129] The Soviet police, KGB, communist doctors, psychiatrists, and philosophers, and even the Kremlin itself questioned Terelya on end for weeks about how he was able to self-manufacture the light that warmed his freezing cell, refusing to believe Terelya's story that it was a light from heaven in which the Blessed Mother appeared to save him from death.)[130]

Exiled from the Soviet Union to Canada in 1987, Josyp Terelya appeared in Washington, D.C. on October 22, 1987, before the Congressional Commission on Security and Cooperation in Europe, attended by such political dignitaries as Senator Alfonse D'Amato of New York and Senator Frank Lautenberg of New Jersey. At that meeting Congressman Chris Smith, professing his deep-held belief in Fátima, questioned Josyp in length on the Hrushiv apparitions and how they were affecting the Soviet government and their policies toward the banned Ukrainian Church—at that time the largest underground church in the world (five million members in the Ukraine and 1.9 million in other parts of the Soviet Union). Terelya replied to the committee that in the first three weeks of the apparitions, 100,000 pilgrims a day were coming to the small chapel in Hrushiv, which greatly upset the Soviet authorities who felt powerless to stop them, and that Mary's apparitions in Hrushiv were significantly strengthening the faith in God throughout the Soviet Union. Terelya went on to say, without going into detail, that the prophecies he received from Mary in Hrushiv were a continuation of the prophecies in Fátima and Medjugorje about the conversion of Russia in the end and an imminent chastisement upon the sinful world. (Following his testimony before Congress, Josyp Terelya was invited to a reception at the White House by Ronald Reagan. Terelya has also had private audiences with Pope John Paul II, Cardinal Ratzinger, the Prefect of the Vatican's Congregation of the Doctrine of the Faith, Canadian Prime Minister Brian Mulroney, Canadian Foreign Minister Joe Clark, and Queen Beatrice of the Netherlands to name a few.[131])

Mary's prophecies in Fátima about the spread of Russia's errors; the attempted assassination of Pope John Paul II in 1981 by Mehmet Ali Aga at the behest of Bulgarian agents working for the Soviet Union; the history of the Romanov Empire; the fall of the Soviet Union on Christmas day in 1991;

Russia's symbol of the bear; the explosion of Chernobyl on April 26, 1986; Mary's appearance in Ukraine on the first anniversary of the Chernobyl nuclear accident; Gorbachev's birthmark that looks like a mortal head wound; and the biblical symbolism behind Judith beheading Holofernes, Jael slaying Sisera, and the Thebezite woman mortally wounding Abimelech, all suggest that the Soviet Union was the Revived Roman Empire of the Book of Revelation—the "Evil Empire" that only former president Ronald Reagan had the courage to call in public. (For those who think that Gorbachev's birth mark is just a coincidence, please refer to the notes section on the extreme importance of the forehead as symbolism in the Bible.[132])

One last comment about the Soviet Union being the Revived Roman Empire: Russia was converted from atheistic communism on the hundredth anniversary of Pope Leo XIII's landmark encyclical, *Rerum Novarum,* in which he "utterly rejected" communism as the "great mistake."

The Catholic Church's consecration of Russia to the Immaculate Heart of Mary, which finally brought down the Soviet Union, was a long time in coming; but as the Lord said to Sister Lucy in August of 1931, *"Like the King of France, they will repent and do it, but it will be late."*

Antichrist—The Eighth King

One very important thing to remember: although the seventh head of the First Beast was mortally wounded by the Virgin Mary in 1991, it will be resurrected before the end of the world as an eighth head or king. We know this for certain from two passages in the Book of Revelation. In Revelation 13:3 it says that the beast's head that seemed mortally wounded was *"healed,"* and in wonderment, *"the whole world followed after it."* This insinuates that the devil's power that resided in the Soviet Union and the six other evil empires will come back to life before the end of time. That is, there will arise another evil world power in the end that will fight against Jesus Christ and his Catholic Church for the final time. The seventeenth chapter of Revelation, which was written by John the Evangelist around the year A.D. 90, ventures the same thing. Here is that chapter in its entirety:

> "Then one of the seven angels who were holding the seven bowls came to me and said: 'Come, I will show you the judgment in store for the great harlot who sits by the waters of the deep. The kings of the earth have committed fornication with her, and the earth's inhabitants have grown drunk on the wine of her lewdness.' The angel then carried me away in spirit to a desolate place where I saw a woman seated on a scarlet beast, which was covered with blasphemous names. This beast had seven heads and ten horns. The woman was dressed in purple and scarlet and adorned with gold and pearls and other jewels. In her hand she held a gold cup

that was filled with the abominable and sordid deeds of her lewdness. On her forehead was written a symbolic name, 'Babylon the great, mother of all harlots and all the world's abominations.' I saw that the woman was drunk with the blood of God's holy ones and the blood of those martyred for their faith in Jesus.

"When I saw her I was greatly astonished. The angel said to me: 'Why are you so taken aback? I will explain to you the symbolism of the woman and the seven-headed and ten-horned beast carrying her. The beast you saw existed once but now exists no longer. It will come up from the abyss once more before going to final ruin. All the men of the earth whose names have not been written in the book of the living from the creation of the world shall be amazed when they see the beast, for it existed once and now exists no longer, and yet it will exist again. Here is the clue for the one who possesses wisdom! The seven heads are the seven hills on which the woman sits enthroned. They are also seven kings: five have already fallen, one lives now, and the last has not yet come; but when he does come he will remain only a short while. The beast, which existed once but now exists no longer, even though it is an eighth king, is really one of the seven and is on its way to ruin. The ten horns you saw represent ten kings who have not yet been crowned; they will possess royal authority along with the beast, but only for an hour. Then they will come to agreement and bestow their power and authority on the beast. They will fight against the Lamb, but the Lamb will conquer them, for he is the Lord of lords and the King of kings; victorious too will be his followers—the ones who were called: the chosen and the faithful.'

"The angel then said to me: 'The waters on which you saw the harlot enthroned are large numbers of peoples and nations and tongues. The ten horns you saw on the beast will turn against the harlot with hatred; they will strip off her finery and leave her naked; they will devour her flesh and set her on fire. For God has put it in their minds to carry out his plan, by making them agree to bestow their sovereignty on the beast until his will is accomplished. The woman you saw is the great city which has sovereignty over the kings of the earth.'"

In A.D. 90, around the time the angel explained to St. John the Evangelist the meaning of the seven-headed and ten-horned beast, the Roman Empire, the "New Babylon," was in power. The previous five evil empires (Egypt, Assyria, Babylon, Medo-Persia, and Greece) had already fallen, and the seventh evil empire (the Soviet Union) had not yet come. St. John was first given a vision of the future, of the period of peace following the upcoming chastisement, and then the angel explained to him the fall of the seven-headed First Beast into the abyss during the chastisement and its resurrection before the end of the world as the eighth head or king, who will really be one of the fallen seven.

Where the eighth king will be born or what his name will be we do not know. This you can be certain of though: like the forerunners of Antichrist, he will deify himself, curse Christianity, change the calendar and feast days, put his own image in the churches and basilicas, fight against the Catholic Church, and try to end the daily sacrifice of the mass, as prophesied in the Book of Daniel, chapter 8. The eighth king, therefore, represents the future Antichrist, the eleventh "little horn" of Daniel 8 that arises out of the ten horns of the beast.

After the brief period of peace (not a literal thousand years as millenarianists think) the devil will come up from the abyss and bestow his full power on the Antichrist, who will align himself with the ten world powers of the future—symbolized by the harlot woman riding the seven-headed, ten-horned beast. Likewise, according to Revelation's symbolism of the seven hills on which the harlot woman sits enthroned, the woman sits on Rome, "the city on seven hills." So Antichrist's throne will be in Rome.

The peaceful, "Second Holy Roman Empire" formed after the chastisement will end with the coming of the eighth king or Antichrist—that "Man of Lawlessness" and "Son of Perdition"—because God has decreed it to be so. You see, everything in the end times must parallel the life of Jesus—his Palm Sunday and apparent triumph, his passion, his betrayal, his death, and his resurrection—only this time it will be experienced by the Roman Catholic Church instead of Christ.

When Antichrist comes three of the beast's ten horns will be overthrown, as mentioned in Daniel 8, leaving only seven nations who will serve Antichrist. The seven remaining powers will then turn against the lewd harlot, whose cup holds the wicked of the earth whom the Roman Antichrist reigns over, and strip her naked and destroy her with fire (which may intimate a nuclear holocaust). Whatever happens, Antichrist's reign will be short, only forty-two months (three and a half years) before he is thrown into the abyss forever with the First Beast and the "False Prophet" or Second Beast. Then, for the last three and a half years of time, Satan himself will reign over the desolated earth. At the end of this seven-year tribulation, the worst in history, Christ will literally and physically come back down from heaven on the clouds and throw Satan into the abyss for all eternity, where the Antichrist and his two beasts await him, and the world as we know it will end.

There is nothing about the future that God wants us to know that can't be understood. Like Sister Lucy said when asked what was in the Third Secret of Fátima: "It is in the Gospel and in the Apocalypse, read them!"

The Second Beast

"The desire of power in excess caused the angels to fall; the desire of knowledge in excess caused man to fall."

Francis Bacon, *Advancement of Learning*, 1605

"Science confers power, not purpose. It is a blessing therefore, if the purpose which it serves is good; it is a curse, if the purpose is bad."
William Poteat, *Can a Man Be a Christian Today*, 1926

If the First Beast of Revelation represents the political power directed against God and is the demon analogous to Michael the Archangel (Power of God), the Second Beast represents the human knowledge that rejects God and is the demon analogous to the Archangel Gabriel (Messenger of God who announces revelations to man). Like Gabriel, the Second Beast gives information and knowledge to man, but he gives it with the intent to make man grow proud and to draw him away from Jesus Christ into mortal sin.

While most people still have enough good in them not to idolize human power, they do worship the human sciences that deny Jesus Christ is God.[133] The Second Beast, therefore, is the silent killer that destroys far more souls than the First Beast because it enters and destroys without being detected. It is a master seducer and false prophet. It is believed to be truthful, when in fact it is a liar like its master, the Dragon. On the outside it appears good, innocent like a lamb, while on the inside it is a ravenous beast—a real wolf in sheep's clothing that devours the souls of the ignorant and unwary.

How many people have lost their faith in Christianity because modern science and philosophy have supposedly disproved it? Legions. Look at the devastating impact rationalism, materialism, Darwinism, communism, secular humanism, Freudianism, Jungianism, and the rest of the antichristian theories have had on our youth: prayer in school was outlawed by the Supreme Court in 1962, the Bible banned from schools in 1963, and the Ten Commandments taken down from classroom walls in 1980. Nowadays, students and teachers cannot mention the name of Jesus in class or sing Christian songs during Christmas, which they now refer to as the Winter Pageant (they want to keep the holiday but get rid of the holy day). God has been taken out of our schools and replaced with a hostile, pagan, antichristian, secular humanistic ideology not unlike communism.

With God now out of our kids' lives, look what prodigies godless human knowledge and technology have replaced him with: computer games are full of graphic violence and demonic characters; the internet allows unlimited and uncensored access to pornography, pedophilia, live sex shows, hidden-camera voyeurism, open-camera exhibitionism, credit card gambling, greedy day-trading, easy access by anyone to dangerous prescription drugs and date-rape drugs, consumer fraud, copyright piracy, privacy invasion, identity thefts, and chatrooms with perverts, child molesters, drug dealers, gun runners, bomb builders, and neo-Nazi hate groups; Hollywood movies and TV are packed with graphic sex, homosexuality, gratuitous violence, and profanity; video and audio tapes, CD's, DVD's, and radio stations disseminate hate-filled, misogynist rap and satanic heavy metal music to impressionable and often fatherless teens; phone companies provide easy access to sex and psychic hotlines; teen books, magazines, and tabloids are rife with smut and gossip; health care organizations, pharmaceutical companies, Planned Parenthood and other "altruistic" community organizations provide free condoms, birth control, and abortion counseling services to our youngsters right in school—without the knowledge or consent of the parents. Because of the knowledge we have obtained from the Second Beast the souls of our children are being destroyed. One only has to look at the recent rise in mass murders, gang violence, and teen pregnancies in our public schools to see the devastating effect of the Second Beast on our kids.

Not content to just destroy our souls and the souls of our children, the devil utilizes the knowledge he gives mankind through the Second Beast to facilitate the aims of the First Beast to physically ruin the earth. Scientists have harnessed the power of the atom only to build more and more weapons of mass destruction. New biological agents have been cultured that can wipe out entire civilizations. Enough chemical bombs have been stockpiled to destroy the earth many times over. Unstable nuclear power plants threaten our fragile ecosystem. We live in an age where Armageddon is just a millisecond away. Like Pope John Paul II said, ours is a "culture of death."

There's no denying that the knowledge given to us by the Second Beast has brought about an increase in human deaths in the world. We prove it by manufacturing birth control and abortifacients that kill our offspring, and by providing lethal doses of medicines to euthanize our sick and elderly. We prove it by artificially procreating life in a petri dish and then destroying the leftover human embryos. We prove it by trying to obtain immortality by cloning new bodies from our own cells or cryogenically freezing our corpses. Our minds have been so blinded by the technical knowledge the Second Beast has given us that we no longer can see that abortion, birth control, sterilization, assisted suicide, artificial insemination, sex selection, fetal tissue research, infanticide, eugenics (selective breeding), surrogate parenting, and human cloning are sins against nature, against the family, against life itself. These are the kinds of sins against nature that will soon bring about God's chastisement upon the world.

Not long after the chastisement, when the world has finally come to recognize the Catholic Church as the One True Church and everyone is converted, the Second Beast, Human Knowledge, will resurrect the mortally-wounded image of the First Beast, Political Power, which will then bestow its full power on Antichrist. The ten kings (nations) of the end time will come to agreement and confer their authority on Antichrist, who, and this is important to remember, will remove three of the kings from power, leaving only seven. With full authority vested in him by the remaining seven nations, Antichrist, the evil offspring of scientific rationalism within the church, will then remove the sacrifice of the mass, abolish the worship of Jesus Christ, perform great wonders, change the calendar and great feast days, and have himself worshiped as God. He will put his own image in the house of God in place of Jesus Christ (the abomination of desolation), and will force everyone to worship it. He, like his father Lucifer, will call himself a god, which will bring down God's wrath and the literal end of the world.

The period of the Antichrist that takes place right before the end of the world will be more violent than any other period in history because mankind will be enslaved by the devil as never before, and the remnant of Christians that remains faithful to the church will be more oppressed than during the time of the ten great Roman persecutions. It will be better to be dead than to be alive during these times.

Here is the second part of Revelation 13 which symbolically portrays what will happen when Human Science resurrects Human Power, which will then give total authority to Antichrist:

> "Then I saw another wild beast come out of the earth; it had two horns like a sheep but it spoke like a dragon. It used the authority of the first beast to promote its interests by making the world and all its inhabitants worship the first beast, whose mortal wound had been healed. It performed great prodigies; it could even make fire come down from heaven to earth as men looked on. Because of the prodigies it was allowed to perform by authority of the first beast, it led astray the earth's inhabitants, telling them to make an idol in honor of the [first] beast that had been wounded by the sword and yet lived. The second beast was then permitted to give life to the [first] beast's image, so that the image had the power of speech and of putting to death anyone who refused to worship it. It forced all men, small and great, rich and poor, slave and free, to accept a stamped image on their right hand and forehead. Moreover, it did not allow a man to buy or sell anything unless he was first marked with the name of the beast or the number that stood for its name.
>
> "A certain wisdom is needed here; with a little ingenuity anyone can calculate the number of the beast, for it is a number that stands for a certain man. The man's number is six hundred sixty-six."

After the chastisement and brief period of peace, man will grow proud of himself again by virtue of the knowledge given him by the Second Beast. He will be able to perform signs and wonders that will cause men to worship the First Beast (the prodigies of making fire come down from the sky in the above passage refers, of course, to man's invention of nuclear weapons and his feeling of invincibility possessing such power). With the resurrection of the mortally-wounded First Beast by the Second Beast, ten nations will come together and confer the devil's power on Antichrist, who will want to be worshiped as God. By the authority of the First Beast, Antichrist will have the power of speech (like Lenin and Hitler did) and of putting anyone who won't follow him to death, in addition to total control over the economy like communism. Eventually, Antichrist, whose number will be 666, will turn against three of the ten nations (kings) who put him in power, which will leave only seven. Perhaps there will be a nuclear attack on three of the nations of the ten-nation confederacy by the other seven nations. Whatever happens, just the threat of a nuclear attack can force nations to bow down before Antichrist, which is symbolized by the stamped images on the right hand and forehead, a mark of slavery once used by the ancient Romans.[134]

The True Meaning of 666

In the Bible the number 6 represents imperfection, rebellion, and sin: man, who fell from god's grace, was created on the 6th day and the satanic number for the unholy trinity of the Dragon and his two beasts, which will be given to Antichrist when he comes, is 666. In the nineteen-hundred-year-old quest to decipher the meaning of 666, many biblical scholars have claimed that the name of Antichrist will total six hundred and sixty-six. The early Christians who believed in an imminent return of Jesus Christ claimed that the Roman emperor Nero, who began the persecution of Christians and whose name supposedly added up to 666, was the Antichrist. He wasn't. More recently, other unravelers of the mystery have said that the World Wide Web, WWW, is the answer to the riddle of 666 (Waw, W, is the sixth consonant of the Hebrew alphabet.) That theory is only partially true: the real truth is any combination of 666 can be used by the devil if he wants to take credit for an evil he authors. Satan's options are limitless and he can use the number 6 any way he wants, but he prefers to use it to symbolize the knowledge, whether it be the truth or lies, that the Second Beast gives us to destroy ourselves. If you look real close with spiritual eyes, you can see the clues to the beast's involvement in Human Science. Lucifer is proud of his intelligence and he loves to autograph his evil with symbolism.

Before giving a few examples of Satan's use of 666, let me first review the biblical story of the downfall of man through the serpent's temptation of the apple of knowledge and its godlike power. Then I will relate the number 666 and the symbol of the apple to modern history.

In the time of Adam and Eve, the apple of the knowledge of good and evil was the forbidden fruit that Adam and Eve, going against God's command, took a bite out of, which caused them to be expelled from the Garden of Eden and which brought a curse upon mankind. Appealing to Eve's lust and envy, the serpent promised that if she ate the fruit she wouldn't die like God had warned, but, instead, would be like God, knowing good from evil:

"Now the serpent was the most cunning of the animals that the Lord God had made. The serpent asked the woman [Eve], 'Did God really tell you not to eat from any of the trees of the Garden?' The woman answered the serpent: 'We may eat of the fruit of the trees in the garden; it is only about the fruit of the tree in the middle of the garden that God said, "'You shall not eat it or even touch it, lest you die.'" But the serpent said to the woman: 'You certainly will not die! No, God knows well that the moment you eat of it your eyes will be opened and you will be like gods who know what is good and what is bad.' The woman saw that the tree was good for food, pleasing to the eyes, and desirable for gaining wisdom. So she took some of its fruit and ate it; and she also gave some to her husband, who was with her, and he ate it. Then the eyes of both of them were opened, and they realized they were naked; so they sewed fig leaves together and made loincloths for themselves.

"When they heard the sound of the Lord God moving about in the garden at the breezy time of the day, the man and his wife hid themselves from the Lord God among the trees of the garden. The Lord God then called to the man and asked him, 'Where are you?' He answered, 'I heard you in the garden; but I was afraid, because I was naked, so I hid myself.' Then he asked, 'Who told you that you were naked? You have eaten, then, from the tree of which I had forbidden you to eat!' The man replied, 'The woman whom you put here with me-she gave me from the tree, so I ate it.' The Lord God then asked the woman, 'Why did you do such a thing?' The woman answered, 'The serpent tricked me into it, so I ate it.'"[135]

We all know the rest of the story: Adam and Eve were banned from the metaphorical Garden of Eden and the serpent was cursed for giving them the knowledge of good and evil. Thus, from the dawn of civilization the apple has been the symbol of the knowledge the devil gives mankind to make him think that he can be like God. Now, here are a few examples of connections between the satanic number 666 and the apple of knowledge the devil has given us in order that we grow proud in our wisdom and destroy ourselves.

In 1666, the year of the great London fire and the year following the great London plague, a brilliant young Englishman named Isaac Newton, who was posthumously born with no father on Christmas day[136] in 1642 and eventually became known as the "Father of Modern Science," was sitting underneath an apple tree one day at Woolsthorpe Manor in Lincolnshire, on leave from his classes at Trinity College in Cambridge, when an apple fell to the ground (some say on his head), inspiring him to formulate the theory of universal gravity.[137] Newton's ingenious discovery of universal gravity, along with his co-invention of calculus and the discovery of the laws of motion, would later be used by scientists to develop long-range nuclear missiles, giving mankind the ability to destroy himself many times over.[138] Once again, such a simple thing as an apple gave us the knowledge to destroy humanity, this time physically rather than spiritually.

Because we worship Human Science and believe most anything it says, most people think of Isaac Newton as a brilliant, godlike scientist; but, in fact, Newton spent the majority of his time engrossed in alchemy,[139] natural magic, astrology, biblical prophecy and numerology.[140] He could quote passages from the Bible from memory and spent a great deal of time predicting the future and interpreting the Book of Revelation, being keenly aware of the tremendous importance of the year 1666, his *annus mirabilis* (year of wonders), in relation to his scientific discoveries.[141]

> "All this was in the two years of 1665-1666, for in those days I was in the prime of age for invention, & minded mathematicks [sic] & philosophy more than any other time."[142]

As a Puritan, Newton publicly professed a belief in God, but like the Arian heretics of the Early Church, he refused to believe in the essential Catholic doctrine of the Trinity—that Jesus is one in being with God the Father and God the Holy Spirit.[143] Although careful to keep his anti-Trinitarian views quiet to avoid being branded a heretic by the church, and his dabbling in alchemy and natural magic a secret to keep from being charged with sorcery, Newton was fearlessly outspoken against the Roman Catholic Church, which he often referred to as the "Whore of Babylon."[144] And although he frequently branded the pope as the devil incarnate, Newton didn't actually believe in a literal, personal being called the devil. Instead, he attributed the existence of evil to disturbances in the human mind and flaws in human character.[145] So confident was Newton that there was no devil or hell, on his deathbed he told his nephew that he had no intention of receiving the last rites, which deeply upset his friends and relatives.[146] John Conduitt, husband of Newton's half-niece and a collector of Newton's anecdotes, tried to apologize for this by insinuating that Newton was so great that he had nothing to confess.[147] History proves otherwise.

Despite being born an intellectual genius, Newton was psychologically disturbed throughout his entire life. Scarred from youth because his mother left him for another man after his real father died before he was born, Isaac Newton the adult was reclusive, anti-social, rarely laughed, never married, hated Catholics, and was extremely egotistical and competitive. (Because of his name Isaac, his birth on Christmas Day, his survival of a low birth weight and the London fire and plague of 1665-1666, and his recognized genius, Newton thought himself superhuman.[148]) But from what historians now know of the real Isaac Newton, the so-called "Father of Modern Science," he is not a very good role model for our kids. Be that as it may, Isaac Newton is the second most recognizable person in all of history, behind Muhammed and ahead of Jesus.[149]

Another possible example of the apple of knowledge that Human Science

The Archangel Michael Throws Out the Rebellious Angels, by Luca Giordano.

Figure 1

Judith Slaying Holofernes, by Artemisia Gentileschi.

Figure 2

Photograph of the actual 1531 *tilma* of Juan Diego.

Figure 3

The Red Dragon and the Woman Clothed with the Sun, by William Blake.

Figure 4

The Great Red Dragon and the Beast from the Sea, by William Blake.

Figure 5

Former General Secretary and President of the Soviet Union,
Mikhail Gorbachev, Poland, 1988.

Figure 6

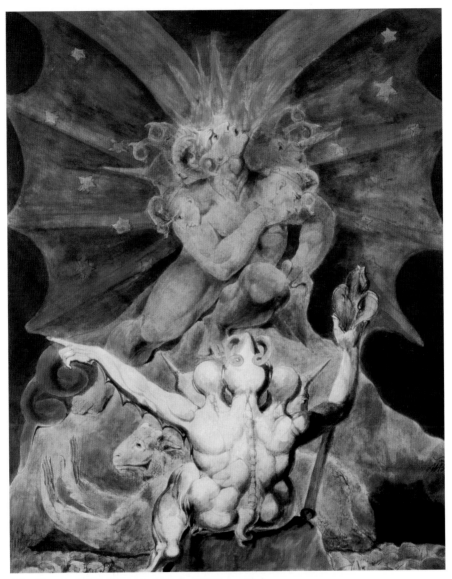

The Number of the Beast is 666, by William Blake.

Figure 7

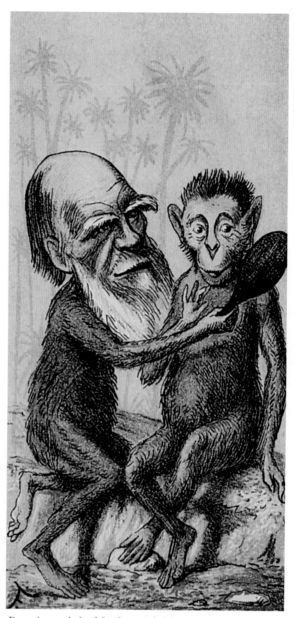

Darwin and the Monkey with Mirror.

Figure 8

Newton Under the Apple Tree.

Figure 9

Hydrogen bomb test, Castle Romeo.

Figure 10

The address on the Tishman Building, 666 Fifth Avenue, New York, NY.

Figure 11

The Whore of Babylon, by William Blake

Figure 12

Our Lady of La Salette, in tears.

Figure 13

The statue of Akita, in tears.

Figure 14

Russian space station, *Mir.*

Figure 15

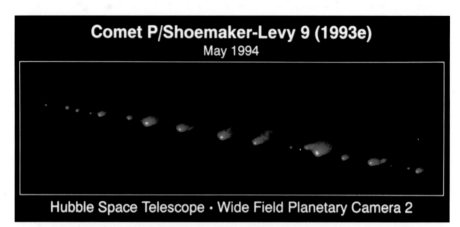

Shoemaker-Levy 9 comet.

Jupiter impact of the Shoemaker-Levy 9 comet.

Figure 16 (top) & Figure 17 (bottom)

gives us in order that we destroy ourselves can be seen in the invention of the personal computer. Was it just a coincidence that the first workable personal computer was called the Apple or that it's original sales price was $666.66?[150] All those involved in the making of the first personal computers, their operating software, and the internet surely knew that the PC would bring to the common person godlike power and knowledge which could be used for good or evil purposes.[151] One only has to look at the flood of uncensored smut and voyeurism on the internet nowadays, which our Supreme Court protects by law, and the deluge of violent, demonic computer games in computer stores to realize that a lot of what personal computers have brought us is bad, very bad—especially to our children. Just look what happened in Columbine High School if you don't think that this latest prodigy of Human Science has thrown open the gates of hell and has become the quickest and broadest gateway to the abyss.[152] Remember what Jesus said in the Gospel of Matthew:

> " . . . *the gate is wide and the road broad that leads to destruction, and those who enter it are many.*"[153]

And don't forget the other computer dilemmas that may someday destroy civilization: terrorist hackers, foreign and domestic computer spies, programming errors like Y2K, system crashes, pandemic computer viruses like the "Melissa" or "Worm" viruses of 1999, the Chernobyl virus that strikes every year on the anniversary of the Chernobyl accident, and the "Love Bug" virus of the year 2000. Our fascinating friend the computer may soon become our worst nightmare—like HAL in Stanley Kubrick's landmark movie *2001: A Space Odyssey.*

Still another possible example of the number of the Second Beast symbolically connected to the destructive knowledge of good and evil can be physically seen on the Tishman building in New York City, until recently the former address of two of the largest publishers of books, both good and evil, in the world. The address I'm referring to on Fifth Avenue in NYC is 666—the number of the Second Beast who gives us knowledge.[154] Remember, Mary in La Salette warned us that in the end times, evil books would be abundant on earth, so be very careful what you read!

There are so many possible ways that Satan can use 666 to symbolize the harmful knowledge he gives mankind that volumes could be written on just that subject.

Chapter Ten

Our Lady of Beauraing and Banneux, Belgium: 1932-1933

"A forerunner of the Antichrist, with his troops gathered from several nations, will fight against the true Christ, the only Savior of the world. He will shed much blood and will want to annihilate the worship of God to make himself be looked upon as a God."

Our Lady of La Salette, 1846

On the Eve of World War II

The tiny nation of Belgium is a mixed Flemish- and French-speaking country in northern Europe with a population of around 10 million, ninety-five percent of whom are Catholic. Belgium is about the size of the state of Maryland, and borders France to the south, the Netherlands to the north, and Germany and Luxembourg to the east. In the early 1930s, within the span of about two weeks, the Blessed Virgin Mary appeared in Belgium on two separate occasions in two different regions: from November to January of 1932-1933 in Beauraing, and from January to March of 1933 in Banneux.

In Beauraing, a small town of about 2,000 in the southern part of Belgium, Mary appeared thirty-three times to five young Catholic children, ranging in age from 9 to 14, whose names were Gilberte and Andrée Degeimbre, and Fernande, Gilberte, and Albert Voisin.

On the evening of November 29, 1932, four of the five children were walking back to their Catholic school, run by the Sisters of Christian Doctrine, to pick up their friend Gilberte Voisin, a semi-boarder who didn't leave school to go home until after 6 o'clock. As they climbed the stairs to ring the doorbell of

194

the academy, young Albert Voisin shouted, "Look, the Blessed Virgin, dressed in white, is walking above the bridge!" Turning to look in the direction in which Albert was pointing, the other three children saw the illuminated figure of a woman wearing a long white gown, appearing to be walking on a cloud. Momentarily frightened, the four children screamed and pounded on the convent door until Sister Valeria came down to open it. Sister Valeria looked in the direction to where the children were pointing, but didn't see anything. She assumed they were playing a practical joke on her until Gilberte Voisin came out of the doorway, after having put on her hat and coat, and shouted, "Oh, look!"

All five children raced home to tell their parents what they'd seen, but their parents, instead of listening, got angry with them for telling such preposterous tales. Meanwhile, Sister Valeria, now believing that the children were sincere, told her Mother Superior what had happened, but was tersely told to forget about such childish nonsense.

The following evening, when the four children came to pick up Gilberte Voisin, they saw the lady on the bridge again. But when they ran back to the Degeimbre's home to report that they'd seen the lady again, Mrs. Degeimbre was furious—she though that someone was playing a cruel practical joke on her children. To catch the culprit, Mrs. Degeimbre followed her children back to school the next night, bringing along some neighbor friends for protection. But no trickster showed up that evening, only the Blessed Mother.

That night, December 1, Our Lady appeared to the children four different times. The first time she came she appeared to the children above a hawthorn tree as soon as they began reciting the Hail Mary. The lovely lady looked to be about eighteen, with beautiful blue eyes and a bright smile. She wore a long, white, heavily-pleated gown without a sash. Rays of light emanated from her head and her dress reflected a bluish tinge. She held her hands together as if in prayer, and parted them whenever she disappeared.

Nothing was said that night by the lady. The following evening, December 2, Albert asked the lady if she was the Immaculate Virgin, and she smiled and nodded her head yes. When asked what she wanted from the children, Mary spoke to the children for the first time:

"Always be good."

Mary disappeared and re-appeared two more times that evening. On her third appearance Mary asked the children:

"Is it true you will always be good?"

"Yes!" a youthfully confident Andrée cried out. "We will always be good." The Blessed Virgin smiled and then disappeared for the rest of the night.

Several times that week the Blessed Virgin requested that they all be present at mass on December 8, the Solemnity of the Immaculate Conception. Expecting to see some Fátima-like miracle, a crowd of about

15,000 showed up for mass that evening. But nothing spectacular happened, except for the tests performed on the children by the skeptical doctors.

The Blessed Mother continued appearing to the children every night over the course of several weeks. On December 17, Our Lady asked for a chapel to be built in her honor, and a week later, on December 23, Fernande asked, "Why do you come?"

"That people might come here on pilgrimages."

On the first of January, the Solemnity of Mary, the Mother of God, Our Lady told Gilberte Voisin:

"Pray always."

The next day the Blessed Mother told the children that she would speak to them separately on January 3. On that day, a huge crowd was on hand for what would be Our Lady's final appearance in Beauraing. When Mary appeared she told all the children except Fernande their secret. The last thing she said before leaving was:

"I am the Mother of God, the Queen of Heaven. Pray always."

Then she left. Alone and disappointed, Fernande remained kneeling in the garden after Our Lady disappeared, while the other four children had been taken into the convent for questioning. Sad that Our Lady had somehow forgotten to give her a secret, Fernande was suddenly jolted by a loud clap of thunder and a flash of lightning that hit the hawthorn tree. All who were present realized by the flash that Mary had returned to Fernande. Our Lady asked Fernande:

"Do you love my Son?"

"Yes," Fernande replied.

"Do you love me?"

"Oh, yes."

"Then sacrifice yourself for me."

That was the last time Our Lady appeared to the five children in Beauraing.

The Blessed Virgin Mary's appearance in Beauraing evoked a tremendous response all over Europe. Over two million pilgrims visited Beauraing in 1933, and reports of miraculous cures were common. People who had fallen away from the Catholic Church or had joined the Socialist Party came back to the Catholic Church in droves. Conversions multiplied exponentially because of the apparitions.

Unexpectedly, just two weeks after her final appearance in Beauraing, Mary appeared to an eleven-year-old Catholic girl by the name of Mariette Beco in Banneux, Belgium, a poor little town about fifty miles to the northeast of Beauraing. Mariette was peering out the window on a cold, wintry evening on January 15, looking for her brother's return for supper, when she suddenly caught a glimpse of a luminous figure in her front yard. "Ah," Mariette said, as she gazed at the beautiful young lady dressed in a dazzling white gown, blue sash, and long, flowing veil that chastely covered her head and shoulders. Mariette could see that on the lady's right arm was a brilliant, diamond-like Rosary, with its golden chain and cross shimmering splendidly in her radiant light. Much to Mariette's surprise, despite the bitter cold, the lady wore no shoes.

Mariette yelled at her mother to quick, come see the beautiful lady. At first, Mariette's mother ignored her, but when curiosity got hold of her she finally came to the window to look for herself and saw some sort of luminous object, although not quite in the same detail that Mariette saw.

When Mariette looked out the window again after saying several decades of the Rosary, the young lady smiled and motioned for her to come outside. But Mariette's mother, out of fear for her daughter's safety, refused to let her go. By the time Mariette ran back to the window and threw open the curtain the lady had disappeared.

Mariette told her father what had happened, but he, being a fallen-away Catholic, refused to believe in such "rubbish." The next evening, trying to convince his daughter and his wife that what they were seeing was an optical illusion, Mariette's father tried several experiments to simulate the conditions that he thought would make it appear as if there were a luminous figure in the yard. He tried reflecting the light of a lamp off the windowpane, but that didn't work. He tried pouring water where the lady stood so it would freeze over and reflect light, but that didn't work either. There was just no way he could simulate the apparition.

For the next two nights, Mariette sat by the window waiting for the lady to return. Meanwhile, a girlfriend of Mariette's told the parish priest, Father Louis Jamin, that Mariette had seen a vision of a luminous lady. Reserving his opinion until all the facts were in, Father Jamin cautioned her not to repeat what she had just told him. He did, however, think it was odd that Mariette had showed a remarkable new enthusiasm for her Wednesday catechism lessons. Maybe there was something to this girl's story after all.

That night, on January 18, Mariette knelt down near the spot where the lady had appeared and began praying the Rosary. All of the sudden a star descended from the heavens, growing bigger and bigger as it came to rest within five feet of the young girl. It was the lady—she had come back to Mariette. When Mariette's father, Julien, peered out the window and saw his daughter frozen in a state of ecstasy, impervious to anything around her, he jumped on his bike and rode to town to get Father Jamin. When he couldn't locate the priest, he asked a practicing Catholic to come and take a look at his daughter. As they approached the Beco's house they saw Mariette walking down the street. When her worried father asked her where she was going, Mariette replied, "She's calling me."

Kneeling down several times along the way, Mariette finally stopped at a stream. The lady, guiding her all the way, said to Mariette:

> *"Plunge your hands into the water."*

Then the lady said:

> *"This spring is reserved for me. Goodnight. Au revoir."*

The lady rose into the sky and returned to heaven. The following night, January 19, the lady returned to Mariette and identified herself as "The Virgin of the Poor"—an appropriate title for 1933 because of the worldwide economic depression. The Blessed Virgin led Mariette back to the spring and the young girl, somewhat confused, asked Mary a simple question, "Why was the spring reserved for me?" The Blessed Mother couldn't help but laugh because Mariette had obviously misunderstood her. Mary said:

> *"This spring is reserved for all nations. To relieve the sick."*

Now Mariette understood—the spring was for healing. Within months pilgrims from all over the world were flocking to Banneux, and reports of miraculous cures came pouring in.

On February 15, Mariette asked the Blessed Virgin Mary for a sign from heaven so that people would know for sure that she was appearing. Mary looked at Mariette and smiled sweetly, saying:

> *"Believe in me, and I will believe in you."*

Our Lady appeared to Mariette for the last time on the evening of March 2, a cold and rainy night. As Mariette was praying, suddenly the rain clouds parted and the luminous figure of the Virgin Mary descended through the opening in the sky to where Mariette was kneeling. More radiant than ever, the Blessed Virgin Mary spoke to Mariette for the last time:

> *"I am the Mother of the Savior. Mother of God. Pray a lot. Adieu."*

Storm Clouds Gather Over Europe

In coming to Belgium in 1932-1933, Mary was preparing the world for the arrival of Adolf Hitler and his Nazi death camps, which Hitler first opened in

March of 1933 to house prisoners who were arrested for the burning of the German Reichstag on February 27, 1933.[1] Hitler used the Reichstag fire, which he blamed on the communists, as a pretext to consolidate his power base in Germany: non-Nazi governors, police chiefs, and city officials were kicked out of office; members of the Catholic Church were attacked; and Jewish enemies were arrested and deported to Dachau. The Jews, of course, were Hitler's primary target.

Hitler's attacks on Jews began in earnest on April Fool's Day, 1933, when he began enforcing a ban on all Jewish merchandise in Germany. A month later, Hitler staged a massive book-burning campaign across from the University of Berlin, protesting the writings of Jewish liberals and intellectuals. Two years later, in 1935, Hitler declared German Jews to be non-citizens of Germany— Jews couldn't marry or have sex with German citizens because they were considered racially impure, subhuman vermin. Hitler drew up plans to exile the Jews to other countries, but no one was willing to accept them. He then began rounding up Jews and putting them into Polish ghettos and Nazi concentration camps.

Trainloads of Jews began arriving in internment camps from all over Europe, creating tremendous overcrowding and a public health nightmare. Upon seeing that his internment camps were unmanageable, Hitler's "final solution" to the Jewish problem was their mass extermination. Beginning in 1941, huge crematoriums were built inside Nazi extermination camps that were capable of burning thousands of corpses per day (Hitler's preferred method of exterminating the Jews was to gas them in the concentration camp showers and then burn their remains).

Top priority was given to the transport of Jews to Nazi extermination camps, even over the transport of troops and armaments to the fronts. By the end of the war in 1945, two-thirds of European Jews and one-third of the world's Jews were exterminated in Hitler's death camps. A total of eleven million people perished in the camps, which were mostly located in Catholic Poland.

When Mary appeared in Belgium the storm clouds of war had already gathered over Europe. On October 14, 1933, Hitler withdrew from the League of Nations, dissolved the German Reichstag, and began a massive rearmament campaign in direct violation of the Treaty of Versailles, which he treated as a Jewish conspiracy. During the infamous "Night of the Long Knives" on June 30, 1934, approximately 200 storm troopers, the original SA "brownshirt" Nazis who helped bring Hitler to power, were executed without trial by the Gestapo for allegedly plotting to overthrow Hitler. All SA members were subsequently disarmed and the SS, the infamous death's head "blackshirts," became the Fuhrer's private army and security force under the second most powerful man in Germany—Heinrich Himmler.

Following the death of President Paul von Hindenburg, Chancellor Hitler became the president of Germany on August 19, 1934. With his rivals conveniently murdered and Himmler's SS protecting him, Hitler secured absolute power over 60 million Germans. But none of this would have happened if the German people hadn't wanted it—he mesmerized them with his thundering anti-Semitic speeches and promises of wealth and glory. For that, the German people were willing to follow Hitler anywhere—even to world war.

On March 7, 1936, the German army entered the Rhineland in direct violation of the Treaty of Versailles. Two years later, on March 12, 1938, Hitler invaded Austria, which signaled the beginning of World War II.

Mary, you recall, predicted in Fátima on July 13, 1917, that the start of a much worse war would be heralded by a light of unknown origin. On the night of January 25, 1938, an unknown blood-red light illuminated the skies over Europe, the Soviet Union, North Africa, and North America. Scientists called it an aurora borealis, but nothing like it had ever been seen before in recorded history. Just a year earlier, on May 6, 1937, the German dirigible Hindenburg had caught fire and exploded over Lakehurst, New Jersey, killing dozens. Both the burning dirigible and the unknown light were seen by many as omens of impending disaster coming from Germany.

Trying to avoid war at any cost, Britain's Prime Minister, Neville Chamberlain, handed over the Sudetenland region of Czechoslovakia to Hitler on September 30, 1938. Chamberlain's cowardice and appeasement in the face of Hitler's naked aggression convinced the Nazis that no one was willing to risk war to stop them, so they could do as they pleased, especially with the Jews. And so the holocaust began. On Crystal Night, November 9, 1938, Nazi thugs in Germany smashed Jewish shops, burned Jewish synagogues and homes, and indiscriminately killed more than 90 Jews in retaliation for the supposed assassination of the Third Secretary of the German Embassy in Paris, Ernst vom Rath, by a young Polish Jew, Herschel Feibel Grynspan.[2]

On March 15, 1939, an emboldened Adolf Hitler roared into Prague, Czechoslovakia, completely unopposed. Then on September 1, the German army blitzkrieged into Poland, and within weeks that once proud Catholic nation was totally annihilated and partitioned between Germany and the Soviet Union. Britain and France declared war on Germany immediately following the invasion of Poland, and in return, an angry Adolf Hitler vowed all out war in Europe. Hitler invaded Scandinavia on April 9, 1940, and steamrolled through Belgium the following month. Despite their courageous and heroic efforts, the Belgian defense forces were no match for the heavily armed *Wehrmacht*. The tiny Catholic nation of Belgium was taken in only a matter of days.

Just seven years prior to this, the Blessed Mother had been in Belgium requesting their prayers and sacrifices. The reason for her appearance now made perfect sense to the Belgians—a forerunner of the Antichrist had arrived in Europe and the fury of hell was being unleashed upon the world. Only God could save them now.

A Wolf in Sheep's Clothing

From the beginning of his life, Adolf Hitler was a satanic parody of Jesus Christ: Hitler was born a Catholic on April 20, 1889, the day before Easter, in an Austrian inn, the Gasthaus Zum Pommer in Braunau-am-Inn, while Jesus Christ, on the other hand, was born in a cave after his mother was turned away from an inn. Hitler hated his father, while Christ loved his. Christ was born a Jew, while Hitler hated Jews and was paranoid that his father was half-Jewish. [3] Hitler was born out of the incestuous union between his parents, who were uncle and niece, while Christ was born out of the holy union between an immaculate virgin and the Holy Spirit. Christ is our High Priest according to the order of Melchizedek, while Hitler considered becoming a priest as a young boy but grew to hate the Catholic Church. Hitler's name, Adolf, means Wolf, while Christ is the Lamb of God.

As a young boy, Adolf Hitler attended the Benedictine Monastery at Lambach from 1897 to 1899. He sang in the choir, went to mass daily, wanted to be a priest someday, and, at 15, was confirmed a Catholic by the bishop. But by the time of his confirmation, Hitler was already starting to hate the Catholic Church—he is even said to have spat on a Communion host when he joined Austria's anti-Catholic *Los Von Rome* (away from Rome) movement. [4]

Throughout his life, Hitler harbored deep-seated fears that his illegitimate father was half Jewish—a legend that has never been proven. [5] Because of this, Hitler developed an unhealthy attachment to his doting and overly protective mother, whose bulging eyes looked just like his. When she died of breast cancer at an early age Hitler, because he hated Jews, naturally blamed her Jewish doctor for her death.

As an adolescent, Hitler was shy, self-conscious, especially over the fact that he had only one testicle, and meticulously dressed to the point of an obsession. He liked painting and planned on applying to art school to study under some of Austria's finest instructors. Adolf's father, however, saw painting as too effeminate and tried to steer his son into a more manly profession like his, civil service. But despite his father's objections, Adolf was determined to become an artist.

Nominally talented in art, Hitler was turned down by the Jewish director of the Vienna Academy of Fine Arts when he applied for admission. This was another reason why Hitler hated the Jews—he blamed them, not himself, for his failed admission to art school. Doing the only thing he knew how, Hitler eked out a living by painting postcards for the windows of rich Jewish merchants, which made him hate them even more.

Wandering from one low-rent apartment to another, Hitler entertained himself for hours by reading books on philosophy, history, evolution, archaeology, world religion, cults, the occult, paganism, rune magic, astrology, Anthroposophy, Theosophy, Eastern mysticism, freemasonry, German folklore, the Knights Templar, Aryanism, anti-Semitism, and Nordic mythology by such notables authors as Madame Helena Blavatsky, Charles Darwin, Lanz von Liebenfels, Guido von List, Arthur Schopenhauer, Friedrich Nietzsche, and Rudolph Steiner. In addition to being a voracious reader, Hitler loved going to operas, especially Wagnerian operas. Richard Wagner, himself a notorious anti-Semite, was Hitler's favorite composer. It is said that Hitler attended Wagner's *Rienzi, Parsifal,* and *Tristan and Isolde* dozens of times each.[6]

Evil books and Wagnerian operas turned Hitler into a superstitious, Christian-hating, anti-Semitic, paranoid schizophrenic. He began having delusions of grandeur about himself being a Nordic messiah, believing it was his destiny to resurrect the master race of blond-haired, blue-eyed Aryans. Apparently, something foreign and extraordinarily powerful was possessing Hitler. He frequently spoke to his closest friends about the "voices" he heard inside his head that were in charge of his life, and he just knew that somehow, someday, these voices would lead him to greatness.

In August of 1914, with both parents dead and his economic future looking bleak, Hitler fell down on his knees and "thanked Heaven" when World War I broke out. The whole of Europe hadn't been at war since the time of Napoleon Bonaparte a hundred years earlier, and was eagerly awaiting the "general war" that Mary had foretold would come in La Salette. But those anxious for war were in for a rude awakening—modern technology had forever changed the theater of war. With the recent invention of machine guns, chemical weapons, improved artillery, and mechanized armor, generals trained in nineteenth-century warfare were ill-prepared for the carnage of the twentieth century.

Millions of lives were lost in the first couple of years of WW I. The war that was expected to last only several months turned into a grueling trench warfare that would drag on for four long years and claim over ten million lives. The entire resources of the European economies had to be mobilized. Private industry retooled for making armaments and everyone sacrificed. Food and supplies were rationed, while anything of value was requisitioned by the governments for the war.

As a lance corporal in the army, Adolf Hitler served as a dispatch messenger for the German High Command—one of the most dangerous assignments in WW I. Dispatchers hand delivered messages from trench to trench, and more often than not, a sniper's bullet was waiting for them as soon as they left the security of the trenches. Miraculously though, Hitler managed to evade that one bullet with his name on it, making him a legend amongst his comrades. Hitler bragged to them of his invincibility and of the supernatural protection that was guarding his life. He was, however, wounded twice, and received the Iron Cross for bravery and valor.

While in the hospital recuperating from being temporarily blinded by mustard gas, Hitler's voices said that he had been "selected by God to be Germany's messiah, and would save Germany from the claws of International Jewry."[7] Hitler's blinding and his great commission to save Germany was, of course, a satanic parody of the blinding of St. Paul on the road to Damascus and his great commission.

When WW I ended, Hitler was employed by the German army to secretly infiltrate and report on right-wing radical groups such as the Thule Society. The Thule Society, which later evolved into the Nazi Party, was a secret, right-wing, occultic, fascist, anti-communist, anti-Semitic organization that championed pan-Germanic nationalism and the overthrow of the Treaty of Versailles. It was during Hitler's investigations of the Thule Society that he secretly joined their ranks on October 19, 1919, as member No. 555 (the first two fives were fictitious to make the party look bigger).

Besides the Thule Society, many occult groups spread throughout Germany after WW I, including the Rosicrucians, the Anthroposophists, the Theosophists, the Freemasons, and the Vril Society (an occultic, gnostic group sometimes referred to as the Luminous Lodge). The Thule Society (a hard-core, neo-Cathar, anti-Semitic group named after a mythical, Scandinavian, hyperborean, Aryan culture existing sometime before the dawn of recorded history) was based partly upon the heretical doctrines of thirteenth-century Catharism, which as previously mentioned in chapter 2, incorporated the heresies of Manichaeanism, Zoroastrianism, and Gnosticism into its creeds.

Hitler joined the Thule Society at age 30, the same age as Christ was when he began his public ministry. A year later, in 1920, the Thule Society evolved into the German Workers' Party, which later became the National Socialist German Worker's Party (NSDAP) or "Nazis" for short. The Nazis chose as their emblem the "crooked cross" (swastika), because they thought it equal in power and symbolism to the Christian cross and Jewish Star of David. The swastika was an ancient design revered in India and the Far East, and ironically, was on the coat of arms of the Benedictine Monastery at Lambach, which graced the arched entryway that Hitler passed through everyday as a young boy.[8]

One of the Nazi's chief ideologues was Alfred Rosenberg, an Estonian-born early member of the Thule Society and assistant to one of the Thule's chief leaders, Dietrich Eckart. Rosenberg, who also went by the pseudonym Rolf Eidhalt—an anagram of Adolf Hitler which means "Oath Keeper"—wrote numerous anti-Semitic articles in Thulian tracts and newspapers in the early

1920s and authored an anti-Semitic book entitled *The Myth of the Twentieth Century,* which was meant to depict the German race as superior to the Jewish. Rosenberg's *Myth* and a forged book called *The Protocols of the Learned Elders of Zion,* which purported to reveal details of an international Jewish conspiracy to dominate the world, became the two bibles of early Nazism. The third bible was Hitler's autobiography, *Mein Kampf* (My Struggle), written when Hitler was imprisoned in 1924 for trying to overthrow the German government.[9]

Rosenberg's *Myth,* in turn, was adapted from Houston Stewart Chamberlain's (1855-1927) two books, *The Foundation of the Nineteenth Century* and *Race and History,* both of which advocated anti-Semitism, master and slave races, and a pan-Germanic new world order. Chamberlain's anti-Semitic books were first introduced to Germany at the turn of the century by Kaiser Wilhelm II. Chamberlain imparted to the kaiser that only Germany was fit to rule over the scientific new world order, and the kaiser, in turn, introduced the German officer corps to Chamberlainism. Hitler's *Mein Kampf* (My Struggle) was basically a rehash of Chamberlainism.

Firmly grounded in the anti-Semitism of Rosenberg and Chamberlain, Hitler's thundering anti-Semitic oratories quickly gained him an enthusiastic following within the Thule Society's *Frei Corps* (free army), who were convinced that Hitler was the messiah of the German people. The leader of the Thule Society, Dietrich Eckart, saw in this electrifying young orator the chosen one predestined to lead the Aryan people to final victory over the Jews. Josef Goebbels, the Nazi's minister of propaganda, went so far as to say that Hitler was Jesus Christ incarnate, or at least St. John the Baptist. With such an enthusiastic following of worshipers within the Thule Society, Hitler prepared himself to begin, according to his voices, his "mission from God."

On November 9, 1923, Hitler led a coup d'état (the "Beer Hall Putsch") against the German national government, but it failed and Hitler was arrested and sentenced on April Fool's Day to five years in prison. While in prison, Hitler dictated his *Mein Kampf* to his assistant Rudolph Hess, and was then freed after serving only eight months in jail. Hitler's two objectives after he was released were to reorganize the German National Socialist Workers Party, which had been banned after the Beer Hall Putsch, and gain control of the German government. He succeeded in both—in just eight years time, as head of the Nazi Party, Hitler was elected Chancellor of Germany.

When Hitler came to power over Germany in 1933 he banned all occult groups in Germany except, of course, his own Nazi Party. Members of other occult groups were sent to Nazi concentration camps or just simply disappeared. By doing so, Hitler concealed his party's satanic origins and eliminated any potential rivals, thereby establishing for himself an air of legitimacy and respectability in the eyes of the international community. With his occult roots now cleverly concealed, Hitler was set to rebuild

Germany into a mystical, pseudo-religious, neo-Cathar kingdom, with himself as the new German messiah.

Medieval gnostic Christian orders such as the Teutonic Knights and the Knights Templar heavily influenced Hitler's social and political reorganization of Germany, as did the Catholic Church. Heinrich Himmler's SS patterned itself after the slavishly obedient Jesuit order, wearing all black uniforms and using Saint Ignatius Loyola's *Spiritual Exercises* as a training manual for officers. Copying the twelve mythical Knights of the Round Table and the twelve apostles of Christ, Himmler always dined with 12 top SS generals—never more, never less.[10] Hitler liked to rib Himmler about this practice, calling him "my Ignatius Loyola." A former Catholic like Hitler, Himmler was much more involved in occult practices than the Fuhrer. Himmler frequently consulted astrological tables and the writings of the mid-sixteenth-century soothsayer Nostradamus to validate Hitler's grandiose predictions of world conquest.

The Prophecies of Nostradamus

Nostradamus was a sixteenth-century French-Jewish physician who converted to Catholicism to avoid suspicion from the Catholic Inquisition because he was practicing the black arts of astrology, soothsaying, and magic, and he knew that if he got caught he would be burned at the stake.[11] Writing in coded messages called quatrains, Nostradamus was highly regarded by the royalty and nobility of his day for his amazingly accurate predictions. By the time of his death, in the year 1566, Nostradamus correctly predicted a young monk's election to the papacy, the death of a king in a joust, King Charles I's execution and the English Civil War, the fire that destroyed London in 1666, the year his coffin would be unearthed (1791), the French Revolution, the overthrow of the French monarchy, the rise of Napoleon, and the rise of Adolf Hitler. In 1555, Nostradamus published several amazing quatrains in his prophecies that speak of the coming of Adolf Hitler, whom he enigmatically referred to as Hister:[12]

> "In the depths of Western Europe,
> a young child will be born of poor people,
> who will seduce many people with his oratory.
> His reputation will grow even greater in the kingdom of the East." [13]

> "Beasts wild with hunger will cross rivers.
> The greater part of the field will be against Hister.
> The great one will be dragged in an iron cage
> when the child of Germany observes nothing."[14]

Hitler's New Religion

As the new messiah of the German people, Hitler ordered Himmler to research world religions and prepare a new religious doctrine for his Thousand-Year Reich, a religion which would be based on Germanic neo-paganism, earth worship, Nordic mythology, occultism, Eastern mysticism, and bastardized Christianity. In this new religion, Hitler would be the Supreme Pontiff and would take the place of Jesus Christ, and Himmler would be the Reich Minister of Religion. Wewelsburg Castle, SS headquarters, would be the Reich's "Vatican," and Nazi holy days would be celebrated on January 30 and November 9. Since orthodox Christianity was antithetical to Naziism, the teaching of Christianity would be banned from all schools and the German children would learn new prayers to Hitler:

> "Adolf Hitler, you are our great leader. Thy name makes the enemy tremble. Thy Reich comes, thy will alone is law upon the Earth. Let us hear daily thy voice and order us by thy leadership, for we will obey to the end with our lives. We praise thee! Heil Hitler!"[15]

> "Fuhrer, Fuhrer, sent to me from God. Protect and maintain me throughout life. Thou hast saved Germany from the deepest need, I thank thee today for my daily bread. Remain at my side and never leave, Fuhrer. My Fuhrer, my faith, my light, Heil Mein Fuhrer."[16]

> "Jesus and Hitler. As Jesus freed men from sin and Hell, so Hitler freed the German people from destruction. Jesus and Hitler were persecuted, but while Jesus was crucified Hitler was raised to the Chancellorship. Jesus strove for Heaven, Hitler for the Germanic people."[17]

Hitler taught the German schoolchildren that Jesus Christ was a bastard child of a Roman soldier who probably raped a Moabite or Elamite woman, and most certainly wasn't a Jew.[18]

According to Hitler, Jesus Christ wasn't the founder of the Catholic Church as the pope claimed, but was some sort of New Age, cosmic spirit like Hitler. The coming of Adolf Hitler heralded a new world order, a thousand year period of unbridled optimism and heaven on earth. The Aryans would be the master race and Hitler their savior. The inferior races, like the Jews, the Slavs, and the gypsies, would be the servants of Aryan man, or eliminated altogether.

To realize his dream, Hitler turned to the occult for power. He spent hundreds of thousands of dollars searching for the Holy Grail (the wine cup of the Last Supper). Legend had it that whoever possessed the Holy Grail or the Spear of Longinus (the lance that was thrust into Christ's side) would have power to rule the world. The Arthurian legends of the thirteenth century, popularized by Wagner's *Parsifal*, had convinced Hitler that the Holy Grail was last possessed by the Cathars in the southern region of France, so Hitler ordered Himmler's SS to search out the castles in that region. But Hitler never found the Holy Grail. He did, however, know where the Spear of Longinus was—in the Hofburg museum in Vienna. When Hitler invaded Austria in 1938, his first priority was to personally confiscate the spear from the museum. Now with the Spear of Longinus in his possession, Hitler finally had the power to rule the world—or so he thought.

In the first two years of WW II, Hitler won a succession of quick, easy victories against Poland, the Netherlands, Belgium, Norway, Denmark, France, Greece, Bulgaria, Yugoslavia, and Northern Africa. But then his fortunes changed. The Allies cracked the German deciphering and encoding machine (Enigma), Allied sonar and radar began zeroing in on Nazi submarines, the horrible Russian winter of 1941-1942 halted Germany's advance on Moscow, the British routed Rommel in North Africa in 1942, Hitler's Sixth Army was captured by the Russians in Stalingrad in 1943, and around the clock Allied aerial bombing devastated Germany's cities and war-making capabilities. The Allied invasion of Normandy (Operation Overlord) on June 6, 1944, sealed Hitler's fate forever—by the spring of 1945, the war in Europe was lost and Hitler contemplated suicide—the coward's way out.

Having miraculously escaped a bullet in WW I, and having survived eleven assassination attempts on his life, Adolf Hitler committed suicide in his Feuhrerbunker, 55 feet beneath the Reichschancellory in Berlin. Just before he committed suicide, Hitler was married to Eva Braun by a municipal official named Herr Wagner. Afterwards, Hitler shot Eva and then turned the gun on himself.[19] Before Hitler committed suicide he left instructions with his aids to take their bodies outside the bunker and douse them with gasoline and then set them on fire. His orders carried out, the remains of Germany's false messiah went up in flames on April 30, 1945—Walpurgis Night—a satanic feast day preceding the first day of the month of May, a month dedicated to the Blessed Virgin Mary.

The Coming Antichrist

As previously mentioned, Adolf Hitler was a wolf in sheep's clothing—promising heaven, delivering hell. He wasn't the Antichrist that the Bible speaks of—he was a forerunner of the Antichrist. When the real Antichrist comes, he, too, will be a Catholic; someone high up in the Catholic Church like a bright, shining star—probably an archbishop or pope. Some have predicted the 266th pope (John Paul II is the 264th) to be the Antichrist. Whoever he is, the Antichrist will be a member of Christ's inner circle, like Judas Iscariot and Lucifer. After practicing chastity he will give in to lust, after living in poverty he will succumb to greed, after vowing obedience he will thirst for power. He will sit in the sanctuary of God, the Holy of Holies, and declare himself to be God. He will do away with the sacrifice of Holy Communion and use the power and knowledge of the First and Second Beasts to have himself worshiped in the place of God. His persecutions of Jews and Christians will make Adolf Hitler's look tame. There will never have been so much suffering in all the world as when the Antichrist comes.

To beget the Antichrist, Satan will unite with a lascivious women and incarnate himself into human flesh, as Jesus incarnated himself into a virgin and became man. When that happened, or will happen, no one knows. Right now we are in the period following the forerunners of the Antichrist (Hitler, Lenin, Stalin). The chastisement or purification of the earth is the next event prophesied to come and is expected to be in this generation. When it comes, billions of people will perish. Whether the Antichrist will be born before or after the chastisement no one knows. But we do know from the dictations of the Italian mystic, Maria Valtorta, that a short period of peace will follow the chastisement and the earth will be spiritually renewed. Christ will pour out his spirit upon those still alive at that time and the Catholic Church will be recognized as the One True Church. After the Catholic Church has its Palm Sunday, its Hosanna day, then it will be the time of its Passion—the coming of Antichrist and the final satanic period before the end of the world. The period of time between the chastisement and the coming of the Antichrist will be a short one, not a literal thousand years as millenarianists think.

If Hitler wasn't the Antichrist, was he demonically possessed? Absolutely. We can be certain of that by the numerous telltale signs of demonic possession: his hearing voices; his obsessive hatred of Jews and Catholics; his delusions of grandeur; his feelings of invincibility; his fascination with the occult; his belief that he could predict the future; his belief that he was God; his wanting to remake man in his own image[20]; his going into an altered state of consciousness while he spoke in public; his going into a rage anytime someone mentioned Jews around him (during which he would spread his arms and act as if he were crucified). All these maniacal personality traits point to demonic possession.

Furthermore, Hitler was known to have been haunted by night demons. He was petrified of the dark and was afraid to go to sleep at night, often staying awake until daybreak. Sentries had to be posted outside his door for him to sleep. Sometimes they reported hearing Hitler scream unintelligibly that they were there to get him. Strange, unearthly sounds and voices hounded him continually. Hitler's left arm trembled uncontrollably and the panicked look in his bulging eyes towards the end of the war revealed the torment going on inside his mind. The powerful evil possessing Hitler also affected those closest to him. Six of the seven women he had intimate relations with—which included Unity Mitford, his half-niece Geli Raubals, and Eva Braun—all committed suicide or at least attempted it.

Arthur Schopenhauer

Any biography of Hitler and the Nazis would be incomplete without at least mentioning three nineteenth-century German intellectuals who were ideological forerunners of the Nazis—Arthur Schopenhauer, Richard Wagner, and Friedrich Nietzsche.

In his two books, *On the Will and Nature* and *The World as Will*, Arthur Schopenhauer (1788-1860) introduced the atheistic philosophical idea that life is but an illusion and the world is but a reflection of our own will. Borrowing from Schopenhauer's atheistic and pessimistic ideologies, Hitler convinced himself that with the strength of his own will, he could be the one to lead Germany out of the despair of WW I back into its former grandeur and glory of the Second Reich. Leni Riefenstahl's epic documentary of the 1934 Nazi rally in Nuremburg, *Triumph of the Will*, glorified Hitler's powerful will to resurrect Germany to greatness again.

Richard Wagner

Hitler's favorite composer was a mid-nineteenth-century German named Richard Wagner (1813-1883). Like Hitler, Wagner hated Jews, whom he lambasted as an inferior race. In his *Judaism in Music,* Wagner wrote that the entire Jewish race was incapable of achieving the highest levels of culture. In fact, Wagner told his second wife, Cosima, that all Jews "should be burned at a performance of Nathan" (SS concentration camp officers played Wagner as they fed their crematoriums with Jewish corpses). Wagner's operas and anti-Semitic writings left such a deep impression on Hitler that he saw Wagner's *Tristan and Isolde* and *Die Meistersinger* at least 100 times each. Hitler's favorite opera, though, was Wagner's *Parsifal,* in which the character of the Parsifilian Christ, in whom Hitler closely identified with, "disdains to be crucified and chooses to live on." Hitler admitted to his closest circle of confidants that he "built up his religion out of *Parsifal.*"

Hitler idolized Wagner, calling him "the greatest prophetic figure the German people have had." At a visit to Wagner's grave, Hitler said his heart "burst with pride" when he recognized his own "psychological kinship with this great man." But Richard Wagner was no great man; he was a racist, a radical, a rebel, a pervert, a degenerate, an adulterer, a wife-stealer, a promoter of incest, a self-absorbed tyrant, an egoist, a blasphemer, and an anti-Christian, free-thinking atheist given to frequent bouts of self-consciousness, depression, loneliness, paranoia, thoughts of suicide, mania, and uncontrollable bursts of anger.

Friedrich Nietzsche—
The Philosophical Antichrist

One of Richard Wagner's best friends and personal admirers, before they got mad at each other and went their separate ways, was Friedrich Wilhelm Nietzsche (1844-1900)—a brilliant nineteenth-century philosopher and linguist from Germany, now recognized as one of the most important philosophers of the nineteenth century. More than any other philosopher, Nietzsche's extremely irreverent, anti-Christian writings encouraged the godless ideologies of the twentieth century, especially within the Nazi Party. Adored by the Nazis, Nietzsche endorsed the overthrow of Christianity, the creation of master and slave races, the selective breeding of a new race of Aryan supermen, the superiority of the heroic German spirit, the propitiatory value of war, and the taking of power by the strong-willed, ruling caste elite.

Nietzsche's anti-Christian writings were a favorite of fascists, radicals, anarchists, libertines, socialists, secular humanists, and bohemians of every stripe—particularly in Germany. They were so nihilistic, so negative, so Dionysian, and so irreverent that they were adopted for just about every profane, rebellious cause imaginable. Non-christian professors at the German universities loved Nietzsche because his books were pure dynamite in the hands of their young, gullible readers not solidly grounded in the Bible and their Christian faith. Continuing to this day, many a young boy and girl have gone off to college only to have his or her belief in Christianity utterly destroyed by Friedrich Nietzsche.

Never one to parse his words, Nietzsche called Christianity a decadent, effeminate, life-negating anachronism, deeming it the "world of pure fiction" and the "greatest misfortune" inflicted upon mankind to date. He claimed that Jesus Christ was an "idiot" and a "sneak," and the Catholic Church was "hostile to life." The Church's notion of morality, Nietzsche said, was "anti-nature," and their concept of "sin" was "an invention against science."

To get a better idea where Nietzsche was coming from, one should know a little about his life. Friedrich Wilhelm Nietzsche was born in a small German village on October 15, 1844, the son of a Lutheran minister. Born nearly blind, Nietzsche was extremely myopic and had to wear thick, coke-bottle lenses to see (his bulging eyes were similar to Hitler's). Bad vision, migraine headaches, and extremely poor health plagued Nietzsche his entire life; no doubt contributing to the lifelong torment he suffered. Named after Friedrich Wilhelm IV, King of Prussia, young Nietzsche was raised in a devout Christian home—his father, his uncles, and both his grandfathers were pastors. Growing up, Friedrich was a pious and talented boy who loved to write poetry, and planned on becoming a Lutheran minister like his father someday—that is, until he went to college. While at Bonn and Leipzig Universities, Nietzsche was introduced for the first time to the godless, anti-Christian writings of Darwin, Schopenhauer, Feuerbach, Spinoza, Rousseau, Goethe, Hume, and Wagner. After the evil books he read totally destroyed his Christian faith, Nietzsche decided to become a professor of linguistics instead of a minister. As a professor of philology (linguistics) at Basel University, Nietzsche quickly gained a following for his irreverent writings and speeches, which were permeated with sarcasm, biting satire, satanic diatribe, and anti-Christian blasphemy. To put it politely, Nietzsche was a wise cracker.

Nietzsche heartlessly encouraged the elimination of the weak, the poor, the disinherited, and the physically impaired from the face of the earth. Ironically, Nietzsche's own physical infirmities eventually forced him to give up his chair at Basel in 1870, and for the remainder of his life he was a drug-addicted, sickly pariah. (In a bit of symbolism, Nietzsche collapsed on Christmas day in 1875, and another time nearly choked to death on a fish-bone, which he saw as full of meaning.) A loner and a sickly recluse, Nietzsche wandered about Europe searching for the right climate and the right cure to relieve his chronic pain and illnesses, but he never found them.

As Nietzsche's health worsened his hatred for Christianity also worsened, becoming more and more evident in his writings. For example, Nietzsche advocated the replacement of Christianity with a new religion of human science—one that would create a superior, worthier race of men, free of the genetically weak and the physically handicapped. He predicted these Aryan supermen (overmen) would someday rule the world, and would be led by a strong-willed, merciless leader who would put Nietzsche's godless ideologies into action. That strong-willed, merciless man turned out to be Adolf Hitler, which made Nietzsche seem like an incredible prophet to the Nazis.

Nietzsche knew that only after his own death would his prophecies and ideologies be recognized as those of a great sage. He relished in the disasters and holocausts that he predicted would come during the twentieth century, and the coming of that strong-willed, merciless leader. But Nietzsche never lived to see those days: he went insane in 1889, the same year Hitler was born, and died in 1900, the first year of the twentieth century he predicted would be so violent.[21]

Friedrich Nietzsche's tremendous influence on the historical events in the twentieth century cannot be understated. For a sampling of some of Nietzsche's most infamous quotes, turn to Appendix B.

Chapter Eleven

Our Lady of Mount Carmel: Garabandal, Spain 1961-1965

"Russia will spread her errors, causing wars and persecutions. The good will be martyred . . . "

Our Lady of Fátima, 1917

"A time will certainly come when people will no longer believe in the truth of our apparitions; no one or almost no one; very few at any rate. We ourselves will one day deny them. When the great majority of people no longer believe, then the great Miracle will come."

Conchita to Avelina Gonzalez, 1961

The Spanish Civil War

The communist pogrom against Christianity in western Europe started in Catholic Spain during the time of the great global depression. In the late 1920s, economic depression had hit Spain hard and its military government under General Primo de Rivera was on the verge of total collapse. Thereafter, many disgruntled peasants, urban workers, union leaders, intellectuals, and students became enamored with the Spanish Communist Party's pie-in-the-sky promises of economic prosperity. Consequently, Primo de Rivera was forced to leave office in January of 1930, and the following year, King Alfonso XIII, the figurehead Spanish monarch, fled the country. A new Spanish Republic with strong ties to the Soviet Union was formed in 1931, and Spanish communists celebrated by burning down 200 Catholic churches.[1] In May and June of 1931, Spain's anti-Catholic leader, Manuel Azaña, vehemently attacked pro-Catholics in the army, wealthy capitalists, and the hierarchy of the Catholic

213

Church: the Jesuits were expelled from Spain, Catholic parochial schools were outlawed, loyalist army officers were dismissed, private estates were confiscated, and banks and railroads were nationalized.[2]

As in the French and Russian Revolutions, following the formation of the Spanish Republic, Catholic churches, monasteries, convents, libraries, and schools were either desecrated or destroyed, and for the first time since the Moorish invasion, Catholicism ceased to be the official religion of Spain. Manuel Azaña proudly boasted to the Spanish legislature in 1931 that "Today, Spain has ceased to be Catholic."

As soon as it became clear that Manuel Azaña was turning Spain into a godless Soviet satellite, Spanish patriots loyal to the Catholic Church (the Traditionalist Communion or "Carlists") began mass demonstrations. Because of their demonstrations, the Republican government of Spain changed hands eighteen times from 1931 to 1936.[3]

To counter the growing Catholic opposition, an extremely left-wing movement called the Spanish Popular Front was organized in 1936, composed mainly of hard-core Freemasons, Socialists, communists, anti-Catholics, Syndicalists, and Basque and Catalan nationalists. Like the Communist Party in the Soviet Union, members of the newly-formed Popular Front had no qualms about resorting to the worst forms of violence and terrorism, and were suspected in the July 13, 1936 assassination of the former finance minister under General Primo de Rivera, Calvo Sotelo.

With armed confrontation between the pro-Catholic Nationalists and the pro-communist Republicans a certainty, the final straw was reached when the leader of the left-wing Republicans, José Giral, promised to speed up the seizure of the remainder of Spain's privately-held farms. Consequently, a pro-Nationalist army revolt broke out on July 18, 1936, which marked the beginning of the Spanish Civil War between the Republicans and the Nationalists.

During this horrible and bloody civil war, which cost the lives of hundreds of thousands of Spaniards, liberal ideologues and communist sympathizers from Western nations volunteered by the thousands to fight on the side of the Republicans. Tragically though, most of these Westerners were unaware that the Republicans whom they were fighting for were at the same time torturing and murdering thousands of innocent priests, monks, and nuns.

Mary's prophesy at Fátima about the spread of Russia's errors and the martyr of the good was fulfilled again during the Spanish Civil War. By war's end in 1939, Spanish Republicans had massacred over 6,800 Catholic priests and religious—many by torture of the cruelest kind. Historian Warren Carroll described the communist-led Spanish Civil War for what it really was—an all out satanic war against the Catholic Church:

> "Almost at once the holocaust of Spain began. The chief target of the revolution was not the wealthy capitalists nor even persons known or thought

to be associated with the military rising [Carlists], but the Catholic Church. During the next three months, the priests and the religious and laity of the Church in Spain who were caught in the half of the county where the Republic [Azaña] retained control, were the victims of the bloodiest persecution the Church has experienced since that of the Roman Emperor Diocletian in the fourth century. In all, 6,549 priests and 283 nuns were martyred, many in the classic circumstances of martyrdom, when they were offered life if they renounced their faith and death if they upheld it. Eighty per cent of them died between July 19 and October 1 [1936]. About a quarter of all the priests in the area retained by the Republic were killed. Thirteen bishops were martyred. In the diocese of Barbastro in Aragon, where the ferocious anarchist Buenaventura Duruti commanded in the first days of the war, 123 of 140 priests perished. In Cuidad Real in the center of Spain, the bishop and every single priest of the diocese were murdered; not one escaped."[4]

At the onset of the Spanish Civil War, anti-Catholics, leftist intellectuals, and communist sympathizers in the Western media were able to convince the American people that the Spanish Republicans were fighting for the ideals of democracy over Spanish fascism. Even today, many historians still portray the Soviet-backed Spanish Popular Front to have been a Republic of the people, by the people, and for the people. But in truth, the Spanish Republic was a ruthless, murderous, tyrannical, anti-Christian, anti-capitalistic, totalitarian regime that was armed and funded by the Soviet Union.

The popular right-wing Catholic leader of the Nationalist uprising, Generalissimo Franco, whom the liberal Western media likened to Hitler, had no choice but to turn to the Axis powers for military assistance after Western democracies refused him help against the communists. But Franco was no Nazi; his pro-Catholic Nationalists were fighting for the very ideals we Americans hold sacred: freedom of speech, freedom of assembly, freedom of religion, and freedom of commerce. In fact, when World War II broke out, Franco infuriated Hitler and Mussolini when he refused to fight along side them against the Allies (although, understandably, Franco did send a division of Spanish volunteers to fight with Germany against the Soviet Union).

Only with military aid supplied by Germany was Franco's pro-Catholic Nationalists able to defeat the Soviet-equipped Spanish Republicans in 1939; thereupon, restoring freedom of worship and freedom of religious education to Spain. After the defeat of the Spanish communists, much to the displeasure of the Western media and the U.N. which ostracized him, Generalissimo Franco remained the undisputed chief of state of Spain until 1975 when he picked Prince Juan Carlos of Bourbon to be king. Under King Juan Carlos I, Spain's economy flourished and the Spanish Catholic Church was rebuilt to its former greatness. The Spanish Communist Party, on the other hand, all but withered away.

Mary Appears in Catholic Spain

In the tiny, isolated mountain village of San Sebastian de Garabandal in northern Spain, the Blessed Virgin Mary, accompanied by St. Michael the Archangel, appeared over 2,000 times to four pre-teen girls—Conchita and Jacinta González, Mari Loli, and Mari Cruz—from 1961 to 1965, asking for sacrifices, prayers, penance, and frequent reception of the Holy Eucharist. Like the visionaries from La Salette and Fátima, the Blessed Mother warned the four girls of an imminent world-wide Chastisement, which would be preceded first by a Warning, followed shortly thereafter by a Miracle, and then a visible, permanent, supernatural Sign for all the world to see.

The Warning

The first to come will be the Warning. Mari Loli knows the year it will come and, according to Conchita, it will warn the wicked and bring the good closer to God. It will be like a mini-chastisement, but shorter in duration. Everyone will be afraid, but Catholics who know about Garabandal will be able to bear it better. The Warning will be visible to everyone in the world and people will know that it comes from God. In that instant, everyone, believer and unbeliever alike, will be able to see the true condition of his or her soul. People will feel it bodily and spiritually, and unbelievers will feel the fear of God inside them, some for the first time. It will be like fire, but it will not burn. It will come suddenly and formidably—like an earthquake but much worse. Many will die of fright because of it. Jacinta said of the Warning:

> "The Warning is something that is first seen in the air, everywhere in the world and immediately is transmitted into the interior of souls. It will last for a little time, but it will seem a very long time because of its effects within us. It will be for the good of our souls, in order to see in ourselves our conscience... the good that we have failed to do, and the bad that we have done. Then we will feel a great love towards our heavenly Parents and ask forgiveness for all our offenses. The Warning is for everybody because God wants our salvation. The Warning is for us to draw closer to Him and to increase our faith. Therefore, one should prepare for that day, but not await it with fear. God does not send things for the sake of fear but rather with justice and love. He does it for the good of all his children so that they might enjoy eternal happiness and not be lost."[5]

On January 1, 1965 (the Solemnity of Mary, Mother of God), the Blessed Mother made known to Conchita the details of the Warning. The Warning itself will be preceded by a pre-warning. The main Warning is designed to bring the good closer to God and to warn the wicked of their plight. Although

Conchita was told not to reveal the contents of the Warning, she did give us a hint of its characteristics on September 13 and 14, and October 22, 1965:

"Everyone will be afraid, but Catholics will bear it with more resignation than others... The Warning will come directly from God. It will be visible in every part of the world no matter where we live... It will be like an interior realization of our sins. Believers as well as unbelievers, wherever they are at that time, will see and feel it... Oh! yes, the Warning will be very formidable! A thousand times more than earthquakes. It will be like fire; it will not burn our flesh, but we will feel it corporeally and interiorly. All nations and every person on earth will feel it. No one shall escape it. And unbelievers will feel the fear of God... One day, we are going to suffer a horrible catastrophe in all parts of the world. No one will escape. It would be preferable to die than to bear for five minutes that which awaits us. It will only last a short time... We could suffer in the daytime as well as the night, whether we are in bed or not. If we die during that time, it will be of fright. I think the best place to be at that time would be in church, near the Blessed Sacrament. Jesus would give us the strength necessary to bear it... It will be a horror of the worst kind. If only I could tell you how the Virgin described it to me! But the Chastisement, that will be worse... We will understand that the Warning comes to us because of our sins... It can happen at any moment. I am expecting it every day... If we but knew what it consists of, we would be horrified in the extreme... We cannot image how much we offend God. The Blessed Mother told me that people know very well there is a heaven and a hell. But can't we see that we think about it only through fear and not love of God?... On account of our sins, we have only ourselves to blame for the Warning. And we must suffer it for Jesus; for the offenses committed against God..."[6]

On August 15, 1972 (the Solemnity of the Assumption of Mary), Conchita González elaborated more on the Warning:

"I [Conchita] want to tell you that first will come the Warning, which is like a chastisement; but it will not injure the body. It will, however, cause us to suffer. Afterwards, if we do not change in spite of all these things (which are truly the last warnings—the last remedies that God will send) He will send us a Chastisement...."[7]

The Miracle

Shortly after the Warning, a Miracle at Garabandal will occur. Conchita knows when the Miracle will take place but cannot reveal its date. The presence of the visionaries won't be necessary for the Miracle to happen, which God will perform at the request of the Blessed Virgin Mary. There will be a general disbelief in Garabandal right before the Miracle happens: even the visionaries' families will believe the seers have lied. The doubts will be caused by the length of time people will have to wait. Before the Miracle transpires, the seers will contradict each other and discredit the apparitions—then the Miracle will come. The Miracle will be announced eight days in advance by Conchita, who knows the date of the Miracle's occurrence. It will be greater than the Miracle of the Sun at Fátima and will be seen in Garabandal and the surrounding countryside. The sick who will be present will be cured. It will be possible to film it. Sinners and non-believers will be converted. The Miracle will take place at 8:30 in the evening, on the feast of a great martyr who was devoted to the Holy Eucharist. It will coincide with an important event in the Catholic Church and will last approximately ten to fifteen minutes.

In an interview on July 27, 1975 with Mari Loli, Needles (now Garabandal magazine) was told that not more than a year would elapse between the Warning and the Miracle, and that on the day of the Warning, the earth would stand still: everything would stop, including the planes in the air. The Warning, which Mari said is near, will last only a few minutes and will make everyone see themselves and their sins as God sees them.[8] It will be horrifying!

The Sign

Immediately after the Miracle has passed, a Sign will remain in the pines at Garabandal for all the world to see. It will be visible, supernatural, and permanent. It will be possible to film the Sign, but not to feel or touch it. Sick persons will be healed and unbelievers will be converted. A blind man, Joey Lomangino, will gain his sight on that day. The pope will see it, and so will Padre Pio (before he died in 1968, Padre Pio testified to his close friend, Fr. Bernardino Cenamo, that he, indeed, saw the Miracle).[9] The Miracle and Sign will be sent as proof of the apparitions of Garabandal and testimony to the Blessed Virgin Mary's appearance there. It will save many souls.

The Chastisement

After the Sign the Chastisement will come. It will come because, despite God's numerous warnings, mankind will persist in its love of evil. But the Blessed Virgin Mary has told the visionaries that all of us have the ability to lessen its severity through prayers, fasting, and penance.

The visionaries have said that the divine punishment will come when we least expect it. Mari Loli, who together with Conchita and Jacinta saw the chastisement in a vision, said it was terrifying:

"Oh! it was horrible to see. We were absolutely terrified... I cannot find words to explain it. We saw the waters in the rivers turn to blood... Fire was falling from heaven... And something worse still which I cannot reveal at this time..."[10]

The chastisement will be a direct intervention from God and the world will know that it comes from heaven, not from the earth. Conchita said in a letter to Fr. Laffineur dated February 2, 1965, that "It will be less terrible for little children to die a natural death than die of the chastisement." In another letter, Conchita acknowledged that "... it will be worse than if we were enveloped in flames; worse than if we had cinders or hot bricks under our feet and on top of our head."[11]

Visionary Mari Loli wrote to a Mexican priest, Fr. Gustavo Morelos, in 1967, explaining the events leading up to the chastisement:

"...During the night of terror, although we could still see the Blessed Virgin, we also saw a great multitude of people who were suffering very much and screaming with great anguish....

"The Blessed Virgin has explained to us that this great tribulation—which was not, as yet, the Chastisement—will arrive because there will come a time when the Church will seem about to disappear; it will undergo a terrible trial. We asked the Blessed Virgin what this trial was called and she told us 'Communism.'

"Then the Virgin made us see how a great Chastisement would come upon mankind and that this Chastisement would come directly from God.

"At a certain time, not a single motor or machine will operate; a terrible heat wave will come down upon the earth and men will start experiencing a great thirst; they will search desperately for water, but due to the great heat, the water will evaporate. Then most people will fall into despair and try to kill one another... but they will not have the strength to do it; they will fall to the ground, one after the other. That is when they will realize that it is God who justly permits this.

"Finally, we saw a large number of people enveloped in flames. They were running to throw themselves into the sea and the lakes, but as they would enter the water, the water seemed to boil and instead of putting out the flames, would make them worse.

"It was so horrible, that I ask the Blessed Virgin to take with her all our little children so that this would not happen to them. But the Virgin told us that when this day comes, the children [of 1967] will have already grown...."[12]

Years later, in August of 1971, Conchita told a group of Americans:

"... The Virgin will ask God to perform the miracle so as to avoid the Chastisement, but the Chastisement cannot be avoided, because we have lost even the meaning of sin. Now we have reached such an extremity, that

God has no choice but to send the Chastisement. But we need it for our own good. As a result of the Chastisement, those who survive will change enormously and then we shall truly live for God until the end of [all] time, which is coming..."[13]

The Visionaries of Garabandal

The apparitions in Garabandal began in the summer of 1961. On June 18, at 8:30 P.M. four young girls around the ages of eleven and twelve were pilfering apples near a stony road leading to a bluff where nine pine trees (the future site of the Sign) are clustered, when, suddenly, they heard a clap of thunder and saw a beautiful angel (St. Michael the Archangel). The angel was there but a few seconds and then disappeared. The following night at 10:00 P.M., each child heard an angelic voice say:

"Do not worry, you will see me again."

On June 20, the four girls simultaneously gathered at the stony road to say the Rosary; alerted beforehand by three interior calls, which they described as joys. A dazzling, blinding light suddenly appeared, frightening them very much. The next afternoon the angel re-appeared wearing a long, blue robe and having large, pink wings. He seemed to be about nine years old. The children asked the angel's name and his purpose for coming, but he remained silent. Altogether, the angel made eight of these silent appearances.

On June 22, 8:30 P.M., the angel reappeared and the children fell into an ecstasy for the first time. Pricking, probing, and poking on the children showed they had no sensitivity to pain while in ecstasy. Two nights later, on June 24, the Feast of St. John the Baptist, St. Michael appeared with an inscription on a plaque that said:

"...One must...XVIII-MCMLXI."

The meaning of the inscription, unclear to the children at that time, was announcing the date of their first message from heaven, October 18, 1961.

On July 1, 1961, the angel announced that the Blessed Virgin Mary would appear on Sunday under the name Our Lady of Mount Carmel, after a holy mountain in Israel. On Sunday, July 2, the Virgin appeared to the children wearing a long white gown with a blue mantle. On her right wrist was the brown scapula of Mount Carmel. St. Michael and an unidentified angel also appeared with her. Three days later the Virgin explained the meaning of the plaque to the children, saying that it represents the first part of a message that was to be made known publicly by October 18, 1961.

In the last two weeks of July of 1961, the visionaries had many ecstasies, lasting anywhere from a few minutes to several hours. The Blessed Virgin Mary made them understand that a time would come when they would deny their visions and contradict one another, causing much division. It would be a period of great trial and suffering for them and their families.

On July 31, the visionaries, while in ecstasy, started moving around on their knees for the first time, reciting the Rosary in perfect synchronization without beads or without counting. But just as Mary said, Conchita began to have doubts about her visions and was pressured by the authorities into signing a prepared document stating them.

On August 2 or 3, the visionaries began having perfectly synchronized "ecstatic falls," which alarmed the crowd of spectators but did no harm to the children. A few days later, on August 5 or 8, the children began having their first "ecstatic walks," walking up, down, backward, forward, on their knees or on their feet, rapidly, over rocky terrain, with the greatest of ease.

During these ecstasies, the children experienced other supernatural phenomena as well: their faces became beautifully transfigured and their voices and laughter changed in quality. They became impervious to the weather, insensitive to bright light, snowflakes, raindrops, and even hailstones on their eyes. They showed a sureness of orientation, an absence of fear, and an absence of fatigue. They had extraordinary changes in their weight, their bodies became rigid when someone tried to move them, they had abnormal strength (some say they levitated), they spoke in foreign tongues (Greek, Latin, and French), they identified unknown persons and blessed objects, and had the charisms of mind-reading, mental telepathy, and clairvoyance.

Jesuit Father Luis Andreu went into an ecstasy on August 8 and followed the children into the nine pines, where he suddenly cried out "Miracle, miracle, miracle, miracle!" On the way home, Fr. Luis said to his friends, "What a wonderful present the Virgin has given me! How lucky we are to have a mother like that in Heaven! Today is the happiest day of my life!" A few hours later, Fr. Luis died of joy—he was only thirty-eight. Following Father Luis's death, the Blessed Virgin appeared to the children and told them that he was with her in heaven and that he had seen a vision of the "Great Miracle" to come before he died.

On August 15, the Solemnity of the Assumption of Mary, cosmic miracles began appearing in the skies over Garabandal. The following day, the children had a conversation with the spirit of Fr. Luis Andreu. Afterwards, they told his brother, Father Ramon Andreu, what he had said. Fr. Ramon knew that it was true because he recognized in their conversation secrets that were known only to him and Fr. Luis.

As promised by St Michael the Archangel, on October 18, 1961, the Blessed Virgin Mary gave the children a message which was read aloud to a crowd of five thousand at the pines and which was to be made known to the whole world:

"We must make many sacrifices, perform much penance, and visit the Blessed Sacrament frequently. But first we must lead good lives. If not, a chastisement will befall us. The cup is already filling up and if we do not change, a very great chastisement will come upon us."[14]

On May 1, 1962, the first day of the month dedicated to the Blessed Mother, the four visionaries began receiving Holy Communion from St. Michael the Archangel. The following month, on June 19 and 20, they received their first visions of the chastisement, which filled them with terror.

On the first anniversary of the apparitions (July 18, 1962), at around midnight, Conchita received a visible Host during Communion from St. Michael the Archangel, which was photographed by a Barcelona businessman named Don Alejandro (the "Miracle of the Visible Communion" was announced beforehand to Conchita on June 22). All present who were close enough to see witnessed the miraculous formation of a visible host on Conchita's tongue.

On September 12, 1962, Maria Cruz had her last ecstasy. After that, doubts began filling her mind—just as the Blessed Mother had predicted.

Antichrist-The Last Pope?

By January 20, 1963, Conchita was the only one who still had ecstasies (her last would be on November 13, 1965 at the nine pines). In June of 1963, Conchita announced that after the death of Pope John XXIII, the 261st pope, there would only be three more popes before the end of time as we know it. So according to Conchita, the chastisement will come during the reign of Pope John Paul II—the 264th pope. If this is true, the world has very little time left to convert: John Paul II turned eighty in the year 2000 and he himself is praying that he lives until the end.

The Virgin Mary also told Conchita that the 264th pope would be the last pope "before the end of time, but not the end of the world"; and Conchita was insistent that there was a difference between the two periods, which means that there would be additional popes after the 264th.

Garabandal's prophesy that the world would not end during the pontificate of the 264th pope is consistent with the prophecies of La Salette, which, if you'll recall, said that the triumph of the Church at the end of the world will take place in the second pontificate after the suffering pope (Pope John Paul II). Both the prophecies of La Salette and Garabandal are in agreement with the famous prophecies of a highly-respected, twelfth-century Irish monk named St. Malachy, whose prophecies were first mentioned in a book called *Lignum Vitae*, published in 1559 by a Benedictine historian, Arnold Wion. Wion listed the 110 slogans of Malachy's, which characterized the future popes, starting in the year 1143 and ending with the 266th pope. After the 266th pope, according to St. Malachy, there will be no more popes.

In addition to being the last pontiff, some visionaries hint that the 266th pope will be the Antichrist. The prophetic writings of the great Italian mystic, Maria Valtorta, which are covered in the epilogue, seem to intimate this. Maria said that the Antichrist will be a heavenly body in Jesus' army; an elect leader who gives in to the rationalism of the Second Beast and political power of the First Beast after being virtuous in the true faith. Another very credible mystic and stigmatist now living in County Mayo, Ireland, Christina Gallagher, has had visions of the Antichrist wearing a bishop's miter and Satan smashing the chair of St. Peter, which, to me, seems to indicate that a future pope will be the Antichrist. If Antichrist turns out to be someone other than the 266th pope, one thing is for sure—he will be someone high up in the Church and his number will be 666.

By the way, in his list of 110 slogans, St. Malachy gave the 264th pope the motto of labor solis, the labor or eclipse of the sun. John Paul II was, in fact, born during an eclipse of the sun on May 18, 1920.

Mary's Last Warnings to Conchita

On June 18, 1965, Conchita received a dire message for the world from the Blessed Mother through the intercession of St. Michael the Archangel:

> *"As my message of October 18, 1961, has not been complied with and has not been made known to the world, I am advising you that this is the last one. Before, the cup was filling up. Now it is flowing over. Many cardinals, many bishops, and many priests are on the road to perdition and are taking many souls with them. Less and less importance is given to the Eucharist. You should turn the wrath of God away from yourselves by your efforts. If you ask his forgiveness with sincere hearts, He will forgive you. I, your mother, through the intercession of St. Michael the Archangel, ask you to amend your lives. You are now receiving the last warnings. I love you very much and do not want your condemnation. Pray to us with sincerity and We will grant your requests. You should make more sacrifices. Think about the passion of Jesus."*[15]

The Blessed Virgin Mary appeared for the last time to Conchita on November 13, 1965. This was the gist of her message:

> *"... Do you remember what I told you on your feast day? That you will have much to suffer on this earth... Conchita, I have not come for you alone. I have come for all my children, with the desire to bring them closer to Our [two] hearts...Do you know, Conchita, why I did not come on June 18 to give you the message for the world? It was because it hurt me to tell you myself. But I must tell you, however, for your own good and, if you accomplish it, for the glory of God...This is the last time*

you will see me here, but I shall always be with you and with all my children...
Conchita, why do you not visit my Son more often in the tabernacle? He waits for
you day and night... Remember what I told you on your feast day. When you appear
before God, your hands must be filled with the deeds you have accomplished for your
brothers and for His glory. Right now, your hands our empty... "16

On February 13, 1966, Conchita had an interior locution with Jesus Christ, who told her that contrary to her wishes she would not become a nun (that proved to be true: Conchita got married on May 26, 1973). Christ also told Conchita that she would have "much to suffer until the Miracle, for there are few who believe you..."

Investigations of Garabandal

The original board of inquiry set up by the bishop of Santander (Garabandal's parish), Bishop Doroteo Fernandez, to investigate Garabandal was comprised of three priests and two psychiatrists. After completing his investigations, one of the leading mental health experts in Spain, Dr. Luis Morales Noriega, declared that the events in Garabandal were totally natural and had a psychological explanation, and thereby dismissed the whole affair as "child's play." The doctor's negative conclusion caused the young visionaries to doubt themselves as Mary said they would: in 1966, they recanted their testimonies but have since taken them back.

On May 30, 1983, Dr. Luis Morales, the leader of the first team of investigators, had a sudden change of heart and publicly retracted his negative report: "I am here today to speak to you on the apparitions of Our Lady of Garabandal. It is because she herself has worked this change in me. Moreover, I am speaking with full permission of the ecclesiastical hierarchy... I will end my conference pleading with the Virgin of Garabandal, that for the rest of my days, she may keep me under her mantle and have mercy on me."17

In 1986, a new commission was appointed by Bishop del Val Gallo to reinvestigate the evidence of Garabandal. By 1991, all studies were completed and sent to Rome for review.

The Church on Garabandal

The Catholic Church has not recognized Garabandal as worthy of belief because since 1961 the bishops of Santandar have said that nothing supernatural has occurred there, and the Vatican has not overturned the local bishops' conclusions. (Mary told the visionaries when she first appeared to them that there would be a disbelief in Garabandal and that the visionaries would even doubt it themselves.)

However, there were some in the Church at the time of the apparitions who definitely believed in Garabandal. Pope Paul VI met with Conchita on her visit to Rome on January 12-19, 1966, and told her "I bless you, and, with me, the whole Church blesses you..."[18]

Before he died, Padre Pio, who believed in Garabandal, wrote Conchita a letter: "I pray to the most Holy Virgin to comfort you and guide you towards sanctity, and I bless you with all my heart."[19] Joey Lomangino, the blind man predicted to gain his sight during the Garabandal Sign, met with Padre Pio and asked him if Our Lady was really appearing in Garabandal, and his reply to Joey was "Yes!"[20]

Like Medjugorje, the apparitions in Garabandal have greatly divided the Catholic Church, yet there has been no official condemnation of it by the Vatican, only the local bishops' conclusions that there was no "supernatural validity" to Garabandal. Private-sponsored pilgrimages to Garabandal are still allowed with some restrictions where mass is said and the banning of the mentioning of the apparitions during mass. The only way we'll ever know for sure if Mary really appeared in Garabandal is if the events prophesied to happen there come true. Until then, we will just have to wait and see. Bishops have been wrong before.

Chapter Twelve

Our Lady of All Peoples:
Akita, Japan 1973-1982

"Throughout this Japanese archipelago, from the northernmost Japanese Island of Hokkaido to the southernmost Island of Okinawa, there are no places which are not soaked with the blood of martyrs. Throughout the history of the Catholic Church worldwide, there are no other countries whose lands absorbed such large quantities of martyrs' blood as has Japan."

Fr. Thomas Teiju Yasuda

Mary Appears in Japan

When people hear the words Akita and Ito they may be reminded of Nicole Brown Simpson's Japanese dog and the Japanese-American judge who presided over the O.J. Simpson murder trial. But the story of "Our Lady of All Peoples" is not about a Japanese dog, nor is it about a Superior Court Judge in L.A.: it's about a Catholic convent on the outskirts of Akita, Japan, in the diocese of a certain bishop named John Ito, where the Blessed Virgin Mary appeared between 1973 and 1982.

Speaking through a statue made out of Judea wood, depicting Mary standing on a globe in front of a cross, the Blessed Mother gave a Japanese Sister several important messages and apocalyptic warnings regarding dire events that would happen in the very near future. As a sign to authenticate her messages, the statue of Mary repeatedly bled from a stigmata wound in the right hand, perspired copious quantities of heavenly-smelling perfume, and cried real human tears on 101 separate occasions.

Japanese television crews were allowed into the convent to film the crying statue, and numerous samples of the *lachrymations* (tears) were carefully collected and sent to a pathologist's lab for analysis, which positively identified them as human in origin. Further scientific analysis of the liquids, performed by Professor Sagisaka of the Faculty of Legal Medicine, found that the blood belonged to blood group B, and the sweat and tears to types AB and O.[1]

Before the lab results had been shared with the Japanese media, skeptics had made scathing allegations on TV, suggesting that the recipient of Mary's messages, Sister Agnes Sasagawa, who is blood type B, was telepathically transporting her own blood, sweat, and tears to the statue from her subconscious mind—a theory that requires far more credulity than believing that the liquids came from God. But when the lab results finally came back and proved that Sister Sasagawa was not perpetrating a hoax, because the samples were of three blood types, her skeptics were silenced, having come up with no other explanations as to how the liquids appeared on the statue.

Since meticulous scientific examination has shown that there was absolutely no physical tampering with the statue and that the liquids couldn't have come from Sister Sasagawa's mind, that leaves only one possible explanation for their origin: they were supernatural.

Another Warning to the World

The miraculous statue of Akita was meant to be a symbolic warning to the world because an awful punishment is about to strike the earth. Human blood is about to be spilled in an unprecedented way. Billions of people are about to perish, all within this generation.

Mary gave Sister Agnes three important warnings concerning the future of mankind and the nearness of God's chastisement. Unfortunately, like La Salette, Fátima, and Garabandal, the warnings in Akita have gone unheeded. Look at the condition the world is in. How many people have ever heard of Akita, let alone believe in it? Satan mocked it in the O. J. Simpson trial and the skeptics who've heard about it dismiss it as a hoax. Unfounded criticisms notwithstanding, the supernatural events in Akita were approved by Bishop John Ito on April 22, 1984, as worthy of belief. May the following account of Akita help to convince you of this.

In the Yuzawadai convent of the Handmaids of the Eucharist, a secular institute founded by Bishop John Ito in 1945—the year the atomic bomb was dropped in Japan—the Blessed Virgin Mary appeared to Sister Agnes Sasagawa with a grave warning for the world. On the 13th of October, 1973, the 56th anniversary of the miracle of Fátima, Mary delivered a dire message concerning an imminent chastisement awaiting the world; a punishment far worse than Noah's flood. Mary warned Sister Agnes:

"... If men do not repent and better themselves, the Father will inflict a terrible punishment on all humanity. It will be a punishment greater than the deluge, such as one will never have seen before. Fire will fall from the sky and will wipe out a great part of humanity, the good as well as the bad, sparing neither priests nor faithful. The survivors will find themselves so desolate that they will envy the dead." [2]

Survivors of the atomic bomb blasts at Hiroshima and Nagasaki should know what it means to envy the dead after fire falls from the sky. That's probably one of the reasons God sent Mary to Japan. Another, perhaps more important, reason is the long history of persecution to Japanese Catholics, some of the bravest religious martyrs in the world. Mary honored the sacrifices those brave Catholic martyrs made by appearing in their country.

Hundreds of thousands of Japanese Catholics have been martyred for their faith since the Jesuit missionary, Francis Xavier, first brought Christianity to Japan on August 15, 1549 (the Feast of the Assumption of Mary). Xavier's first act, when he arrived in the Japanese islands at the port of Kagoshima, was to consecrate Japan to the Immaculate Heart of Mary. This consecration was necessary because the Japanese people were a pagan, superstitious, war-like people, worshiping idols like the spirits of their dead ancestors, the emperor of Japan, and the violent forces of nature, which occur all too frequently in Japan because it sits on the Pacific rim's volatile ring of fire.

Because of her geographic location, earthquakes, volcanoes, tidal waves, and typhoons are commonplace in Japan, and have claimed the lives of hundreds of thousands of Japanese. A major earthquake hit Edo (Tokyo) on December 30, 1703, killing 200,000. Another earthquake struck the island of Hokkaido on December 30, 1730, exactly twenty-seven years later, killing another 137,000. The great Ansei earthquake leveled Tokyo again in December of 1855, killing tens of thousands more. One of the most devastating earthquakes in history hit Tokyo on September 1, 1923, killing 300,000 and leaving 2.5 million homeless. And on January 17, 1995, exactly one year after the Los Angeles earthquake, a major earthquake hit Kobe, Japan (Kobe means "Door of God"), killing at least 5,500 and causing billions of dollars worth of damage. January 17, by the way, is the anniversary of Our Lady of Pontmain and a satanic feast day on some occult calendars: it was also the beginning of the Persian Gulf War in 1991.

Huge tidal waves—*tsunamis*—caused by earthquakes underneath the ocean floor have done their fair share of damage, too. On June 15, 1896, a tsunami struck the island of Honshu, killing 27,000. Another tsunami hit Honshu on December 21, 1946, killing 1,000 more. And on September 15-19, 1947, tsunamis hit the islands of Honshu and Shikoku, leaving another 1,000 dead.

Typhoons, likewise, have plagued Japan. A typhoon struck Japan on August 15, 1910, killing 800 and leaving 400,000 homeless. Another typhoon hit Honshu on September 21, 1934, killing 4,000. And it was a tremendous *kamikaze* or "divine wind" that was said to have saved Japan in the 13th century from the invading Mongol hoards of Kublai Khan.

Atomic bombs, earthquakes, volcanoes, tsunamis, typhoons: the Japanese people should be very receptive to Mary's warnings of an imminent disaster, but they aren't. Catholicism is a minority religion in Japan and isn't taken very seriously by that secular, highly westernized society where suicides are becoming epidemic. In fact, Catholics have made very little progress in converting that pagan nation to Christianity, and have suffered tremendous persecutions in the past from Japanese emperors and shoguns (warlords). Ever since the time of St. Francis Xavier, the islands of Japan have been soaked red with the blood of countless Catholic martyrs. Like Fr. Thomas Teiju Yasuda said, no other country in the world has produced as many martyrs for the Catholic faith as Japan. The following history of Catholicism in Japan tells why.

Japan Persecutes the Catholic Church

At the time of the arrival of the first Christian missionaries in 1549, the Japanese people were practicing four pagan religions: Shintoism, Confucianism, Taoism, and Zen Buddhism—the latter of these being the preferred religion of the ruthless shoguns of Japan. Buddhist monks, however, were often adversaries of the powerful shogun rulers, which was one of the reasons why shoguns allowed Christian missionaries into Japan.

Japanese shoguns were powerful military governors, first appointed by the emperor in 1192, who quickly became the real rulers in Japan. The Japanese emperors were still revered as divine, but, nonetheless, powerless over the militant shoguns. To maintain their absolute hold on power, shoguns hired professional fighters extremely adept in the martial arts—the samurai warriors. Samurai warriors were very formal, very conservative, and very fanatical. Honor and fighting skills meant everything, and an enemy's life, nothing: it could be taken at the slightest provocation. Many poor, unarmed Japanese peasants were beheaded when they unwittingly dishonored a samurai warrior.

Long before the arrival of St. Francis Xavier, Japan had lapsed into a state of continual warfare between competing shoguns. In the middle of the 16th century, General Toyotomi Hideyoshi (1536-98) became the most powerful overlord in Japan, and gradually brought feudal warfare under control. When Francis Xavier landed on Kagoshima in southern Kyushu in 1549, Japan was at peace. Shogun Hideyoshi greeted him respectfully, and for political reasons already mentioned, permitted St. Francis to evangelize the Japanese people (Hideyoshi saw Christianity as a way of keeping power-hungry Buddhist monks in check).

On the southern island of Kyushu, Francis Xavier won many converts to

Catholicism. The city of Nagasaki became a Christian boomtown and was referred to as the "Rome of the East," particularly the district of Urakami.

But before long, Christianity, which was rapidly spreading throughout Japan, was seen as a major threat to the power and influence of the shoguns, who enjoyed subjugating the peasants through the fear and intimidation of the samurais rather than through the love and forgiveness that the missionaries preached. As a result, the feudal prince of Satsuma issued an edict in 1550 to make it a capital offense for any of his subjects to become Christians. Alarmed at this sudden change in attitude by one of the warlords, Francis Xavier fled Kyushu for Kyoto on the island of Honshu, winning many new Japanese converts along the way. When Xavier's work was finally accomplished in Japan, he sailed for China and India in 1551, leaving behind two Jesuit priests and a thriving Catholic mission. By 1570, Japan had twenty Jesuit priests of its own.

At first tolerant towards Christianity, Shogun Hideyoshi helped the Jesuits establish a church near Osaka in the 1580s, making no protests when some of his closest advisors and concubines became converts to Catholicism. By 1586, some 200,000 Japanese had converted to Christianity and Shogun Hideyoshi even hinted to a visiting senior Jesuit that Japan could become a Christian nation, once, of course, China had been conquered. But that never happened. When Franciscan missionaries arrived in Japan, a quarrel between the two religious orders started over the trading policies of the Franciscans, which seemed to favor Spain over Japan and which confused the shoguns about the missionaries' real intentions. Jealous Buddhist monks convinced Shogun Hideyoshi that Christianity was really a diversionary tactic for an imminent military invasion from the West, so Hideyoshi ordered the missionaries' expulsion on trumped- up charges; falsely accusing the Jesuits of selling the Japanese as slaves, and smashing Buddhist images.

On July 25, 1587, all Jesuit missionaries were ordered to leave Japan within 20 days (although their expulsion wasn't strictly enforced and most of the Jesuits went into hiding). For ten years Hideyoshi did nothing more. But then suddenly, for reasons unknown, on February 5, 1597, he seized a Portuguese ship and raided the Franciscan community, crucifying seven Franciscan missionaries and nineteen Japanese Catholics upside down on Nishizaka hill, outside Nagasaki, after forcing the martyrs to walk thirty miles in the snow to their crosses. Hideyoshi's samurais used long spears to pierce the chests of the dying martyrs as they sang hymns of praise on the crosses. The martyrs' crucified bodies were then taken down and dragged from city to city in a degrading fashion as a warning to others to abandon Christianity, or die.

Hideyoshi's successor, Shogun Tokugawa Iyeyasu (1542-1616), was even more cruel. At first tolerant towards the Christians, like Hideyoshi, Iyeyasu inexplicably turned on them without provocation, murdering 5,000 converts and burning down their churches. Iyeyasu almost succeeded in completely eradicating Christianity from Japan by committing unspeakable crimes against Japanese Catholics: children were burned in their mothers' arms and martyrs were hung upside down over boiling hot sulfur springs. Japanese Christians, who wanted to stay alive, were forced to renounce their Catholic faith by treading over copper images of Jesus and Mary. Those who refused were knifed and thrown into boiling sulfur pits.[3]

Iyeyasu's son, Shogun Hidetada (1579-1632), continued his father's evil persecution of Catholics. In 1614, he required all Japanese citizens to register as Buddhists and ordered all remaining Christian missionaries to leave Japan (although not all missionaries obeyed his order). To show that he meant business, Hidetada publicly executed several priests in 1617. Most of the remaining missionaries fled Japan, but some of the braver ones went into hiding. In 1622, Hidetada sought out the remaining missionaries, and when those in hiding were caught, they were beheaded or hung upside down in pits, with tiny holes pierced in their ears so that they would slowly bleed to death. Thousands of Japanese Catholics were executed in this sadistic way.

In his book, *History of the Christians of Akita: Snow, Blood, and the Holy Cross,* Tetsujo Muto recounted the history of the early Catholic martyrs of Akita. In 1624, Muto wrote, the first Christians of Akita were executed by the feared Masakage, who wrote an account of his activities on June 3rd: "One, I left the castle with my musket. Two, I had 32 Christians burned, 20 of them men and 12 women. Three, it was a nice day."[4] Such was the callous disregard for Catholics by Japanese shoguns.

In 1637-38, the Shimabara Revolt, a peasants' uprising against the Tokugawa shogunate around the area of Nagasaki, was brought on by the cruelty of Hidetada's son, Shogun Iyemitsu (1604-1651). Peasant demonstrators carrying banners bearing Christian crosses convinced the suspicious shoguns that Christians were behind the revolt, so the shoguns unleashed their samurai warriors on them. Thirty-seven thousand peasants were massacred and thousands more were rounded up and executed. The Dutch and the Chinese, the last of the remaining foreigners in Japan, were forcibly exiled to a walled compound on the island of Deshima near Nagasaki, and for the next 200 years, no more missionaries and no more sacraments were allowed into Japan, which had cut itself off from the outside world.

The persecutions of the Tokugawa shogunate forced the Christian community in Japan to go underground for the next two centuries. "Hidden Christians," poor peasants and farmers who had a special devotion to Mary, practiced Buddhism outwardly to avoid suspicion but were secretly Christians. Hidden statues of the Virgin Mary, called *Nando Gami*, which means "God in cupboard," were taken out at night for silent prayer and veneration. Infants were secretly baptized without priests, and selected members of the underground Catholic Church kept the liturgy and the feast days alive.[5]

The xenophobic "Exclusion Policy" of the Tokugawa shogunate which had cut Japan off from the rest of the world allowed no foreigners into the Japanese ports except for ten Chinese and one Dutch ship each year on the small island of Deshima off Nagasaki. Trying to root out the last vestiges of Catholicism, the shoguns ordered the searching out of all Christian converts, the arrest of any missionaries still working underground, and the detention of anyone being smuggled into Japanese ports. All Feudal warlords were ordered to exclude Christianity from their fiefdoms. No one was allowed to leave Japan, and Japanese citizens living abroad were put to death upon their return. The last of the foreigners in Japan were moved to Deshima in 1636 and were allowed some trade with the Japanese, but only under strict surveillance.

The 1637-38 Shimabara Peasant Revolt against the repressive Tokugawan regime in western Kyushu lead to the edict of 1639, which prohibited Portuguese ships from docking at Japanese ports upon pain of death. Hoping to persuade Shogun Iyemitsu to reconsider, a Portuguese ship from Macao reached Japan in 1640, but the ship was torched and 57 Portuguese delegates were beheaded. Thirteen delegates were spared and sent back to Macao as a warning for Westerners to keep out.

A softening of Japan's hard-line Exclusion Policy began in the middle of the nineteenth century, as the old-guard could no longer stop those in favor of re-opening trade with the West and a return to imperial rule. Foreigners were once again allowed to practice their Catholic faith, but not Japanese natives.

A French missionary priest named Fr. Petitjean came to Japan in 1863 and built a church for foreigners at O'ura in Nagasaki. Fr. Petitjean dedicated the church to the Virgin Mary and the 26 crucified martyrs of 1597. On March 17, 1865, "Hidden Christians" from the Urakami Village outside of Nagasaki came out of hiding for the first time in 200 years by entering the church and revealing their faith to Fr. Petitjean. "Our faith is the same as yours," they said. "Where is the statue of the Virgin?" The "Hidden Christians" had summoned up great courage to enter Fr. Petitjean's church because a warning had been posted that any Japanese citizen found inside the church would be severely punished. When the Japanese authorities found out about the "Hidden Christians," 68 of them were arrested and tortured, and then the subsequent administration ordered all Japanese to renounce Christianity. When they refused, 3,349 Japanese Christians were exiled in 1867 to 19 detention camps across western Japan: 644 died in exile and 64 more were tortured and killed. Those who eventually returned home found their houses in ruin.[6]

The Meiji Period

In 1853, Commodore Perry of the U.S. Navy arrived in Japan with a flotilla of warships to end Japan's "Bamboo Curtain" against the West. The Treaty of

Kanagawa was signed the following year on March 31, 1854, which opened up the ports of Shimoda and Hakodate to the United States. Similar treaties were made with Britain and Russia.

The isolationist samurais known as the *shishi* (men of spirit) boycotted the signing of the so-called "Unequal Treaties," and accused the pro-Western Tokugawa shogunate of high treason. Trying to overthrow the pro-Western shoguns by intimidation, the shishi assassinated leading Japanese officials and foreigners. Their plan worked: the Japanese emperor, who was on the side of the shishi, asserted his imperial powers over the shogunate for the first time in 700 years by summoning the ruling shogun to court, ordering him to inform the foreign envoys that he was reinstating the Exclusion Policy against the West.

In 1863, the anti-Western shogun of Choshu fired on American ships passing through the Straits of Shimoneski. A year later, British, Dutch, French, and U.S. warships retaliated in force. Acknowledging the futility of fighting the superior Western navies, another peace treaty was signed with the West on October 22, 1864.

The centuries-old Tokugawa shogunate finally crumbled in 1867, ending 700 years of domination by the shoguns. Emperor Mitsuhito (1852-1912) assumed power in 1868 under a ruling oligarchy and moved the imperial palace to Tokyo. Another new period of openness with the West was inaugurated.

During the Meiji Period (1868-1912) of enlightened rule, Western technology inundated Japan, resulting in rapid advances in education, economic development, urbanization, and military industrialization. Japan became an industrial and military giant unrivaled in the East. But some old-style Japanese didn't like the westernization of Japan, and it wasn't long before nostalgia for the old Japanese military institutions and customs returned.

Imperial Japan

A new wave of militant imperialism and anti-Western xenophobia pervaded Japanese politics in the late-eighteenth and early-nineteenth centuries, as land-hungry politicians were eager to expand the territories of their burgeoning population. The Japanese Navy engaged and defeated the Chinese Navy in 1895, then the Russian Navy in 1904-05. The Japanese army then annexed Korea in 1910, seized Manchuria in 1931-32, and invaded China in 1937, mercilessly bombing and slaughtering unarmed Chinese civilians in Nanjing in a satanic orgy of blood and mayhem. In Nanjing, Chinese women were dragged from their homes and raped and butchered. Pregnant mothers were run through with bayonets—baby included.

Militant imperialists in the Japanese army took control of Japan in the 1930s and made Emperor Hirohito a virtual prisoner in his own palace.

General Tojo's imperialistic militancy came under increasing criticism from the West, and a "moral embargo" of oil and steel was imposed on Japan by the U.S. to limit its war-making capabilities. A Japanese attack on the U.S. was inevitable.

To Die for the Emperor

Overconfident of their naval superiority and military alliances with fascist Germany and Italy, and convinced of their supernatural protection as a divine race, Japanese military leaders invaded the Philippines and the Dutch East Indies in 1941 to commandeer the iron and oil that the U.S. had embargoed. When the U.S. responded to the Japanese invasion of Indochina by freezing Japanese assets, the Japanese retaliated by attacking Pearl Harbor on December 7, 1941. On December 8, 1941, the Solemnity of the Immaculate Conception of Mary, the United States declared war on the Japanese empire.

On January 1, 1942, the Japanese army entered Manila, the capital of the predominately Catholic country of the Philippines. In the infamous Bataan Death March that spring, 75,000 soldiers on Bataan and Corregidor were forced to march to a prisoner of war camp 60 miles away. Ten thousand American and Filipino prisoners died as a result of the march. Torture and starving of prisoners, slave labor camps, hideous medical experiments—a total disregard for the sanctity of human life characterized the barbarity of imperial Japan.

Soon after the Battle of Midway in 1942, which turned the tide of the war in favor of the Allies, it became apparent that the Japanese were never going to surrender to the West, and were prepared to die for their "divine" emperor. Suicide dive-bombers called *kamikazes* wreaked havoc on American warships, and scores of Americans were killed on the islands of the South Pacific. Faced with this kind of suicidal fanaticism, U.S. military planners calculated that an Allied invasion of the Japanese islands would probably cost at least one million American lives: a figure totally unacceptable to the commander-in-chief of the American armed forces, President Harry S Truman.

In the summer of 1945, Truman informed the Japanese government that the Americans would unleash a horrible new weapon unless their armed forces immediately surrendered. Undaunted by Truman's ultimatum, the Japanese continued their suicidal fighting. President Truman then made good on his threat: on August 6, 1945, the Feast of the Transfiguration of Christ, the first atomic bomb ever used against human beings was dropped on Hiroshima, instantly killing 100,000 civilians.[7] Still refusing to surrender, a second atomic bomb was dropped on Nagasaki on August 9: 74,000 died instantly and another 80,000 later succumbed from radiation poisoning.

Nagasaki was not the primary target but was secondarily chosen when poor visibility prevented the bombing of the first target. Because of mechanical failures, the atom bomb went off target and its blast was centered directly over the small Christian community of Urakami, completely obliterating the Cathedral of the Assumption of Mary—the largest Cathedral in the Orient. It was no coincidence that Nagasaki, already soiled with the blood of so many Catholic martyrs, was once again chosen to be the site of another Catholic holocaust.

Because of Truman's willingness to use atomic weapons, Emperor Hirohito publicly accepted the Allies' terms of surrender on V-J Day, August 15, 1945—the 396th anniversary of the arrival of St. Francis Xavier in Japan, and the Solemnity of the Assumption of Mary. The surrender documents were formally signed on the Battleship Missouri on September 2, 1945, in honor of President Truman's hometown of Independence, Missouri. According to the terms of the surrender agreement, Emperor Hirohito was forced to make a public proclamation on January 1, 1946—the Solemnity of Mary, Mother of God—that the Japanese Emperor was no longer a god, but an ordinary man, and that the emperor's divinity was "a false conception." You cannot imagine how humiliating that was for Hirohito and the Japanese people to accept.

The Japanese people were stunned by their emperor's announcement of his false divinity because since ancient times, they had been raised to believe that he was descended from the Sun Goddess Amaterasu, and that they were a divine race incapable of suffering defeat. But World War II had taught the Japanese people a bitter lesson: only one man is truly divine, and his name is Jesus Christ.

Looking back, the Second World War was, in reality, a battle between Satan and Christ; between the dark, satanic forces of fascism and imperialism and the democratic ideals of Christianity. Spiritual symbolism was everywhere in that war of conflicting ideals; even the Western victors had Christian-sounding names like Winston Church hill and Harry True man.[8]

Sister Agnes Sasagawa

In 1945, the year the war ended, Bishop John Ito established the convent of the Handmaids of the Eucharist near Akita on the island of Honshu. Little did he know that thirty years later one of its lowliest, sickliest members, Sister Agnes Sasagawa, would be visited by the Blessed Virgin Mary.

Sister Agnes Sasagawa was born premature and suffered ill health most of her life; having to be hospitalized many times and forced to undergo numerous operations. When Agnes was 19 she was struck with central nervous paralysis from a surgical mistake made during a routine appendectomy, which immobilized her for the next 16 years. While immobilized in the hospital, a kindly old Catholic nurse at a clinic in Myoko recommended to Agnes, who was brought up a Buddhist, that she read about the Catholic Church in the *Bells of Nagasaki*, an inspirational book about the true meaning of suffering written by a horribly-disfigured victim of the Nagasaki bomb. Upon reading the book, Agnes immediately fell in love with the Catholic faith, and despite her family's objections, entered the Sisters of Notre Dame of Junshin in Nagasaki when her health improved.

Just four months after she began her novitiate, Agnes had a severe relapse and was put back in the hospital, where she lapsed into a coma. Ten days into her coma she was put on the critical list and wasn't expected to live. As a last resort, the Sisters of Junshin gave Agnes some Lourdes water and she miraculously began to regain her health. When Agnes was fully recovered, she was given permission by the bishop to join the secular institute of the Handmaids of the Eucharist.

The diminutive Sister Agnes was given yet another physical trial to bear in early 1973, when she began losing her hearing. By March 16 of that year, Sister Agnes went completely deaf (although she was still capable of communicating by lip reading). Totally deaf, Sister Agnes arrived at the Handmaid's convent in Yuzawadai on the outskirts of Akita on May 12, 1973. On June 12, while Sister Agnes was alone in the chapel, a brilliant light appeared from inside the open tabernacle as Agnes was worshiping the Holy Eucharist. Not knowing what to do, Agnes fell prostrate on the floor and remained there for an hour until the light disappeared. The following morning Sister Agnes arrived earlier than the others and witnessed the return of the brilliant light.

On June 14, while praying with her Sisters before the Blessed Sacrament, a brilliant light emanated from inside the tabernacle and engulfed the altar with reddish-gold flames, which only Sister Agnes could see. Sister Agnes felt an extraordinary sense of peace from the light despite persistent thoughts in her mind that she was going crazy.

On June 29, the eve of the Feast of the Sacred Heart, the brilliant light shone forth again from the Blessed Sacrament; but this time a fog surrounded the altar and a multitude of angelic beings appeared kneeling in adoration. When Sister Agnes told Bishop Ito what had happened that day, he advised her not to tell anyone, but to continue meditating and praying before the Blessed Sacrament: for these things were entirely possible and she needn't worry about losing her mind because something similar had already happened in Fátima.

On the Feast of the Sacred Heart, Sister Agnes was getting ready to pray the Rosary with her superiors, when suddenly, at the instant she took the Rosary in her hand, Sister Agnes's guardian angel appeared on her right side. The guardian angel recited the Rosary with Agnes, then disappeared as quickly as she came. Sister Agnes recognized this angelic being as the same one who had appeared to her four years earlier in Myoko while she was hospitalized in a coma. On the second day of her coma, as the priest was administering the Sacrament of the Sick, Agnes, without knowing it, recited the Our Father, the Hail Mary, the Gloria, and the Apostles Creed in Latin—a language she didn't know. In her comatose state, Agnes saw a beautiful angel on her right side who recited the Rosary with her. At the end of each decade, the angel told Agnes to add these words:

> *"Oh my Jesus, forgive us our sins, save us from the fires of hell, lead all souls to heaven and especially those in most need of your mercy."*[9]

After Agnes recovered, a friend who was visiting her while she was in a coma told her about the prayer she had recited. Later, a Salesian priest told Sister Agnes that the prayer was the Prayer of Fátima that the Virgin Mary had taught the three children.

On June 29, while Sister Agnes and her guardian angel were saying the Rosary together, a brilliant, luminous mist appeared around the altar together with a multitude of angels chanting, *"Holy, Holy, Holy."* When they finished, an angelic voice on the Sister's right side began praying the prayer of the Handmaids of the Eucharist:

> *"Most Sacred Heart of Jesus, present in the Holy Eucharist, I consecrate my body and soul to be entirely one with Your Heart, being sacrificed at every instant on all the altars of the world and giving praise to the Father, pleading for the coming of His Kingdom.*
>
> *"Please receive this humble offering of myself. Use me as You will for the glory of the Father and the salvation of souls.*
>
> *"Most Holy Mother of God, never let me be separated from Your Divine Son. Please defend and protect me as Your special child."*[10]

The Statue and Stigmata

On Thursday evening, June 28, while praying in the chapel, Sister Agnes began feeling a sharp pain in the palm of her left hand. When she opened her hand she was amazed to find a rose-colored cross engraved in her epidermis. The following Thursday, July 5, Sister Agnes's guardian angel appeared beside her again to recite the Rosary. A new pain, like that of an ice pick, now jabbed the middle of her palm. When Agnes opened her left hand, she saw blood trickling from a puncture wound in the center of the engraved cross. Like Saints Francis of Assisi and Catherine of Siena, Sister Agnes had received the stigmata of Christ.

The pain in her hand had prevented Sister Agnes from sleeping that night. Around 3 o'clock in the morning, she got up to change her dressing. While praying, her guardian angel appeared to her and said:

"Do not fear. Pray with fervor not only because of your sins, but in reparation for those of all men. The world today wounds the most Sacred Heart of Our Lord by its ingratitude and injuries. The wounds of Mary are much deeper and more sorrowful than yours. Let us go to pray together in the chapel."[11]

The angel escorted Sister Agnes into the chapel and then disappeared, leaving Agnes all alone. Praying before the wooden statue of Our Lady of All Peoples, Agnes got the sense that the statue was about to come to life. Suddenly, a light of indescribable beauty burst forth from the statue. As Sister Agnes threw herself on the floor, a heavenly voice sweeter than a thousand angels began to speak. It was the voice of Our Lady:

"My daughter, my novice, you have obeyed me well in abandoning all to follow me. Is the infirmity of your ears painful? Your deafness will be healed, be sure. Be patient. It is the last trial. Does the wound of your hand cause you to suffer? Pray in reparation for the sins of men. Each person in this community is my irreplaceable daughter. Do you say well the prayer of the Handmaids of the Eucharist? Then, let us pray together."[12]

As they began to pray, Sister Agnes's guardian angel joined in. When they got to the part, "Jesus present in the Eucharist," Mary stopped Agnes and instructed her to say from now on *"Truly present."* When the prayer was finished Mary said:

"Pray very much for the Pope, Bishops and Priests. Since your Baptism you have always prayed faithfully for them. Continue to pray very much... very much. Tell your superior all that passed today and obey him in everything that he will tell. He has asked that you pray with fervor."[13]

That morning, Sister Agnes asked the Mistress of Novices to check the hands of the statue of Mary, for she had a strange feeling that they were bleeding too. Sure enough, in the center of Mary's right hand was a thin, perfectly inscribed black cross; looking as if it had been drawn in black ink, with blood trickling from a small hole about the size of a needle at the intersection of the two lines. Dumbfounded at the sight of the miracle, the Sisters fell prostrate in homage.

As time progressed, the cross on Mary's statue seemed to be truly cut into flesh: the edge of the cross had the aspect of open skin, and one even saw the grain of the epidermis like in a fingerprint. The bleeding of the statue coincided with important Catholic feast days or the bleeding of Sister Agnes's hand. Agnes's stigmata always began with a sharp pain in the palm of her hand on Thursday nights, followed by swelling and bleeding on Fridays, and then healing on Saturdays—all corresponding with the Passion and crucifixion of Christ.

Bishop Ito counseled Sister Agnes that the stigmata was meant not only for her, but for everyone. Above all, it was necessary for her to remain humble.

During the afternoon of the First Friday of July 1973, a tremendously sharp pain jabbed the middle of Sister Agnes's left hand. Unable to bear the pain any longer, she fell on the floor in agony. Immediately, Sister Agnes's guardian angel appeared to console her:

> *"Your sufferings will end today. Carefully engrave in the depth of your heart the thought of the blood of Mary. The blood shed by Mary has a profound meaning. This precious blood was shed to ask your conversion, to ask for peace, in reparation for the ingratitude and the outrages towards the Lord. As with devotion to the Sacred Heart, apply yourself to devotion to the most Precious Blood. Pray in reparation for all men.* "[14]

The angel continued:

> *"Say to your superior that the blood is shed today for the last time. Your pain also ends today. Tell them what happened today. He will understand all immediately. And you, observe his directions.* "[15]

The angel smiled and then disappeared. Immediately, the pain left Sister Agnes's hand.

Agnes's stigmata wound disappeared on July 27, the Feast of Saint Pantaleon, a martyr whose blood liquefies each year on his feast day like the blood of St. Januarius.

Mary Warns Sister Agnes

On August 3, 1973, Sister Agnes received the voice of Mary from the statue for the second time, with the following message:

> *"My daughter, my novice, do you love the Lord? If you love the Lord, listen to what I have to say to you.*
>
> *"It is very important. You will convey it to your superior.*
>
> *"Many men in the world afflict the Lord. I desire souls to console Him to soften the anger of the Heavenly Father. I wish, with my Son, for souls who will repair by their suffering and their poverty for the sinners and the ingrates.*
>
> *"In order that the world might know His anger, the Heavenly Father is preparing to inflict a great chastisement on all mankind. With my Son, I have intervened so many times to appease the wrath of the Father. I have prevented the coming of calamities by offering Him the sufferings of the Son of the Cross, His Precious Blood, and beloved souls who console Him forming a cohort of victim souls. Prayer, penance and courageous sacrifices can soften the Father's anger. I desire this also from your community... that it love poverty, that it sanctify itself and pray in reparation for the ingratitudes and outrages of so many men. Recite the prayer of the Handmaids of the Eucharist with awareness of its meaning; put it into practice; offer in reparation for sins. Let each one endeavor, according to capacity and position, to offer herself entirely to the Lord.*

"Even in a secular institute prayer is necessary. Already souls who wish to pray are on their way to being gathered together. Without attracting too much attention to the form, be faithful and fervent in prayer to console the Master.

"Is what you think in your heart true? Are you truly decided to become the rejected stone? My novice, you who wish to belong without reserve to the Lord, to become the spouse worthy of the Spouse make your vows knowing that you must be fastened to the Cross with three nails. These three nails are poverty, chastity and obedience. Of the three, obedience is the foundation. In total abandon, let yourself be led by your superior. He will know how to understand you and direct you."[16]

The statue's blood flowed for the last time on July 27, 1973, but the trace of the wound remained until September 29, the day the statue broke out in a heavenly-smelling perspiration. Even after the Sisters thoroughly dried the statue, the sweet odor of an unknown perfume remained in the chapel until the 15th of October. Lab analysis by a forensic pathologist later showed the liquid samples to be human perspiration.

The blood on Sister Agnes's hand also disappeared on July 27. On October 2, the Feast of the Guardian Angels, eight angels appeared around the altar during the morning mass. On October 13, 1973, the anniversary of the miracle of Fátima, the Blessed Virgin Mary appeared to Sister Agnes with her third and most important message:

"My dear daughter, listen well to what I have to say to you. You will inform your superior.

"As I told you, if men do not repent and better themselves, the Father will inflict a terrible punishment on all humanity. It will be a punishment greater than the deluge, such as one will never have seen before. Fire will fall from the sky and will wipe out a great part of humanity, the good as well as the bad, sparing neither priests nor faithful. The survivors will find themselves so desolate that they will envy the dead. The only arms which will remain for you will be the Rosary and the Sign left by My Son. Each day recite the prayers of the Rosary. With the Rosary, pray for the Pope, the bishops and the priests.

"The work of the devil will infiltrate even into the Church in such a way that one will see cardinals opposing cardinals, bishops against other bishops. The priests who venerate me will be scorned and opposed by their confreres... churches and altars sacked; the Church will be full of those who accept compromises and the demon will press many priests and consecrated souls to leave the service of the Lord.

"The demon will be especially implacable against souls consecrated to God. The thought of the loss of so many souls is the cause of My sadness. If sins increase in number and gravity, there will be no longer pardon for them.

"With courage, speak to your superior. He will know how to encourage each of you to pray and to accomplish works of reparation....

"Pray very much the prayers of the Rosary. I alone am able still to save you from the calamities which approach. Those who place their confidence in me will be saved.[17]

The message of October 13 is extremely important because it predicts the increasing apostasy within the Church; the loss of many priests and religious to the devil; the abandonment of sound Catholic doctrine for a more palatable, politically-correct ecumenism; the hostility amongst Christians towards Marian devotion; and the nearness of an inevitable chastisement through which devotion to the Blessed Mother is the only means of protection.

On October 16, the day after the heavenly perfume stopped, the chapel was filled with a hellish stench that lasted for three days, with maggot-like worms appearing on the floor. Satan intended to frighten the Sisters and God permitted it to prove that hell exists and that Satan is real.

This wasn't the first time that Satan appeared to Sister Agnes. The devil in the form of a dark, menacing shadow with long, powerful claws once grabbed Sister Agnes from behind and tried keeping her away from the chapel. Another time, after she prayed for the conversion of a dying unbeliever, a dark vapor appeared to her from behind the soul of the person she had just saved and reached out to grab her just before she fainted. And yet another time the devil appeared to her in a dream as a huge snake, followed by the discovery the next morning of a huge serpent in the convent.

Although he tried, Satan couldn't deter Sister Agnes from her destiny: her guardian angel protected her from any real harm he could do. On one occasion, Agnes's guardian angel woke her up and warned her about a burning kettle left on the stove that surely would have caused a terrible fire. Another time, her angel appeared to Sister Agnes in a dream and told her to get up and shore up the roof. The reason: six feet of snow had fallen that night and was about to collapse on top of the Sisters. A maintenance repairman was amazed that the braces were still holding, and said that Sister Agnes had probably saved their lives.

On January 4, 1975, the miraculous statue of Our Lady of All Peoples wept tears for the first time. Sister Agnes's guardian angel appeared and said:

> *"The Holy Virgin... loves Japan. She has therefore chosen this land of Akita to communicate Her messages... She awaits you with open arms to pour forth graces. Spread devotion to the Virgin."*[18]

On May 31, 1974, the Feast of the Visitation, the face of the statue of Mary changed color, becoming darker than the rest of the wood. It began changing expressions on different occasions too.

Two weeks before, on May 18, following morning adoration of the Eucharist, Sister Agnes's guardian angel had come to her and announced the healing of her deafness:

> *"You will hear, you will be healed. But that will last for only a moment because the*

Lord still wishes this offering and you will become deaf again. In seeing that your ears are restored again, the heart of those who still doubt will melt and they will believe. Have confidence and pray with good intention... [19]

Sister Agnes is Miraculously Healed

On October 13, 1974, Sister Agnes was temporarily healed of her deafness after a year and seven months in total silence, but by Ash Wednesday 1975, she was deaf again.

By now word was spreading throughout Japan about the miracles at the Yuzawadai convent. Many post-modernists and skeptics within the Catholic Church, however, refused to come to Akita because they didn't believe in the existence of supernatural miracles and believed this to be some kind of attention-seeking hoax.

In January of 1975, Sister Agnes's guardian angel appeared to her during the Rosary with this message:

"Do not be so surprised to see the Blessed Virgin weeping. She weeps because she wishes the conversion of the greatest number; She desires that souls be consecrated to Jesus and to the Father by Her intercession.

"He who directs you told you during the last sermon today; your faith diminishes when you do not see. It is because your faith is weak. The Blessed Virgin rejoices in the consecration of Japan to Her Immaculate Heart because She loves Japan. But She is sad to see that this devotion is not taken seriously. Even though She has chosen this land of Akita to give Her messages, the local pastor doesn't dare to come for fear of what one would say. Do not be afraid. The Blessed Virgin awaits you all. Her hands extended to pour forth graces. Spread devotion to the Virgin...

"You who have believed while seeing the tears of Mary, when you have permission of your superior speak to the greatest number in order to console the hearts of Jesus and Mary. Spread this devotion with courage for their greater glory... "[20]

On May 1-2, 1976, during the Feast of Saint Joseph, fifty-five eyewitnesses, including four doctors, witnessed the lachrymations of the statue. Later on, Sister Agnes's guardian angel appeared to her with the following message:

"Many men in this world afflict the Lord. Our Lady awaits souls to console Him. Remain in poverty, sanctify yourself and pray in reparation of the ingratitudes and the outrages of so many men. The Rosary is your weapon. Say it with care and more often for the intention of the pope, of bishops and priests.

"You must not forget these words [of Mary]. The Blessed Virgin prays continually for the conversion of the greatest possible number and weeps, hoping to lead to Jesus and the Father souls offered to Them by Her intercession. For this intention, and to overcome exterior obstacles, achieve interior unity, from a single heart. Let believers lead a life more worthy of believers! Pray with a new heart... "[21]

The Church on Akita

The first commission set up by Bishop Ito in 1976 to investigate the miracles of Akita was headed by a priest well known for research in Mariology, but who seemed totally unsupportive of supernatural miracles. If that wasn't bad enough, he was the only member of the seven-member committee to even bother to visit the convent. This priest concluded that the liquids emanating from the statue of Mary were "ectoplasms" generated from the mind of Sister Agnes—a manifestation of her subconscious desires. How Freudian! A perfect example of how modern psychology has ruined the minds of so many good priests and religious.

Unsatisfied with the negative conclusion of the First Commission, Bishop Ito visited the Congregation for the Doctrine of the Faith in Rome for guidance on the matter. Their recommendation was that if he wasn't satisfied with the findings of the First Commission, set up a Second Commission—only proceed cautiously. A Second Commission was formed by Bishop Ito to investigate Akita in 1979.

On December 8, 1979, the Solemnity of the Immaculate Conception of Mary, television crews filmed live footage of the statue's 96th tears. On September 12, 1981, the day the statue wept for the 100th time, the Second Commission held their last meeting: four were in favor, three against. The Second Commission decided that to declare the events supernatural, they needed more important miracles. Angered at their request, Sister Agnes's guardian angel appeared to her and said there would be no more miracles.

The Meaning of Mary's Tears

On September 15, 1981, the Feast of Our Lady of Sorrows, the statue wept for the 101st and final time. Two weeks later, on September 28, Sister Agnes had a vision of a huge Bible opened at Genesis 3:15. The voice of her guardian angel then explained the significance of the number 101:

> "*There is a meaning to the figure one hundred and one. This signifies that sin came into the world by a woman and it is also by a woman that salvation came to the world. The zero between the two signifies the Eternal God who is from all eternity until eternity. The first one represents Eve and the last one the Virgin Mary...* "[22]

May 1, 1982, was the last time the angel appeared to Sister Agnes. As promised, Sister Agnes's deafness was totally cured on May 30, 1982—Pentecost Sunday (also the vigil of the day when the Catholic Church of Japan commemorates the discovery in 1865 of the descendants of the "Hidden Christians" on the site of O'ura in Nagasaki.[23] Sister Agnes had first lost her hearing on March 16, 1973, then regained it on October 13, 1974, and then lost it again on March 6, 1975. The final cure came on May 30, 1982, and was the heavenly sign to authenticate Akita. Many more cures and conversions have since been attributed to Akita.

Chapter Thirteen

The Mother of the Word:
Kibeho, Rwanda 1981-1989

"There are no devils left in Hell...They are all in Rwanda."

Cover of *Time* magazine, May 16, 1994

Tribal Hatreds

Rwanda is one of the tiniest countries in Central Africa, about the size of the state of Vermont. One of the poorest and most densely populated countries in the world (265 people for every square kilometer), Rwanda needs every bit of its arable land to feed its 7.5 million inhabitants. Food shortages, overcrowding, and long-standing tribal conflicts between the Hutus and Tutsis have put constant pressure on Rwanda's political and economic stability, the horrible results of which we now know.

Rwanda is inhabited primarily by two different ethnic groups: the Hutus and the Tutsis (or Watusis). The Hutus make up the majority of the population and number around six million. They are a short, dark, thick-set people whose ancestors were primarily sedentary farmers. The Tutsis, on the other hand, are much taller and lighter-skinned, and descended from nomadic cattle-herders. They number about one million and currently control the Rwandan government.

Rwanda descended from the former colony of Rwanda-Urundi, which was colonized by Germany in 1899 and then made a Belgian protectorate by the League of Nations following World War I. Rwanda's occupation by German and Belgian colonists only worsened the long-standing divisions between its two competing tribes. The Hutus accused the Belgian government of showing preferential treatment towards the taller, lighter-skinned, more European-looking Tutsis, claiming that the Belgians helped the Tutsis oust them from their key posts in government and education in the elections of 1952.

With the two rival tribes unable to come to a peaceful agreement over power-sharing, a much-anticipated tribal war between the Hutus and Tutsis broke out in 1956. Following the death of King Mutara III, the Hutus gained control of the Rwandan-Urundi government in 1959, and the ruling Tutsi elite had to flee for their lives to neighboring Uganda. The following year, Rwanda-Urundi split from the Belgian Congo and became two separate countries, Rwanda and Burundi. With the departure of the Belgians from Rwanda, a new round of tribal skirmishes was touched off in the early 1960s; by 1965, 105,000 Africans had been killed in tribal fighting. After a period of relative calm, fighting flared up again in 1972, resulting in an additional 150,000 deaths.

Anti-Tutsi hard-liners remained in power in Rwanda until a coup by the moderate Hutu general, Juvenal Habyarimana, in July of 1973. On December 17, 1978, a new Rwandan constitution was adopted and Juvenal Habyarimana was elected president. He would go on to serve two consecutive terms, being re-elected in 1983 and again in 1988.

When a famine struck Rwanda in the 1980s, a coup by Hutu hard-liners who wanted their power back threatened the moderate Habyarimana regime. To counter the hard-liners' threat, Habyarimana stacked his government and military with friendly Tutsis and Hutu moderates. In 1990, the Tutsi Rebel Patriotic Front (RPF) from Uganda invaded Burundi and began a three-year civil war to reestablish their minority rule and fulfill Ugandan President Yoweri Mueveni's dreams of becoming ruler of a greater Tutsi Empire. The Tutsi's invasion of Burundi resulted in an estimated 100,000-200,000 deaths before a peace accord was signed in August of 1993. Included amongst the dead was the Hutu president of Burundi, Melchior Ndadaye, who had been assassinated by the Tutsis in a failed coup attempt. During the fighting in Burundi, an estimated one million Burundis fled into neighboring Rwanda, already burgeoning with too many residents, making that tiny nation an ethnic powder keg ready to explode. It was only a matter of time before another tribal war broke out.

Apparitions and Warnings in Kibeho

By the beginning of the 1980s, Rwanda had the largest number of Catholics in any African country: between 55 and 65 percent of the population was Catholic. In November of 1981, the Blessed Virgin Mary began appearing in

Kibeho, Rwanda, to six girls and one boy: Alphonsine Mumureke, Anathalie Mukamazimpaka, Marie-Claire Mukangango, Stephanie Mukamurenzi, Agnes Kamagaju, Vestine Salina, and Emmanuel Segastasha. Three of the girls were boarders at the Kibeho College run by the Benebikira Sisters and the other three girls lived in the bush country. One of the other girls, Vestine Salina, was a Muslim, and the boy, Emmanuel Segastasha, was a farmer who converted to Christianity and changed his name to Emmanuel, which means "God is with us."

Sixteen-year-old Alphonsine Mumureke was at the Sisters' college when she received the first apparition in Kibeho on November 28, 1981. While serving dinner at the noon hour, Alphonsine heard a beautiful voice calling out to her from the corridor: *"My daughter,"* the voice called.

Alphonsine turned around and saw a beautiful lady about twenty-five years old, barefoot, wearing a white dress with white veil and no seam. Alphonsine dropped to her knees and asked "Who are you?" The lady replied in Kinyarwanda, the regional language: *"Ndi Nyina wa Jambo" ("I am the Mother of the Word").*[1]

During their conversation, the Virgin Mary asked Alphonsine, *"Of the religions, what do you like?"*

Alphonsine responded immediately: *"I love God and His Mother who has given us Their Son who has saved us."* Mary replied, *"It is true. I have come to assure you of this. I have heard your prayers. I would like it if your companions had more faith because some of them do not believe enough."*[2]

Alphonsine's apparitions of Mary continued until November 28, 1989. During her apparitions, Alphonsine would sometimes cry and sometimes laugh. When the Blessed Mother finished her conversation and departed, Alphonsine would lose strength and faint. Straw had to be put around Alphonsine to cushion her fall and keep her from injuring herself. When she regained consciousness, Alphonsine was totally exhausted and had to go to bed right away. Alphonsine later asked Mary why this happened, and Mary told her that it is she who supported her, and without her support she was helpless.

The Virgin Mary requested to Alphonsine that she be recognized as the Mother of God, and that the children prepare the world for the return of her son Jesus. She urged Rwandans to forsake worldly things and follow the narrow road to heaven. Mary's central message was one of prayer from the heart, penance, conversion, the Rosary, and preparation for the return of Jesus. She advised the visionaries to be ready for their deaths and the end of the world. Mary also requested that a chapel at Kibeho be named "The Gathering of the Displaced." That peculiar name would make much more sense in 1994.

Between 1982 and 1983, each visionary was given prophetic warnings of what was about to take place, and messages to relay to the world. During one particularly terrifying apparition on October 2, 1982, Alphonsine fell to the ground seven times and implored Mary tearfully, "On the day you will come to call your children, have mercy on us!"

Skeptics accused Alphonsine of faking her apparitions, so Mary appeared to a second Catholic student, sixteen-year-old Anathalie Mukamazimpaka, on January 12, 1982. Mary told Anathalie, *"Wake up, stand up, wash yourselves and look up attentively. We must dedicate ourselves to prayer, we must develop in us the virtues of charity, availability, and humility."*[3]

With Motherly concern, Mary instructed Anathalie to *"Return to God, the Source of Living Water.*[4]

Mary appeared to a third young Catholic visionary, Marie-Claire Mukangango, on March 22, 1982. She was one of those skeptics who hadn't believed in Alphonsine's visions. Mary told Marie-Claire, now a believer, *"We must meditate on the passion of Jesus and on the deep sorrow of his Mother. We must recite the Rosary and the beads of the Seven Sorrows of Our Lady to obtain the grace of repentance.*[5] On another occasion, Mary said to Marie-Claire, *"The world has turned against God. We must repent and ask for pardon.*[6]

Word spread quickly that the Virgin Mary was appearing to three teenagers in Kibeho, Rwanda, and curiosity seekers started pouring in from around the world. A platform had to be built outside the school so that the thousands of pilgrims could better see the visionaries' ecstasies.

On March 27, 1983, the Virgin Mary told Marie-Claire that her messages were ecumenical and meant for everyone, not just for Rwandans:

> *"When I show myself to someone and talk to them, I want to turn to the whole world. If I am now turning to the parish of Kibeho it does not mean I am only concerned for Kibeho or for the Diocese of Butare, or for Rwanda, or for the whole of Africa. I am concerned with and am turning to the whole world."*[7]

To end the persistent criticisms that this was a hoax put on by the Benebikira Sisters, Mary started appearing to youngsters who didn't go to the Sisters' college. On May 25, 1982, Mary appeared to Stephanie Mukamurenzi, a young student at the local public school, saying, *"We must be converted, we must pray and mortify ourselves. Satan tries to ruin us. God wants our prayers from the heart."*[8] Mary also told Stephanie: *"We must remain humble and available. Let us learn to pray from the heart."*[9]

On June 2, 1982, twenty-two-year-old Agnes Kamagaju received her first apparition of Mary in her home. Two months later, Agnes received a message from Jesus regarding the sins of the flesh. Jesus' message was one of penance, conversion, prayer, and faith, and renunciation of idolatry and fornication. His message was particularly relevant for Africa, where upwards of one-fourth of the adult population is said to be infected with HIV:

> *"They [young girls] should not use their bodies as an instrument of pleasure. They are using all means to love and be loved and they forget that true love comes from God. Instead of being at the service of God, they are at the service of money. They*

must make of their body an instrument destined to the glory of God and not an object of pleasure at the service of men. They should pray to Mary to show them the right way to God. "10

In a related message, the Blessed Mother told Agnes:

"I have come to prepare the way for my Son for your good and you do not want to understand. The time remaining is short and you are absent-minded. You are distracted by the goods of this world which are passing... Do not forget that God is more powerful than all the evil of the world. Tell the youth not to spoil their future by the wrong way of living, which can weigh heavily on their future. Don't lose Heaven for the world. The intellectuals have received learning to help others arrive at the truth, which is God. To profess atheism is to insult and mocks God..."

Twenty-four-year-old Vestine Salina, a Muslim convert, began having her visions of Mary on September 15, 1982. Mary said to Vestine, *"[Seek] detachment from the goods of this world and search for the goods prepared by God."* Our Lady also told Vestine how hard it is to get into heaven: *"The walk to heaven is through a narrow road. It is not easy to get through. The road to Satan is wide. You will go fast, you will run because there are no obstacles."*11

The last to receive apparitions was Emmanuel Segastasha. A shining figure of a black man dressed in native African garb and surrounded by a bright light appeared to this unschooled, fifteen-year-old pagan boy as he was returning home from the bean fields on July 2, 1982. Emmanuel heard a voice inside him ask, *"Child, if you receive a mission, will you be able to accomplish it?"* In his heart, Emmanuel responded with "Yes." Then the man led Emmanuel toward a crowd of villagers and said, *"Tell them to purify their hearts because the time is near."*

When Emmanuel asked the man his name, the man replied, *"If I told you my name, no one would believe you. My name is Jesus. Go, and bring the message to the people."* Jesus taught Emmanuel the Lord's Prayer and reassured him that he was the God of all men, not just white men. Jesus said, *"I am neither black nor white. I am simply the Lord."*12 Jesus told Emmanuel that what was needed was a turning away from sin and a return to the sacraments, especially the sacrament of Penance: *"Often we say that we are weak, but God has given us the sacrament of reconciliation."*13

In another message, Jesus told Emmanuel to look for religious fighting before his Second Coming: *"Too many people treat their neighbors dishonestly. The world is full of hatred. You know my Second Coming is at hand when you see the outbreak of religious wars. Then, know that I am on the way."*14 Jesus confided in Emmanuel that time was running out for the world: *"There's not much time to prepare for the Last Judgment."* Our Lady confirmed to Emmanuel that, indeed, little time was left and that we must all be prepared to die:

"There isn't much time left for preparing for the Last Judgment. We must change our lives, renounce sin. Pray and prepare for our death and for the end of the world.

We must prepare while there is still time. Those who do well will go to Heaven. If they do evil, they will condemn themselves with no hope of appeal. Do not lose time in doing good and praying. There is not much time and Jesus will come. [15]

All seven Rwandan visionaries were shown visions of heaven, hell, purgatory, and terrifying glimpses into Rwanda's future: a tree in flames, a river of blood, abandoned bodies with no one to bury them, and piles and piles of decapitated corpses. *"The world,"* explained Our Lady to a crying Marie-Claire, *"is on the edge of a catastrophe."*

All Hell Breaks Loose in Rwanda

Mary and Jesus came to Rwanda to forewarn that country about impending civil war, and to lead it back to salvation before it happened. On April 6, 1994, all hell broke loose when a pre-planned ethnic genocide, orchestrated by extremist Hutu members of the Rwandan Presidential Guard together with Hutu militiamen, massacred over a half-million Tutsis; creating the largest human exodus in modern history (two and a half million Rwandans fled into neighboring Tanzania, Zaire, Burundi, and Uganda). U.N. Secretary General Boutros Boutros Ghali called the ethnic massacres and mass exodus from Rwanda one of the most hideous events in recent times." [16]

In the first three days of war, tens of thousands of innocent Africans were killed. The carnage was so bad that Western journalists likened Rwanda to the Apocalypse. "There are no devils left in Hell...They are all in Rwanda," said the May 16th cover of *Time* magazine; "Deeper into the Abyss" and "Escape from Hell" read the captions of articles in the May issues of *Newsweek. U.S. News and World Report* described Rwanda as "A Descent into Hell," and *Macleans* magazine called Rwanda "A Scene from Hell." The May 18, 1994, issue of *The New York Times,* with its caption, "Blood in the River," validated Mary's prophetic warning of a "river of blood."

Rwanda's orgy of blood started on April 6, 1994, when its President, Juvenal Habyarimana, and Burundi President Cyprien Ntaryamira, were killed on their way back from a peace conference in Tanzania, after their jet was hit by a rocket and crashed on approach to Kigali airport. It was believed that Hutu political extremists had orchestrated the attack on their own President at least eighteen months in advance, with the intent to blame the Tutsi Rebel Patriotic Front (RPF). The Hutu elite were angry with Habyarimana because he had assigned key political posts to Tutsis in accords with the peace agreement of 1993. Hutu political extremists vowed to keep their hold on political power by preventing Habyarimana's democratization of the Hutu-led government, and to prevent the repatriation of exiled Tutsi rebels living in Burundi.

Hutu militiamen and soldiers of the Presidential Guard, armed and trained by France, took to the streets and began hunting down Tutsis. Since all Rwandans were required to carry race identification cards, anyone identified as a Tutsi was butchered on the spot. Those who merely resembled Tutsis were also murdered. Mobs of drunken youths called the *interahamwe* ("those who attack together") joined in the frenzy of killing and indiscriminately stabbed, hacked, bludgeoned, and shot to death any Tutsi they happened upon. Propaganda from the Hutu-controlled radio station Radio Mile Collines urged Hutu youth gangs to strike first because the Tutsi RPF was planning their genocide.

A hit list was circulated amongst the Hutu death squads that contained the names of any human-rights figures, clerics, aid workers, intellectuals, journalists, and moderate Hutus who posed a threat to the radical Hutu elite. Moderate Hutu Prime Minister Agathe Uwilingiyimana was hunted down by Hutu government soldiers and raped and murdered, along with ten Belgian U.N. peacekeepers, who were on their way to protect her. The ten captured Belgian soldiers were taken back to their barracks, tortured by the Hutus, and then shot. Three other Tutsi ministers were similarly murdered.

With a dull, blank stare in their eyes, Hutu street gangs dressed in outlandish clothes and armed themselves with anything they could find: machine guns, grenades, spears, *pangas*, (machetes), clubs, and axes. Anyone suspected of opposing the Hutu government was executed on sight. Elderly African males, women, and children, on their knees begging for their lives, were hacked, clubbed, and shot. Some of these gruesome scenes were captured on video and shown on TV in the West. Exactly as the children of Kibeho had seen in their visions, decapitated bodies and severed limbs were piled high in the streets, houses, and churches of practically every town in Rwanda. The stench of rotting corpses permeated the air and made it hard to breathe. Bodies lay rotting in fields, flowerbeds, and on roads. On one particularly gruesome occasion, six wounded patients were dragged from a Red Cross ambulance at a barricade and bayoneted to death in the street. Blood flowed so much that it formed pools in the roads, causing fleeing cars to spin out of control. Whole communities were wiped out and dumped into the rivers. Dead bodies bobbed in the Rusumo River like mannequins. Corpses floated sixty miles down the rain-swollen Kagera River in Rwanda to Lake Victoria in Uganda, where at least 40,000 dead bodies were counted floating on the lake.

Extremist Hutu government soldiers moved from house to house in search of Tutsis in hiding. Anyone caught sheltering them was executed. Innocent Hutus were forced to murder their Tutsi neighbors or else be killed themselves. Parents were forced to watch their children be dismembered alive. Helpless infants were chopped in half or tossed alive into the rivers to drown. Many victims had their abdomens slit open and died a slow and painful death. Others chose suicide in order to put an immediate end to their agony.

No Sanctuaries from the Slaughter

Nowhere in Rwanda could Tutsis find safety from the slaughter. Twelve thousand Tutsis under U.N. protection in Kigali took refuge in the national sports stadium and the city hospitals, but were mortared and machine gunned to death by crazed Hutu mobs. Fearful health care workers in public hospitals and mental asylums abandoned their patients to a certain death.

That Satan was behind the slaughter in Rwanda was obvious: most victims were killed on church property. Rwandans had felt a degree of safety in Church sanctuaries because those who sought refuge there in the intertribal fighting of 1959, 1963, and 1973, were spared. But this time churches were used as bait. Local Hutu officials lured fleeing Tutsis into their churches and then called in the Hutu death squads. The following are a few examples of the atrocities committed on church property:

- Thirteen hundred Tutsis were killed in a Nyarubuye parish at Kabarondo: women and children were slaughtered in a church as they cried, sang songs, and prayed.
- Twelve hundred Tutsi civilians, more than half children, were murdered in a church just east of Kigali.
- Five priests and twelve young women gathered for a retreat were killed at a Jesuit center near Kigali airport.
- At a Catholic mission in Rukara, where hundreds of refugees had gathered for safety, dozens of corpses were found on the altar, in the pews, in the aisles, and in the church library. Skeletons were found still hugging each other. One woman, even in death, was still cradling her infant.
- Sixty Rwandan boys, who were taken from a church, were found in a mass grave.
- Thirteen clergymen in Kabgaye were slain by Rwandan rebel soldiers assigned to protect them.

The Rwandan Catholic Church is Decimated

The Catholic Church in Rwanda was deliberately attacked by Satan in an attempt to destroy the heart and soul of the Rwandan people: three bishops, 96 diocesan priests, five religious priests, 45 brothers, 64 nuns, and 28 lay missionaries were murdered.[17] Over one half of the Rwandan priests and a third of the bishops were killed.[18] Tutsis blamed the Catholic Church for complicity in the ethnic cleansing because, they said, the hierarchical church had "failed to separate itself" from the Hutu regime. They accused church leaders of being "too silent" when Tutsis were being massacred by the Hutus, and therefore targeted them for retribution. Archbishop Vincent Nsengiyumva, Bishop Thaddee Nsengiyumva of Kabgayi, and Bishop Joseph Ruzindana of Byumba were shot in cold blood by their Tutsi guards assigned to protect them, to avenge the massacres of Tutsis.

Shamefully, a handful of Roman Catholic priests and nuns were accused of aiding and abetting the Hutu death squads by helping identify Tutsis for slaughter. Father Wencelas Munyeshyaka, a Rwandan priest, was said to have planned and participated in one massacre, and another unidentified Hutu priest was accused of shooting ten of his own parishioners to death when they came to his church for protection. Two Benedictine Hutu nuns, Sisters Gertrude Mukangango and Julienne Kizito, were accused of handing over frightened Tutsi refugees who were hiding in their Benedictine convent at Sovu in southern Rwanda on April 25, 1994. The survivors of that massacre said that Sister Julienne even supplied the Hutu mob with gasoline to burn down the building in which the terrified Tutsis had locked themselves, and then participated in looting their corpses. In their own defense, the nuns, now seeking refuge in Belgium, have testified that they were forced to hand over the Tutsis at the threat of their own deaths, and did so only after the Hutu mob had guaranteed the refugees' safety. In all, at least a dozen Rwandan priests and nuns were accused by human rights groups of aiding and abetting the murderers. On April 17, 1998, two Rwandan priests were condemned to death by judges in Kibuye, Rwanda, for crimes against humanity. They were Father Edouard Nturiye, 49, and Father Emmanuel Kayiranga, 36. Both were found guilty of killing about 2,000 Tutsis, who had sought refuge at Nayange Church in Kivumi.

Three of the Kibeho visionaries—Vestine Salina, Emmanuel Segastasha and Marie-Claire Mukangango—were rumored to have been killed during the Rwandan Civil War.[19] Emmanuel was said to have been shot in the head and Marie-Claire killed with her husband. No wonder the Blessed Virgin Mary had forewarned the visionaries to prepare for their deaths.

Suffer the Innocents

As in all wars, innocent children suffered the most. At least 150,000 children were left orphaned by the Rwandan Civil War. Countless numbers of Tutsi children were mentally traumatized when they saw their parents and family members hacked to pieces by machete-wielding Hutus. With no one left to care for them, orphans were packed off to overcrowded orphanages. At one orphanage built to house 40 children, 40,000 were crowded together in appallingly unsanitary conditions. Malnourished and dehydrated, Rwandan children in orphanages and refugee camps contracted tuberculosis, lice, cholera, dysentery, malaria, scabies, and severe diarrhea. Many died as a result.

Western Indifference

The United Nations had 2,000 peacekeepers in Rwanda at the time of the massacres, but they were ordered confined to their barracks. The U.N. Security Council ordered the withdrawal of the barracked peacekeepers with the exception of 400 U.N. soldiers, who were joined by 800 Belgian troops flown-in to keep the Kigali airport open and to help evacuate foreigners, most of whom got out alive.

Indifference permeated the governments of the West over the genocide going on in Rwanda. Westerners didn't want to become involved because they said there were no vital economic interests there. White, liberal, Western population-control advocates looked upon Rwanda as Darwinian "natural selection" in action—nature's way to reduce the burgeoning black African population; a survival of the fittest. Eco-feminists and earth worshipers seemed more upset about the danger to the 600 gorillas living in the mountains of Rwanda than the plight of the 7.5 million Rwandans.

At first, President Clinton tried downplaying Rwanda by refusing to call it genocide. He turned a deaf ear to Rwanda's pleas for help because, for one reason, he didn't want to become involved in another Somalia fiasco. But nightly news coverage of the horrible carnage going on sparked a global outcry and forced the Clinton administration to act. Clinton ordered airdrops of relief supplies and brought in 330 Marines to help evacuate foreigners. By the time Clinton sent in 2,000 U.S. troops in Operation Support Hope, more than a half million Rwandans had already been butchered.

When the capitol of Kigali fell to the better-equipped Tutsi RPF pouring in from Uganda in July of 1994, Hutu government soldiers and militiamen fled for their lives to refugee camps on the borders of Rwanda and in surrounding countries. Refugee camps inside Zaire and Tanzania were dominated by Hutu militia, and thousands of them went around terrorizing the hapless refugees by controlling the distribution of relief supplies. In some refugee camps, Hutu militiamen were known to have held Tutsi women as sex slaves.

The Zairian army was able to dislodge many of the Hutu militiamen from their refugee camps, thereby thwarting the Hutus' attempts to try to retake Rwanda from the outside. With the Hutu militia momentarily disabled, the government of Zaire tried to repatriate the Rwandan refugees; but that didn't work because the Hutu militia had spread false rumors in the refugee camps that returning Hutus were being tortured and slaughtered in revenge killings by the Tutsi RPF. As a result, frightened Rwandans refused to leave the refugee camps.

The plight of Rwandans in refugee camps was horrible: over 2,000 died each day from cholera, pneumonia, and tuberculosis. Since upwards of 25% of the adult population in Rwanda were already infected with HIV, the U.N. had a humanitarian crisis of cataclysmic proportions[20]

The U.N. Assistance Mission in Rwanda (UNAMIR) was incapable of coping with Rwanda's humanitarian nightmare. Much of the relief aid destined for the Tutsi refugees wound up in the hands of the Hutus, who had started the genocide. Aid workers were helpless to do anything about it because they were overwhelmed and exhausted with all the people dying in the camps, forcing them to become undertakers rather than care providers.

Slaughter in Camp Kibeho

The new Rwandan government of the Tutsi RPF began efforts in October of 1994 to close refugee camps in southwestern Rwanda. Starting in January of 1995, in Operation Retour, members of the Rwandan government and UNAMIR tried to persuade the displaced refugees to return to their homes voluntarily, but met with little success because the rumors of disappearances and arrests of returnees had frightened the refugees into staying put. So on April 18, 1995, the RPF decided to forcibly close the Rwandan refugee camps in Kibeho, Munini, Kamana, and Ndago, where a total of 200,000 refugees were camped.

During the evenings of April 20-21, 1995, extremist Hutu militiamen inside the Kibeho camp, where 100,000 refugees were kept, began attacking the refugees with machetes. Several of the refugees were killed and dozens more were wounded by the Hutus. Tutsi RPF guards fired into the crowded camp with machine guns on both nights when, they said, the panicked refugees rushed at them, threw stones at them, and shot at them, although no cases of RPF soldiers wounded by gunfire was reported.

The next day, April 22, at least 2,000 civilians in the Kibeho camp were murdered and about 600 more wounded when Tutsi government troops attempted to forcibly close the camps. Eighty thousand refugees living on a single hill inside the camp attempted to break out of the RPF cordon, having spent five days without adequate food, shelter, water, and sanitation. According to the Rwandan government, the RPF had been concerned that the camp was a haven for former Hutu government soldiers and militiamen. A gun battle between the Hutu militia and the RPF started a stampede and many refugees were trampled to death. Around noon, the Tutsi RPF fired a two-hour sustained volley directly into the camp, then resumed again at 5:00 P.M. that evening. Rocket-propelled grenades and mortars were also used.

When the shooting was finally over, at least 2,000 Rwandans were dead. RPF soldiers hastily buried many of the corpses during the night of April 22-23 to prevent the U.N. military presence at the camp from recording an accurate body count. Many of the bodies were later found thrown into latrines. Despite a hasty attempt to cover-up the massacre, the U.N. estimated that somewhere between 2,000 and 4,000 refugees in Kibeho had been killed—from both the Tutsis and the Hutus.

The surviving refugees in Camp Kibeho finally began returning home on April 23. The taunting RPF soldiers chased, shot at, and threw grenades at the fleeing refugees, mostly women and children, forcing them to leave their only worldly possessions behind. Those fortunate enough to make it back home alive were deprived of everything they had.

All but 1,000 of Camp Kibeho's original 100,000 inhabitants left the camp. The remainder held up in the camp hospital and surrounding buildings, determined to make a stand against the RPF. When it became evident that the RPF was going to wait them out rather than attack, the holdouts decided to surrender rather than starve.

Where were the U.N. peacekeepers all this time? The 200-man U.N. contingency stationed inside the camp with authorization to use military force to protect the camp's 100,000 inhabitants hid inside their two command posts within the center of the camp, protecting themselves with tens of thousands of human shields.

Rwanda Spills Over to Neighboring Countries

In neighboring Burundi, an estimated 100 people are being murdered each day in tribal conflicts, and that country could explode at any moment. Here are just a few examples of the atrocities that have taken place in Burundi since the outbreak of the Rwandan Civil War: On April 10, 1996, a Roman Catholic seminary in Burundi was attacked by a mob of 200 people who killed two priests and a nun; on June 4, 1996, three Swiss Red Cross workers were killed by Burundis in an ambush; in July of the same year the last elected President of Burundi had to flee for his life into the U.S. embassy after a coup ousted him from power; Burundi's religious fighter for peace, Archbishop Ruhuna, was shot to death in a car on September 10, 1996, a along with six others, including a nun.

In neighboring Zaire (now the Democratic Republic of Congo), American troops were sent in 1995 to monitor the volatile refugee situation, as hundreds of thousands of Rwandan refugees headed back home to Rwanda. Even with the presence of American troops, Hutu refugees in Zaire began attacking ethnic Tutsis with the help of the Zairian army, who began expelling the Tutsis from Zaire in 1995. The following year, hundreds of thousands of returning ethnic Tutsis counterattacked the Zairian army, driving the Hutu refugees deeper into the interior of Zaire. On December 1, 1996, a volcano in eastern Zaire erupted, spewing a plume of lava and ash into the air about 30 miles from the Goma border crossing, where Rwandan refugees were straggling homeward from the Kahale and Kahindo camps. Hundreds of thousands of Rwandan refugees remained behind in the forests surrounding the volcano, held there by Hutu militia trying to escape the fighting in Zaire between government troops and anti-government rebels.

In 1997, Zairian rebels ousted their government from power and renamed Zaire the Democratic Republic of Congo. Like Burundi, fighting between the Hutus and Tutsis in the Democratic Republic of Congo could turn that country into another Rwandan bloodbath. Over in Uganda, in March of 1999, eight tourists were murdered outside Uganda's Bwindi National Park by Rwandan Hutus.

Rape as a Weapon of War

Nine months after the carnage in Rwanda, thousands of babies were being born to women who had been raped by marauding Hutu soldiers and militiamen. Often the father of the baby was the one who had killed the rape victim's family. Many of the victims contracted sexually-transmitted diseases, including AIDS, from their attackers, and most Rwandan "rape babies" were abandoned after birth and died.

The number of rapes and sexual mutilations in Rwanda was staggering. Every women or girl who was spared her life from the massacre by the militias had been raped. They even raped corpses and women who had just given birth.[21] Many women and young girls were sexually mutilated and killed after being raped. Some were allowed to live if they became sex slaves for their rapists; others not. Many of those who survived the slaughter and rapes committed suicide.

The Aftermath of Rwanda

U.N. chief Kofi Annan, the head of U.N. peacekeeping operations in 1994, was accused by *New Yorker* magazine in April of 1998 of knowing about the Rwandan government's plans to exterminate minority Tutsis, and allegedly ordering his U.N. peacekeepers not to intervene; a charge Annan has denied, saying that he briefed diplomats from the U.S., France, and Belgium about a Hutu plot to exterminate the Tutsis, but that they had refused to send in additional U.N. forces. On his recent visit to Rwanda in the spring of 1998, Annan was visibly upset by the hostile reception he received. But what did he expect after the *New Yorker* released a copy of Annan's own fax, ordering the U.N. peacekeepers not to intervene in the genocide of Tutsis?

Secretary of State Madeleine Albright visited Rwanda in mid-December of 1997 and apologized for the West's slow response to the Rwandan Civil War, and President Clinton did the same in March of 1998. To some critics of the Clinton administration, their visits appeared politically timed to win public support for the Democrats, and nothing but a show for the media. The people in Rwanda greeted Clinton coldly.

The U.N. War Crimes Tribunal

An International War Crimes Tribunal for Rwanda was set up by the U.N. in November of 1994 to try those suspected of genocide, but it has been charged with rampant corruption, nepotism, and foot dragging. By June of 1998, only 36 suspected war criminals have been indicted by the U.N., with 35 of those 36 given life sentences. The new Rwandan government, however, imprisoned over 125,000 suspected war criminals by June of 1998, and as of that date has executed 22 of 116 sentenced to death, despite pleas from Pope John Paul II for clemency. Another nine Rwandans were sentenced to die in July of 1999. The new head of the Rwandan government reassured the pope that the judges on his courts weren't sadists but were only carrying out justice.

Jean Kambanda, the former Hutu prime minister of Rwanda during the massacres, plead guilty to genocide in May of 1998 and has been found guilty by the U.N. tribunal and sentenced to life imprisonment. A Rwandan pastor of the Seventh-Day Adventist Church, Elizaphan Ntakirutimana, accused by the international war crimes tribunal of taking part in the Rwandan massacres, is awaiting extradition from the United States. The U.S. Supreme Court rejected his lawyer's argument in January of 2000 that he can't be extradited to Rwanda because no treaty exists between the U.S. and the U.N. war crimes tribunal.

The Church on Rwanda

A team of doctors and theologians was commissioned by Bishop Jean-Baptiste Gahamanyi of Butare to investigate the apparitions of Mary in Kibeho. The apparitions were approved by the local bishop on August 15, 1988, in the first stage of the investigation. A final decision by the Church on Kibeho has not, as yet, been made, but it is generally agreed that Kibeho will be approved as worthy of belief. The historical facts strongly support the visionaries' testimonies that Mary and Jesus appeared there.

Chapter Fourteen

The Queen of Peace: Medjugorje, Bosnia-Herzegovina, 1981

"To those who believe no proof is necessary; to those who doubt no proof is sufficient."

Unknown

Mary Appears in Medjugorje

Medjugorje, which is Slavic for "among the hills," is a tiny village that lies at the foot of a large, rocky hill in southwestern Bosnia-Herzegovina called Mount Krizevac, which means "the hill of the cross." On top of Mount Krizevac is a huge concrete cross that was erected in 1933 in commemoration of the nineteen-hundredth anniversary of the crucifixion of Jesus Christ. According to local legend, a priest in Medjugorje, Brno Smoljan, was summoned to Rome in 1933 and informed that Pope Pius XI had been instructed by God in a dream to raise a cross "on the highest Golgotha in Herzegovina." The cross was erected according to the pope's wishes.[1]

Just to the west of Medjugorje is the hill of Crnica, which contains a rocky mound that juts out from it called Podbrdo. At the base of Podbrdo lies the little village of Bijakovici. In-between Bijakovici and Medjugorje is the parish church of St. James, which was constructed during the 1970s to serve the needs of the two Catholic villages.

The people living in these two villages are Croatians and earn their living by raising tobacco or grapes in the valley, or tending livestock in the hills. Theirs is a simple life of hard work and meager wages, and not much excitement. But on the night of June 23, 1981, a terrible electrical storm suddenly arose. The local post office in Medjugorje was hit by a lightning bolt and

259

caught fire, as did several other buildings. The villagers were amazed at the suddenness and ferocity of the storm, and wondered why Satan was voicing his anger at Medjugorje. The following day, however, turned out to be sunny and clear. It was June 24, the Feast of St. John the Baptist.

Fifteen-year-old Ivanka Ivankovic, visiting her grandmother in Bijakovici during summer vacation, joined her friend, Mirjana Dragicevic, a sixteen-year-old from Sarajevo also visiting her grandmother, for a leisurely walk up the hill of Crnica for a cigarette. At about five o'clock in the evening, on their way down the hill, Ivanka spotted a luminous shape of a woman hovering above the rocky terrain of Podbrdo. Ivanka cried out, "Mirjana, look there, it's the Madonna." Mirjana refused to look where Ivanka was pointing and snapped back at her, "Don't be idiotic. Why on earth would the Madonna appear to us?" But Ivanka's strange look frightened Mirjana, so they both ran down the hill as fast as they could. As they reached Bijakovici at the bottom of the hill, they saw another friend of theirs, Milka Pavlovic, setting out to gather her sheep on Podbrdo.

The three girls retraced their steps back to the location where Ivanka had seen the luminous figure. By now it was about a quarter past six in the evening. As they neared the spot, Ivanka shouted out, "Look, there she is!" At 200 meters' distance, Mirjana and Milka could make out the figure of a young woman, dressed in gray, holding something in her hands. From that distance they couldn't make out her face, but they knew in their hearts that the luminous figure had to be the *Gospa* (Our Lady).

Feeling a rush of elation with a tinge of fear, the three girls didn't know what to do. About that time, a local villager, sixteen-year-old Vicka Ivankovic (no relation to Ivanka), found the message that Ivanka and Mirjana had left earlier in the day for her to join them on the hill for a smoke, so she made her way up the footpath without delay. When Vicka neared the girls, who were standing in the middle of the footpath and staring intently up the hill, they shouted for her to hurry up. When Vicka finally caught up they pointed towards the hill and shouted, "Look, it's the Madonna!" Vicka was so frightened that she kicked off her slippers and ran down the hill. When she reached the houses she burst into tears. About that time, twenty-year-old Ivan Ivankovic and sixteen-year-old Ivan Dragicevic (no relation to Mirjana) happened upon Vicka. Vicka asked the boys to go up the hill to see if there was really something up there. The younger Ivan confidently reassured Vicka that there was nothing up there to be afraid of, but when the boys reached the spot on Podbrdo where Ivanka and Mirjana were standing, Ivan bolted down the hill like he'd seen a ghost, locking himself in his room for the rest of the night. Vicka finally got the courage to look up in the direction of the apparition and plainly saw a beautiful young woman floating off the ground in a gray dress with white veil, blue eyes, dark hair, and rosy cheeks. On her head she wore a crown of twelve stars, like the

Woman depicted in the twelfth chapter of Revelation. In her left hand she held something unrecognizable at that distance.

The *Gospa* called for them to come nearer, but none of them dared. Frightened and yet thrilled, the teenagers made their way back down the hill to tell their families, but, of course, no one believed them. Their families' disbelief didn't stop the visionaries from insisting on what they saw though, and word spread rapidly in Bijakovici that the Madonna had been seen on Podbrdo hill.

Across the valley in Medjugorje, when one of the young Bijakovici boys reported that the *Gospa* had been seen on the hill, Iva Vasilj recalled the stormy weather of the night before: "Ah, so that's why there was all that thunder and lightening last night. The mother of God is visiting the earth."[2]

On the following day, June 25, Ivanka and Mirjana felt an irresistible urge to go back up Podbrdo Hill. After they had finished their jobs of picking tobacco leaves in the late afternoon, the two girls joined Ivan, Vicka, Iva Vasilj, Mirjana's uncle, and a couple of curious children and headed up the hill. It was about six o'clock in the evening when Ivanka spotted the *Gospa* again: "Look, the Madonna!" she shouted. Mirjana and Vicka both looked up and cried out in wonder. Vicka rushed down the hill to call her friend Marija, Milka's sister, whom she promised to call if they saw the *Gospa* again. Vicka found Marija with ten-year-old Jakov Colo, and both immediately dropped what they were doing, ran up the hill as fast as they could, and saw the lady, too. The lady motioned for them to come closer, so they sprinted up to within a few feet of the apparition before being thrown down on their knees by some mysterious force. The lady said:

> *"Praise be Jesus."*

At the sound of her voice, the six young visionaries—Vicka Ivankovic, Marija Pavlovic, Ivan Dragicevic, Mirjana Dragicevic, Ivanka Ivankovic, and Jakov Colo—began to cry and pray. Ivanka, whose mother had just recently died in May, asked the *Gospa* about her fate, and was reassured that she was well and happy. Since Ivanka's mother died alone in the hospital, Ivanka asked if there was anything she wanted to say to her daughter. The *Gospa* replied:

> *"Just that you should obey your grandmother and take special care of her now that she's old and unable to work."*

Mirjana, the most mature of the group, voiced the group's concern to Mary about what people would say: "Dear Madonna, they won't believe us, you know. They'll say we're mad." The *Gospa* just looked at Mirjana and smiled. After answering a few more personal questions and promising to return the next day, the Virgin Mary parted with these words:

"Go in the peace of God."

June 25 became the official anniversary of the apparitions at Medjugorje because that was the day when Mary appeared to all six visionaries at once (neither Milka nor the older Ivan would ever see the *Gospa* again). The following evening, on Friday the 26th around 6:15, three bright flashes of light lit up the village of Bijakovici and the surrounding areas. The six children scurried up Podbrdo (now known as Apparition Hill), followed by a large crowd of excited spectatorsthat would grow to several thousand in number. Having climbed about 300 meters higher than the previous day, near an old wooden cross, all six visionaries suddenly stopped, turned to the northeast, and dropped to their knees in front of Our Lady. Vicka threw salt and holy water at the apparition and commanded, "If you really are the Madonna, please stay with us; but if you are not, go away and leave us alone." The *Gospa* smiled and stayed where she was. "Who are you?" Mirjana asked.

"I am the Blessed Virgin Mary."

"And why have you come?"

"I have chosen this place specially, because there are many faithful believers here. I wish to be with you to convert and reconcile the whole world."

Why were these six children selected to receive apparitions from Mary? They were just average kids, and by no means very religious—they only went to church on special occasions like Christmas and Easter, or when their parents made them. They knew nothing of Marian apparitions like those recorded at Fàtima and Lourdes, and didn't know what to expect. When they asked Mary why she chose them, the Blessed Mother responded matter-of-factly:

"I do not necessarily choose the best."

At the end of this apparition, the children were instructed by Mary to stand and pray. The whole crowd joined in as they recited together seven Our Fathers, seven Hail Mary's, seven Gloria's, and at the Madonna's request, the Apostles' Creed. Then the Madonna said she would meet them again at the original spot lower down the hill and parted with her usual farewell.

Marija, however, felt a strong compulsion to go down the hill on a path to the left. On the way down, she saw a vision of an empty cross, shining with a kaleidoscope of colors. The Madonna stood in front of the cross and wept bitterly:

"Peace, peace, peace, you must seek peace. Be reconciled with God and with each other. For that it is necessary to believe, to pray, to fast, and to go to confession."

On June 27, the visionaries requested the lady to post a sign near the site of the apparitions to prove that the apparition was truly the Blessed Mother, and that they hadn't been lying, hallucinating, or under the influence of drugs at the time of the sightings.. Mary tried reassuring them:

"My angels, do not be afraid of injustices. They have always existed."

The children's worry about what people were saying wasn't without merit: Father Zrinko, the Franciscan friar temporarily in charge of the Medjugorje parish while the parish priest, Fr. Jozo Zovko, was away visiting his sick mother in the hospital, was angry with the visionaries because he thought they had gotten themselves involved in a communist hoax to discredit the Catholic Church. The Yugoslav police (SUP), on the other hand, feared that Medjugorje was the beginning of a Franciscan plot to stir up old feelings of Croatian nationalism and anti-communism, and were quietly making plans to put a halt to the gatherings in Medjugorje.

Communist Yugoslavia

Let me pause here and explain how Yugoslavia came into existence and how it turned into a communist state. This is vitally important in order to understand why Mary appeared in Medjugorje in the first place.

In the sixth century, the Southern Slavs (Yugoslavs) migrated into the Balkans from what is now modern day Belarus and the Ukraine, and came under the rule of two Turkish (Muslim) people living in the Balkan Peninsula, the Avars and the Bulgars. By the end of the seventh century, the Slavic language and culture dominated the Balkan Peninsula, and the Turks were either forced out of the Balkans or assimilated into the Slavic culture. In A.D. 748, the Slovene people of the northeastern Balkan Peninsula incorporated themselves into the Carolingian Empire of the Franks, whereby they converted to Roman Catholicism. The Slavs, who had migrated in 877 into the western part of the Balkans, now known as Croatia, also converted to Catholicism, but were ruled by the Orthodox Christians of the Byzantine Roman Empire. Around 910, the Catholic Croats successfully rebelled against the Orthodox Christians and formed their first Kingdom of Croatia.

The first Serbian state in the eastern Balkans came into existence in the middle of the ninth century, when southern Serb tribes united in opposition to the southeastern expansion of the Turkish Bulgars, and made an alliance with the Orthodox Christian Byzantine Empire. At this time the Serbs adopted the Eastern Orthodox Christian religion and Cyrillic alphabet. In the tenth century, however, the Serbian kingdom once again fell under the control of the Muslim Bulgars, and in the eleventh century was ruled by the

Macedonians from the southern Balkans. In 1018, the Byzantine Empire rescued the Serbs and overthrew the Macedonians, giving rise to the short-lived kingdom of Herzegovina (in the center of the Balkan Peninsula) and the kingdom of Montenegro, just below Croatia. A new Serbian kingdom then arose in the eastern Balkans around 1282, which resisted the territorial expansion of both the Catholics and Muslims.

The Orthodox Serbs fought with their hated enemy, the Catholic Church, and tried just as hard to stamp out a Bosnian heresy known as Bogomilism, which, like Catharism and Manichaenism, believed in the existence of a good god and a bad god, and denied the divinity of Christ. Bogomilism had arrived in the Balkans around the tenth century and was probably brought in from Constantinople by Bosnian and Dalmatian merchants.

Serbian efforts to eradicate Bogomilism eased up when the Ottoman Turks invaded Gallipoli in 1354 and defeated the Serbs at Kosovo in 1389. In order to enlist military help from the West against the invading Muslims, the Bogomil king of Bosnia-Herzegovina converted to Catholicism in 1450. But the majority of Bogomils in Bosnia chose to convert to Islam rather than join the Catholic Church, which they hated even more than Islam because of prior Catholic attempts to eradicate Bogomilism from Bosnia.

By 1463, the invading Turks occupied all of Bosnia, and by 1483, all of Herzegovina. As Catholics fled from northern Bosnia into the former kingdom of Croatia, hundreds of thousands of Serbian Orthodox came in to take their place. As a result, Bosnia-Herzegovina became a volatile mixture of Croatian Catholics, Bosnian Muslims, and Orthodox Serbs, with the Bosnian Muslim majority, backed by the Ottoman Turks, controlling the local governments.

The Turkish Ottoman Empire, which tried unsuccessfully to conquer Christian Europe and convert it to Islam, reached the zenith of its power during the reign of Suleiman the Magnificent (1520-1566), but was finally driven out of Europe in 1914 in the Balkan Wars. The beginning of the end of the Turk's foray into Europe came when the Polish-German army under John Sobieski repulsed the Turks at Vienna, Austria, in 1683. In the 1699 Peace of Karlowitz, the Hapsburg Empire of Austria won from the Turks the nations of Hungary, Transylvania, Slovenia, and Croatia. The Turks then lost northern Bosnia and northern Serbia to the Austrians in 1718 and 1815 respectively. After the Russo-Turkish War of 1828-29, the remainder of Serbia was made a Russian protectorate, but technically was still under the suzerainty of the Turkish Ottoman Empire.

In 1875, Bosnia-Herzegovina rose in revolt against their Austro-Hungarian occupiers, whereby the central powers of Europe (Germany and Austro-Hungary) began to fear a possible pan-Slavic Bosnian alliance with Serbia and Russia. Thus, the Congress of Berlin sent Austro-Hungarian occupation forces into Bosnia-Herzegovina.

In 1876, Serbia declared war on Turkey and won its independence from the Muslims two years later when the Russians intervened on the side of the Serbs. The land-hungry Serbs fought against the Bulgarians in 1885-86, and almost went to war with Austria in 1908, when the Serbian king's quest for a "Greater Serbia" brought it into confrontation with the Austrians, who had annexed Bosnia-Herzegovina that same year. Austria had acquired these lands in the Treaty of Berlin in 1878, but had not, as yet, formally annexed them. War in the Balkans was averted for now, but the seeds of WWI had already been sown.

In 1909, Austro-Hungary formally proclaimed the annexation of Bosnia-Herzegovina, and in three years' time the Balkan Wars of 1912-13 ended the 400-year-old Turkish presence in Europe. The Bosnian Serbs were intent on creating a "Greater Serbia," so in 1911 Serbia sponsored the organization of a radical new anti-Austrian terrorist group called the "Black Hand." On June 28, 1914, nineteen-year-old Gavrilo Princip, a Serbian nationalist and a member of the Black Hand, shot to death the heir to the Austrian throne, Archduke Francis Ferdinand, and his wife, the Duchess of Hohenberg, as their motorcade was riding through the streets of Sarajevo. An earlier assassination attempt on that same day had been unsuccessful, when a young Serb named Gabrinovics threw a bomb into the Archduke's car. (The Archduke managed to pick up the bomb from the seat of his car and throw it back on the street before it detonated.) Serbia failed to agree to the full demands of an Austrian-led investigation into the murder, so Austro-Hungary declared war on Serbia in the summer of 1914. That's how the first world war began.

The Central Powers of Germany, Austro-Hungary, and Turkey declared war against France, Britain, Italy, Russia, and the U.S. By 1918, the Central Powers had been defeated and ten million lives had been lost. It was the worst war in history.

With the defeat of the Central Powers, the Balkans became the Kingdom of the Serbs, Croats, and Slovenes, and the Serbs, in the majority, gained control of the Balkan government and economy. In 1929, Serbian King Alexander threw out the kingdom's constitution and declared a new dictatorship named Yugoslavia, which means land of the Southern Slav. The ruthless Serbian auxiliary police, the *Chetniks*, became King Alexander's instrument of oppression as they brutally terrorized the Catholic Croats who had previously sought independence from Yugoslavia. Because of the Chetniks, many Croats chose to emigrate from Yugoslavia to the West. Under the leadership of the Croat Ante Pavelic, members of the ultra-nationalist Croatian opposition movement, the *Ustashis*, fled to Italy in the 1930s and were welcomed with open arms by Italy's fascist dictator, Benito Mussolini. Armed and trained by Mussolini, the Ustashis made frequent hit-and-run terrorist raids on Serbian-controlled Yugoslavia.

With the coming of World War II, Hitler made secret plans with the

Croatian Ustashis to annex the Balkans with the Third Reich. Hitler pressured Yugoslavia into signing a pact with the Axis powers in 1941, but following a military coup the Serb-dominated Yugoslav army announced a new policy of neutrality. Infuriated at the Serbs for breaking their pact with him, Hitler attacked Yugoslavia ten days later and easily defeated the Serbs, then partitioned Yugoslavia between Germany, Italy, Bulgaria, and Hungary. What land was left after the Nazi partitioning was given the title of the "Independent State of Croatia" under Ante Pavelic. Pavelic's puppet countries included Bosnia-Herzegovina, Slovenia, and parts of Dalmatia.

With the arrival of the Nazis in Yugoslavia, the Ustashis waged a brutal campaign of retribution against the Serb Chetniks. Dozens of Orthodox Serbs were hurled by a band of Croat thugs into a deep natural cavern on the other side of Podbrdo (Apparition Hill) and were abandoned to perish from exposure and starvation.[3] Trainloads of prisoners—men, women, and children—were taken to Surmanci, a village within the parish of Medjugorje, and led up the hills to be thrown off cliffs.[4] Outside the diocesan town of Mostar, Serbian prisoners were machine-gunned by the hundreds. The entire community of Orthodox monks at the Monastery of Zitomislic was buried alive by the Ustashis (some Franciscan friars helped the Ustashis commit their atrocities against the Serbs).[5] Concentration camps were set up by the Croats and many members of the Serbian Orthodox Church were sent there. The number of Serbs killed by the Ustashis ranged from 60,000 to 750,000. It is estimated that between 200,000 and 300,000 Serbs converted to Catholicism to escape the brutality of the Ustashis.[6]

A Partisan resistance movement headed by a Croatian communist named Josip Tito surfaced during WWII to fight the Nazis and the Ustashis. Sponsored by the Soviet Union and armed with the captured provisions of the Italian army, who surrendered in 1943, Tito's communist Partisans wreaked havoc on the fascists and Ustashis.

Belgrade was liberated by the Russians and Yugoslav Partisans in October of 1944, and by February of 1945, the Nazis were defeated in Europe and the Ustashis were on the run from the Partisans. Ustashis fled to the hilltop monastery of Siroki-Brijeg in Herzegovina, thirty kilometers from Medjugorje, but were surrounded by the Partisans. Everyone in the monastery, Ustashi and priest alike, were massacred. An estimated 758 Siroki-Brijeg parishioners and thirty friars of the monastery were murdered.[7] Captured government officials and thousands of Croatian soldiers were forced by the communist Partisans to dig their own graves. Many prisoners were tied up and thrown in the river Drava to drown. Many others were sent to die in Serb concentration camps or shot along the way as they fell from exhaustion.[8]

At the end of World War II, Marshall Tito became Premier of Yugoslavia, and declared it a Federal People's Republic. With the communists' ascension to power in Yugoslavia, one terrorist group had simply replaced another, which had replaced another (the Ustashis had succeeded the Chetniks and now the communists succeeded the Ustashis). The Yugoslav people were glad that the fascists had left but were just as worried about the brutality of the communists. Their worries were not unfounded either: Tito immediately went to work to build more concentration camps, filling them with members of both the Catholic and Orthodox Churches.

Tito's communists waged war on Christianity, closing 49 Catholic seminaries and numerous Catholic schools, hospitals, nursing homes, and orphanages. By the end of 1945, Tito had killed 245 priests and religious, and imprisoned 169 in concentration camps (89 were listed as missing). Orthodox Bishops Simrak, Carevich, and Garich were executed by Tito, while Bishops Sarich and Rozman were exiled.

Yugoslav communists were every bit as bad as Soviet communists: they severed ties with the Vatican, arranged for show trials of church members, intimidated and beat up bishops, and pressured believers into renouncing their Christian faith. The Catholic prelate of Zagreb, Archbishop Stepanic, was unjustly tried for complicity with the Nazis and the Ustashis and sentenced to sixteen years hard labor, but he served only five and died in 1960 while still under house arrest.[9] (Although convicted by Tito's kangaroo courts, Stepanic was innocent of all charges against him: he had spoken out publicly in 1943 against atrocities being committed on both sides during the war, and personally intervened to save the lives of thousands of Serbs and Jews. Pope John Paul II beatified Cardinal Aloysius Stepanic on October 3, 1998, which has outraged some Jews and Serbs.)

Typical of repressive communist regimes, Tito nationalized private businesses, confiscated private property, and turned Yugoslavian farmland into huge collectives modeled after the Soviet agricultural system. Religion was allowed to exist only so long as the priests stayed out of politics and didn't teach religion in the public schools.

After Vatican II, Tito's relations with the Catholic and Orthodox Churches improved, but when he died in May of 1980, a year and a month before the first apparitions in Medjugorje, the communists were on heightened alert for any renewed signs of Croatian nationalism. That's why Medjugorje was immediately suspected by the Yugoslav communists as fostering a new movement for Croatian Catholic independence, and that's why they were determined to put a stop to it.

The Regime Fights Medjugorje

Fearful that the apparitions in Medjugorje were the beginnings of a Franciscan plot to incite the people against the communist government, the Yugoslav police quickly whisked the visionaries away to Citluk on June 27,

1981, for "routine medical tests." To the displeasure of the authorities, the attending physician, Ante Bijevic, found nothing physically or mentally wrong with the children, nor any evidence that they were involved in any subversive political plot. He diagnosed them to be normal, healthy kids, and advised the police to let them go—which they did, albeit reluctantly.

On the evening after their release, Podbrdo was bathed in light again and the children gathered together for another apparition. When the Blessed Virgin Mary appeared to the children they asked her why she doesn't appear to everyone so that they would believe, too. Our Lady quoted the Bible in reply:

"Blessed are those who have not seen and who believe."

"What do you want of these people?" asked the children.

"That they should persevere in their faith. Let all those who do not see me believe just as they did see me. Let them [priests] be strong in their faith and give you all the help they can."

The children again asked for a sign from the Madonna so that skeptics would believe. Mary only said:

"Go in the peace of God"

Perturbed by the gatherings on Apparition Hill, the local Franciscan Fathers Jozo and Zrinko announced at mass the following day, June 29, that there were no "public revelations" taking place on the hill. Everyone, it seemed, believed in the children except the police and the local priests.

Despite the dismissals by the local priests, the crowds on Apparition Hill grew larger each day. People from all over Yugoslavia, including Muslims and Orthodox Christians, waited for hours on the hill for the apparitions to occur. Many walked barefoot on the brambles and rocks, while others prayed and sang. The visionaries asked Mary if she was happy to see so many people present:

"More than happy."

The children then asked Mary on the hill at Bijakovici how long she would stay.

"As long as you want me to, my angels."

Regarding the faiths of the different people who were coming to Medjugorje in droves, Mary told the children:

"There is only one God, one faith. Let the people believe firmly and do not fear anything."

The visionaries then asked Mary what she expected from them.

"That you have a solid faith and that you maintain confidence."

"Will we be strong enough to endure persecutions because of our beliefs?" they asked.

"You will be able to, my angels. Do not fear. You will be able to endure everything. You must believe and have confidence in me."

Not satisfied with the Citluk doctor's report, the police took the children to the capital city of Mostar to be examined by a state psychiatrist, Dr. Dzuda, on the morning of June 29. The new doctor was belligerent and accusatory, and was determined to get a confession from the children. At one point Vicka was taken down to the morgue and had a gun pointed to her head by an interrogator.[10] But the children held to their stories and the police were forced to return them to their homes, just in time for their evening apparition. In the meantime, an atheist doctor, Darinka Glamuzina, had been instructed by the police to follow the children up the hill. During the apparition, Dr. Glamuzina asked Vicka if she could touch Our Lady. Vicka, in turn, asked Mary if it was all right, and Mary replied:

"There have always been Judases who don't believe, but she can approach."

The doctor touched the left shoulder of Our Lady and reported she felt a violent tremor go up and down her arm—she refused to ever go up the hill again.[11]

On June 30, Frs. Jozo and Zrinko were ordered to a meeting of the League of Communists headquartered in nearby Citluk. At the meeting, the communists told Fr. Jozo that they were holding them personally responsible for the disruptive gatherings at Medjugorje and were planning to halt the hillside apparitions. But instead of halting them altogether, a compromise was worked out to move the people into the church of St. James.

Early the next day, two female state (communist) social workers "volunteered" to drive the visionaries (Ivan wasn't with them) on a "sightseeing tour" of the surrounding area; purposely making them miss their scheduled evening apparition on the hill. Realizing what they were up to, at about six-thirty in the evening the children begged the social workers to let them out of the car. When the driver refused they threatened to jump out. Finally, stopping at Cerno, on the other side of Apparition Hill, the children got out and fell down on their knees and began to pray. Suddenly, a light from on top of Apparition Hill rushed towards them, and the Blessed Mother appeared. The two social workers later admitted to their superiors that they saw the light descend upon the children. Deeply shaken by this inexplicable incident, one of the social workers moved to Sarajevo and the other emigrated to Germany. Apologizing, the children told the Madonna that the authorities had forbidden them to go up the hill and Mary agreed to visit them the next evening in the church.

On July 1, the police announced at a meeting that the children were banned from both the hill and the church. That afternoon, policemen kidnapped Vicka, Marija, and Ivanka to keep them away from the church of St. James, but let them go because the Virgin appeared to the three right there in the police van. Apparently, the look on the visionaries' faces spooked the policemen so intensely that they ordered the children out of their van.

On the evening of July 2, with huge crowds still thronging to Apparition Hill, Father Jozo, still unconvinced that the apparitions were real, prayed in the church for God's guidance. At the moment he began to pray, Jozo heard a voice just like his own say:

"Go outside now and protect the children."

As he went to open the door, the children came rushing in asking for his help because the police were after them. Fr. Jozo now believed.[12] That afternoon the Blessed Mother appeared to the children in the clergy house where Fr. Jozo had hidden them. For the time being, the visions would take place in the clergy house, and Father Jozo would witness one of them.

After the eighteenth apparition, the visions began to occur randomly, whether the children were at home, at church, in a neighbor's house, or outdoors.

On July 4, the state-run *TV Sarajevo* publicly announced for the first time that a "clerico-nationalist" conspiracy against the communist regime was taking place in Medjugorje. The communists' news story of the Franciscans' hoax of the "Ustashi Madonna" brought in journalists from all over Europe wanting to know what exactly was behind the alleged sightings of the Virgin Mary. Ironically, the state's public announcement of a Franciscan conspiracy against their regime had the opposite effect that it was hoping for: more people than ever were coming to Medjugorje to see if the Blessed Mother was really appearing there.

The six visionaries continued their requests for a sign from Our Lady, but on July 21, 1981, Mary courteously replied to them:

"My sweet angels, even if I were to leave a sign, many people will not believe. Many people will only come here and bow down, but people must be converted and do penance."

Miracles, Signs, and Secrets

Many signs and wonders were occurring, however, in Medjugorje. A miraculous cure took place on July 4, 1981, on the fortieth anniversary of the Partisan communist uprising in Yugoslavia. Jozo Vasilj, blind and ridden with chronic sores on his left arm, took some mud and wild thyme from the site of the apparitions and washed his face with the mixture and immediately regained his sight. He then put plaster over his diseased arm and the next morning his sores disappeared.[13]

Even more spectacular reports of miracles came in the days that followed. On July 14, at eleven o'clock at night, about fifty people, including the visionaries, saw a shaft of brilliant light coming from the dark sky, which fell on the ground where a hole was being dug and where a cross had been placed. They said it was as if a balloon of light had broken and thousands of tiny stars burst forth. Over the cross of Krizevac people saw two Madonna-shaped figures, one glowing like fire.[14]

Around the end of July of 1981, the word MIR appeared in big red letters in the sky above the cross on Mount Krizevac and was seen by at least 150 people, including Fr. Jozo. The word MIR, which is Slavic for "PEACE," would be especially meaningful for Bosnia-Herzegovina because Yugoslavia would soon become embroiled in a horrible civil war. The word MIR might also have been one of the "signs in the sky" that Jesus said would occur before the end times. *Mir* is also the name of the Russian space station that carried U.S. astronaut Shannon Lucid in 1996, the first woman to orbit the earth in a space station. (*Lucid*, by the way, means translucent, clear, understandable.) Not coincidentally, on June 25, 1997, the sixteenth anniversary of the appearance of Mary in Medjugorje, the Russian cargo ship Progress crashed into Mir's *Spektr* module, causing extensive damage and endangering the lives of the joint Russian and American crew. The name for the damaged module, "Specter," in English, means a disembodied spirit or a haunting ghost. *Spektr* is an appropriate name for the module because the Mir space station, having had over 1,500 malfunctions since it was first deployed in 1986, seems to be haunted by a malicious spirit. Here are just a few of the things that have gone wrong with Mir: in July of 1993 a *Soyuz* spacecraft bumped into Mir as it was taking pictures of the space station. On February 23, 1997, an oxygen canister burst into flames and filled the space station with life-threatening vapors and smoke. In March of the same year two oxygen generators failed, and the following month the station's temperature control system began to leak antifreeze and then the air-purification system broke down. And if that wasn't trouble enough, soon afterwards, the Russian commander of Mir, Vasily Tsibliyev, who began having heart trouble in July, accidentally pulled a power cord connected to the space station's main computer, deactivating the guidance system, causing the space station to tumble out of control. A replacement crew was launched on August 5, 1997, to repair the beleaguered space station and to relieve the exhausted Russian crew. But on the same day of the rescue launch, another disaster struck: Mir's oxygen-generating system failed once again and its crew was forced to use emergency oxygen canisters in order to breathe. Before they were launched from the *Baikonur Cosmodrome,* two replacement cosmonauts were blessed and prayed over by a black-robed Russian Orthodox priest, which was a first for the Russian space program.

Even the widely-read Russian publication *Komsomolskaya Pravda* admitted that non-believers were beginning to think that Mir was being haunted by a ghost. In an article that appeared on August 15, 1997, one writer from *Pravda* was quoted as saying, "How and why fortune declared war on this crew is unclear. But even confirmed materialists have started shouting, 'Something spooky's going on here.'"[15]

As you well know, the Mir space station has become the brunt of numerous jokes by Western cartoonists and talk-show hosts because of its seemingly never-ending troubles, but it isn't the only "Mir" to be associated with trouble. See the notes section for a couple more examples.[16]

On the Feast of the Transfiguration of Jesus Christ (August 6, 1981), Our Lady announced for the first time that she was The Queen of Peace (The Queen of "MIR"). The significance of Mary's name for herself wouldn't be fully understood until the outbreak of the Yugoslav Civil War a decade later, but should have been a tip off to believers that war was about to break out in the former Yugoslavia.

Many signs and wonders were worked in Medjugorje. One day the Virgin Mary asked Marija and forty others to go the meadow of Gumno. Mary said that everyone there would be allowed to touch her—atheists and believers alike. The atheists and hardened sinners who touched Mary, however, turned her robe black because of their sins.[17] Horrified at the sight of so much sin in people, the visionaries encouraged everyone there to go to confession. That same day the sun seemed to dance and spin like it did in Fátima, and the people could look directly at it without hurting their eyes. Rainbow rays of light rested on the apparition site and the church tower, on which a clear image of the Virgin Mary appeared. Some present saw figures surrounding the sun in the shape of a cross, with six small hearts appearing in the sky surrounding a larger heart. A white cloud came down the mountain towards the apparition site and then moved toward the sun, which became normal again. Two days later, Fra Umberto Loncar saw a huge red and violet cloud over nearby Cerno, moving towards Krizevac at tremendous speed. A red and violet figure of a woman arose from the hill of Crnica, with a brilliant white scarf dangling from her feet.[18]

On October 28, 1981, a burning fire that didn't consume anything was seen by hundreds of people, including non-believers, on the hill of the first apparition. However, local firefighters and police investigating the fire found no evidence that anything was burned. When asked why, Mary told the children:

"The fire, seen by the faithful, was of a supernatural character. It is one of the signs, a forerunner of the great sign."

When questioned by the visionaries about when the great sign would appear, Mary said:

"The sign will be given at the end of the apparitions."

The great sign is supposedly one of ten individual secrets given each vision-ary by Mary regarding events (warnings, signs, and punishments) that would take place in the very near future. According to the visionaries, after the first few secrets or admonitions, the rest of the secrets will follow in rather short order, and the people will have little time left for conversion. Before the visi-ble sign is given to mankind as an authentication of Medjugorje, there will be three quick warnings to the world. The warnings will be in the form of events on earth.

The ten secrets were invisibly written on a supernatural parchment, which was given to Mirjana by Mary. Ten days before the occurrence of each secret Mirjana will inform Father Pero Ljubicic, and he, in turn, will publicly announce the secret three days before it happens; that way the public will know that the event comes from God. The rest of the secrets will remain invis-ible until their scheduled time of occurrence. Fr. Ljubicic's witness will be a confirmation of the apparitions in Medjugorje and a stimulus for the conver-sion of the world. After the appearance of the first few admonitions, a visible sign will appear on the site of the apparitions in Medjugorje for all the world to see. After the sign, unbelievers will no longer be able to say that there is no God. Therefore, it is imperative that people convert before the visible sign, because afterwards it will be too late. Mary said in the spring of 1983:

> *"Hasten your conversion. Do not await the sign which has been announced for those who do not believe; it will be too late. You who believe, be converted and deepen your faith."*

The first two secrets are essentially warnings. After the warnings the perma-nent sign will come; after the sign, the seven punishments—possibly the seven plagues of Revelation Chapter 15. The punishments get worse with their numerical order. Mirjana said: "The eighth secret is worse than the seven before it. I begged for it to be made less severe. Every day I beseech the Madonna to get it mitigated, and at last she said that if everyone prayed it might be averted. But then she told me the ninth secret and it was even worse. As for the tenth, it is terrible, and nothing can alter it. It will happen."[19] Fr. Vlasic asked Mirjana if we could prepare for it in any way. "Yes, the Madonna said the people must prepare themselves spiritually...and not panic. They should accept God now so that they will not be afraid. If they commit their lives to God, he will accept them."[20] The ninth and tenth secrets, which follow shortly after the visible sign, are serious and pertain to the divine punishment of the world.

God's chastisement is unavoidable, for the world cannot be expected to convert, and imminent because it will definitely occur within the lifetime of the visionaries (the visionaries will be in their mid-sixties by the year 2030). It will come from God and will follow shortly after the sign so that the world will know it's being punished for its sins. It will not be a global thermonuclear holocaust, as many false prophets have maintained, because Mary told the visionaries on July 12, 1982, that the Third World War will not take place. Many tend to think it will be something natural, like a comet or an asteroid, so they know it comes from God and not man: something akin to the Shoemaker-Levy 9 comet that hit Jupiter in July of 1994. Many scientists are warning that an asteroid the size of the one that probably killed the dinosaurs hundreds of millions of years ago could hit the earth at any moment. Each year large asteroids come extremely close to the earth and it's only a matter of time before one the size of a mountain finally hits the earth. It's no coincidence that Hollywood and the media have recently made several movies about comets, asteroids, volcanoes, and natural disasters, for God has put it in their minds to warn the world before he acts.

Certainly, God is sending us other warnings in the form of earthquakes, volcanoes, floods, mudslides, heat waves, droughts, fires, tornadoes, typhoons, and hurricanes, all of which have increased in intensity and frequency within the last twenty-years: a fact which scientists have no logical explanation for except to blame it all on *El Nino.* Jesus said in Matthew 24:3-8 that when these things start to occur, know that the birth pangs of the end times have already begun. When Jesus was sitting on the Mount of Olives one day, the disciples approached him privately and said, "Tell us, when will this happen, and what sign will there be of your coming, and of the end of the age?" Jesus said to them in reply:

> *"See that no one deceives you. For many will come in my name, saying, 'I am the Messiah,' and they will deceive many. You will hear of wars and rumors of wars; see that you are not alarmed, for these things must happen, but it will not yet be the end. Nation will rise against nation, and kingdom against kingdom; there will be famines and earthquakes from place to place. All these are the beginning of the labor pains."*

Everything that Jesus said must occur before the end time has already occurred in the twentieth century, so the chastisement could happen at any moment.

When the chastisement comes, billions of people are expected to die, both the good and the bad. Everyone must be prepared for his or her own death, like the visionaries were told to do in Kibeho. Those who seek to outwit God and avoid the chastisement by digging shelters and stockpiling supplies will fare poorly. The severity of the chastisement, however, can be lessened by frequent prayer and fasting. The seventh secret, according to Mirjana, has already been lessened this way.

On October 25, 1985, with Fr. Pero Ljubicic present, Mary gave Mirjana a vision of the first secret, with all its chaos and destruction. Mirjana wept and asked Mary why so soon?

> *"Because there is so much sin in the world."*

Then Mirjana asked the Blessed Mother how God could have such a hard heart. Mary replied:

"God's heart is not hard. Look around and see how people behave. How can you say it is God who is hard-hearted? ...The time that remains is a time of grace. Use it well and change your lives."

An unavoidable punishment is about to befall mankind and our time is short. This time of grace, the period we are in now, will soon be followed by the admonitions that will end with the visible sign to the world. When the sign appears, no one will be able to doubt God's existence anymore; for many, however, it will be too late. Those who have chosen not to believe or have chosen to live an ungodly life will be devastated by the sign. People will tear their hair out because they know they'll be condemned for having lived their lives apart from God.

As mentioned, after the first two admonitions, a visible sign will appear on the site of the apparitions in Medjugorje for all the world to see. The sign will be given as a testimony to the apparitions and in order to call people back to the true faith. The sign will be permanent, indestructible, beautiful, and visible to all. Vicka has seen the sign and says it is very beautiful. She said people will flock to the hill and be forgiven for their sins.

The Parish Priest is Jailed

Fr. Jozo was called into SUP headquarters on August 11, 1981. He was ordered to stop people from assembling on the hill and abolish the evening mass, and told if he failed, he would be imprisoned.[21] The hill was closed by police guards on August 12, so the Virgin Mary appeared to the visionaries behind a house. The following day, police roadblocks were set up to prevent cars from entering Medjugorje. On August 17, two agents of the Mostar Ministry came for Fr. Jozo, arrested him, and drove him to Mostar, where he was beaten and incarcerated. Meanwhile, five Franciscan nuns from the convent near Medjugorje were accused of having secret projection devices on their persons and were humiliatingly strip-searched, but no such devices were found.[22]

Mary told the children not to worry about Fr. Jozo because she would protect him in jail (it was later discovered that Father Jozo's cell would supernaturally illuminate and his chains would free themselves, and the policeman who had severely beaten him when he was jailed died ten days later of a heart attack).

On August 28, the visionaries patiently waited for Our Lady in Father Jozo's room, but she didn't come. This was the second time this happened. The first was when Ivan entered seminary on August 22, and Mary was late appearing to the other five on the evening of August 23. Mary said later that she didn't show up because she had visited Fr. Jozo in jail and that he sends his greetings.

Fr. Jozo was put on trial in October for supposedly making hidden reference to the forty years of communist rule in Yugoslavia when police informants overheard him preaching on the Israelites wandering forty years in the desert. Because of this sermon, Jozo was charged with "inciting nationalistic-fascist sentiments for a popular Croat uprising." To prove their case, the government brought in false witnesses to swear that Jozo was intending to overthrow the communists.[23]

On October 21, 1981, the day before Jozo's sentencing, Mary told Vicka:

> *"Jozo looks well and he greets you warmly. Do not fear for Jozo. He is a saint. I have already told you. Sentence will not be pronounced this evening. Do not be afraid, he will not be condemned to a severe punishment. Pray only, because Jozo asks for your prayer and perseverance. Do not be afraid because I am with you."*

Father Jozo was sentenced to three and a half years on October 22, but would only serve about half his sentence. He was released from prison in February of 1983, and transferred to the parish of St. Elijah in Tihaljina, with orders not to return to Medjugorje. Jozo's associate, Fr. Ferdo Vlasic was sentenced to eight years for publishing articles on Medjugorje in the Franciscan magazine *Our Hearths*. Ferdo's assistant, Fra Jozo Krizic was given five years.[24] On the day the friars were sentenced, about seventy people, including priests and nuns, saw the silhouette of a woman with outstretched arms in place of the cross on Krizevac.

Prophecies of Medjugorje

Father Jozo's replacement, Fr. Tomislav Vlasic, arrived in Medjugorje on June 29, 1981, five days after the apparitions had already begun. Vlasic supposedly knew beforehand that the Blessed Mother was about to appear in Yugoslavia because a fellow friar, Franciscan Father Branko, formerly of the parish of Medjugorje, supposedly received two prophetic messages in 1979 while attending a meeting of the Charismatic Renewal Movement in Italy, which Vlasic was also part of. In one of the prophetic messages, given to the world-famous mystic, Sister Briege McKenna, Fr. Vlasic was seen in the midst of a fast-growing multitude, where streams of living water flowed. In the other message, received by Sacred Heart Father Emilien Tardif, Vlasic was told: *"Do not worry; I shall send you My Mother and everyone shall listen to her."*[25]

After receiving the two prophetic messages, Father Branko returned immediately to his parish of Medjugorje, and while there, told his catechism class of the "special grace" that God was about to grant Medjugorje, and instructed them to pray for its hastening. Not long afterwards, miracles began occurring in Medjugorje. In 1980, two village children fell seriously ill and their mothers sought the help of Father Branko after exhausting all medical means. Father Branko formed prayer groups from his catechism class to pray for healing, and after several weeks of fervent prayer, the children recovered. In thanksgiving, a pilgrimage was made to the Marian shrine of Marija Bistrica, and a special devotion to Mary was set up at Medjugorje.

In the spring of 1981, just a couple months before Mary appeared in Medjugorje, several old and precious Franciscan rosaries were found in the vicinity. After determining that they belonged to no one, Father Branko declared the rosaries "clear signs of the Medjugorje's selection by God and His coming grace." Vicka was later told by the Virgin Mary that the antique rosaries were supernaturally placed in Medjugorje as an invitation to prayer.

Other Visionaries in Herzegovina

The six visionaries from Bijakovici weren't the only ones to receive visions and messages from Our Lady. Eighteen people from Izbicno, sixty kilometers away, had apparitions from 1982-83, and Mary confirmed to the six from Medjugorje that their visions had come from God. The Blessed Mother also appeared to two eleven-year-old girls, Jelena Vasilj and Marijana Vasilj (no relation), beginning in February of 1982, through interior locutions (interior locutions differ from exterior, three-dimensional apparitions in that they are seen two-dimensionally, like in a dream).

On December 29, 1982, Jelena asked Mary if she, too, could have ten secrets entrusted to her. The Blessed Mother respectfully explained to the young girl:

"I do not appear to you as to the other six because my plan is different. To them I entrusted messages and secrets. Forgive me if I cannot tell you the secrets which I have entrusted to them. This is a grace which is for them, but not for you. I appeared to you for the purpose of helping you to progress in spiritual life and through your intermediary I want to lead people to holiness."

In 1983, Jelena asked Our Lady about the authenticity of the apparitions received by the six, and the contents of the great sign:

"Pardon me, but you cannot know it; it is a special gift for them. You will have to believe it like all the others. In the meantime, everything that they say corresponds to the truth."

Jelena and Marijana were asked by Mary to form a prayer group consisting of young children to meet regularly and pray for the intentions of the world, especially the young.

Our Lady's messages to Jelena and Marijana lasted until July 30, 1987. In one locution, Jelena was shown starving children in Africa, fighting in Asia, and American children smoking dope and injecting drugs.

When asked why she was appearing in so many places in Bosnia-Herzegovina, Mary replied:

"...It is necessary to awaken the faith. It is a gift from God. If it is necessary, I will appear in each home."

Frustrated by the two girls' never-ending questions regarding future events and the contents of the ten secrets, the Madonna stressed to them the importance of reading the Gospels for that information:

"Why ask so many questions? Everything is there in the Gospels."

Our Lady's True Birthday

In May of 1984, Our Lady announced for the first time to Jelena that the true date of her birthday is on August 5 rather than September 8, her traditionally celebrated birthday.[26] Mary asked Jelena to relay a message to all Christians requesting that they prepare a three-day celebration in honor of her 2,000th birthday, which would take place on August 5, 1984 (the year that the Winter Olympics were held in Sarajevo):

"This message is dedicated to the Pope and to all Christians. Prepare the second millennium of my birth which will take place August 5, 1984. Throughout the centuries, I consecrated my entire life to you. Is it too much for you to consecrate three days for me? Do not work on that day, but take up the Rosary and pray."

Mary then told Jelena:

"The priests who will hear confessions will have great joy on that day."

Father Vlasic sent the pope this message on June 2, but for diplomatic reasons, he elected not to act on it.

In August of 1984, however, tens of thousands of jubilant well-wishers were on hand for the 2,000th anniversary of Mary's birthday: many had been there the entire three days celebrating, fasting, and praying. About seventy priests heard confessions around the clock. The priests related that they have never felt such joy in all their lives.

On August 5, Mary appeared to the visionaries dressed in golden splendor, weeping with joy:

"Never in my life have I cried with sorrow, as I have cried this evening in joy. Thank you!"

To all that came Mary gave a Special Blessing.

Just the day before, on August 4, Father Tomislav Vlasic was at a meeting with Jelena's prayer groups. During the praying of the Our Father, Fr. Vlasic noticed a strange thing happen: during part of the prayer, Jelena was unable to utter a sound, despite her struggle to pray. This only lasted several seconds and then Jelena got her voice back. Afterwards, Father Tomislav took her aside and asked what had happened. Jelena told him that during the Our Father Satan appeared to her and physically prevented her from praying. He was on the ground before her, in great pain, and crying bitterly. She said he begged her to ask the Gospa not to bless the world tomorrow. Jelena ignored him and Satan disappeared. A short time later, the Blessed Mother reappeared to Jelena and explained the reason for Satan's tears:[27]

> *"He knows well what he is asking! He knows that during these days he will not be able to do anything in this place [Medjugorje] because he will be tied. The Almighty has permitted me to bless the world with a solemn blessing."*

The Bishop of Mostar Attacks Medjugorje

Higher-ups in the communist government had demanded that Pavao Zanic, the bishop of Mostar, put a halt to the celebrations at Medjugorje, but, at first, he refused. The bishop was apparently elated when he first learned that the Virgin Mary was appearing in his parish in Medjugorje, acting as though he believed, too. Zanic was even quoted early in a statement that appeared in the Croatian Catholic paper, *The Voice of the Council,* on August 16, 1981, that the Medjugorje children were telling the truth and no one had forced them or influenced them in any manner.[28]

Bishop Zanic interviewed the visionaries in Medjugorje on July 21, 1981, recorded their conversations and put them under oath regarding their apparitions. While in Medjugorje on the feast day of the church's patron saint, the bishop preached a sermon on the great significance of the apparitions:

> "I declare and guarantee that none of the priests has had any aim whatsoever in this affair, nor has any of them tried to influence the boys and girls for any ulterior motive. I am equally convinced that the boys and girls are not lying."[29]

At that time Bishop Zanic supported Medjugorje and all was peaceful. But afterwards, when the visionaries told the bishop that Mary had been critical of him for expelling two young Franciscan friars from his diocese in June of 1981 during the controversial "two-priests affair of Herzegovina," Zanic became enraged. Doing a complete about-face, the bishop started telling his colleagues that he had been suspicious of the visionaries all along, and that he only acted as though he believed because he was reserving judgment. The bishop's ego had been deflated by the Blessed Mother's defense of the two Franciscan friars, Ivica Vego and Ivan Prusina, who Zanic had wrongfully expelled from the diocese just two weeks before the beginning of the apparitions in Medjugorje, and the bishop was not about to admit that he made a mistake. Thus, Bishop Zanic became the second means by which Satan attacked Medjugorje.

The Catholic Church in Bosnia

The hostility between the secular bishops of Mostar and the Franciscan friars that led up to the controversial "two-priest affair" and Bishop Zanic's relentless attacks on Medjugorje is best understood if one knows a little of the history of the Catholic Church in Bosnia-Herzegovina.

As previously mentioned, the Slavs of east-central Europe migrated to the Balkans and took control of the region in the late sixth and early seventh centuries. The Croats settled in the western part of the Balkans, the Serbs in the eastern, and the Slovenes in the northern. The Croats and Slovenes, who settled in the north and the west, converted to Roman Catholicism because that region was loyal to the pope, while the Serbs, who settled in the east, converted to Orthodoxy, which was the faith of the Eastern Roman Empire after it split with Rome in 1054.

Around the tenth century, the heresy of Bogomilism arrived in the Balkans from the Middle East and infiltrated Bosnia, where it became the state religion. Bosnian Bogomils called themselves Christians but rejected the doctrines of Christianity, which led to Bogomilism's condemnation as a heresy by both the Roman Catholic and the Greek Orthodox Churches. The Catholic Crusaders of the thirteenth century attempted to stamp out Bogomilism by laying waste to Bosnia, but it survived and flourished and by the end of the thirteenth century, it had become the state religion of Bosnia. When the first Franciscan missionaries arrived in Bosnia-Herzegovina in 1339, they found it overrun with Bogomil heretics.[30] The Franciscans' simplicity and humility, however, won the heart of the Bogomil king, Stephen II, and he converted to Catholicism. Because of this, Franciscans were allowed to establish monasteries and preach to the Bogomils.

When the Ottoman Turks invaded Serbia and Bosnia at the end of the fourteenth century, most Bogomil leaders and Bosnian aristocrats allied themselves with the Muslims rather than the Catholics because of their hatred towards the Catholic Church for what they did to them during the Crusades. Most of the Bosnian peasants, however, remained Christian because of their love for the Franciscan friars. When the Turks invaded Herzegovina in1483, most Catholics fled into Croatia, but pockets of believers still remained in the area of Medjugorje.

With their churches and monasteries all but destroyed by the invading Turks, many of the Franciscan friars fled to the countryside to live secretly and preach amongst the peasants. Those friars unfortunate enough to be caught by the Turks were impaled, skinned-alive, stoned, hanged, or cudgeled.[31]

In July of 1875, Christian peasants in central Bosnia-Herzegovina rose in revolt against the Turks. Serbia, Montenegro, and Russia then entered the war in 1876-77 and defeated the Ottoman Turks in 1878.

After the Turks' defeat in Bosnia-Herzegovina, the Hapsburg rulers of the Austro-Hungarian Empire sought to install a secular clergy and slowly phase out the dominance of the independent-minded Franciscan friars, whom they thought had too much of the people's loyalty. Bosnia-Herzegovina was divided into secular dioceses and new bishops and priests were appointed to run them. A regular clergy was installed in Bosnia-Herzegovina by Pope Leo XIII on July 5, 1881, with an archbishopric at Sarajevo and episcopal sees at Mostar and Banja Luka.

In 1923, an agreement was ratified in Rome whereby the Franciscans would keep the majority of their parishes and could claim as theirs all the parishes they would build up through missionary activity amongst the Orthodox and Muslims. In return, the Franciscans priests would contribute to a diocesan seminary and help in the recruitment of seminarians, which, of course, they were reluctant to do. As a result, an intense rivalry for parishioners and seminarians was started between the secular dioceses and the Franciscan Order.

By the early 1940s, the Franciscans controlled 63 of 79 parishes, 29 monasteries, 5 seminaries, a few hospitals, some businesses and a number of landownings. But with the coming to power of Josip Tito during WWII, the communists confiscated much of the Franciscans' possessions. Tito outlawed all Franciscan missionary activity and a secular priest was appointed Bishop of Mostar for the first time in 1942. The Franciscan friars defended their parishes against the communists as best they could; some even joined the anti-communist Ustashis.

By 1966, when relations between Yugoslavia's communist government and the Franciscan Order had improved somewhat, an agreement was signed by the Vatican guaranteeing each party's rights and obligations towards each other. That same year, however, the secular diocesan bishop of Mostar signed a secret agreement with the communist government of Bosnia-Herzegovina guaranteeing educational grants for priests and other facilities in exchange for a degree of state control over the selection of seminarians and the appointment of parish priests. The bishop of Mostar managed to convince Rome to transfer 33 of the 63 remaining Franciscan parishes to diocesan jurisdiction, which, of course, infuriated the Franciscans. The Franciscan Order in Bosnia-Herzegovina had every right to be upset: by 1967, their jurisdiction had shrunk from 79 parishes to just 30.

Most of the Bosnian peasants were fiercely loyal to the Franciscans and looked upon the introduction of the diocesan clergy into their urban parishes with deep suspicion, considering them an extension of the communist regime. Sometimes it was necessary for the police to wrest away control of the parishes from the peasants and the Franciscans by force. Diocesan priests and Franciscan friars even came to blows on occasions.

In 1975, when five key Franciscan parishes were being considered for transfer to the bishop of Mostar's control, the Father Superior of the Franciscan Order sent a letter to the Vatican stating in no uncertain terms his fierce opposition to the transfer. As a result of his protest, the Vatican suspended the Franciscan Father Superior from his office. The secular bishop of Mostar wrongly interpreted this suspension as an excommunication of the Father Superior and immediately pronounced the presence of all Franciscan parishes in Bosnia-Herzegovina to be in conflict with Catholic Church law, which, of course, they weren't.

Because of the ongoing bickering between the Franciscans and the Bosnian bishops over the division of parishes, in 1978 the Vatican abolished the Franciscan Herzegovina Province, suspended its entire leadership, and made the friars answerable to their Father General in Rome. When Pavao Zanic became bishop of Mostar in 1980 he immediately cut the Franciscans' jurisdiction in half; taking three-quarters of Mostar's churches away from the Franciscans and then building a new cathedral in Mostar to replace the older Franciscan one. Bishop Zanic intentionally falsified the agreement that was worked out between his diocese and the Franciscans, claiming that the Franciscans had agreed to his divisions—which they hadn't. Many of the Franciscans' parishioners were so upset at Zanic that they refused to attend mass with his secular priests. Masses were celebrated, instead, in private homes and chapels by the Franciscans. Two of the most vocal critics of Bishop Zanic were the Franciscan Friars Ivica Vego and Ivan Prusina, who were expelled from their order because of their protests against Zanic.

Mary Blames the Bishop

Because of their outspoken opposition to Bishop Zanic, Franciscan friars Ivica Vego and Ivan Prusina were expelled in June of 1981, just two weeks before the beginning of the apparitions in Medjugorje. In messages received by the bishop from Vicka regarding the recent "two-priests affair," Our Lady said that the guiltiest person was Bishop Zanic, not the two expelled friars. Mary told Vicka on January 3, 1982:

> *"Ivica isn't guilty. If he is expelled by the friars he must be brave! I say every day, Peace, Peace, and there is more and more trouble. Ivica is not guilty. Let him stay where he is...The bishop isn't attempting to resolve the friction so he is guilty. But he won't always be bishop..."*[32]

In a follow-up message on April 26, 1982, Mary said:

"The bishop has none of the real love of God for those two. Let Ivica and Ivan stop worrying about the bishop, since he has saddled them with a great weight in order to shift it from his own shoulders. He has begun with the younger friars and intends to feel his way forward a little at a time. I know this has all been a big shock for them, but they mustn't worry. They should try and forget about it, and learn how to suffer in silence for justice. What the bishop is doing is not in accordance with God's will. Innocent, blameless young men, and punished in this way. God would never want such a thing."[33]

As previously mentioned, when Vicka informed Bishop Zanic of Mary's January 3rd message in support of the two expelled friars, the bishop blew up: "Go away," he yelled. "And when your Lady finally reveals her true colors and curses God, be sure and let me know."[34]

The Blessed Mother's siding with two lowly friars against a diocesan bishop was too much for Zanic to take, so he convinced himself that Medjugorje must be a Franciscan conspiracy against him. "The real aim," the bishop said, "of this group of Franciscans is to point out to the simple people and the foreign pilgrims, with the authority of Our Lady, that they are in the right while the bishop and the legitimate Superiors of their Province and their Order are in the wrong concerning the famous problem of the divisions of the parishes. The sad case of the ex-chaplains of Mostar, expelled from the [Franciscan] Order for their misdemeanors and then defended by 'Our Lady of Medjugorje' despite the decrees of the Holy See and the Franciscan Order, is clear proof that they are manipulating the whole affair."[35]

Bishop Zanic was determined to prove that the apparitions in Medjugorje were a fantastic hoax conceived by the Franciscans in order to discredit him in the eyes of the Catholic Church.

The First Commission

On January 10, 1982, Bishop Zanic assembled a four-man panel to investigate Medjugorje. The four theologians selected, however, included only one Franciscan, and he was the only one to show enough enthusiasm to visit Medjugorje regularly. The First Commission's findings were inconclusive: voting was secret and the results were never published, but it is generally thought that they voted against Medjugorje.

In the spring of 1982, two Commission members were sent to Medjugorje and Sarajevo (where Mirjana was) to get the visionaries to write down on a piece of paper the contents of the sign, including the date of its expected occurrence. The letter containing the sign, they promised, would be put it in a sealed envelope in the bishop's archives for safe-keeping. But the children's spiritual advisor, Fr. Vlasic, was tipped off by the only Franciscan on the Commission that they were coming to get the secret, so he recommended that the children ask the Lady's permission first. On May 6, 1982, the children asked the Blessed Mother's permission to write the sign down and she resolutely said no:

> "No! I have entrusted that only to you. You will unveil it when I tell you. Many persons will not believe you, I know, and you will suffer very much for it. But you will endure everything and you will finally be the happiest."

The Blessed Mother knew what the bishop's real intention was: he hoped to catch the children in a lie by forcing them to write down a sign that wouldn't occur.

All the visionaries except Ivan, who was away at Visoko seminary, politely refused the bishop's request. Secluded in seminary, Ivan had no contact with the outside world and was unaware that the bishop was trying to trap the others in a lie. Acting quickly, Zanic phoned the seminary to make sure that Ivan wasn't allowed any outside phone calls or visitors to warn him they were coming. When the Commission members arrived on May 6, 1982, Ivan was totally unaware of what their intentions were.

Not the brightest of the six visionaries, Ivan was struggling at the seminary and was full of self-doubt and anxiety (he had already failed his first round of tests). When the commissioners arrived and ordered Ivan to write down the sign and put it into a sealed envelope, Ivan panicked—not knowing what he should do. Should he obey Our Lady's request to keep the sign a secret, or obey the request of his bishop? Thus began the well-publicized "Ivan affair," which Bishop Zanic used as one of his main "proofs" that Medjugorje was a fraud.

Not using his head, Ivan tried satisfying everybody by writing down a fictitious account of the sign. He reasoned that since it would be put in a sealed envelope and locked away in the bishop's archives, no one would be the wiser if the contents were false. On the paper Ivan wrote that the great sign would be a Marian shrine built within six months at Medjugorje.

As he had hoped, when the First Commission broke its promise and opened the sealed envelope on March 7, 1985, Bishop Zanic was delighted to find out that it was false. Since the predicted sign had not occurred, Zanic was now sure that everyone would realize that Medjugorje was a fraud. Bishop Zanic exuberantly revealed that Ivan's secret sign had not come true, and Medjugorje's credibility was thrown into serious doubt with the world. If Medjugorje was to survive, Ivan needed to do some explaining, and fast.

Panicking, Ivan gave two different accounts at two different times of what happened. At first, he claimed that he put a blank piece of paper in the envelope, but when the Commissioners proved that the letter was in Ivan's handwriting, he admitted that he did write something down, but that it wasn't the real sign.

Thinking he had gotten the proof he needed to discredit Medjugorje, a jubilant Bishop Zanic went to Rome to report the "Ivan affair," but to his dismay was ordered to tone down his opposition and let Medjugorje take its course. Our Lady of Medjugorje still had some powerful friends in the Vatican, which included Pope John Paul II.

Ivan made several dumb mistakes, there is no doubt, and the Blessed Mother thoroughly scolded him for them. When Franciscan Father Slavko Barbaric came to visit Ivan at the seminary, a tearful Ivan told him that the Madonna was visibly angry when she appeared to him again and had reprimanded him sternly. Ivan told Barbaric that Mary had told him that he should not have written anything and told everyone so, instead of trying to deceive people, and that he'd wept with shame because of it.

When the subject of Ivan was brought up again on March 13, 1985, after the bishop revealed the phony contents of the sealed envelope, the Madonna told Vicka to pray so that she would not repeat Ivan's mistake:

> *"Pray, pray, pray! It is only with prayer that you will be able to avoid Ivan's error. He should not have written; and after that, he had to acknowledge it so as not to plant any doubts."*

When Mary appeared to Mirjana on Mirjana's birthday (March 18, 1985), Our Lady tried putting the whole "Ivan affair" behind them:

> *"...Ivan did not make a big mistake. I've scolded him enough. It is not necessary to scold him anymore. Let him alone."*

The bishop, however, refused to let the "Ivan affair" die because two years earlier, in 1983, Ivan had infuriated him with a sworn statement that said Our Lady had demanded that the bishop be converted to Medjugorje before it was too late. This was Our Lady's message to Ivan concerning the bishop's unbelief and her warning to him:

> *"I am sending him the last warning but one. If he doesn't accept these events [concerning Medjugorje] and behave accordingly, he will hear my judgment and that of Jesus, my Son. If he does not heed my message, then he is not walking in the Way of my Son."*36

Zanic sent this statement off to Rome in protest, but continued to receive more calls for repentance from Our Lady. The following are more of Mary's messages given through the visionaries concerning Bishop Zanic's refusal to believe in Medjugorje:

> *"Tell the bishop that I beg him most earnestly to endorse the events in the parish of Medjugorje before it is too late... I want him to approach these events with great understanding, love and a deep sense of responsibility. I don't want him to cause friction among the priests or to draw public attention to their negative attitudes. The Holy Father has told all the bishops to carry out their diocesan duties and problems. The bishop is father-in-chief to all the Herzegovina parishes, and head of the Church in that province. For this reason, I beg him to accept what is happening there."*37

"I have sent the bishop many messages. But he has not wanted to receive them. I have also sent you. Yet he is still not prepared to listen to the Queen of Peace, because his heart is full of anxiety, an anxiety that will not leave him alone."[38]

"Pray for the bishop every day, [because] he carries a heavy burden."

"Fast two days a week for the intentions of the bishop, who bears a heavy responsibility. If there is a need to, I will ask for a third day."

On December 2, 1983, Fr. Vlasic wrote a letter to a "Roman friend" saying that the Blessed Mother was appealing directly to Pope John Paul II to get Medjugorje removed from Zanic's jurisdiction, and for the Vatican to create an international, non-biased commission to investigate Medjugorje. Vlasic's letter denouncing Zanic's attempts to discredit Medjugorje, which was properly sent to Bishop Zanic for his notification, accused the bishop of being "in the grip of the forces of evil."[39]

Zanic's outrage against Medjugorje grew worse with time, giving additional fodder to Medjugorje's critics. In an interview given to the Italian journal, *Il Sabato*, on September 17, 1983, Bishop Zanic hinted to a reporter that Satan, not the Blessed Mother, was behind the events in Medjugorje: "These events may indeed be of diabolic origin," Zanic said. "Those children are little liars."[40]

Father René Laurentin, a world-renowned and highly respected Mariologist from France, and author of one of the first books supporting the apparitions in Medjugorje,[41] met with Bishop Zanic on December 26, 1983, to ask him to please refrain from publicly attacking Medjugorje, saying it was always best to wash one's dirty laundry *within* the family.[42] Fr. Laurentin was in Medjugorje to conduct scientific studies on the apparitions and had heard that Zanic was telling anyone and everyone who'd listen that Medjugorje was the work of the devil. To prove its satanic connection, the bishop cited the non-appearance of the promised sign, the ludicrous banality and repetition of Mary's messages, Vicka's alleged secret diary that she refused to hand over, the implausibility of Our Lady's support of the two expelled friars, the visionaries' differing stories of why they had gone up Podbrdo Hill on June 24, Ivan's deception with the letter and his attempts at intimidating him with warnings from the Lady, and the deaths of some of the people who had supposedly been cured of their illnesses at Medjugorje.

Finally going too far, Bishop Zanic began attacking Fr. Laurentin's personal integrity and credibility by accusing him in the Catholic press of being a Franciscan dupe and profiteering from his book on Medjugorje. In response to Laurentin's criticism of Zanic's dismissal of the apparitions as the result of a "collective hallucination," Zanic shot back at Laurentin: "The word hallucination is too flattering for what goes on in that apparition room. There are witnesses to testify that there are no ecstasies, no hallucinations, but simply parrot-like performances of a comic show. Therefore, I declare the word 'hallucination' too generous a description for such wicked play-acting. It will all blow up in your face sooner or later, and then your [Laurentin's] precious encephalograms and cardiograms and all your scientific apparatus will sink without a trace."[43]

Bishop Zanic's personal attacks on Fr. René Laurentin's integrity and scientific investigations caused those who were unsure about Medjugorje to finally see Zanic's criticisms for what they really were: a personal vendetta against the Franciscans friars and the six visionaries who had bruised his ego.

Trying desperately to repair Medjugorje's credibility, Frane Franic, Archbishop of Split and Makarska, came to Medjugorje's defense by saying that the visionaries had done far more for popular religion in Yugoslavia in three years "than all the pastoral letters in forty."[44] Soon after Franic's defense of Medjugorje, Zanic went to Cardinal Casaroli of the Secretariat of State to stop Franic from interfering with his condemnation of Medjugorje, but then Franic went to Cardinal Ratzinger, head of the Vatican's Congregation for the Doctrine of Faith, to do something about Zanic, who, he said, was out of control. Archbishop Franic cited to the Vatican the huge number of pilgrims coming to Medjugorje and the authenticated cures as testimony of the working of the Holy Spirit. Franic pleaded with Ratzinger to set up an international commission and to stop Bishop Zanic from prohibiting pilgrimages, but both he and Cardinal Kuharic, another supporter of Medjugorje, were ordered by the Vatican to tone down their rhetoric against Zanic. Zanic, however, wasn't about to tone down his.

The Bishop's Document Blasts Medjugorje

Bishop Zanic desperately wanted to silence Franic and the rest of his critics, so on October 30, 1984, he wrote a 23-page document called *The Present (Unofficial) Position of the Diocese of Mostar on the Medjugorje Events,* in which he thoroughly bashed Medjugorje and its defenders as frauds. Zanic's article, which had no legal authority whatsoever, was sent to Catholic prelates around the world. Signed and adorned with Zanic's episcopal seal, the report had the look of a definitive pronouncement, which it wasn't. In this unofficial document, Zanic said that he was "morally certain" that Medjugorje was a case of "collective hallucination," cleverly exploited by a group of unscrupulous Franciscan friars. He claimed that he had "invited the Franciscans of Medjugorje not to divulge in unbridled propaganda but the desire to push themselves forward in order to defend their position on the notorious Herzegovina issue—plus their desire for not inconsiderable material gain—has swayed their every action."[45]

Bishop Zanic was so convinced that Medjugorje was the result of a

Franciscan conspiracy against him that he bragged if one day the events at Medjugorje proved true, that he would "walk there barefoot."[46] He even went so far as to call the visionaries "mindless robots" who were "taught what to say to journalists and how to conduct themselves with doctors. It is all a lie," he said.[47] And Zanic proclaimed that Fr. Tomislav Vlasic, the visionaries' spiritual advisor, was a "confidence trickster" and a "charismatic sorcerer." "Irresponsible theologians," "shallow journalists," and "excitable charismatics" were, according to Zanic, the real ones responsible for creating a false euphoria over Medjugorje.[48]

Unfortunately for Medjugorje, the world press misinterpreted Zanic's unofficial document as an official Vatican denunciation and began printing it as such. Doubt was immediately thrown over the apparitions, and Medjugorje's reputation suffered for it: pilgrimages were canceled, charter flights were left vacant, books on Medjugorje were removed form shelves, and priests and bishops discouraged their parishioners from believing in it.

By publishing his belittling document and not biding his time until investigations were over, as he was recommended to do by his superiors in the Vatican, Bishop Zanic degraded his office and severely harmed the reputation of Medjugorje, especially within the Catholic clergy. His unofficial document should never have been taken seriously. It completely ignored the scientific findings of French and Italian doctors, who, in 1983 and 1984, concluded that the children were normal in every way and that the apparitions were not a mental aberration or a pious hoax, as Zanic was maintaining. Also conveniently ignored in Zanic's document were all the wondrous signs, miracles, testimonies, and conversions taking place in Medjugorje, as well as the many documented cures.

Cardinal Hans von Balthasar, one of the most highly respected theologians of the twentieth century, wrote to Bishop Zanic expressing in no uncertain terms his displeasure about his degrading document on Medjugorje:

> "Monsignor! What a simply sad document you have dispatched throughout the world! I was deeply hurt to see the office of the Bishop degraded in this fashion. Instead of having patience as you were advised by your superiors, you thunder and hurl Jupiter's arrows, blackening renowned and innocent people, worthy of your respect and protection. You repeatedly come up with accusations that have been proven untrue a hundred times over."[49]

But no amount of criticism changed Bishop Zanic's opinion about Medjugorje—he wanted it banned for good.

Bishop Zanic Bans Medjugorje

In July of 1984, Bishop Zanic ordered Fr. Vlasic to ban the visionaries from the church of St. James, but Fr. Vlasic refused. For his disobedience, Zanic had Vlasic's superior transfer him to a parish in Vitina, and Father Slavko Barbaric replaced Vlasic as the visionaries' spiritual advisor.[50]

Towards the end of 1984, the bishop ordered the parish priest of Medjugorje, Father Tomislav Pervan, to "cool and gradually extinguish" the events taking place there, but like Fr. Vlasic before him, Fr. Pervan refused. On March 25, 1985, the Solemnity of the Annunciation, Zanic wrote a letter to Fr. Pervan demanding to know why he hadn't taken the necessary steps to "cool and extinguish" things as he had been ordered to a few months prior.[51] When Pervan failed to come up with a satisfactory answer, Bishop Zanic gave him a list of eight demands, effective immediately:

1. The visionaries were to make no further public appearances.
2. The visionaries were to have no more apparitions in the church.
3. The statue of Our Lady of Medjugorje was to be removed from in front of the altar.
4. There was to be no more mention of apparitions nor messages from Our Lady in the homilies.
5. Practices and devotions related to Medjugorje were to stop.
6. No publications or souvenirs of Our Lady of Medjugorje were to be sold.
7. Fathers Jozo, Vlasic, and Rupcic were banned from preaching or celebrating mass in Medjugorje.
8. The visionaries were to hand over to the bishop everything they had written down concerning the apparitions, including secrets given only to the visionaries.

Bishop Zanic ordered the Franciscans to extinguish all pilgrimages to Medjugorje. Violators, he said, would be prohibited from receiving the sacraments.

The visionaries' new spiritual advisor, Fr. Slavko Barbaric, a trained psychologist, came to believe in Medjugorje and was subsequently transferred to Blagaj on September 15, 1985, by his superior on pressure from Bishop Zanic.[52] Zanic, quite confident of Barbaric's mistaken belief in the visionaries, said: "...I'm quite convinced the only way those children have seen Our Lady is on a statue or a holy picture." Revealing his underlying prejudice against women visionaries, Zanic was quoted as saying, "I have always been extremely suspicious of religious women who claim to have seen this, that or the other thing. These fantasies of theirs, usually no more than hallucinations, can do the Church a lot of harm."[53]

Bishop Zanic had abused the powers of his office to succeed where the communist regime had failed: not even they had the audacity to order the visionaries and their spiritual advisors out of their own church, or to try to stop parishioners and pilgrims from mentioning the apparitions in Medjugorje.

The Second Commission

A second, larger and more critical Commission was assembled by Bishop Zanic in 1983-84 at the request of Cardinal Kuharic of Zagreb. But the 15-member Commission, which included physicians and psychiatrists, was stacked with opponents of Medjugorje (eleven of the fifteen were known opponents). The new Commission was so biased against Medjugorje that one of Zanic's fellow-bishops commented wryly that disapproval of Medjugorje seemed to be a condition of selection.[54]

At the Commission's first meeting in April, Bishop Zanic proclaimed himself chairman and president of the Commission, and announced his intention of "crushing the apparitions." "I am the Commission," Zanic boasted.[55] When Fr. Robert Faricy asked Zanic what would happen if the Commission failed to reach an agreement, Faricy said, "[he] replied that the judgment of events at Medjugorje would not come from the Commission but from him, and that he had already made up his mind that the Blessed Virgin was not appearing in Medjugorje."[56]

The Second Commission published a report deploring the organization of pilgrimages and demanded silence on Medjugorje until they released their findings. When they voted in May of 1986, Bishop Zanic collected the ballots and spirited them away. Not even the Commission members knew how each one voted. The results were never officially published, but the bishop spoke openly about the results: eleven were against, two were for it, one said it could have had a supernatural character at the beginning, and the other abstained from voting.[57]

Doubt was immediately cast on the true outcome of the Second Commission's votes because the bishop had overstepped the rules of protocol when he spirited the ballots away. When Bishop Zanic sent the ballots to Rome, Cardinal Ratzinger dissolved the Second Commission in May of 1986 and ordered the Yugoslav Bishops' Conference to set up a new investigative committee, though not an international one as Archbishop Franic had hoped. The Yugoslav Bishops' Conference, under the direction of Cardinal Ratzinger, issued a communique to be read aloud from the pulpit at all masses that the Catholic Church was against "official" (Church-sponsored) pilgrimages to Medjugorje; however, unofficial pilgrimages were not forbidden. It remains that way to this day.

Bishop Zanic, however, took the new communique one step further: in a pastoral letter, he forbade all his parishioners from making pilgrimages to Medjugorje, threatening to withhold the sacraments from violators. Zanic's threatening letter was largely ignored, though: his parishioners poured into Medjugorje by the thousands, which forced the Franciscans in the diocese of Mostar to add an additional forty pastors.

Bishop Zanic's banning of Medjugorje and the negative conclusions of his

Second Commission failed to put an end to people's belief in Medjugorje. Each year, millions of pilgrims from around the world continue to stream into the tiny village.

Frustrated by the bishop's failure to halt Medjugorje by an episcopal order, Satan decided it was now time for drastic action—he would destroy it by force.

Civil War in the Former Yugoslavia

God, out of his mercy, frequently sends the Blessed Virgin Mary to areas of the world that have undergone persecution for their faith or which are about to suffer satanic persecution, as was the case in Rwanda. In fact, the best substantiation of any alleged Marian apparition is the history surrounding the area where the Marian apparition allegedly took place. Was there first a tremendous outpouring of love and faith and conversions followed by a horrible outbreak of evil? If so, then rest assured that the Blessed Mother was truly appearing there and that Satan was trying his best to destroy her work. So it would be in Medjugorje.

On June 25, 1991, the tenth anniversary of the appearance of the Blessed Virgin Mary in Medjugorje and the feast day of the Queen of Peace, the Republics of Croatia and Slovenia declared their independence from the atheistic regime of Yugoslavia—the last bastion of communism in Europe. This date is particularly meaningful because it marked the beginning of the four-year Yugoslav Civil War, which claimed over 300,000 Yugoslavian lives and left millions of Yugoslavians homeless and traumatized.

Fighting in Bosnia-Herzegovina broke out on April 6, 1992, exactly two years to the day before the start of the civil war in Rwanda. Mary did not specifically say to the visionaries in either Medjugorje or Kibeho that a war would erupt in their homeland on a specific date, but she did say several times that the peace of the world was in grave danger, and hinted that a terrible carnage was looming on the horizon in those two countries, which could only be prevented if people amended their lives and turned back to God.

In 1987, Mary pleaded with the Croatians in Medjugorje to "love their Serbian, Orthodox and Muslim brothers, and the atheists who persecuted them." There was a very good reason for this message: Yugoslavia would become embroiled in a horrible civil war in four years' time, which would pit Catholics, Orthodox Christians, and Muslims against one another.

The person most responsible for the outbreak of the Yugoslav Civil War was the evil communist leader, Slobodan Milosevic, the Serbian president and head of the Federal Republic of Yugoslavia. Alarmed by the wave of nationalistic sentiment sweeping throughout the communist countries of Eastern Europe during the late 1980s, Milosevic conspired to keep Yugoslavia under his dictatorial communist rule. Purposely whipping up Serb nationalism to foment a civil war that he knew he could win with his superior forces, and thereby force the Croats and Bosnians and Slovenians into submission, Milosevic and his fellow conspirators inflamed Serbian anger and hatred towards those who were calling for democracy and independence from Yugoslavia by reminding the Serbs of all the past atrocities committed against them by Catholics and Muslims. Lying to the Serbian people that they were about to be attacked by the independence-minded Catholics and Muslims, Milosevic ordered the Serb militias in Croatia and Bosnia to strike first. Thus, by using the Serb paramilitary units as his proxies, Milosevic cleverly avoided any direct involvement of himself and his communist Yugoslav army, which would have brought upon him worldwide condemnation and possible military intervention by NATO.

In the summer of 1991, Milosevic ordered Serbian troops to attack Catholic Slovenia and Croatia, and then Muslim-dominated Bosnia-Herzegovina in April of 1992. As a result, by the end of 1992 three of the world's major religions—Catholicism, Orthodoxy, and Islam—were at war with one another. Ten years earlier, Jesus had told one of the visionaries from Rwanda, Emmanuel Segastasha, that the coming of religious wars would be one of the heralds of the end times:

> "...You know my Second Coming is at hand when you see the outbreak of religious wars. Then, know that I am on the way."

Like the civil war in Rwanda that would follow two years later on the exact same day (April 6, 1994), the war in the former Yugoslavia was really a satanic war against religion. The brutal murder of clergymen and other religious affiliates, and the vicious and deliberate attacks on churches, monasteries, convents, synagogues, and mosques proved that these wars weren't just wars over territory, but against the spirit. Photographs in major magazines and newspapers around the world captured on film the horrible desecrations of houses of worship, fulfilling what Mary had prophesied back on October 13, 1973 in Akita, Japan to Sister Sasagawa:

> "...churches and altars [will be] sacked..."

Altogether, over 700 hundred churches, monasteries, convents, and cemeteries were destroyed in three and a half years of fighting in the former Yugoslavia. Sacred buildings and houses of worship were the first places targeted by the Serbs.[58]

Here is a detailed historical account of how the religious civil war in Yugoslavia actually got started.

In 1989, the tension in Yugoslavia worsened when Slobodan Milosevic became the President of Serbia and began to assert his dominance over what he called the growing "regionalism" that he claimed was pulling Yugoslavia apart, especially within the autonomous regions of nearby Serbian Kosovo and Vojvodina. The worsening economy and high inflation rate of Yugoslavia during the 1980s was tearing at the seams that held the fragile six-nation communist federation of Slovenia, Croatia, Serbia, Montenegro, Bosnia-Herzegovina, and Macedonia together. When the Yugoslav government finally collapsed on December 30, 1988, and the inflation rate reached as high as 2,000% the following year, a movement towards a multiparty system, already several years in the making, was pushed by Ciril Ribicic of Slovenia. President Milosevic regarded Ribicic's movement towards a multiparty democratic system as a serious threat to his dictatorial communist rule and began plans to quash it militarily.

In April of 1990, Slovenia held multiparty elections and, campaigning on the slogan "independence within a year," the Slovenian Party for democracy won a majority vote over the Slovenian Communist Party. A referendum on independence was held in Slovenia eight months later on December 23, with 88.5% voting for either independence from Yugoslavia or a looser confederation of Yugoslavian states. Milosevic immediately retaliated to the Slovenian referendum for independence by boycotting Slovenian goods. It was only a matter of time before he would finish preparing his military to force the Slovenes and Croats, who were also voting on independence from Yugoslavia, back into line.

On June 25, 1991, (the tenth anniversary of the Queen of Peace in Medjugorje), without provocation, Slobodan Milosevic's Serbian army began the invasion of Catholic Slovenia. When Slovenia moved to take control of its international borders on June 27, Slobodan Milosevic sent in his tanks. Milosevic felt he was given the green light to invade Slovenia because the Bush Administration had publicly voiced its opposition to Croatian and Slovenian independence "under any circumstances."

The Catholic Slovenes fought back valiantly, much to the Serb's surprise, but were outgunned by the Serb's heavy armor. After three EC-brokered cease-fires, both Slovenia and Croatia finally agreed to suspend their declarations of independence from Yugoslavia for ninety days, which stopped the fighting in Slovenia, but only shifted it over to Croatia.

Proving that the Serbs never wanted peace in the first place, the Chief of the Serbian Army's General Staff, General Blagoje Adzic, announced in an interview on Belgrade television on July 2, 1991 that he repudiated the EC-brokered cease-fire, and that his Serbian (Yugoslav) army "accepted the challenge of total war that had been opposed on it," and would soon put an end to it by a complete military victory. The following day, General Adzic, acting on orders from Slobodan Milosevic, sent an armored column from Belgrade into Southern Croatia.

A year prior, in April of 1990, Croatian President Franjo Tudjman's democratic party had won the legally-held elections in Croatia, and President Milosevic, who was dead-set against Croatian independence from Yugoslavia, retaliated by trying to bankrupt Croatia's economy. Following Tudjman's victory in the elections, Milosevic called on Serbs in Croatia and Slovenia to keep Yugoslavia together at all costs and not allow their breakaway. To allay Croatian Serb fears, Tudjman promised to guarantee their safety, but the Croatian Serbs weren't convinced. The Serbs in Croatia organized two independent regions within Croatia with the purpose of annexing them to Serbia to form a "Greater Serbia." On July 6, 1991, Milosevic gave a speech telling Croatian Serbs to be ready to defend themselves at a moment's notice. The following day, the paramilitary Croatian Serbs declared their loyalty to Milosevic's Socialist Federal Republic of Yugoslavia and immediately began attacking Croatian Catholics. For the record, it was the Serbs who fired the first shots in Croatia and Slovenia.

Milosevic's intention was to use the Croatian Serb militia attacks as justification for sending in his Yugoslav army regulars so that he could pound Croatia into submission. The same day that the Croatian Serb paramilitary units launched their attacks, Serbian army tanks arrived in Croatia and they joined forces. Regular army units and the Croatian Serb militias ruthlessly hammered Croatian territory despite Franjo Tudjman's orders to Catholic Croatians not to attack Serbian-held territorial units. At first, Tudjman was reluctant to fight the Serbs, but had no choice when it became apparent that Milosevic had already made plans to seize one-third of Croatia and incorporate it into a "Greater Serbia"—a brazen plan if there ever was one, because the Serbian population in Croatia was only 12%. But in all fairness to the Bosnian Muslims, the Croatian government was not totally devoid of its own proponents, who wanted to create a "Greater Croatia." Tudjman admitted that certain members of his own government secretly conspired with the Serbs in the summer of 1991 to partition Bosnia-Herzegovina between the Bosnian Croats and the Bosnian Serbs, leaving the majority Bosnian Muslim population without a home.[59] Tudjman later reversed himself and announced a Bosnian Muslim-Croat federation after the Western nations issued an ultimatum in February of 1994, demanding that Serbian forces withdraw their artillery from around Sarajevo.

During the latter half of 1992, Milosevic's navy blockaded the tourist ports of Dalmatia, while Serbian artillery pounded one Croatian city after another. Split and the Croatian capital city of Zagreb were heavily bombarded, as well as the historic towns of Vukovar and Dubrovnik (the place where Commerce Secretary Ron Brown would later die in a plane crash). As Serbian President Slobodan Milosevic had hoped, approximately thirty percent of Croatia was now controlled by the Serbs. The Serbian Republic of Krajina was created in the southern part of Croatia and a cease-fire was declared on January 15, 1992, with the introduction of U.N. peacekeeping forces to Croatia to monitor the cease-fire.

When peace negotiations by the EC and threats of economic sanctions repeatedly failed to stop the Serbs from attacking, it finally became clear to the world what Serbia's real intention was—total victory against the breakaway republics. Germany and Austria, Croatia's historic allies, pushed for EC recognition of Croatian and Slovenian independence from Yugoslavia in the winter of 1991, and the reluctant British and French eventually went along when the Germans threatened to proceed unilaterally if the EC took no action. With the Bush Administration still adamantly supporting the hard-line communist Serbs, the EC finally recognized the independence of Croatia and Slovenia on January 15, 1992, but not the independence of Macedonia or Bosnia-Herzegovina for fear the fighting would spread to Bosnia-Herzegovina. In the meantime, the Bosnian Serbs were arming themselves and making plans to link the Serbian areas of Bosnia and Croatia into one big communist "Republic of *Srpska.*"

Slobodan Milosevic and the EC finally reached an agreement on a new cease-fire in Croatia, the fifteenth so far, whereby the Serbian army would pull out of three Serbian-held enclaves and would be replaced by U.N. peace-keeping forces (UNPROFOR), who would supposedly disarm the local militias and police the regions. Meanwhile in Bosnia, a referendum was held on March 1, 1992, which produced a two-thirds majority in favor of Bosnian independence from Yugoslavia. Boycotting the referendum, the Bosnian Serbs retaliated by barricading the capital city of Sarajevo. The crisis in Sarajevo was temporarily defused by an emergency meeting between the Bosnian Serb leaders and Bosnian President Alija Izetbegovic. An agreement was reached on March 18 between the Bosnian Muslims, Croats, and Serbs for the restructuring of Bosnia into three constituent units based on ethnicity. Control for each autonomous unit would go to that ethnic group that was in the majority; in effect, creating one autonomous unit each for the Bosnian Muslims, the Bosnian Croats, and the Bosnian Serbs. But the peacekeeping agreement never got off the ground: Bosnian Serb leader Radovan Karadzic attacked the Muslim-led Bosnian government on April 6, 1992, and the much-feared war in Bosnia began. If the wars in Slovenia and Croatia between the Catholics and the Orthodox Christians had been bad, the war in Bosnia would be hell, because the Bosnian Serbs and the Bosnian Muslims truly hated one another.

Of the six republics that made up the Yugoslav federation (Slovenia, Bosnia-Herzegovina, Croatia, Macedonia, Montenegro, and Serbia), Bosnia-Herzegovina was the most ethnically, politically, and religiously volatile. Muslims made up 44% of Bosnia, Orthodox Serbs 33%, and Catholic Croats 17%. Multiparty elections were held for the first time in Bosnia in November of 1990, and Alija Izetbegovic was elected President of Bosnia the following month. At first, Izetbegovic favored a continuation of the Federation of Yugoslavia, but with major economic reforms, repudiation of communist leaders, and a more decentralized government. Only when the Serbian army invaded Croatia in July of 1991, and it became clear to him what the true aims of the Serbs were, did Izetbegovic begin planning for the inevitable break-up of Bosnia.

On December 20, 1991, the Bosnian leadership appealed to the EC for recognition of their independence from Yugoslavia. Bosnia's government, however, was split on the issue of independence: the Muslims and Croats were in favor of it, while the Bosnian Serbs were opposed. With the Bosnian Serbs threatening to form their own "Republic of Srpska" out of Bosnian Serb territory, the leaders of the three ethnic groups met again on March 18, 1992, and agreed in principle to peacefully partition Bosnia into three independent ethnic regions. But the following month, when the EC and the United States formally recognized Bosnia's independence, the Bosnian Serbs immediately announced their intention to create their own republic and to remain within the Yugoslav federation. On April 6, 1992, exactly two years before the start of the Rwandan Civil War, the Bosnian Serbs, under the leadership of Radovan Karadzic and General Ratko Mladic, launched an all-out attack on Izetbegovic's Muslim government. The following day, the U.S. recognized the independence of Slovenia, Croatia, and Bosnia. Now, after four of the six Yugoslav Republics had declared their independence from Yugoslavia, Serbia and Montenegro reacted on April 27 by declaring themselves the "new" Federal Republic of Yugoslavia.

Now that war in Bosnia was fully underway, the Yugoslav People's Army (Serbian army) stationed in Bosnia split into two factions: those with ties to Bosnia stayed to help the Bosnian Serbs fight the Muslims, while the rest returned to Serbia or Montenegro. In their departure, the Serbian regular army units left behind huge numbers of tanks, artillery pieces, rockets, missiles, and all the ammunition and equipment needed to stage a prolonged and bloody campaign. General Ratko Mladic took command of the Bosnian Serb military forces while Radovan Karadzic remained in power as the Bosnian Serb's defiant political leader.

The lightly-armed Bosnian government forces of Alija Izetbegovic, although superior in numbers, were no match for the heavily-armed Bosnian Serbs. Within three months the Bosnian Serbs controlled 70% of Bosnia-Herzegovina's territory. The hapless Bosnian Muslims were cut off in several isolated enclaves. Their capital city of Sarajevo, home of the 1984 Winter Olympics, was surrounded by the Serbs, who controlled the high ground above the city, from which Serb artillery shells could reign down with impunity. The Serbs tried to strangulate Sarajevo by blocking relief convoys from entering it, closing off its runways, and shutting off its water and electricity. Serb artillery purposely shelled U.N. peacekeeping stations in Sarajevo, children's hospitals, hotels, media centers, religious buildings, and funeral mourners. Thousands of innocent civilians in Sarajevo were indiscriminately shot by Serb snipers. A newly married young couple, a Serb and a Muslim, trying to flee Sarajevo, were gunned down in open territory after they were guaranteed safe passage by the Serbs. The photo of the two young lovers lying next to each other in an open field plastered the covers of magazines and newspapers throughout the world, causing a universal outcry against the brutality of the Serbs.

Under threats of NATO air strikes, the Serbs pulled back from the mountains surrounding Sarajevo time after time, only to return in a few days; constantly challenging the resolve of Western leaders with an "in your face" attitude. The Bosnian Serbs were convinced that the West had no backbone and was unwilling to use force. They were right: over 10,000 Sarajevians lost their lives by the constant Serb shelling and sniping before the West finally had enough of the Serbs' lies and decided to intervene militarily in 1995, to stop the Serbian siege of Sarajevo.

By July of 1992, the Bosnian Serbs had captured 70% of Bosnia-Herzegovina and had rounded up thousands of Bosnian Muslims and Catholics from their homes and sent them off to Serb concentration camps, where they were "ethnically cleansed." Serbian extermination camps, the likes of which had not been seen since WWII, sprang up throughout Bosnia.

A campaign of systematic rape was ordered by the Serbian leaders to destroy the hearts and souls of the Muslims and Croats. Bosnian women were tortured and raped in Serbian "sex camps" and forced to work in Serbian brothels. Rape scenes were filmed and shown on Serbian news channels with the ethnic identities of victim and rapist reversed to incite anti-Muslim propaganda and hatred. Pregnant Muslim and Catholic rape victims weren't released until the sixth or seventh months of pregnancy so that they couldn't abort their "little Chetniks." Many of these "rape babies" were abandoned by their mothers after birth and left to die. The number of Bosnian rape victims was estimated to be 20,000 by the European Union, and 50,000 by the Bosnian Interior Ministry.

As the Bosnian crisis intensified, on June 17, 1992, the U.S. State Department singled out the Bosnian towns of Medjugorje, Sarajevo, and Mostar as places for American travelers to avoid. Pilgrimages to Medjugorje were reduced by eighty per cent in 1992 and 1993, but slowly started picking back up again after the U.N. declared Medjugorje a safe-haven and center for humanitarian aid. Two hundred Spanish Blue Helmets (U.N. peacekeepers) were stationed in Medjugorje in the latter part of 1992 to protect the refugee center from the Serbs. Ironically, the peacekeepers were housed in the same apartment buildings just recently constructed to house the hundreds of thousands of pilgrims that visited Medjugorje each year.

Bill Clinton, John Major, Boutros Ghali, Lord David Owen, and the rest of the Western leaders wanted "peace at all costs" in Bosnia, and were ready to sacrifice the Bosnian Muslims to the Serbs. No one wanted a repeat of WWI, which had started in Sarajevo with the assassination of Archduke Ferdinand

and his wife. Intense international pressure was put on the Bosnian government to capitulate to the Serb's outrageous demands, but the Bosnian government courageously refused. With the Western nations denying them any real military assistance to defend themselves, the Bosnian government had no choice but to turn to the Islamic nations for help. Arms were smuggled into Bosnia from the Middle East and professional fighters called *Moujahidin* were brought in from Turkey and Iran. As Western leaders feared, the Muslim Moujahidin committed terrible atrocities against the Croats and the Serbs, because to kill a Christian is to earn a free ticket to paradise for a Muslim.

As the war in Bosnia became more and more of an embarrassment for Western leaders, the credibility of the U.N., NATO, and the U.S. as protectors of world peace was questioned. The Serbs acted with impunity because they knew the West was afraid of the Russians coming to their defense and triggering World War III. George Bush, Colin Powell, Robert McNamara, John Major, Boutros Ghali, General Michael Rose, Lord David Owen—all impeded, directly or indirectly, the stopping of the Bosnian War. If they had acted quickly and decisively at the very start with limited military force they could have stopped the Serb aggressors and saved hundreds of thousands of Bosnian lives. But the West preferred the safety of diplomacy over military action, which, of course, played right into the hands of the Bosnian Serbs who were liars from the start, breaking one peace agreement after another. If President Bush had stood up to the Serbs, the people of the United States would have supported him as they did in Operation Desert Storm, and he probably would've been re-elected for a second term. But Bush preferred appeasement over action, and wound up losing the 1992 election to Bill Clinton. George Kenney, Deputy Chief for Yugoslav affairs in the Bush Administration, was so disgusted with President Bush's "do-nothing" policy in Bosnia that he resigned in protest in 1992.

Perhaps in response to the growing criticisms of his failure to adequately respond to the plight of the Bosnian Muslims, President Clinton began parachuting in relief to starving Muslims in March of 1993, but it did more harm than good, as Serb snipers waited until Muslims went to retrieve the airdrops, then gunned them down in the open.

Clinton tried to appear tough by responding to the naked aggression of the Bosnian Serbs with threats of air strikes, but his repeated failure to follow through on his threats only convinced the Serbs that they could act without retribution. Marshall Freeman Harris of the State Department, dealing with Bosnian affairs in the Clinton Administration, was so disgusted with Clinton that he resigned from office on August 5, 1993, over what he said was President Clinton's inaction against "genocide and the Serbs who perpetrate it." Echoing Harris' sentiments, holocaust survivors Simon Wiesenthal and Elie Wiesel publicly shamed Bill Clinton over allowing another holocaust in

Europe. Even the peace-loving Pope John Paul II called on the West to intervene militarily to stop the genocide in Bosnia.

With international outrage growing, the U.N. Security Council adopted Resolutions 816 and 836 that created a "no-fly zone" over Bosnia and so-called "safe havens" for Muslim refugees. The nightly pictures of tens of thousands of beleaguered Muslim and Catholic refugees heading towards U.N. "safe havens" was a pathetic sight to behold. In one instance, dozens of frightened Muslim refugees fleeing the besieged town of Srebrenica were killed in a stampede as they tried boarding convoys headed for the safe haven of Tuzla in the spring of 1992.

For many Bosnians, the U.N. resolutions were too little, too late. Tens of thousands of Srebrenican men and young boys turned up missing and were presumed executed by the Serbs. Mass graves uncovered in parts of Bosnia in March of 1996 were found to contain the remains of the missing Srebrenicans. Some estimates have put the numbered of murdered Srebrenicans as high as 42,000.

U.N.-declared safe havens offered little in the way of real protection for Muslim refugees, even with the presence of U.N. peacekeeping forces. The safe haven of Zepa was attacked by Serb forces in May of 1993, and Bihac in November of 1994. The mayor of Bihac begged the West for help, but again, NATO refused to use air strikes on the attacking Serbs, who were promising the West a cease-fire as they were attacking.

By 1994, the Yugoslav Civil War had produced one million Croat and Bosnian refugees, the largest since WWII. Many refugees in the U.N. safe havens chose to commit suicide rather than fall into the hands of the Serbs, which usually meant torture and a slow, agonizing death, like having one's throat slit. Suicide was the leading cause of deaths in the safe haven of Tuzla in 1995.

The Bosnian Serbs, however, weren't the only ones committing crimes against humanity: the Croats were guilty of committing atrocities too. The Croatian Defense Council (HVO) murdered Muslims in Capljina, Stupni Do, Jablanica, Dreznica, and Mostar. Croatian leaders wanted the Herzegovina city of Mostar as their capital and launched a paramilitary offensive against the city in 1993—an action which was condemned by the U.N. Security Council. Seeing that their offensive against Mostar was causing an international outcry, the Croats halted their offensive but then tried starving the Muslims out by turning back relief convoys bound for the city. On August 25, 1993, a U.N. relief convoy bound for Mostar was taken hostage by fifty panicked Muslim women and children, who stood in their way and wouldn't let them go unless they promised to protect them. In the summer of 1993, Mostar was the most dangerous city in Bosnia.

Symbolizing the break in religious tolerance between the East and the

West, the old Mostar bridge built by the Ottoman Turks in 1566, which linked the Muslim and Christian sections of Mostar, was completely destroyed by artillery fire on November 9, 1993.

Seeming as though the horrors in Bosnia would never end, on February 5, 1994, a Serbian shell landed in a crowded Sarajevo marketplace killing at least 68 civilians. The media coverage of the carnage created an international outcry for the West to retaliate with actions instead of words, so the U.N. threatened the use of air strikes if the Serbs didn't pull back from a twelve-mile exclusion zone and surrender their heavy weapons by February 21. The Serbs complied for a while, but later recaptured their guns and moved right back into position.

On August 5, 1994, U.S. and NATO airplanes finally attacked Serb heavy-weapons stations around Sarajevo, but the limited air strikes amounted to nothing more than a pinprick. By November of 1994, the tide turned somewhat for the beleaguered Bosnian army: the Bosnian Croats and Bosnian Muslims joined forces against the Bosnian Serbs, and President Clinton lifted the arms embargo against Bosnia. That same month, NATO got tougher with the Serbs. On November 21-23, thirty-nine NATO jets attacked Serbian airfields and missile and artillery sites in Bosnia and Croatia in retaliation for Serbian attacks on NATO Harriers.

Responding to NATO's attacks, the Serbs stepped up their attacks on the Muslim enclaves, and the U.N. once again backed down. After the Serbs invaded the safe haven of Bihac in November of 1994 and took 500 U.N. peacekeepers hostage, the U.N. threatened to pull all of its peacekeepers out of Bosnia. The U.N. commander in Bosnia, General Michael Rose, resigned in November, saying there is little he can do to stop Bosnia from falling to the Serbs. Clinton, who up to this point had been unwilling to commit U.S. ground troops to Bosnia, now said he would send U.S. ground troops in to help evacuate U.N. peacekeepers, but a U.N. Security Council resolution that would've condemned the Bosnian Serbs as the aggressors, was vetoed by the Russians in December.

In May of 1995, another Serb shell was lobbed into the safe haven of Tuzla, and killed seventy more innocent civilians. When NATO forces responded to the attack on May 25 with pinprick air strikes against Serbian targets in Pale, the Bosnian Serb capital, the Bosnian Serbs retaliated by taking 370 U.N. peacekeepers hostage, handcuffing them to ammunition dumps, flagpoles, and other strategic locations, to deter NATO retaliation. The sight of U.N. peacekeepers being used as human shields was another tremendous humiliation for the West. The U.N. finally admitted in June of 1995 that it couldn't control the Serbs anymore, and its ineffectiveness as an international peacekeeping institution was finally acknowledged by the world.

With the U.N. admitting defeat, a 10,000 man Rapid Reaction NATO force was sent into Bosnia in June of 1995 to defend the safety of the 22,500 U.N. peacekeepers stationed there. The Serbs responded to the buildup of NATO forces by attacking the U.N. headquarters, a TV compound housing foreign press corps, and blocking food convoys carrying humanitarian relief to besieged towns. The following month, the Bosnian Serbs captured the safe haven of Zepa and Srebrenica where several hundred Dutch peacekeepers were held hostage by the panic-stricken Muslims, who were afraid to let them leave lest they be massacred by the Serbs. And that is precisely what the Serbs did: tens of thousands of Srebrenicans were murdered and buried in mass graves throughout Bosnia.

With the NATO Rapid Reaction force proving ineffective, the U.S., U.K., and France issued an ultimatum to the Serbs in July of 1995, warning them that any attacks on the remaining safe-havens of Tuzla, Gorazde, and Bihac would this time be met with substantial force. The Serbs, of course, ignored NATO's warning and launched an attack on Gorazde and Banja Luka, and NATO retaliated with the largest military action in Europe since WWII. Beginning on August 28, NATO forces launched Tomahawk cruise missiles and HARM and SLAM weapons against selected Bosnian Serb targets with the intention of sending the Serbs a wake-up call that they were no longer going to get by with just a slap on the wrist. As expected, Russian President Boris Yeltsin condemned the NATO air strikes, but failed to come to the Bosnian Serbs' rescue, as many in the West had feared. NATO air strikes lasted for a number of days and destroyed a considerable portion of the Serbs' war-making capabilities. The effect was to greatly increase the morale of Bosnian Muslim and Croat troops, who had been slowly building up their arsenals in preparation for a massive counterattack against the Serbs. Consequently, the Serbs were defeated in Bihac by the Muslims, and the Croats recaptured Krajina in August of 1995, removing 150,000 Serbs, who had captured that region from the Croats in 1992. The Croats had tried reclaiming the Krajina region in 1993 and 1994, but were unsuccessful because Serbs retaliated with massive artillery attacks on Zagreb and other Croatian towns. In an ironic twist of fate, many of the Serb refugees fleeing the Krajina region ended up in former Serb concentration camps.

Medjugorje is Unharmed

On April 6, 1992, the first day of fighting in Bosnia-Herzegovina, the village of Siroki-Brijeg, only thirty kilometers from Medjugorje, was bombed by Serbian MIG jets.[60] Croatian defense forces retaliated against the air strike by shelling Mostar's airport, where the Serbian jets were stationed. The Bosnian Serbs, in turn, threatened to "take" the parish of Medjugorje as reprisal for the Croats bombing their airport.[61] The Serbs knew very well what Medjugorje meant to the world, especially to Catholics. Destroying Medjugorje and the church of St. James would prove that Mary really wasn't appearing there and that the Catholic Church wasn't really the One True Church of God.

The Croatian residents of Medjugorje took the Serb's threat very seriously and prepared the town's defenses. On April 8, trenches were dug on Apparition Hill and in the fields that separate it from Mount Krizevac. While they were digging, Serbs burned down the houses in Vionica, just a little over ten kilometers from Medjugorje.[62]

On April 9, six unexploded cluster bombs were found embedded in the ground in Citluk, approximately six kilometers from Medjugorje.[63] By now, all the nearby towns close to Medjugorje had been bombed—Capljina, Citluk, Grude, Ljubuski, Metkovic, and Siroki-Brijeg—and the Serbs were closing in on Medjugorje, vowing to raise the little village and turn it into a "desert."[64]

On April 11, the first Serbian bombs fell on the parish of Medjugorje in a harmless section away from the population centers.[65] Providentially, within a few days, 200 U.N. peacekeepers began arriving in Medjugorje.

By May, two-thirds of the population of Medjugorje had evacuated and the pilgrimages had virtually stopped. The threat of a full-scale ground attack by the Serbs was lessened somewhat by the presence of the U.N. peacekeepers, but not the threat of bombing from the air. On May 8, six Serb rockets fell on Medjugorje, but with little damage and no human casualties. Two homes had their fronts damaged and some others had their windows blown out. Miraculously, a cow, a dog, and a chicken were the only ones killed. One of the rockets fell a hundred and fifty meters from the bridge, and another only four hundred meters from the church of St. James. Two rockets also fell near the access road to Medjugorje.[66]

Everyone agreed that the Serbs were purposely targeting the church of St. James with their rockets, but that the Queen of Peace was protecting it with her mantle, as she had promised back on August 1, 1985:

> *"I wish to tell you that I have chosen this parish and that I am guarding it in my hands like a little flower that does not want to die."*

On May 10, 1992, several more rockets fell just 300 hundred meters from the visionaries' village of Bijakovici at the foot of Apparition Hill, near the unpaved route that leads to the Neretva just left of the hill, but did no damage. That same day, more Serb bombs dropped on the area of Krstine, only one kilometer away from the church of St. James, then over the area of Tromedja, three hundred meters from the new gasoline pump.[67] The loud explosions of the shells were heard inside the cellar of the presbytery where mass was being said.

A Serbian pilot on his way to bomb the church of St. James was downed by Croatian anti-aircraft fire in May of 1992, and held prisoner in Ljubuski. Upon interrogation, the pilot, who just happened to be an atheist, told his captors that when he came above the valley of Medjugorje on his bomb run, for reasons unknown, a fog came up from out of nowhere, blocking his view so that he was unable to release his bombs on the church. Only when he reached a deserted spot away from Medjugorje was he finally able to release his payload. At that instant, an anti-aircraft battery targeting his plane ripped his plane apart, but he ejected safely. If the bombs meant for St. James had still been on board, the pilot and his plane would have blown up. [68]

The Croatian police chief in Ljubuski named Valentin, admitted to Sister Emmanuel, a French nun living in Medjugorje who documented all these events, that Medjugorje has received a level of protection from destruction that he is unable to explain militarily. Apparently, Medjugorje's miraculous reputation for avoiding destruction was one of the main reasons the U.N. stationed 200 Spanish Blue Helmets there.

Franciscan Father Slavko Barbaric told Sister Emmanuel about another miracle related to Medjugorje: "One of my friends from Medjugorje was sent with a dozen soldiers into a very dangerous zone near the plain of Medjugorje, near the Neretva; the Serb planes started firing all over this zone. For hours they endured a rain of fragmentary bombs, which were outlawed by the Geneva Convention. Once the storm was over, they realized that the whole plain was burned. There were bullet holes everywhere—except for the few square meters they were on. These men then understood that they had benefited from an unimaginable protection, and they promised God to never blaspheme again."[69]

Miracles of other sorts were reported in Medjugorje during the war, proving God's divine protection over the tiny hamlet. In one instance, a resident named Vinko, whose impaired eyes were cured by the Queen of Peace, reported that his meager food and money supply would multiply by itself whenever he gave help to the droves of refugees who flocked to Medjugorje.[70]

Pope John Paul II commented on the divine protection awarded to Medjugorje, saying to the Franciscan General: "Isn't it a miracle that nothing was destroyed at Medjugorje?"[71] God, indeed, was protecting Medjugorje, but not the residence of Bishop Zanic, who had declared his own personal war on Medjugorje ten years earlier.

The Bishop's See is Destroyed

"But if it comes from God, you will not be able to destroy them; you may even find yourselves fighting against God."

Acts 5:39

Just as Bishop Zanic was preparing to apply further restrictions to pilgrimages to Medjugorje, his diocesan see in Mostar was completely destroyed. The Bishop's residence was bombed on May 7, 1992, and burned from the inside out. Zanic barely escaped with his life, leaving his chancellery exactly five minutes before it exploded.[72] A 30,000 book library and the diocesan archives, including negative reports on the investigation of Medjugorje by the Bishop's Committee, were said to have been destroyed. What wasn't destroyed was confiscated by the Mostar police.[73] Zanic, who said back in the mid-1980s, "Either I or Medjugorje must die," and "we are preparing for war [against Medjugorje]," lamented the destruction of his residence: "Faced with these devouring flames, I could see Satan at work. I took refuge in the Cathedral. Only God can save."[74] But the secular Cathedral, which was built by Bishop Zanic to replace the older Franciscan one around the time of the controversial "two-priests affair," offered no safe sanctuary to the fleeing Presbyter—it, too, was eventually reduced by bombs to nothing but walls without a roof.

Up until one month before the start of the war in 1991, most of the twenty bishops on the Episcopal Commission investigating Medjugorje were said to be against it. One of the few members of the Yugoslav Commission known to have supported the apparitions was Archbishop Frane Franic. During the Bosnian war, Franic's Archdiocese in Split was miraculously spared the destruction seen in Mostar. Tragically though, Franic's auxiliary bishop, Monsignor Petar Solic, another of the members of the Yugoslav Bishops' Commission investigating Medjugorje, died in an auto accident in December of 1992. He was only 44.[75] It's not clear which way he would have voted on Medjugorje because the investigations by the Yugoslav Bishops' Commission set up by Cardinal Ratzinger in 1986, was temporarily halted by the war.

Was the terrible destruction of Mostar the judgment imposed on Bishop Zanic and his two biased Commissions for opposing Medjugorje? One has to remember Mary's warning to Bishop Zanic through Ivan in 1983, the one that enraged Zanic so much:

> *"I am sending him the last warning but one. If he doesn't accept these events and behave accordingly, he will hear my judgment and that of Jesus, my Son. If he does not heed my message, then he is not walking in the Way of my Son."*

The End of the War in Bosnia

In her message on February 24, 1994, the Blessed Mother reassured the visionaries that the war in Bosnia would soon end:

> *"I thank you for your prayers. You have all helped me so that this war will stop as soon as possible..."*

The Dayton Peace Accord was signed by the Serbs, Croats, and Muslims on November 21, 1995, putting an end to the hostilities in the former Yugoslavia. By May of 1996, 60,000 NATO troops, including Americans, were stationed there to protect the Dayton Accord.

The Serbs never realized their dreams of forming a "Greater Serbia." Bosnia remained unpartitioned and Alija Izetbegovic won the Bosnian presidential election. The future of Bosnia remains uncertain though. The Bosnian Serbs still grumble about their "Greater Serbia" and the land they lost back to the Muslims (at one point in the war they had captured 70% of Bosnia, but gave 25% of it back in the Croat-Muslim counteroffensive).

The cost of the civil war in the former Yugoslavia was horrendous: 300,000 died and millions more were displaced from their homes. Thousands of children were orphaned, tens of thousands of women were raped, entire areas were "ethnically cleansed," and whole communities and towns were annihilated. Abortions, rapes, infanticides, suicides, tortures, executions, concentration camps, vicious attacks on churches and mosques—Satan tried his best to destroy Medjugorje, but failed.

Over in Serbia, the situation remained tense as President Slobodan Milosevic threatened to use force against the millions of demonstrators who began marching in the streets of Belgrade on November 17, 1996, demanding Milosevic's resignation after he nullified elections which were clearly won by the opposition party *Zajedno,* or "Together." Milosevic orchestrated well-publicized counter-rallies of his own in December of 1996, in Krusevac, Yugoslavia, to make it appear that the majority of the Serbian people were behind him. But his tactic fooled no one. The demands of the opposition party to honor the election results were eventually met by Milosevic after months of protests in the heart of Belgrade, and opposition leaders called off their protests. Milosevic, however, remained in power as president, but his hold on that power remains tenuous.

Ethnic Cleansing

Although war crimes were committed on all sides during the Yugoslav Civil War, the CIA reported that eighty percent of the atrocities were committed by the Serbs.[76] On May 25, 1993, U.N. Security Council Resolution 827 established an international war crimes tribunal in the Hague, Netherlands, to prosecute the war criminals who committed crimes against humanity and genocide in the former Yugoslavia, the first such war crimes tribunal since Nuremberg and Tokyo. As of June 1999, eighty-nine have been indicted by the tribunal, twenty-seven have been apprehended or confirmed dead, and thirteen remain at large. Since most of those indicted by the war crimes tribunal were Serbs, Bosnian Serbs voided all relations with the U.N. in May of 1995.

The kinds of war crimes the Serbs committed are unforgivable. Here are just a few examples: torturing, mutilating, and murdering thousands of prisoners at concentration camps in Brcko, Omarska, and Doboj; murdering tens of thousands of Muslim men and boys from the safe haven of Srebrenica, burying them in shallow graves throughout Bosnia-Herzegovina; assassinating Bosnian Deputy Prime Minister Hakija Turajlic through the open door of the U.N. armored car he was riding in, in the presence of five French peacekeepers; kidnapping Catholic Bishop Franjo Komarica and several priests of Banja Luka in northwest Bosnia, placing them under house arrest and threatening to shoot the entire Catholic population of Banja Luka if Croats didn't immediately release their Serbian prisoners; throwing teenagers alive into fire in Tuzla in May of 1992;[77] draining the blood of Croatian and Muslim prisoners for Serb transfusions;[78] forcing Croat and Muslim refugees and prisoners of war to fight against their own people on the Serb front lines; drugging their own Serbian soldiers to make them fearless;[79] dragging young Serbian men away from their homes and threatening to shoot them if they didn't fight, and chaining them to their artillery cannons so they wouldn't desert.[80]

Practically everyone in Bosnia-Herzegovina knew someone who was a victim of war crimes. One of the Medjugorje visionaries, Mirjana Dragicevic, had twenty relatives massacred in Dojani, Bosnia. No wonder Mary came to Medjugorje in 1981, pleading for peace between the Orthodox Christians, Catholics, Muslims, and atheists.

The Crisis In Kosovo

After the Ottoman Turks drove the Serbs out of Kosovo in 1389, large numbers of Albanian Muslims immigrated into that small area in southwestern Serbia, and by the twentieth century they made up ninety percent of the Kosovar population. In 1929, Kosovo was assimilated into the Kingdom of Yugoslavia, and in an act of consideration for the Muslims, was given political and economic autonomy by the Yugoslav Communist Party Boss, Josip Tito, in 1974. In 1989, however, on the 600th anniversary of the Serb defeat in Kosovo, Serbian President Slobodan Milosevic stripped Kosovo of its political and economic autonomy. Seeking to solidify his dictatorial hold on power over Yugoslavia by whipping up Serb nationalism and anti-Muslim passion, Milosevic went to Kosovo in 1987 and vowed to the Kosovar Serbs that "no one will be allowed to beat you."

A former lawyer, technician, and a banker in the U.S. whose parents had committed suicide, Milosevic was a crafty politician. He had risen quickly through the ranks of Yugoslavia's Communist Party by becoming the leader of Belgrade's Communist Party in 1984, leader of the Serbian Communist Party in 1987, and President of Serbia in 1989. Already a Communist Party zealot at the young age of 18, Slobodan Milosevic aspired to rise to the top of the Yugoslav Communist Party. He was such an ardent communist that his colleagues in Serbia nicknamed him "Little Lenin."

Fearful of losing his autocratic rule over Yugoslavia with the crumbling of the Iron Curtain and the worsening Yugoslav economy in the late 1980s, Milosevic deftly changed his public image from an old-style Communist Party member to a Serb ultra-nationalist, who promised a "Greater Serbia" for the land-hungry Serbian people—and they loved him for it. Fomenting one political crisis after another to rally the Serbs behind him and to prevent his political opponents from ousting him from power, Milosevic started wars in Slovenia and Croatia in 1991, and Bosnia-Herzegovina in 1992. However, when the tide of the war in Bosnia turned in 1995 and Serb forces were on the run in Bosnia and Croatia, the chameleon Slobodan Milosevic quickly turned into a peace negotiator at the Dayton Peace Accords, to make it look like he was for a peaceful settlement all along. He wanted his Serb military intact, to keep him in power.

In 1992, after they had their autonomy stripped away, Kosovar Albanians voted to secede from Yugoslavia, demanding that all Serb military and security forces pull out of Kosovo. Milosevic, if he wanted to stay in power, could never allow Kosovo's independence from Serbia because of the historic significance it held for the Serbian people and because of all the Orthodox monasteries there, so he, in turn, launched a crackdown on that independence-minded province. In response, ethnic Albanians formed the Kosovo Liberation Army (KLA) and orchestrated a campaign of retribution and terrorism on Serb security units to drive them out of Kosovo. Milosevic responded to the KLA attacks with brutal reprisals on innocent ethnic Albanians and suspected KLA members. In response to the KLA's murder of two Serb policemen on February 28, 1998, Milosevic's security and paramilitary forces killed 300 ethnic Albanians and drove 65,000 Muslims from their homes. By the end of 1998, tens of thousands of ethnic Albanians were fleeing for the mountains of Kosovo from Serb paramilitary units, and NATO was threatening to use military force if the Serbs didn't sign a peace treaty with the KLA and allow the fleeing refugees to return home. The KLA agreed to the terms of the Rambouillet Peace Treaty in March of 1999, but Milosevic adamantly refused to sign. Instead, he massed 40,000 Serb troops on the northern border of Kosovo, daring NATO to stop him from invading his own province.

With U.S. special envoy Richard Holbrooke warning Milosevic that if he invaded Kosovo NATO would respond with substantial military force, not just with a few military air strikes, as in Bosnia, Milosevic defiantly invaded Kosovo anyway. True to their word, on March 24, 1999, NATO began launching significant air strikes against the Serbs. At first, the Serbian people in Belgrade responded insolently to the NATO bombs by holding mass rallies at rock concerts and standing on bridges with targets painted on their backs. But after a few days of bombing in Belgrade that claimed civilian lives and took out several key bridges, the Serbs stopped their protests and started taking refuge in bomb shelters.

Making the mistake of ruling out the use of ground forces at the onset of the bombing campaign, President Clinton sent a message to Milosevic that he and NATO weren't really willing to sustain casualties to save the Kosovar Albanians. As a result, the emboldened Serbs butchered tens of thousands of ethnic Albanians and drove 800,000 of them from their homes into neighboring Bosnia, Macedonia, and Montenegro, creating a humanitarian crisis of enormous proportions. True to his lying nature, Milosevic tried blaming the refugee crisis on NATO bombs and even accused Hollywood of paying Albanian actors to stage a phony war as in the movie, *Wag the Dog*. No one in the West, of course, was that stupid.

With U.S. public opinion varying from wanting a complete cessation of the bombing to sending in ground troops, NATO elected to step up the pressure on Milosevic by intensifying the air strikes. After 74 days of intensive bombing that showed no signs of letting up, it became clear to Milosevic that NATO was going to bomb Serbia back to the Stone Age and that the Russians weren't going to intervene militarily on the Serbs' side. Thus, Milosevic agreed to pull out of Kosovo. NATO members from France, Italy, Germany, Britain, and the U.S. sent peacekeeping forces into Kosovo to restore order and disarm the KLA, and the Russians—the historic allies of the Serbs—insisted on sending in a peacekeeping force of their own.

On May 27, 1999, Yugoslav President Slobodan Milosevic was indicted by the U.N. war crimes tribunal in the Hague, Netherlands, for committing crimes against humanity in Kososvo, along with Serbia President Milan Milutinovic, Yugoslav Deputy Prime Minister Nikola Sainovic, and Serbian Minister Vlajko Stojilkovic. We will never know just how many Kosovar Albanians Milosevic killed until all the mass graves and execution sites are discovered. Retreating Serb army units looted and burned houses, laid millions of booby traps and land mines, and tortured and murdered as many Muslims as they could before they withdrew from Kosovo.

On June 24, 1999, the U.S. State Department offered a five million dollar reward for the arrest of Slobodan Milosevic and his return to the Hague for trial. Starting four wars in eight years and losing them all, Milosevic has attacked Slovenia, Croatia, Bosnia-Herzegovina, and Kosovo, and brought untold misery to the former Yugoslavia. In an ironic twist of fate, the Serbs who sought to ethnically cleanse Kosovo of an estimated two million Albanians cleansed themselves instead, as tens of thousands of Kosovar Serbs, fearing revenge killings by the KLA, have fled to Serbia with nothing but what they could carry.

The situation in Kosovo remains tense, as NATO forces are stationed alongside Russian peacekeeping units, who are gradually bringing in reinforcements and showing no signs of a willingness to cooperate with NATO. The most volatile place in the world and only a few miles away from Medjugorje, the eyes of the world are looking anxiously upon Kosovo.

Scientific Studies on Medjugorje

Medjugorje is unique among previous Marian apparitions because, for the first time in history, medical science could accurately test the apparitions while they occurred, leaving no doubt as to whether or not the children were faking it. Numerous tests were conducted on the visionaries by several well-qualified teams of physicians and psychiatrists. The following is what they found.

The apparitions take place in three phases: an ecstatic contemplation before the arrival of the apparition, prayer with the apparition, and conversations with Mary before the end of the apparition. During the ecstatic contemplation phase, the visionaries are praying individually and their movements and actions are random and asynchronous. At the moment Mary appears, the group shows simultaneity in key movements: their wide-open eyes converge upwards towards a fixed point, all eyeball movement (except blinking) is ceased, they lose all perception of time and space, and remaining semi-rigid, they become insensitive to outside stimuli and pain.

When Mary arrives, she begins with the Our Father, and the children simultaneously join in at "Who art in Heaven." During the apparitions, Mary speaks to the children individually or as a group. Sometimes the children move their lips and vocal chords as if responding to questions, but their words remain inaudible, as if Mary did not want to make their conversations public. At the end of the apparition, the synchronized gaze and rigidity ceases, the children's movements return to normal, and one of the visionaries usually announces that she is gone.

The first to examine the visionaries in ecstasy was Dr. Ludvik Stopar, a Yugoslav psychiatrist/parapsychologist and the director of *Polyclinic* in Maribor, Yugoslavia. He examined the visionaries on four occasions from 1982 to 1983, once while they were under hypnosis, and concluded that they were absolutely normal, and not suffering from any mental derangement.[81]

An Italian team of doctors examined the children in 1983. Dr. Mario Botta, a heart surgeon from Milan, conducted an EKG on Ivan and found him to be quite normal. Dr. Enzo Gabrici, a neuro-psychiatrist, conducted psychiatric examinations on the visionaries in April of 1984, and excluded the possibility of collective hallucinations, epilepsy, hypnotic autosuggestion, or altered states of consciousness. Dr. Gabrici commented that the visionaries differ from mediums who are taken over by a different personality because the visionaries retain perfect consciousness of their identity.[82]

A French team of medical doctors under Professor Henri Joyeux, a hospital surgeon and director of a nutrition and experimental oncology lab in Montpellier, France, conducted the most rigorous testing of all, using the most up to date medical, scientific, and photographic equipment available to test the brain, heart, lungs, circulation, eyes, and vocal chords. During his testing in 1984, Joyeux noted that EEG's showed calm alpha brain wave activity of wakefulness and receptivity, therefore excluding hyperactivity, sleeping, epilepsy, hallucinations, or hysteria. Blood pressure tests, pulse rate, eye tests, hearing and vocal tests, and EKG's were all normal. The French team found that the visionaries were not totally disconnected to the outside world while in ecstasy: they experience joy and sadness, their breathing and circulation were normal, they were not rigidly immobile during ecstasy, not anxious or nervous, but quite relaxed; they spoke inaudibly and audibly, and they responded in unison to the vision but not in perfect synchronicity. In the absence of anything "pathological," the French doctors excluded the possibility of individual or collective hallucinations, pretense, invention, individual or collective hysteria, neurosis, trance, catalepsy, pathological ecstasy, sleep state, dreaming, visual or auditory pathology or hallucination, or organic abnormalities. Concluding that the apparitions were scientifically inexplicable, Joyeux said, "The conclusions clearly show that we are dealing with a perception which is essentially objective both in its causality and its scope . . . The most obvious answer is that given by the visionaries, who claim to meet the Virgin Mary, Mother of God."[83]

Italian Dr. Maria Federica Magatti tested the visionaries in February and March of 1984 during ecstasies and found them insensitive to external stimulation (bright lights, skin pricks, physical manipulation) and deduced their "absolute neurological normality."[84] Dr. Lucia Capello from Mostar observed the visionaries during the same period and concluded there was no agitation, no psychic conditioning, and no ulterior motive.[85] Dr. Anna Maria Franchini observed them in April of 1984, and found them to be normal in every way.[86] In a report by Dr. Giorio Sanguinati, a teacher of Psychiatry at Milan's Faculty of Criminal Anthropology in 1985, he said, "Neither before, during nor after the apparition did I find any trace—in gesture, behavior or word—of psychopathology, whether delirium, hallucination or hysteria."[87]

Fr. Nicholas Bulat, a member of the Commission set up to investigate Medjugorje, stabbed Vicka's left shoulder blade with a long needle while she was in ecstasy, but she felt no pain.[88] Dr. Slavko Barbaric, a social psychologist and the spiritual advisor to the children, studied them in 1982 and concluded that, "This phenomenon is not explicable as the action of a leader, nor as the activity of an external manipulator, but only as the action of the apparition which forms and directs the group."[89]

With all this scientific testing, no one can say that there is no way to prove that the visionaries in Medjugorje are telling the truth. Science has done all the tests and concluded that the children aren't lying, nor are they collectively hallucinating. Still, there are always those who refuse to believe, no matter what the evidence shows.

Criticisms of Medjugorje

Critics of Medjugorje generally make one of two claims regarding the apparitions: that the visionaries are reporting non-occurring events (i.e., lying), or that their apparitions appear real, but are, in reality, collective hallucinations. Exaggerated stories of people's rosaries turning gold, miraculous snapshots of Mary, or reports of the sun spinning and dancing, only fuels the criticism against Medjugorje.

Medjugorje's critics give a number of reasons why they think the visionaries are frauds, but most feel the same way as Bishop Zanic did, that the local Franciscans used the children for political purposes, whipping up popular support for their cause against the secular diocese by coaxing the children into pretending that the Virgin Mary was appearing to them in Medjugorje. According to these critics, the Franciscans concocted Medjugorje to undermine the bishop's authority and manipulated the children like puppets, coaching them on what to say and how to act. Zanic even suggested that the whole thing was the work of a former Franciscan friar from Medjugorje, who had fathered a child by an ex-Franciscan nun.

The communist authorities, on the other hand, thought that the Franciscans were behind the apparitions but for an entirely different reason. Medjugorje, they said, was a "fascist plot" to promote Croatian nationalism for the sole purpose of undermining the authority of the communist state. When communist authorities failed to uncover any secret Franciscan plot for independence and realized how much foreign currency was being brought into their local economies by tourists, they no longer tried to stop Medjugorje: it was making them too much money. Other critics of Medjugorje, especially in Europe, said Medjugorje was a greedy scheme concocted by the local Franciscans to take their tourists dollars away from them. A critic in America, an exiled Franciscan Father living in St. Louis, Ivo Sivric—author of *The Hidden Face of Medjugorje,* which claimed Medjugorje to be a "pious fraud"— said that the children read about the apparitions in Lourdes before experiencing their own apparitions and were simply imitating Bernadette Soubirous.[90] Sivric said that the culture in Herzegovina tends to over-dramatize and exaggerate, and the peasant children's imaginations overflowed into fantasies of Mary appearing to them. Countering Sivric's accusation, Father Jozo attested that the visionaries were completely ignorant of prior Marian apparitions, and that he gave them the book on Lourdes to read only after their visions had already started. You will recall that Father Jozo was away for three days when the apparitions started, and that when he came back and interrogated them, he didn't believe their stories, either. He only changed his mind a few days later when, praying for guidance, he heard the heavenly instruction to "go out and protect the children." Mary then appeared to Fr. Jozo in the church of St. James to confirm the apparitions as authentic, and later visited him while he was in jail. Father Jozo also saw the words MIR written in the sky above Medjugorje before he was arrested. He is the most credible witness to the authenticity of the apparitions.

If the children are indeed lying, as Bishop Zanic and the rest of Medjugorje's detractors claim, how could they keep up their charade for two decades without having a slip of the tongue or a nervous breakdown? Those simple kids could never stand up under the constant pressure of all the questions, the examinations, the insults and slanderous attacks against their character, not to mention the tourists, their speaking appearances, their constant travel, and the wars in Bosnia and Kosovo. The visionaries have gained nothing personally. In fact, they've suffered many trials over their apparitions, just as Mary said they would. Besides, what "normal" children would go to such unparalleled lengths as to lie, deceive, and perjure themselves for so many years without changing their story or admitting it to be a hoax?

Bishop Zanic's fifteen-member Second Commission reported after two years of investigating that the children were "normal" in every respect, but that the apparitions were inauthentic because "some of the messages conflicted with the New Testament" and that their "individual testimonies conflicted."[91] It appears that some of the children testified to the Commission that they were going up the hill for a smoke, while others said they were going up after the sheep. Actually, both accounts are true: Mirjana and Ivanka were going up the hill for a smoke and left word for Vicka to join them, while Milka Pavlovic, Marija's sister, was tending sheep. And regarding messages conflicting with the New Testament, none of them do. Since the Yugoslav bishops didn't make their findings public, how are we to agree with their condemnations? Bishop Zanic's Commission only brought up as proof against Medjugorje Ivan's lie about the sign, the refusal of the other five visionaries to write down the sign, and the June 30, 1981, message from Our Lady that mentioned "three more days," which Mirjana mistook for meaning that the apparitions would end in three days.. Fr. Tadija Pavlovic testified that the visionaries said to him on July 3 that the Lady confirmed that it was her last appearance.[92] What was probably said to Mirjana on June 30 was similar to the messages of May 2, 1982, and June 23, 1982, when Mary told the visionaries that these were her last apparitions in the world, that she wouldn't appear any more on earth. Mirjana just misinterpreted the content or meaning of the message. This has happened before with other visionaries, like the little girl in Banneaux, who thought the healing spring was for her instead of Mary.

Skeptics who won't go so far as to accuse the children of outright lying try to account for the apparitions psychologically, calling them (like Bishop Zanic did) a case of "collective hallucination." They say that a picture of Mary hanging in the church of St. James since 1971, together with the sudden appearance of mysterious rosaries and the prophetic messages of Mary's coming, triggered hallucinatory images in the minds of the children through a mental process which medical science calls "autosuggestion." They claim that the Franciscan friars had so brainwashed the children's minds into expecting an appearance from the Virgin Mary that their collective unconscious actually hallucinated her right into their minds; that a false, hallucinatory image of Mary appeared to them, which the children mistook as real; that the children themselves aren't liars but their minds are. This is the same old rationalistic argument that critics of Fátima used in which to deny the Miracle of the Sun, which was witnessed by 70,000 spectators on October 13, 1917. Believing in simultaneously shared visual, auditory, olfactory, gustatory, and tactile hallucinations by a collective group of individuals takes far more credulity than believing in apparitions from heaven.

Other people have honest doubts about Medjugorje because Mary never mentioned the coming of the Bosnian War or the Kosovo War, or because the messages have gone on for so long, or because the end of the world hasn't come yet. Regarding the wars in Bosnia and Kosovo, as I mentioned before, Mary alluded to them by saying as early as 1981 that the peace of the world was in danger. Bosnia and Kosovo weren't one of the ten secrets because the secrets deal exclusively with events surrounding the coming chastisement, which hasn't arrived yet. The Blessed Mother gave us hints about the looming wars in Yugoslavia by announcing herself as the Queen of Peace, and exhorting Croatian Catholics to "love your Serbian, Orthodox and Muslim brothers," who were "equal before God." As a reminder to seek peace and avoid conflict, the Slavic word for peace (MIR) appeared in the sky above Medjugorje. Now think about it: if Mary had told the children that the Serbs would be attacking their homeland on the tenth anniversary of the Queen of Peace, wouldn't the Croats and Muslims have attacked the Serbs first, thus causing them to commit a major crime in the eyes of God? That's why God never gives specific details about imminent wars, he just tells us to repent or prepare to face the consequences.

Mary gave Yugoslavia the remedy to avoid the two wars (through prayer and fasting), but her pleas went unheeded. We now know the consequences of what happens when we ignore God's directives. Regarding the skeptics' objections about the messages going on for so long and the delay in announcing the secrets, remember that this is a period of grace we are in, and that's why God is allowing Medjugorje to go on for so long: he wants as many people to convert as possible. Mirjana told René Laurentin that it is because so few people have accepted Mary's messages and changed their lives that God delays his chastisement. "There are more unbelievers than ever," she said. This delay is a merciful delay. It is for our own benefit. Remember, it took over seventy years for Russia to convert, but the Immaculate of Heart of Mary finally triumphed over Russian communism.

There is another group of people who don't believe in Medjugorje because it affirms the Catholic Church as the One True Church of God. Many Protestants and other non-Catholics don't believe in Medjugorje because they don't believe in Marian apparitions and are brainwashed from their youth to believe that the Mary of the Catholic Church is the "Whore of Babylon." As far as most Protestants are concerned, all revelations from God ended with the Gospels, so anything coming from Medjugorje can't be from God and must be from the devil, and, therefore, the Queen of Peace is Satan in disguise. Those who do so blaspheme Mary and the Holy Spirit and are risking the fires of hell, as Jesus warned in Fátima.

On the other hand, liberals and post-modernists within the Catholic Church don't like Medjugorje because they say it's "a return to discarded theologies and fear-ridden religiosity."[93] They are scandalized by Medjugorje's apocalyptic undertones and threats of a global punishment for the sins of the world. The idea of a vengeful God and everlasting punishment in hell belongs, they say, to the forgotten era of witch-hunts, black magic, and super-stition. One such liberal Catholic cynic (whose name I will not mention here but whose syndicated columns appear in many diocesan newspapers through-out the U.S.), recently asked his readers who believe in Medjugorje why the Queen of Peace didn't appear to Slobodan Milosevic and give him a good spiritual whipping, and thus avoid the horrible evils that have taken place. But that ignorant question, which came from a well-respected theologian of all people, is no different than asking why God allows evil in the world, or why God allows Satan to exist, or why God allows bad things to happen to good people. The answer is: We live in a fallen world.

Just as bad as the liberals are the extreme right-wing religious conservatives and Christian fundamentalists, who don't believe in Medjugorje because of Mary's ecumenical message that says all men are created equal and salvation is open to everyone, not just Christians alone. These modern-day Pharisees want to believe in a God of exclusivity, like the ancient Pharisees did in Israel, or like the Islamic extremists do today. People of all faiths can go to heaven if they have good will, obey the dictates of their conscience, love God with all their heart, and love their neighbor as they love themselves. Only when you know Jesus Christ and consciously reject him and his teachings do you go to hell for not being a Christian.

Still other Catholics don't believe in Medjugorje because of the negative conclusions of Bishop Pavao Zanic, or because the current Yugoslav Commission investigating Medjugorje has yet to make an official pronounce-ment one way or the other. They are afraid to decide for themselves without first having the approval of the Church, which, for good reasons, is sometimes too slow in approving apparitions.

As you can see, there are many reasons why people don't believe in Medjugorje, which has caused a deep split within the Catholic Church.

Medjugorje Divides the Church

Despite what some people say, the Catholic Church is terribly divided over Medjugorje. There are many members of the Church who are vehemently opposed to Medjugorje, believing wholeheartedly that there is nothing supernatural going on there. Their colleagues who do believe in Medjugorje are often ridiculed as gullible and superstitious. The Blessed Mother told Sister Agnes on October 13, 1973, that someday this would happen:

> *"The work of the devil will infiltrate even into the Church in such a way that one will see cardinals opposing cardinals, bishops against other bishops. The priests who venerate me will be scorned and opposed by their confreres..."*

Medjugorje was never intended by God to divide the Catholic Church. On the contrary, it was meant to unify it. On seeing how divisive the Catholic Church was becoming over Medjugorje, Mary confided her sadness to the visionaries on August 29, 1982:

> *"I have not desired your division. On the contrary, I desire that you be united..."*

Medjugorje's biggest opponent came from within the Catholic Church itself, from the local bishop. It's only logical for Satan to try to get to the local bishop because he has the authority to declare any apparitions in his diocese valid or invalid. Yet however hard Bishop Zanic tried to convince people that Medjugorje was a fraud (Zanic was quoted once as saying, "In my opinion, Medjugorje is the greatest deceit and swindle in the history of the Church."[94]) he never succeeded because the Holy Spirit convinced people otherwise. In fact, more than twenty-five million pilgrims have visited Medjugorje since 1981, and they continue to come to this day.

Unfortunately, Bishop Zanic was allowed to choose his successor when he retired in 1992.[95] As his replacement, Bishop Zanic picked Monsignor Ratko Peric, who was as much opposed to Medjugorje as Zanic; maybe even more so. On September 14, 1992, Peric publicly denounced Medjugorje as a hoax, parroting all the objections of his predecessor. But Bishop Peric, like Bishop Zanic before him, has failed to stop the belief in Medjugorje.

Pope John Paul II on Medjugorje

How does the head of the Roman Catholic Church, Pope John Paul II, feel about Medjugorje? The following are some of his comments:

"Let the people go to Medjugorje if they convert, pray, confess, do penance and fast."[96]

"If I wasn't the Pope, I'd been in Medjugorje already!"[97]

"Medjugorje, I know, I know, Medjugorje... Protect Medjugorje. I am with you. I bless you. Courage, courage, I am with you. Support Medjugorje. Greet them all for me. I bless all of them. I know you are suffering in this war."[98]

"Authorize everything that regards to Medjugorje."[99]

"Today's world has lost its sense of the supernatural, but many are searching for it-and find it in Medjugorje, through prayer, penance, and fasting."[100]

"There are bishops, like in Yugoslavia for example, who are against this [Medjugorje] . . . But it's important to look at the great number of people who are answering her invitations, the amount of conversions . . . All this is underlined in the Gospel, all these facts have to be seriously investigated."[101]

Pope John Paul II called for a pilgrimage of peace to Bosnia in 1993. The pope planned to visit Sarajevo on September 8, 1994, but canceled it for fear of retaliation on that city by the Serbs. The Pontiff instead celebrated a mass for peace on that day in Castle Gandolfo. John Paul honored Medjugorje with the following prayer: "Mary, Queen of Peace, pray for us." A papal Mass was said in Zagreb, Croatia on September 23, 1994.

Medjugorje—The Continuation of Fátima

Medjugorje is recognized as a place of prayer and pilgrimage, but the supernatural characteristic of the apparitions has not, as yet, been officially established by the Catholic Church. The declaration of the ex-Yugoslav Bishop Commission assigned to investigate Medjugorje, announced in Zadar on April 10, 1991, that, "On the basis of the investigations so far it can not be confirmed that one is dealing with supernatural apparitions and revelations." The Commission, which released its report one year before the outbreak of the Bosnian War, could not, however, disprove that Mary was appearing there, so private pilgrimages to Medjugorje are still being allowed by the Catholic Church, just no official church-sponsored trips. Meanwhile, the Catholic Church continues to investigate Medjugorje, but it is only a matter of time before it recognizes Medjugorje as worthy of belief. That day will come when the sign that Mary has promised in Medjugorje materializes.

Why did God choose to send Mary to Medjugorje? Because Yugoslavia was the last vestige of Russian communism in Eastern Europe, and because the peace of Yugoslavia was about to destroyed. Another reason is to call people to conversion before the chastisement comes, and to finish the work she began in Fátima regarding Russia's conversion. Mary revealed to the visionaries on August 25, 1991, the year that the Soviet Union died, that Medjugorje was the fulfillment of her prophecies in Fátima:

"[So that] the secrets I began in Fátima may be fulfilled."

Pope John Paul II also said that Medjugorje is the continuation of Fátima:

"Medjugorje is a continuation of Fátima. The world has lost its sense of the supernatural. It will find it again in Medjugorje through prayer, fasting, and sacramental penance."[102]

Medjugorje as a Sign of the Times

Mary told the visionary Marija Pavlovic on January 25, 1993, that her appearances in Medjugorje were meant to help people discern the "signs of the times":

"Today I call you to accept and live my messages with seriousness. These days are days when you need to decide for God, for peace and for good. May every hatred and jealousy disappear from your thoughts, and may there only dwell love for God and for your neighbor. Thus, only thus, shall you be able to discern the signs of this time. I am with you, and I guide you into a new time, a time which God gives you as grace, so that you may get to know him more."[103]

The Message of Medjugorje

Mary's central messages in Medjugorje are surrender to God; conversion; prayer without ceasing, especially before the crucifix; penance; sacrifice; renunciation; mortification; self-denial; daily communion; monthly confession; reading the Bible; saying the Rosary; fasting on Wednesday and Fridays; and reconciliation on first Fridays, Saturdays, and Sundays. She also recommends the display of blessed objects in the home and on the person. For more about Mary's messages from Medjugorje, turn to Appendix C.

Epilogue

In no way is this book meant to be an exhaustive study of the apparitions of Mary. I've only touched on the most important Marian apparitions and the historical circumstances surrounding them to emphasize the tremendous role that the Virgin Mary is playing in helping Jesus win the battle against Satan. If every Marian apparition that had ever occurred in the past two thousand years was fully documented a single book could not record them all. In fact, the majority of Mary's appearances on earth will probably remain unknown. Nonetheless, working unceasingly and without complaint, and not for her own glory, Mary has given her entire life to the salvation of our souls.

Within the last fifty years the number of reported sightings of the Virgin Mary have skyrocketed. The Catholic Church sees this as a sign that the battle between heaven and hell has intensified. Many of the reports of Marian appearances, of course, are phony, because some unscrupulous people pretend to see apparitions from heaven for their own personal glory and greed. Mary says this is a very serious sin and we should pray very much for these people. Some purported visions may indeed be demonic in origin and must be scrutinized very carefully.

For obvious reasons, the Catholic Church is very, very cautious in declaring apparitions to be worthy of belief, sometimes taking too long to reach a decision. But this is entirely understandable because the church's reputation is at stake. Historically, perhaps the most embarrassing charge the church ever made was against Galileo, in 1633. In a vain attempt to defend certain passages of the Bible that metaphorically speak of the earth as being the center of the universe, the church censored Galileo for upholding the Copernican theory, that the earth revolves around the sun and is not the stationary center of the universe. The church is still apologizing for that mistake, which many scientists, like the late Dr. Carl Sagan, have used as "proof" of the fallibility of the Catholic Church and the non-existence of God. Whatever the critics think about the Catholic Church, she has given rise to many credible saints and visionaries. The following are messages from Jesus and Mary to two twentieth-century Catholic visionaries, who were not cited in the previous chapters of this book, whose messages compliment the afore-mentioned apparitions of Mary and have extreme relevance for our time.

319

The Revelations of Saint Faustina Kowalska

Reports of apparitions of Jesus and Mary have come from all over the globe: Poland, Italy, the Ukraine, Egypt, Venezuela, the United States, and Asia to name a few. One particular visionary from Plock, Poland, Sister Faustina Kowalska (1905-1938) of the Congregation of the Sisters of Our Lady of Mercy, recorded a diary of her apparitions, which took place just a few years before Hitler and Stalin invaded Poland, a country which has arguably suffered more persecutions for its faith than any other nation in history. For twenty years organized devotionals to Sister Faustina's writings in her note-book were prohibited by the church, but were finally allowed after the Catholic Church completed its investigations of the writings and allowed them to be published. Faustina's notebook was first published in English in 1987, and the messages quoted here are excerpted from *Divine Mercy in My Soul,* copyright 1987, published by the Marians of the Immaculate Conception with the permission and help of Father Seraphim Michalenko, M.I.C., of the Marian Helpers Center in Stockbridge, Massachusetts.

Karol Cardinal Wojtyla, now Pope John Paul II, has led the way for the beat-ification of Sister Faustina, and declared her Blessed in 1993. On April 30, 2000, John Paul II canonized her a Saint. Beginning in 1931, Christ appeared in a vision to Sister Faustina to have her inform the world of the nearness of the last days and of the infinite mercy he is waiting to pour out on all those who are willing to accept it. For those poor souls who reject Christ's mercy, they'll soon have to deal not with the merciful Savior but with the just Judge. On February 22, 1931, Sister Faustina had a vision of Jesus, who appeared to her clothed in a white garment, with one hand raised in the gesture of bless-ing and the other hand touching his garment at the breast. From under Jesus' garment, two large rays emanated—one red, the other pale. Jesus said to Sister Faustina:

> *"Paint an image according to the pattern you see, with the signature, 'Jesus, I trust in You.' I desire that this image be venerated, first in your chapel, and throughout the world. I promise that the soul that will venerate this image shall not perish. I also promise victory over [its] enemies already here on earth, especially at the hour of death. I Myself will defend it as My own glory... Let the sinner not be afraid to approach Me. The flames of mercy are burning Me—clamoring to be spent; I want to pour them out upon these souls..."*[1]

Upon the request of her spiritual advisor, Sister Faustina asked Jesus whether the words "Christ, the King of Mercy" should be the inscription on the image. Jesus replied:

> *"I am the King of Mercy. I desire that this image be displayed in public on the First Sunday after Easter. That Sunday is the Feast of Mercy."*[2]

While in prayer one day, Sister Faustina received an interior message that the words "Jesus, I trust in You" must be displayed on the image. When her spiritual director asked the meaning of the image, Jesus explained it to Sister Faustina:

> *"The two rays denote Blood and Water. The pale ray stands for the Water that makes the soul righteous. The red rays stands for the Blood which is the Life of souls... These two rays issued forth from the very depths of My tender mercy when My agonized Heart was opened by a lance on the Cross. These rays shield souls from the wrath of the Father. Happy is the one who will dwell in their shelter, for the just hand of God shall not lay hold of him. I desire that the first Sunday after Easter be the Feast of Mercy. Ask of my faithful servant [Father Sopocko] that, on this day, he tell the whole world of My great mercy; that whoever approaches the Fount of Life on this day will be granted complete remission of sins and punishment... Proclaim that mercy is the greatest attribute of God. All the works of My hands are crowned with mercy."[3]*

In 1935, Jesus told Sister Faustina the reason for his appearance to her:

> *"You will prepare the world for My final coming."[4]*

Jesus then told Sister Faustina what would occur just before the Day of Justice, which is looming near:

> *"Write this: before I come as the just Judge, I am coming first as the King of Mercy. Before the day of justice arrives, there will be given to people a sign in the heavens of this sort: All light in the heavens will be extinguished, and there will be great darkness over the whole earth. Then the sign of the cross will be seen from the sky, and from the openings where the hands and feet of the Savior were nailed will come forth great lights which will light up the earth for a period of time. This will take place shortly before the last day."[5]*

On August 5, 1935, the Patronal Feast Day of the Congregation of the Sisters of Our Lady of Mercy, Mary appeared to Sister Faustina during mass with these words:

> *"I am Mother to you all, thanks to the unfathomable mercy of God. Most pleasing to Me is that soul which faithfully carries out the will of God..."[6]*

The Blessed Mother appeared again to Sister Faustina on March 25, 1936, on the Solemnity of the Annunciation, with the following message:

> *"Oh, how pleasing to God is the soul that follows faithfully the inspirations of his grace! I gave the Savior to the world; as for you, you have to speak to the world about His great mercy and prepare the world for the Second Coming of Him who will come, not as a merciful Savior, but as a just Judge. Oh, how terrible is that day! Determined is the day of justice, the day of divine wrath. The angels tremble before it. Speak to souls of this great mercy while it is still the time for [granting] mercy. If you keep silent now, you will be answering for a great number of souls on that terrible day. Fear nothing. Be faithful to the end. I sympathize with you.[7]*

Our Lord appeared to Sister Faustina a year later with the following request:

> "*Say unceasingly the chaplet [of Divine Mercy] that I have taught you. Whoever will recite it will receive great mercy at the hour of death. Priests will recommend it to sinners as their last hope of salvation. Even if they were a sinner most hardened, if he were to recite this chaplet only once, he would receive grace from My infinite mercy. I desire to grant unimaginable graces to those souls who trust in My mercy.*"[8]

The chaplet of Divine Mercy can be said anytime, but the Lord especially requested that it be said as a novena nine days before the Feast of Mercy. Jesus promised that by this novena, he would grant *"every possible grace to souls."* The chaplet is recited using ordinary Rosary beads. Begin with the Our Father, the Hail Mary, the Apostles' Creed; then on the Our Father beads before each decade, recite: "Eternal Father, I offer You the Body and Blood, Soul and Divinity of Your dearly beloved Son, Our Lord Jesus Christ, in atonement for our sins and those of the whole world." On the ten Hail Mary beads of each decade, say: "For the sake of His sorrowful Passion, have mercy on us and on the whole world." Conclude with saying three times: "Holy God, Holy Mighty One, Holy Immortal One, have mercy on us and on the whole world."

Sister Faustina was made to know that her sacrifices, and that of her fellow religious, were used by God to help sanctify the world: she suffered constantly from poor health and from the onslaughts of Satan. Satan was enraged at the number of souls being saved by the divine chaplet, which, if said at the hour of death, or having it said for you, placates the wrath of God and opens his most tender mercy:

> "*At the hour of death, I defend as My own glory every soul that will say the chaplet; or when others say it for a dying person, the pardon is the same. When this chaplet is said by the bedside of a dying person, God's anger is placated, unfathomable mercy envelops the soul, and the very depths of My tender mercy are moved for the sake of the sorrowful Passion of My Son.*"[9]

Jesus said that for those who spread the honor of his mercy, he would protect them for the remainder of their lives:

> "*Souls who spread the honor of My mercy I shield through their entire lives as a tender mother her infant, and at the hour of death I will not be a Judge for them, but the Merciful Savior...*"[10]

Jesus told Sister Faustina that many souls obstinately refuse the mercies offered by God, even at the moment of their deaths. They choose hell rather than God because that is what they want.

Sister Faustina's guardian angel took her on a tour of the abyss in 1936. This is what she recorded seeing:

> "Today, I was led by an Angel to the chasm of hell. It is a place of great torture; how awesomely large and extensive it is! The kinds of torture I

saw: the first torture that constitutes hell is the loss of God; the second is perpetual remorse of conscience; the third is that one's condition will never change; the fourth is the fire that will penetrate the soul without destroying it—a terrible suffering, since it is purely a spiritual fire, lit by God's anger; the fifth suffering is continual darkness and a terrible suffocating smell, and, despite the darkness, the devils and the souls of the damned see each other and all the evil, both of others and their own; the sixth torture is the constant company of Satan; the seventh torture is horrible despair, hatred of God, vile words, curses and blasphemies. These are the tortures suffered by all the damned together, but that is not the end of the sufferings. There are special tortures destined for particular souls. These are the torments of the senses. Each soul undergoes terrible and indescribable sufferings, related in the manner in which it has sinned. There are caverns and pits of torture where one form of agony differs from another. I would have died at the very sight of these tortures if the omnipotence of God had not supported me. Let the sinner know that he will be tortured throughout all eternity, in these senses he made use to sin. I am writing this at the command of God, so that no soul may find an excuse by saying there is no hell, or that nobody has ever been there, and so no one can say what it is like.

"I, Sister Faustina, by the order of God, have visited the abysses of hell so that I might tell souls about it and testify to its existence. I cannot speak about it now; but I have received a command from God to leave it in writing. The devils were full of hatred for me, but they had to obey me at the command of God. What I have written is but a pale shadow of what I saw. But I noticed one thing: that most of the souls there disbelieved that there is a hell. When I came to, I could hardly recover from the fright. How terribly souls suffer there! Consequently, I pray even more fervently for the conversions of sinners. I incessantly plead God's mercy upon them. O my Jesus, I would rather be in agony until the end of the world, amidst the greatest sufferings, than offend You by the least sin." [11]

Jesus revealed to Sister Faustina that his divine mercy was a sign of the nearness of the end times and must be accepted before it's too late:

"... *Speak to the world about My mercy; let all men recognize My unfathomable mercy. It is a sign for the end times; after it will come the day of justice....* "[12]

Then Jesus warned:

"*Secretary of My Mercy, write, tell souls about this great mercy of Mine, because the awful day, the day of My justice is near.*"[13]

Even though the day of justice is near, Jesus doesn't want us to despair: even the most hardened sinners have recourse to his mercy. Jesus said:

"*[Let] the greatest sinners place their trust in My mercy. They have the right before others to trust in the abyss of My mercy. My daughter, write about My mercy towards tormented souls. Souls that make an appeal to My mercy delight Me. To such souls*

I grant even more graces than they ask. I cannot punish even the greatest sinner if he makes an appeal to My compassion, but on the contrary, I justify him in My unfathomable and inscrutable mercy. Write: before I come as a just Judge, I first open the door of My mercy. He who refuses to pass through the door of My mercy must pass through the door of My justice... "[14]

Christ spoke to Sister Faustina in 1936 on the necessity of performing good works in addition to having faith in his mercy; contrary to the Protestant heresy of *sola fide:*

"*My daughter, if I demand through you that people revere My mercy, you should be the first to distinguish yourself by this confidence in My mercy. I demand from you deeds of mercy, which arise out of love for Me. You are to show mercy to your neighbor always and everywhere. You must not shrink from this or try to excuse or absolve yourself from it.*

"*I am giving you three ways of exercising mercy toward your neighbor: the first—by deed, the second—by word, the third—by prayer. In these three degrees is contained the fullness of mercy, and it is an unquestionable proof of love for Me. By this means a soul glorifies and pays reverence to Me. Yes, the first Sunday after Easter is the Feast of Mercy, but there must also be acts of mercy, and I demand the worship of My mercy through the solemn celebration of the Feast and through the veneration of the image which is painted. By means of this image I shall grant many graces to souls. It is to be a reminder of the demands of My mercy, because even the strongest faith is no avail without works.*" [15]

Sister Faustina was plagued by poor health most of her short adult life, and died from tuberculosis on October 5, 1938. Before she died, Christ assured her that her physical and spiritual sacrifices and sufferings would help save a multitude of souls. Jesus also promised that her homeland would help prepare the way for his Second Coming (perhaps Jesus was referring to Karol Cardinal Wojtyla, the future Pope John Paul II):

"*I bear a special love for Poland, and if she will be obedient to My will, I will exalt her in might and holiness. From her will come a spark that will prepare the world for My final coming.*" [16]

Revelations of the End Times by Maria Valtorta—The Little John the Evangelist

The most prolific mystical writer of the twentieth century, and perhaps of all time, was an invalid from Viareggio, Italy, named Maria Valtorta (1897-1961), who received innumerable dictations and visions from Jesus during WWII about the life of Christ, the way of holiness, and prophecies of the end times.

When Maria Valtorta was twenty-three she received a crippling blow to her back from a delinquent youth wielding an iron bar, which caused her to became permanently disabled at the relatively young age of thirty-seven, and be confined to bed for the rest of her life. Maria's bed-ridden infirmity was all in God's plan though: he meant to use her as his "mouthpiece of the end times"; his "Little John the Evangelist."

Confined to her bed, Maria felt herself being drawn closer and closer to God through dreams, premonitions, and other "strange things." Seeing the great spiritual change coming over her, Maria was instructed in 1943 by her spiritual advisor, Fr. Romuald M. Migliorini of the Servants of Mary, to write her autobiography. After having completed this in 1942, Maria began receiving her visions from Christ on Good Friday, the 23rd of April, 1943. Jesus instructed Maria to record an autobiography of his life, spanning from the birth of his Mother, his childhood, and his public life, to Mary's assumption into heaven.

During her visions of Christ's life, Maria was spiritually transported back in time to the Holy Land, and wrote about what she saw, with narrations and explanations dictated by Jesus and sometimes Mary. Maria's visions were unprecedented in church history, consisting of 700 visions illustrating the stories of the Gospels, and around 1000 dictations and commentaries.[17]

Most of Maria's visions occurred during and after WWII, between 1943 and 1947. By 1953, Maria's notebook included almost 15,000 pages of hand-written notes. Her 5,000 page *Poem of the Man-God*, which is an expanded narrative of the Gospels, was finished in 1947. Other published books compiled from Maria's notes include *The Notebooks: 1943, The End Times*, which were dictated by Jesus, and *The Book of Azariah*, which was dictated by Maria's guardian angel, Azariah.

Fr. Corrado M. Berti O.S.M., professor at Marianum Pontifical Faculty of Theology at Rome, submitted the first typewritten copy of *Poem of the Man-God to Pope Pius XII* in 1947. On February 26, 1948, the pope received in private audience three Servite priests: Fr. Berti, Fr. R. Migliorini, and Fr. A. Cecchin. Before these three witnesses, Pope Pius XII declared:

"Publish this work as it is. There is no need to give an opinion about its origin, whether it be extraordinary or not. Who reads it will understand. One hears of many visions and revelations. I will not say they are all authentic; but there are some of which it could be said they are."[18]

When consulted, Edouard Cardinal Gagnon, Head of the Pontifical Council for the Family and Doctor in Canon Law, wrote from the Vatican in 1987:

"...this judgment by the Holy Father in 1948 was an official Imprimatur of the type given before witnesses."[19]

Post-modernists and liberals within the Catholic Church, however, hate Maria Valtorta and have fought desperately to keep her manuscripts from being published. In 1949, they attempted to seize the manuscripts from the publishers and destroy them, but were unsuccessful in their attempt. Thankfully, the publisher and the Servites of Mary in charge of the writings remained faithful and protected them. Their plans thus thwarted, post-modernists succeeded in getting the first 1956-1959 edition of *Poem of the Man-God* placed on the Index of Forbidden Books. But in 1962, the Holy Office approved the master edition of *Poem of the Man-God*, and it is now a bestseller many times over, having been read throughout the entire world.[20] Now, the only thing left for modernists to do is slander Maria personally by claiming she was a mad woman. But multitudes of humble believers have read the *Poem of the Man-God* and have recognized the voice of their Great Shepherd in it. As Jesus said in the Gospel of John:

"My sheep hear my voice; I know them, and they follow me."[21]

Critics and skeptics of Maria Valtorta have spent many hours pouring through *Poem of the Man—God* to sift out the historical and biblical inaccuracies, but haven't found any. That's because they don't exist. All dictations and visions to Maria were supernatural and inerrant. If Maria was a mad woman pulling off a gargantuan hoax, she would have had to have had access to vast libraries to do all the necessary scholarly research. This would have been impossible for her to do because she was a cripple and couldn't get out of bed: her only references were her Bible and the Catholic Catechism. Maria's bed-ridden infirmity is precisely why God chose her: it was impossible for her to have faked it. Furthermore, many times Maria didn't understand what was being dictated to her, but Jesus told her to write it down anyway.

When the visionaries of Medjugorje questioned the Virgin Mary about the authenticity of Maria Valtorta's *Poem of the Man-God*, Mary replied that it was true.

The *Poem of the Man-God* contains over 700 visions of Christ's life and countless spiritual teachings. If you really want to get to know the heart and mind of the Savior, this is the book to read. As far as knowing prophecy about the end times, Maria Valtorta's *The End Times* is the better of the two.

According to dictations given to Maria Valtorta from Jesus, which are documented in Maria's book *The End Times*, (published by Éditions Paulines, Centro Editoriale Valtortiano, Sherbrooke, QC, Canada, 1994, and excerpted here with their permission) the final years consist of three major scourges by Satan and a short period of peace in between:

- The period of the forerunners of the Antichrist (Lenin, Stalin, Hitler, Mussolini), well under way by 1943, will culminate in the rationalistic period of the spiritual Antichrist (the Great Apostasy) at the end of the twentieth century. This is the anti-Christian period of time we are now in and that is rapidly leading up to the chastisement. Following the chastisement, which will kill billions of people, a short period of peace will occur in which Satan will be chained up and the renewing spirit of Jesus Christ will flood the earth and give mankind a time to regroup under his sign. In this short period of peace, which is not at all a literal millennium, the Catholic Church will be recognized by all survivors of all faiths as the One True Church.

- After the Catholic Church has its hosanna day, the period of the *real* incarnate Antichrist—where Satan incarnates himself into his chosen one to wage all-out war on the Catholic Church—will follow, bringing to the earth destruction and misery as never before seen. The period of Antichrist will only last three and a half years (42 months).
- After Antichrist unlocks the gates of hell with his wickedness, Satan and all his minions will be loosened from their chains and the final period of Satan will begin. This horrific tribulation will last for another three and a half years, and ends with the Second Coming of Jesus Christ and the final defeat of Satan. Christ will defeat the devil and cast him down into hell forever, where the Antichrist, the two beasts, the false prophets, demons, and human reprobates await him. The dead will then be resurrected for the Last Judgment and the world will come to an end. At the Last Judgment, the just will be given a glorified body and will inherit a new heaven and earth, while the damned will be given horrified bodies and will be cast back down into hell forever.

When will the Second Coming occur? Jesus said he would only come at the last hour (the end of the world).[22] By saying this, Jesus dispels the heresy of millenarianism, the mistaken belief that Christians will be "raptured" to heaven before a "seven-year tribulation" on earth, preceding Christ's physical coming to earth and his literal reign for a thousand years. I hate to be the one to give them the bad news, but millenarianists will have to face the coming chastisement like everyone else, even though they've been led to believe by their false prophets that they'll be "raptured" into heaven beforehand. How terrible will be the day when they see the coming of the chastisement and they haven't been raptured out of it. Like the Bible says, they'll tear their hair out in fright. False prophets who've made millions of dollars with their false assurances of salvation through "faith alone" and the "rapture of the elect" will have to answer to God for misleading so many of his children.

Jesus told Maria that when he comes at the physical end of the world, for the majority it will be as a just Judge, not a merciful Savior:

"My second coming will be a coming of stern, inflexible, general Judgment, and for the majority of you, it will be a judgment of punishment."[23]

Jesus then explained to Maria what he meant by "majority":

"In truth I tell you that over two thirds of the human race belong to the category that lives under the sign of the Beast. For them I died uselessly."[24]

As the end of the world draws nearer, many priests and ministers will fall;

not so much to sensuality and lasciviousness, which have scandalized Christianity, but to post-modernism, which denies the faith and makes a god out of man:

> "When the time comes, many stars [priests] will be swept away by the coils of Lucifer who, to prevail, needs to lessen the light of souls.... The plan of Satan's shrewd malice is to put out, by sweeping them away, these stars that are lights reflecting My Light for the crowds.... Satan knows it and scatters his seed to prepare the weakness of the priesthood, to be able to sweep it away easily into sins, not so much as their senses as of their minds. In a mental chaos, it will be easy for him to bring about a spiritual chaos. In the spiritual chaos the weak, confronted with the torrents of persecution, will commit the sin of faint-heartedness, when they deny the faith.[25]

But the Catholic Church will never completely die: a faithful remnant will always remain. Jesus assured us of this when he promised to Peter two thousand years ago that the jaws of death shall not prevail against his church. Jesus explained to Maria the reason for the persecution of the church:

> "The Church shall not die because I will be with it. But it shall experience hours of darkness and horror like those of My Passion, hours multiplied in time because it must needs be. It must needs be that the Church suffer what its Creator suffered, before dying to rise in eternal form. It must needs be that the Church suffer much longer because it is not, in its members, perfect like its Creator, and if I suffered for hours, it must suffer for weeks and weeks of hours. In the early times the Church was persecuted and fed by a supernatural power in her best children and then she sprang up. She will have the same lot when the times come, in which she will exist, subsist, and resist the satanical tide and the battle of the Antichrist with her best children: a painful, albeit just selection."[26]

Just who will the Antichrist be? The Antichrist will be a satanic mockery of the Son of God, an incarnation of the devil himself:

> "In a world in which so many spiritual lights will have died, it is logical that there openly begins the brief but dreadful reign of the Antichrist, begotten by Satan just as Christ was begotten by the Father. Christ is the Father's Son procreated by love with Purity. The Antichrist will be Satan's son procreated by Hatred and triple Impurity."[27]

Jesus added:

> "Lucifer strives to imitate God, in evil of course. He takes on, I will say, the lifestyle and form of court that the Son of God had. The devil poses as Christ, and like Christ, has apostles and disciples. Among these he will choose the perfect one to turn him into the Antichrist. For now [1943] we are in the preparatory period of the forerunners of the Antichrist."[28]

Jesus gave Maria hints about the identity of the future Antichrist, insinuating that he will be someone high up in the Catholic Church—maybe even the

266th Archbishop of Rome, whom Catholic prophets like St. Malachy have already predicted to be the last pope. Jesus said:

> "*He will be someone very high up, high up like a heavenly body: not a human star that shines in a human sky, but a heavenly body from a supernatural sphere. Giving up to the Enemies enticement, he will experience pride after humility, atheism after faith, lust after charity, the craving for gold after evangelical poverty, the thirst for honors after concealment.*
>
> "*It will be less frightful to see a star of the vault of Heaven shoot down than it will be to see this elect creature hurtle down into Satan's coils, copying the sin of his chosen father. Lucifer, out of pride, became the Cursed and Dark One. The Antichrist, out of pride of one hour, will become the cursed and dark one after having been a heavenly body in My Army.*
>
> "*His abjuration shall shake the heavens under a deep shudder of horror and make the pillars of my Church tremble in the dismay brought upon by his fall. As a reward for his abjuration, he shall get Satan's help in full. Satan will give him the keys of the whole abyss for him to open it, in fact to throw it completely open to let out the instruments of horror which Satan has been putting together for thousands of years to drive people to utter hopelessness, so that on their own they would call upon Satan as King and rush after the Antichrist to follow him. The Antichrist will be the one who can throw the gates of the abyss open to let the King of the abyss out, just as Christ opened the gates of the Heavens to let out grace and forgiveness which turn human beings into gods like God and kings of an eternal Kingdom in which I am the King of kings.*
>
> "*As the Father gave me all power, so will Satan give the Antichrist all power, and especially all power of seduction, to sway into his retinue the weak and those corroded by the fevers of ambitions as he, their head is. But in his unbridled ambition he will find Satan's supernatural forms of help still too little and he will seek other help in Christ's enemies. These shall be armed with deadlier and deadlier weapons, such as their lust for Evil was able to lead them to create in order to spread hopelessness among the crowds. They will help him until God utters His 'Enough!' and reduces them to ashes with the radiance of his countenance.*"[29]

The "Abomination of Desolation" mentioned in Daniel 9:27, when Antichrist seats himself in the Temple of God, will result from a priesthood that loves rationalism and serves political power too much, and will be the forerunning sign of the end of the world. Jesus elaborated:

> "*In the past centuries, from these errors there came the antipopes and the schisms, which, the antipopes as well as the schisms, split consciences into two opposite camps thus causing countless downfall of souls. In the centuries to come, these same errors will be able to bring about the Error, namely the Abomination in God's house, the forerunning sign of the end of the world. What will it consist in? When will it happen? You do not need to know that. I will only tell you that from a priesthood that loves rationalism too much and serves political power too much, there can but fatally come a very dark period for the Church.*"[30]

During the short period of peace following the imminent chastisement, the world will recognize the Catholic Church as the One True Church; but at the last hour before the final scourge of Satan, three quarters of the church will disown Christ. Jesus told Maria:

> "*During my short rule over the world, I will be the One reigning, I and the rest of My people, in other words the real faithful, those who do not disown Christ and cover the sign of Christ with Satan's [fake] tiara. Then the false gods of excessive power will fall, as well as the indecent doctrines that disown God, the almighty Lord.*
>
> "*My Church, before the hour of the world comes to an end, will have its glittering triumph. Nothing differs in the Mystical Body's life from that which was in Christ's life. There will be the hosanna on the eve of Passion, the hosanna when the nations, seized by fascination of the Divinity, bend the knee before the Lord. Then the Passion of My Church militant will come, and finally the glory of eternal Resurrection in Heaven.*
>
> "*O bliss of that day when conspiracies, retaliations, struggles of this earth, of Satan, of the flesh will be over forever! My Church will then be made up of real Christians, in that time, in the next-to-last day. Few as in the beginning, but holy as in the beginning. The Church will end in holiness as it began in holiness. Liars, betrayers, idolaters will stay outside, those who on the last day will imitate Judas and sell their souls to Satan, harming Christ's Mystical Body. In them the Beast will have its replacements for its last war.*
>
> "*And woe betide those in Jerusalem, in the end times, who become guilty of sin. Woe betide those who in Jerusalem will exploit their authority for human advantage. Woe betide those who let their brothers and sisters perish and will neglect to turn to the Word I entrusted to them into bread for the soul hungering for God. Woe betide them. Between those who openly disown God and those who disown Him by their actions, I will make no difference. And in truth I tell all of you, with the sorrow of a sublime Founder, that at the last hour three quarters of My Church will disown Me, and I will have to cut them off from the tree-trunk as dead branches infected by an unclean leprosy.*"[31]

Elaborating further, Jesus said:

> "*I already told you. My Church will have its hosanna day before its passion. Then the everlasting triumph will come. At that time the whole world will know the Church of Rome, because the Gospel will resound from the poles to the equator and the Word will go from one side of the globe to the other, like a belt of love.... Like a march of millions and millions of tribes, people will go towards Christ with their spirits and will put their trust in Earth's only being in whom there is no craving for oppression or longing for revenge.*
>
> "*It will be Rome that speaks. But not the more or less great, more or less lastingly great Rome which rabble rousers [like Mussolini] can win. It will be the Rome of Christ. The one that conquered the Caesars, conquering them without weapons, without battles, with only one force, love; with the one weapon only, the Cross; with one rhetoric only, prayer. It will be the Rome of the Pontiffs which, in a world darkened*

*by barbarian invasions and dazed by their destructions, was able to preserve civi-
lization and to spread it among the uncivilized. It will be the Rome that stood up to
arrogant men and through its holy, Venerable Old Men was able to stand for the weak
and sting with a spiritual punishment even those who appeared to be immune to any
remorse.*[32]

The final Satanic period immediately preceding the Second Coming of
Christ will be the most turbulent time in the history of the world. But out of
God's mercy, it will be short. Jesus said:

*"The satanic period will be three times more ferocious than the period of the
Antichrist. But it will be short because for those living at the hour the whole Church
triumphant will pray amidst the lights of Heaven, the Church suffering will pray
amidst the cleansing flames of love, the Church militant will pray with the last
martyr's blood.*[33]

In the last days, following the coming of Antichrist, Israel will have united
with the Roman Catholic Church and both will suffer their greatest tribulation in all of history. By then the Holy Mass will have been outlawed and the
abomination of desolation will have occurred. Jesus told Maria:

*"The archangel [Michael] who defeated Lucifer, and who watches over My
Kingdom and its children, is the one who will rise as a heavenly sign in the last
time. This shall be the time when Israel is joined on again to the Rome of Christ:
there no longer will be two branches of God's people, the one blessed and the other
cursed for its deicide; there shall be only one treetrunk known as of Christ, because
it will be alive in Me....*

*"The last time of three years and six months will be more awful than what
mankind ever experienced. Satan shall be inflamed with the utmost spite, because
even the split between the two branches of God's people will be over, and with it the
cause of so many material, moral, and spiritual evils. Satan, through his son
[Antichrist], shall use his absolute, ultimate wiles to harm, ruin, kill Christ within
hearts and kill hearts belonging to Christ...*

*"Then the time shall come when, crushed to an extent never reached before, the
Church is no longer free to celebrate the perpetual Sacrifice [the Mass], and the
abomination of desolation shall be lifted up on the Holy Place [Jerusalem] and the
holy places....*[34]

Summarizing the sequence of events of the three anti-Christian periods of
the end times which was already under way by WWII, Jesus informed Maria:

*"After the forerunners of the Antichrist, the Antichrist himself will come. The
antichristian period is symbolized by the Beast armed with ten horns, Satan's ten
slaves, who consider themselves kings. (Three of these—note well—will be torn off
and cast into nothingness, namely into the abyss where God is not and so where
Nothingness is, the opposite of God who is Everything.) The antichristian period
will climax in the birth and the growth, until its greatest power, of the eleventh horn,
the reason for the fall of its three forerunners, and the seat of the real Antichrist. The*

Antichrist will blaspheme God as no son of man has ever done. He will ride roughshod over God's saints and torture Christ's Church. He will think, because he is the son [of the union of] demonic pride with lust, that 'he can do great things, changing the times and the laws,' and for three and a half years he will be Horror ruling over the world.

"Then the Father will say: 'Enough' in front of the great chorus which will be made in Heaven by the 'noise of the great words' of the saints; and the wicked Beast shall be killed and thrown into the shaft of the abyss and with all the lesser beasts to remain there with Satan, their breeder, for eternity.

"I shall then be called by the Father to 'judge the living and the dead' in accordance with what is said in the Symbol of the Faith. And the 'living,' those who have kept life within them by having kept Grace and Faith alive, shall inherit 'the kingdom, the power and the majesty of God.' The dead of the spirit shall have never-ending Death in accordance with what their will chose to have.

"And there shall no longer be Earth and carnal human beings. But there shall be only 'children of God,' creatures free from every sorrow, and there shall no longer be sin, and there shall no longer be darkness, and there shall no longer be fear. But only joy, joy, immense, everlasting joy inconceivable to human beings. Joy to see God, to possess Him, to understand His thoughts and His Love."[35]

For those who want to be redeemed to a life of everlasting joy, the secret is the veneration of Mary. Jesus confessed:

"... Mary is your Salvation in this terrifying end of this terrifying [twentieth] century in which the complete opening of the seven seals may happen due to God's punishment... Truly, many of the seals have already been opened. But woe if they were all opened. Woe if they are opened! Anticipate the hour of the triumph of the Woman, foundress of the family of those marked with the sign of God's servants, of the elect whose home is Heaven. Anticipate the hour of Mary's triumph over Satan, over the world, matter, and death—death which was vanquished by us twice, vanquished in her, a creature, even in her non-experiencing the spiritual death of sin, as well as in her flesh which does not corrupt and lives [in Heaven]. Anticipate the hour of Mary's triumph. Let men, women, and children of the One, Holy, Catholic, Apostolic Church of Rome join the Angels, captained by Michael [the Archangel], so that the seven-headed dragon with the ten horns and seven cursed crowns—the seven seductions—be thrown down for a time, and so that Christendom have time to be reunited and strengthened in charity and in faith and squeeze together to defend themselves in the last battle [against Antichrist].

"Woe if the woman dressed in purple and scarlet [the earth], whose throne is the loathsome beast with blasphemous names, were proclaimed queen before the Woman clothed with the sun, whose feet tread on the moon and whose head is crowned with stars was proclaimed, with infallible words, Queen of angels and of mankind.

"There cannot be a second Redemption carried out by Me, Christ. But there can still be one to save a greater number of souls from hell's coils: the one by Mary in glory. THE SECRET OF THE LAST REDEMPTION IS FOUND IN THE VENERATION OF MARY."[36]

Appendix A: Proud Boasts and Blasphemies from the Mortally Wounded Beast

Communist Manifesto, 1848, co-authored by Karl Marx and Friedrich Engels

"A specter is haunting Europe—the specter of communism. All the powers of old Europe have entered into a holy alliance to exorcize this specter..."

"The immediate aim of the communists is the same as that of all the other proletarian parties: formation of the proletariat into a class, overthrow of the bourgeois supremacy, *conquest of political power* by the proletariat."

"The communists disdain to conceal their views and aims. They openly declare that their ends can be attained only by the enforceable overthrow of all existing social conditions. Let the ruling classes tremble at a communist revolution. The proletarians have nothing to lose but their chains. They have a world to win. Workingmen of all countries, unite!"

"In this sense, the theory of communists may be summed up in the single sentence: *Abolition of private property.*"

"*Abolition of the family!* Even the most radical flare up at this infamous proposal of the communists."

Karl Marx (1818-1883)

"The policy of Russia is changeless... Its methods, its tactics, its maneuvers may change, but the polar star of its policy—*world domination*—is a fixed star."

"Religion is the sigh of the oppressed creature, the feeling of a heartless world, just as it is the spirit of unspiritual conditions. *It is the opium of the people.*"[1]

"The first requisite for the happiness of the people is the abolition of religion."[2]

"The Emancipation of the Jews in its last significance is the emancipation of mankind from Judaism."[3]

Friedrich Engels (1820-1895)

"Outside man and nature nothing exists, and the higher beings which our religious phantasies have created are only the fantastic reflection of our individuality."[4]

"For Marx, science was a motive force of history, was a revolutionary force."[5]

"Just as Darwin discovered the law of evolution in organic nature, so Marx discovered the law of evolution in human history."[6]

"Our evolutionary conception of the universe allows no place at all for a Creator."[7]

Vladimir Lenin (1870-1924)

"I hate God as I do my personal enemies."[8]

"Atheism is a natural and inseparable part of Marxism."[9]

"The dictatorship of the proletariat is nothing else than power based upon force and limited by nothing—by no law and by absolutely no rule."[10]

"Outside of Socialism there is no salvation of mankind from wars, hunger, and the further destruction of millions and millions of human beings."[11]

"In the end, one or the other will triumph—a funeral dirge will be sung over the Soviet Republic or over world capitalism."[12]

"The roots of modern religion are deeply imbedded in the social oppression of the working classes, and their apparently complete helplessness before the blind forces of capitalism."[13]

"The modern proletariat ranges himself on the side of Socialism, which, with the help of science, is dispersing the fog of religion and is liberating the workers from their faith in a life after death."[14]

"Religion teaches those who toil in poverty all their lives to be resigned and patient in this world, and consoles them with the hope of reward in heaven. As for those who live upon the labors of others, religion teaches them to be charitable in earthly life, thus providing a cheap justification for their whole exploiting existence and selling them at a reasonable price tickets to heavenly bliss.... Religion is a kind of spiritual intoxicant, in which the slaves of capital drown their humanity and blunt their desires for some sort of decent human existence."[15]

"Of course, we say that we do not believe in God. We know perfectly well that the clergy, the landlords, and the bourgeoisie all claimed to speak in the name of god, in order to protect their own interests as exploiters."[16]

"We must engage in a most decisive battle against reactionary clergy and suppress their resistance with such cruelty that they will remember it for decades to come."[17]

The Cheka (Soviet Secret Police)

"All things are permitted us, because we were the first in the world to take up the sword... Who is to reproach us, armed as we are with this sacred sword, who is to reproach us for the manner of our struggle?"[18] (Refer to Revelation 13 and William Blake's drawing of the "Beast from the Sea" for the symbolism of the sword of the Beast.)

"...Communism and religion are mutually exclusive.... No machinery can destroy religion except that of the [Cheka]. In its plans to demoralize the church the Cheka has recently focused its attention on the rank and file of the priesthood. Only through them, by long, intensive, and painstaking work, shall we succeed in destroying and dismantling the church completely."[19]

Joseph Stalin (1879-1953)

"The Pope! How many divisions has *he* got?"[20]

"The Communist Party cannot be neutral toward religion. It stands for science, and all religion is opposed to science."[21]

"The scientific concept, dictatorship, means nothing more or less than power which directly rests on violence, which is not limited by any laws or restricted by any rules... Dictatorship means unlimited power, resting on violence and not on law."[22]

"Kill the eunuch priests and you kill this Christ."[23]

Nikita Khrushchev (1894-1971)

"Whether you like it or not, history is on our side. We will bury you."[24]

"If anyone believes that our smiles involve abandonment of the teaching of Marx, Engels, and Lenin he deceives himself poorly. Those who wait for that must wait until a shrimp learns to whistle."[25]

Appendix B: Infamous Quotes from Friedrich Nietzsche— The Philosophical Antichrist (1844-1900)

On the Non-Existence of God

"God is dead. God remains dead. And we have killed him."[1]

"The greatest recent event—[is] that 'God is dead,' that the belief in the Christian God has ceased to be believable..."[2]

"God is a conjecture..."[3]

"...there are gods, but no God."[4]

Against Christianity

"I condemn Christianity. I raise against the Christian church the most terrible of all accusations that any accuser ever uttered. It is to me the highest of all conceivable corruptions."[5]

"Buddhism is a hundred times more realistic than Christianity... Buddhism is the only genuinely positivistic religion in history... In my terms, it stands beyond good and evil."[6]

"Buddhism does not promise but fulfills; Christianity promises everything but fulfills nothing."[7]

"What is more harmful than any vice? Active pity for all the failures and the weak: Christianity."[8]

"Christianity is called the religion of pity... Pity is the *practice* of nihilism."[9]

On the Blessed Virgin Mary

"I should sooner believe in the man in the moon than in the woman [clothed with the sun]."[10]

On the Non-Existence of Sin and Immorality

"Let us remove the concept of sin from the world—and let us soon send the concept of punishment after it."[11]

"Morality is the herd-instinct in the individual."[12]

"Morality and religion belong altogether to the psychology of error..."[13]

On the Non-Existence of an Afterlife

"The great lie about immortality destroys every kind of reason, every kind of naturalness in the instincts."[14]

Belief that Man is God

"All of us are nailed to the cross, consequently we are divine. We alone are divine."[15]

"Formerly, the proof of man's higher origin, of his divinity, was found in his consciousness, in his spirit."[16]

"God is dead... I teach you the overman [superman]. Man is something to be surpassed."[17]

"Christianity... has waged deadly war against this higher type of man."[18]

On Selective Breeding and Eugenics

"The problem I thus pose is not what shall succeed mankind in the sequence of living things (man is an *end*), but what type of man shall be bred, shall be *willed*, for higher value, worthier of a life, more certain of a future."[19]

"Christianity... represents the counter-movement to any morality of breeding, of race, of privilege: it is the *anti-Aryan* religion par excellence."[20] (Nietzsche once nearly choked to death on a fishbone, which he saw as full of "symbolism and meaning".)

On the Goodness of Power, the Selfish-Will, War, and the Coming of a Hitler

"Life itself is to my mind the instinct for growth, for durability, for accumulation of forces, for *power*: where the will to power is lacking there is decline."[21]

"The man who has renounced war has renounced a grand life."[22]

"He shall be the greatest who can be the loneliest, the most hidden, the most deviating, the human being beyond good and evil, the master of his virtues, he that is overrich in will."[23]

On the Coming of Horrible Wars

"The concept of politics will be assimilated wholly into ideological warfare, all the power structures of the old society will be blown up—they are all founded on lies. There will be wars such as there have never been on earth."[24]

Prophesying His Own Impact on the Twentieth Century

"My time has not yet come... some are born posthumously."[25]

"...deeds require time even after they are done, before they can be seen and heard."[26]

"One day my name will be associated with something catastrophic—a crisis such as there has never been on earth, the most profound collision of conscience... I am not a man, I am dynamite."[27]

Appendix C: Our Lady's Messages from Medjugorje

On Christmas day, 1982, the daily apparitions of Our Lady ended for Mirjana. That day she received her tenth and final secret: Mirjana said it was very grave. Mary continues to appear to Mirjana once a year at Christmas, and on special occasions such as her birthday. Ivanka's apparitions ended on May 7, 1985: she got to see her mother in heaven and kiss her goodbye. She continues to receive visitations from Mary each year on June 25, the anniversary of the apparitions, or on special occasions. On one special occasion Ivanka received a vision of multitudes of black people dying terrible deaths. Mary informed Ivanka that the event was near and would be a sign or warning. That event turned out to be Rwanda.

The other four visionaries, Jakov, Ivan, Marija, and Vicka, continue to receive apparitions from Our Lady. Mary began giving a series of public messages to Marija once a week, beginning on March 1, 1984, which turned into monthly messages in January of 1987, and which have continued to this day. The Madonna also revealed the story of her life to the visionaries and Vicka has transcribed Our Lady's biography into three books.

The following are some of the more important messages that the Blessed Mother has given the Medjugorje visionaries, which have appeared in countless books, magazines, newsletters, prayer cards, telephone messages, and web pages about Medjugorje—far too many to list here.

Regarding the real existence of Satan

"Satan exists! He seeks only to destroy."

"This is the time of the devil."

"Darkness reigns over the world."

"The hour has come when the demon is authorized to act with all his force and power. The present hour, is the hour of Satan."

"Be on your guard. This period is dangerous for you. The devil is trying to lead you astray from the way. Those who give themselves to God will be the object of attacks."

"Satan is enraged against those who fast and those who are converted."

"Satan wants to impose hardships on the Catholic Church."

"Satan is strong and is waiting to test each one of you."

"...Every disorder comes from Satan."

"My Son wants to win all souls to Him, but the Devil strives to obtain something. The Devil makes a great effort to infiltrate among you, at all costs."

"Whatever be the place where I appear, and where my Son comes with me, Satan also comes. You permitted him to subdue you without realizing you were being led by him."

"You are ready to commit sin, and to put yourselves in the hands of Satan without reflecting. I call on each of you to consciously decide for God and against Satan..."

"My Son struggles for each of you, but Satan fights Him also."

On September 2, 1981, Vicka asked about the fate of a young person who hanged himself. Mary's answer should be a warning to anyone contemplating suicide or euthanasia to escape suffering and despair:

"Satan took hold of him. This young man should not have done that. The Devil tries to reign over the people. He takes everything into his hands, but the force of God is more powerful, and God will conquer."

Horrible looking and black all over, Satan appeared one day to Mirjana in 1982, causing her to faint. When she came around he was laughing at her. Then Satan asked her to renounce the Blessed Mother and follow him: that way she could be very beautiful and happy in love and in life. He said that following the Virgin would only lead to suffering and hardships. When Mirjana rebuked the devil, the Blessed Mother immediately appeared and said:

"Excuse me for this, but you must realize that Satan exists. One day he appeared before the throne of God and asked permission to submit the Church to a period of trial. God gave him permission to try the Church for one century. This century is

under the power of the Devil, but when the secrets confided to you come to pass, his power will be destroyed. Even now he is beginning to lose his power and has become aggressive. He is destroying marriages, creating divisions amongst priests and is responsible for obsessions and murder..."

Satan exists! Not figuratively, not anthropomorphically, not as a personification of our shadowy self, but literally. He's an extremely intelligent and crafty being whose powers are second only to God's. His best deception is getting people to believe he doesn't exist. For those of you who don't believe in him, let me ask you: Why then do we need a Savior? Why did God have to sacrifice his only begotten Son? Why would Jesus take upon himself our sins and suffer the horrible, ignominious death of crucifixion if there were no Satan or hell to save us from?

Regarding the real existence of hell

The Medjugorje visionaries were shown a vision of the crucified Christ on All Souls Day, November 2, 1981. Four days later some of the visionaries saw a horrendous vision of hell. Naked people walked in the flames and came out blackened, unrecognizable: you couldn't tell the men from the women. Vicka described a beautiful young girl who went into the flames and came out looking like a grotesque, blackened beast. After their visit to hell, the Blessed Mother had to comfort the frightened children lest they lose heart:

"Do not be afraid! I have shown you Hell so that you may know the state of those who are there."

Mary told the visionaries on July 25, 1982 why so many people go to hell:

"Today many persons go to Hell. God allows His children to suffer in Hell due to the fact that they have committed grave, unpardonable sins. Those in Hell no longer have a chance to know a better lot."

When Mirjana asked Mary on January 10, 1983, why God so "mercilessly" sends sinners to hell forever, Mary told her:

"Men who go to Hell no longer want to receive any benefit from God. They do not repent nor do they cease to revolt and to blaspheme. They make up their mind to live in Hell [while on earth] and do not contemplate leaving it."

In essence, people who go to hell choose to do so while alive. They hate God/good and love the Devil/evil. They love their wickedness and evil so much that they never contemplate giving it up; so they, in effect, send themselves to hell. God, for his part, takes no pleasure in sending people to hell; he only does it because his Justice demands it. People forget that God is not just a God of Love and Mercy, he is also a God of Justice. He repays each person for the good that person has done as well as the bad. So don't blame God for sending people to hell: God puts the rewards and punishments in front of people and they choose what they want—God and Life, or the Devil and Death.

The Bible says that the beginning of wisdom is the fear of God. The world, however, has lost its fear of God. The vast majority of people, if they believe in hell at all, don't believe they'll ever go there. A March 25, 1991, article in *U. S. News & World Report* reported that only 60% of 1,108 people surveyed believed in the existence of hell; and of that 60% only 4% believed they had an excellent or good chance of going there. By their calculations, this figures out to be only about 23 out of a 1,000 people winding up in hell, which is not very many. But the Bible says, and Mary reiterates, that many people go to hell. "Wide is the road," Mary says, "and many people there are who choose it."

The devil deceives people into believing that hell doesn't exist, or if it does exist then only serial killers and child molesters will go there—certainly none of us. Wrong! One of Satan's best deceptions is getting people to believe that they are good, or that a compassionate, loving God would never send anyone to hell for all eternity. Having bought the devil's lie, most post-modernists and liberals within Christianity don't believe in the real existence of hell anymore. How often these days do you hear someone preaching about it? Hardly ever. This would offend their congregation too much and hurt their collection plate. Even the well-respected Billy Graham is afraid to teach that hell is everlasting fire and eternal torment. Billy prefers to call hell an "eternal separation from God," which probably sounds like heaven to atheists. With all due respect, Mr. Graham, the torments of hell are real and for all eternity. Not figuratively, as liberals and unbelievers contend, but literally. Jesus spoke about the literal existence of hell more than any other topic in the New Testament. That's why it's so important that we take hell seriously and do everything we can to avoid going there.

Furthermore, the damned don't cease to exist after a certain period of time in hell as some theologians claim, because as spiritual creatures we are all made in the likeness of God and are, therefore, eternal beings. And God won't eventually free the damned from hell, as others claim, because the wicked and rebellious are eternally unrepentant and will always hate and blaspheme God—like the demons do. If hell's demons could, they would tear heaven and earth to pieces. Besides, if wicked people like Hitler and Stalin were eventually rewarded with the same eternal bliss of heaven as the saints, what's the use of being good? No, the Justice of God demands there be an everlasting hell, both as a punishment for the wicked and as a deterrent against those contemplating wickedness.

People should know what hell is really like. From the many documentations of Catholic priests who have performed exorcisms, from people who have had near-death experiences and were sent to hell as a warning, and from the true accounts of visionaries and mystics who were given glimpses of hell, we know for certain that hell is total physical and spiritual torment—just as Jesus said in the Gospels. Fire and ice burns the body while the worm that does not die eats away at the flesh. The sulfur that fuels the everlasting fire and smoke stinks like putrefying garbage and rotten eggs, permeating the nostrils with a horrifying stench and the mouth with an equally caustic taste. The ears constantly hear screams, cursing, moans, and blaspheming. The eyes never see light again; hell's darkness is lit only by a fire hotter than the sun. The parched tongue is never quenched with water. The parts of the body that sinned are physically tortured by demons who love to inflict you with pain. Equilibrium and balance is disoriented as souls, burning like sparks from a fire, are tossed to and fro in the blazing whirlwind.

Worse than the physical torments are the spiritual sufferings: never again to be able to have God (peace and love); mental depression from the constant darkness and physical tortures; total isolation from friends and family; no fellowship, no companionship; loss of all hope for a better life; remorse of conscience for having refused to listen to God's Word and accept his offer of salvation; constant remembering of the sins that condemned you; hatred, anger, rage, fear, anxiety, despair, helplessness, powerlessness (mortals have no power in hell and are totally at the mercy of demons and devils), rejection, loneliness, insanity—that is hell.

Regarding purgatory

Purgatory was described by the visionaries as a dark place where they saw no people, only gray ash. There were no walls or floors but you could hear the people knocking as if they wanted out. The Gospa said to pray for the people in purgatory.

> *"There are many souls in Purgatory. There are also persons who have been consecrated to God... There are a large number of souls who have been in Purgatory for a long time because no one prays for them."*

> *"In Purgatory there are different levels; the lowest is close to Hell and the highest gradually draws near to Heaven. It is not on All Souls Day, but at Christmas, that the greatest number of souls leave Purgatory. There are in Purgatory, souls who pray ardently to God, but for whom no relative or friend prays on earth. God makes them benefit from the prayers of other people. It happens that God permits them to manifest*

346 THE WOMAN AND THE DRAGON

themselves in different ways, close to relatives on earth, in order to remind men of the existence of Purgatory and to solicit their prayers to come close to God who is just, but good. The majority of people go to Purgatory. Many go to Hell. A small number go directly to Heaven."

As Mary said, many people go to hell, but most people go to a temporary place of suffering called purgatory, to be "purged" of their sins. The worse your sins, the closer you are to hell and its punishments, and the longer your stay. But those in purgatory benefit from the prayers of the living, so it is important that we remember to pray for them.

"These persons wait for your prayers and your sacrifices."

Regarding the need for conversion

"If you would be strong in the faith, Satan would not be able to do anything against you. Begin to walk the path of my messages. Be converted, be converted, be converted."

"Dear children, all the prayers which you recite in the evening in your homes, dedicate them to the conversion of sinners because the world is immersed in a great moral decay. Recite the Rosary every evening."

"...There are many Christians who live like pagans. There are always so few true believers."

"God does not want you lukewarm or undecided, but that you totally surrender to Him...."

"...Do not deceive yourselves into thinking, 'I am good, but my brother next door is no good.' You would be wrong..."

Oh how many people think that they are good and don't need to go to church, or confession, or take Holy Communion. They are only deceiving themselves. Fooling people into thinking that they are good but other people are bad is Satan's biggest victory. Only with Jesus in your heart can you be halfway good.

"Some don't even want to hear about Jesus, but they still want peace and satisfaction."

Too many people nowadays want peace in their lives but aren't willing to pray to Jesus, or read the Bible, or make sacrifices. If people only knew the real way to happiness they would follow Jesus.

Regarding the chances of getting into heaven

"Whoever has done very much evil during his life can go straight to Heaven if he confesses, is sorry for what he has done, and receives Communion at the end of his life."

"The most important thing is to believe."

Regarding the danger of unbelief

Every man, no matter what faith or belief, has knowledge of God and the Ten Commandments written on his heart. No one can plead ignorance of the law or say that he didn't know there was a God at the time of his personal judgment. Agnosticism doesn't exist.

"In your life you have all experienced light and darkness. God grants to every person recognition of light and darkness..."

"My angel, pray for unbelievers. People will tear their hair, brothers will plead with brothers, they will curse their past lives without God. They will repent, but it will be too late ..."

"Those who say, 'I do not believe in God,' how difficult it will be for them when they will approach the Throne of God and hear the voice: 'Enter into Hell.'"

"They [unbelievers] are my children. I suffer because of them. They do not know what awaits them. You must pray for them."

"If they [unbelievers] can't believe in God, they should spend at least five minutes a day in silent meditation. During that time, they should think about the God they say doesn't exist."

On the glut of false visionaries and false prophets

"Many pretend to see Jesus and me, and to understand our [alleged, false, untrue] words, but they are, in fact, lying. It is a very grave sin, and it is necessary to pray very much for them."

On the disbelief in Marian apparitions

"It is necessary to tell them from the very beginning I have been conveying the message of God to the world. It is a great pity not to believe in it. Faith is a vital element, but one cannot compel a person to believe. Faith is the foundation from which everything flows."

On what God wants for our vocations

In early August of 1981, the children asked the Gospa what she would like them to be. Mary responded that we are free to choose for ourselves:

"I would like you to become priests and religious, but only if you, yourselves, would want it. It is up to you to decide."

Regarding other faiths

"...In God divisions do not exist... and there are not many religions. It is you in the world who make divisions..."

"Members of all faiths are equal before God. God rules over each faith just like a sovereign over his kingdom. In the world, all religions are not the same because all people have not complied with the commandments of God... They reject and disparage them."

All men are created equal, but not all religions are equal

"...The Muslims and the Orthodox, for the same reason as Catholics, are equal before My Son and me. You are all my children. Certainly, all religions are not equal, but all men are equal before God, as St. Paul says. It does not suffice to belong to the Catholic Church to be saved, but is necessary to respect the commandments of God in following one's conscience.

"Those who are not Catholic, are no less creatures made in the image of God, and destined to rejoin someday, the House of the Father. Salvation is available to everyone, without exception. Only those who refuse God deliberately are condemned. To him who has been given little, little will be asked for. To whomever has been given

much, very much will be required. It is God alone, in His infinite justice, Who determines the degree of responsibility and pronounces judgment."

Regarding Eastern religions and Oriental meditations such as Zen and Transcendental Meditation

"Why do you call them 'meditations,' when it deals with human works? The true meditation is a meeting with Jesus. When you discover joy, interior peace, you must know there is only one God, and only one Mediator, Jesus Christ."

On mixed marriages

"In my eyes and in the sight of God, everything is equal. But for you, it is not the same thing because you are divided. If it is possible, it is better if she [a Catholic] were not to marry this man [an Orthodox] because she will suffer and her children also. She will be able to live and follow only with difficulty, the way of her faith."

Regarding the false belief in reincarnation

"You go to Heaven in full conscience: that which you have now. At the moment of death you are conscious of the separation of the body and the soul. It is false to teach people that you are reborn many times and that you pass to different bodies. One is born only once. The body, drawn from the earth, decomposes after death. It never comes back to life again. Man receives a transfigured body."

We only have one life to live, so the condition of our souls at the moment of death determines are destiny. People can be lost or saved in their last breath. Once dead, there are no second chances. It's wrong to believe in past lives and reincarnation as New Agers and Eastern religions teach. If you want a chance to start all over, fine: do it in this life. Be born again now.

Regarding other mediators besides Jesus Christ

"There is only one mediator between God and man, and it is Jesus Christ."

"Jesus prefers that you address yourselves directly to Him rather than through an intermediary. In the meantime, if you wish to give yourselves completely to God and if you wish that I be your protector, than confide to me all your intentions, your fasts, and your sacrifices so that I can dispose of them according to the will of God."

Regarding Mary's role as the Co-Mediatrix

"I cannot do anything without the help of God. I, too, must pray like you..."

"I do not dispose all graces. I receive from God what I obtain through prayer."

"I cannot cure. God alone cures. Pray! I will pray with you. Believe firmly. Fast, do penance. I will help as long as it is in my power to do it. God comes to help everyone. I am not God. I need your sacrifices and prayers to help me."

"I beseech you, pray to Jesus! I am His Mother, and I intercede for you with Him. But all prayers go to Jesus. I will help, I will pray, but everything does not depend solely on me, but also on your strength, and the strength of those who pray."

"...I am the Mediatrix between you and God..."

Regarding the Catholic doctrine of the Assumption

"I am the Mother of God and Queen of Peace. I went to Heaven before death."

Regarding the imminent chastisement and the warnings and the sign that precede it

"Take my message seriously for God is not joking with mankind."

"Be converted! It will be too late when the sign comes. Beforehand, several warnings will be given to the world..."

Concerning the eighth secret, Mirjana is frightened and prays to Our Lady for mercy:

"I have prayed; the punishment has been softened. Repeated prayers and fasting reduce punishment from God, but it is not possible to entirely avoid the chastisement. Go on the streets of the city, count those who glorify God and those who offend Him. God can no longer endure that."

"You cannot imagine what is going to happen nor what the Eternal Father will send to earth."

The Blessed Mother showed Mirjana a vision of the first secret—the earth was a desolate place:

"It is the upheaval of a region of the world. In the world there are many sins. What can I do, if you do not help me? Remember that I love you. God does not have a hard heart. Look around you and see what men do, then you will no longer say that God has a hard heart. How many people come to church, to the house of God, with respect, a strong faith, and love God? Very few!"

Why we should fear God

"You cannot even image how powerful God is."

Regarding World War III

"The third world war will not take place."

Regarding Christians who are obsessed with rumors of wars, calamities, and false prophesy

"The only [proper] attitude of the Christian toward the future is hope of salvation. Those who think only of wars, evils, punishment do not do well. If you think of evil, punishment, wars, you are on the road to meeting them. Your responsibility is to accept Divine peace, live it, and spread it."

On the situation in Poland in 1981 between Solidarity and the communists

"There will be great conflicts, but in the end, the just will take over."

As we know from history, Poland was the first of the Eastern Bloc nations to declare its freedom from the Soviet Union and began the process that precipitated its downfall on Christmas Day in 1991.

Regarding Russia's conversion and the West's decadency

"The Russian people will be the people who will glorify God the most. The West has made civilization progress, but without God, as if they were their own creators."

The Soviet Union fell on December 25, 1991. Russia was converted and was allowed to became a Christian nation again, just as Mary had predicted in Fátima. But in the West, self-gratification, greed, and materialism has supplanted Christianity. The United States is now a secular nation like China, not a Christian nation as it was when it was founded. It allows people to practice their faiths privately, but separates itself from religion.

Regarding Pope John Paul II

"His enemies have wanted to kill him, but I protected him."

"Have him consider himself the father of all mankind and not only of Christians. Have him spread untiringly the message of peace and love among all mankind."

On the importance of love

"Love is a gift from God. Therefore, pray that God may give you the gift to love."

"Without love, dear children, you can do nothing."

"I am beautiful because I love. If you want to be beautiful, love. There is no one in the world who does not desire beauty."

"Let your only instruments always be love. By love turn everything into good which Satan desires to destroy and possess. Only that way shall you be completely mine and I shall be able to keep you."

On the power of prayer

"Through prayer you can prevent wars from happening; with prayer you can stop wars."

"With prayer you can change the laws of nature."

"Pray. When I give you this message, do not be content to just listen to it. Increase your prayer and see how it makes you happy. All graces are at your disposal. All you have to do is gain them. In order to do that, I tell you—Pray."

"The most beautiful prayer is the [Apostles'] Creed."

"Your days will not be the same according to whether you pray, or you do not pray."

"When you pray you must feel more. Prayer is a conversation with God. Prayer is useful for you because after prayer everything is clear. Prayer makes one know happiness. Prayer can teach you how to cry. Prayer can teach you how to blossom. Prayer is not a joke. Prayer is a dialogue with God."

"By prayer you can completely disarm him [Satan]."

"Advance against Satan by means of prayer... Put on the armor for battle and with the Rosary in your hand defeat him."

"In prayer, you shall find... the way out of every situation that has no exit."

"Do not be afraid of Satan. That isn't worth the trouble, because with a humble prayer and an ardent love, one can disarm him."

"Prayer is the only way to save the human race."

How to pray properly

Mary suggests a minimum of seven Our Fathers, Hail Mary's, Glory Be's, and an Apostles' Creed each day.

"One has to be already prepared. If there are some sins, one must pull them out. Otherwise, one will not be able to enter into prayer. If one has concerns, he should submit them to God."

"You must not preoccupy yourselves during prayer. During prayer, you must not be preoccupied with your sins. Sins must remain behind."

"...I do not need the Lord's Prayer said a hundred or two hundred times. It is better to pray only one, but with a desire to encounter God..."

"Pray before the Crucifix. Special graces come from the Crucifix. Consecrate your-selves to the Cross. Do not blaspheme either Jesus or the Crucifix."

On the necessity of fasting

"The best fast is on bread and water. Through fasting and prayer one can stop wars, one can suspend the laws of nature. Works of charity cannot replace fasting... every-one except the sick, has to fast."

"...If you do not have the strength to fast on bread and water, you can give up a number of things. It would be a good thing to give up television, because after seeing some programs, you are distracted and unable to pray. You can give up alcohol, cigarettes, and other pleasures. You yourselves know what you have to do."

"Fast strictly on Wednesdays and Fridays."

"Repeated prayers and fasting reduce punishments from God."

On the importance of reading
the Bible every day

"You have forgotten the Bible."

"Dear children, today I call you to read the Bible everyday in your homes and let it be in a visible place so as always to encourage you to read and to pray."

On the power of sacramentals

"Dear children, today I call you to place more blessed objects in your homes and call everyone to put some blessed objects on their person. Bless all the objects and thus Satan will attack you less because you will have armor against him. Thank you for having responded to my call."

On the necessity of going to confession

"Make your peace with God and among yourselves. For that, it is necessary to believe, to pray, to fast, and to go to confession."

"Pray, pray! It is necessary to believe firmly, to go to confession regularly, and likewise, to receive Holy Communion."

"Monthly confession will be a remedy for the Church in the West. One must convey this message to the West."

"Do not go to confession through habit, to remain the same after it. No, it is not good. Confession should give an impulse to your faith. It should stimulate you and bring you closer to Jesus. If confession does not mean anything for you, really, you will be converted with great difficulty."

On the Eucharist

"You do not celebrate the Eucharist as you should. If you knew what great grace and what gifts you receive, you would prepare yourselves for it each day for an hour at least."

Christ is "truly" in the Eucharist, as Mary told Sister Sasagawa in Akita, Japan. Not symbolically, but truly—body, blood, soul, and divinity. Rearranging the letters of EUCHARIST (a Greek word for thanksgiving) to A-EU-CHRIST transliterates into "A True Christ" ("eu" is a Latin/Greek prefix meaning true or truly). Truly, Christ is in the Eucharist.

The Holy Mass

"Mass is the greatest prayer of God. You will never be able to understand its greatness. This is why you must be perfect and humble at Mass, and you should prepare yourselves for it."

"Let the Holy Mass be your life."

"The Mass is the most important and the most holy moment in your lives."

On the Holy Spirit

"When you have the Holy Spirit, you have everything."

"Begin by calling on the Holy Spirit each day. The most important thing is to pray to the Holy Spirit. When the Holy Spirit descends on earth, then everything becomes clear and everything is transformed."

"Ask the Holy Spirit to renew your souls, to renew the entire world."

"The most important thing in the spiritual life is to ask for the Holy Spirit. When the Holy Spirit comes, the peace will be established. When that occurs, everything changes around you."

"Pray to the Holy Spirit for enlightenment."

Regarding holiness

"If you live the messages, you are living the seeds of holiness."

"I desire to lead you on the way to holiness."

"I am calling you to pray with your whole heart and day by day to change your life.... I am calling that by your prayers and sacrifices you begin to live in holiness..., daily change your life in order to become holy."

"Dear children, you know that for your sake I have remained a long time so I might teach you how to make progress on the way to holiness."

"If you abandon yourselves to me, you will not even feel the passage from this life to the next life. You will begin to live the life of Heaven from this earth."

On the importance of these apparitions in Medjugorje

"I have come to call the world to conversion for the last time. Afterwards, I will not appear any more on this earth."

"These apparitions are the last in the world."

"...there will be in the future signs concerning sinners, unbelievers, alcoholics, and young people. They will accept me again."

"I wish to keep on giving you messages as it has never been done in history from the beginning of the world."

'Dear children, behold, also today I want to call you to start living a new life as of today. Dear children, I want you to comprehend that God has chosen EACH ONE OF YOU, in order to use you in a great plan for the salvation of mankind. You are not able to comprehend how great your role is in God's design. Therefore, dear children, pray so that in prayer you may be able to comprehend what is God's plan through you. I am with you in order that you may bring it about in its fullness. Thank you for having responded to my call."

"Dear children, to be chosen by God is really something great, but it is also a responsibility for you to pray more, for you, the chosen ones, to encourage others, so you can be a light for people in darkness... Dear children, this is the reason for my presence among you for such a long time: to lead you on the path of Jesus. I want to save you and, THROUGH YOU, TO SAVE THE WHOLE WORLD."

Regarding the cross on Mount Krizevac in Medjugorje which was erected in 1933 for the 1,900th anniversary of the Crucifixion

"I love the cross which you have providentially erected on Mount Krizevac in a very special way. Go there more often and pray."

Medjugorje as a "Sign"

"...Medjugorje is a sign to all of you and a call to pray and live the days of grace God is giving you...."

Medjugorje is a symbol, a sign from God regarding the end times we live in. The hill, the cross, the miracles, the signs in the sky, the sheep, the vineyards, the harvests, war, good vs. evil—all these symbols are contained in the New Testament and are present in Medjugorje, Bosnia-Herzegovina.

Notes

Preface

1 *The End Times: As Revealed to Maria Valtorta,* Editions Paulines, Centro Editoriale Valtortiano, Sherbrooke, QC, Canada, copyright 1994, pp. 5, 6, 59.
2 Two good books on the subject of the reality of the devil are Malachi Martin's *Hostage to the Devil,"* Harper and Row, and Fr. Gabriele Amorth's *An Excorcist Tells His Story,* Ignatius Press.
3 Luke 21:11.
4 Matthew 24:12.
5 Roman Polanski, the Jewish son of Polish parents who died in a Nazi concentration camp, was the producer of the smash hit *Rosemary's Baby,* which was released by Paramount Pictures in 1968. The film, starring Mia Farrow, was about the naïve wife of a devil worshiper who gives birth to the devil's son in June of 1966 (6-66). In real life, Polanski's pregnant wife, Sharon Tate, was stabbed to death at the Polanski residence in August of 1969 by members of the Charlie Manson gang. Murdered along with Tate were Wojtek Frykowski, Abigail Folger, Jay Sebring, and Steven Parent. Before her murder, Tate was an up-and-coming twenty-six-year-old actress who starred in the movies *Eye of the Devil, Fearless Vampire Killers,* and *Valley of the Dolls.* Roman, whose first successful movie was named *Knife in the Water,* was a thirty-three-year-old writer/director who had written scripts for *Repulsion, Fearless Vampire Killers,* and *Cul-de-Sac,* and just recently produced the devil-worshiping movie *Ninth Gate.*

Introduction: The Doctrine of Mary

1 Maria Valtorta, *The Book of Azariah,* Centro Editoriale Valtortiano, pp. 280-281.
2 Luke 1:28.
3 Luke 1:48-49.
4 *Catholic Encyclopedia,* Our Sunday Visitor, 1991, p. 496.
5 *Catholic Almanac,* Our Sunday Visitor Publishing Div., 1991, p. 246.
6 Romans 3:23.
7 Matthew 19:17; Mark 10:18.
8 Luke 1:47.

9 Similarly, Romans 3:23, Matthew 19:17, and Mark 10:18 speak in generalities about the sinfulness of the human race and are not including the Immaculate Heart of the Blessed Mother.

10 Luke 1:46-55.

11 The name "Mary" means "to suffer."

12 Pope Pius XII, *Ad Caeli Reginam,* October 11, 1954.

13 Pope Benedict XV, 1918.

14 Pope Leo XIII, 1896; Pope Pius X, *Ad diem illum laetissimum,* 1904.

15 1 Timothy 2:5.

16 Pope Leo XIII, *Octobri Mense,* 1891.

17 John 2:1-12.

18 John 2:5.

19 Isaiah 7:14; Matthew 1:18-23.

20 John 19:26-27.

21 Matthew 13:54-58.

22 Matthew 1:25.

23 Luke 2:7.

24 Luke 2:23.

25 Now celebrated on August 15.

26 Remember that in the Old Testament, if any man laid hands on the Ark of the Covenant he was immediately struck dead. Refer to the death of Uzzah in 2 Samuel 6:6-10.

27 Luke 1:43.

Chapter 1: The Woman and the Dragon

1 Pope Paul VI, Vatican II.

2 The name "Satan" means "Adversary."

3 Isaiah 14:12-15

4 Luke 1:38

5 Judith and parts of Esther are in the apocryphal books in the Protestant canon, but are canonical in the Catholic Church.

6 Agagites were historical enemies of the Jews.

7 Matthew 2:16.

8 Matthew 2:13-15.

9 Revelation 12:1-17.

10 Christ was born on the winter solstice (back then on December 25), the birth of the sun [son], the day when darkness gives way to light.

11 John 1:11.

Chapter 2: The Dragon Attacks the Church

1 Acts 2:1-4.

2 Smyr. 8:2.

3 Matthew 16:15-19.

4 *Kepha* in Aramaic, *Petros* in Greek.

5 Tertullian, *De praescritione haereticorim*, 36, I, 32, 2; Ignatius of Antioch, *Epistula ad Romanos*, 4, 3; Irenaeus, *Adversus haereses*, 3, 3, 3; fragment in Eusebius Pamphilius, *Historia ecclesiastica*, 6, 14, I; Eusebius Pamphilius, *Chronic on* ad an. Dom. 42, ad an Dom. 68.

6 Fulfilling Christ's prophecy of the destruction of the temple in Matthew 24:2.

7 Irenaeus, *Adversus haereses*, 3, 3, 3.

8 The title "Patriarch" originated in the East and is the title of a bishop who, being second only to the pope, has the highest rank in the hierarchy of his jurisdiction. In 325, the Catholic Council of Nicaea recognized three Patriarchs—the Bishop of Rome in the West, and the Bishops of Alexandria and Antioch in the East. The Council of Constance in 381 added a fourth Patriarch, the Bishop of Constantinople, and gave him rank second only to the Bishop of Rome. This action was seconded by the Council of Chalcedon in 451 and fully recognized by the Fourth Lateran Council in 1215. Thus, the pope has always been recognized by the early ecumenical Christian councils as the supreme head of the One True Church—the Roman Catholic Church.

9 Ecclesiastes 1:9-10.

10 The ten great Roman persecutions of Christians came from Nero (64-68), Domitian (95-96), Trajan (106-117), Marcus Aurelius (161-180), Septimus Severus (202-211), Maximin the Thracian (235-238), Decius (249-251), Valerian (257-260), Aurelian (274-275), and the reigns of Diocletian and Galerius (303-311).

11 Genesis 16:12.

12 2 Corinthians 11:4-15.

13 The term *jihad*, usually translated "holy war," designates the struggle toward the Islamic goal of "reforming the earth," which may include the use of armed force to assume political power in order to implement the principles of Islam through public institutions.

14 The Christian Crusades to retake the Holy Land from the Muslims in the thirteenth century started with great success, but faltered after they strayed from their original plans and became too self-serving. Thereafter, Jerusalem and the Holy Lands remained in the possession of the Muslims until the Israelis retook them in 1967. Students of Bible prophecy see the return of Israel to Zion as a major prerequisite for the Second Coming.

15 After the Albigensians were crushed in the fifteenth century, the surviving Waldenses became the victims of the Inquisition in France. In 1487, Pope Innocent VIII (1432-92) organized a crusade against them in Dauphine and Savoy (both now part of France). From there, many Waldenses took refuge in Switzerland and Germany, merging gradually with the Bohemian Brethren. The Waldenses became openly Calvinistic during the Reformation and repudiated the Catholic Church at the Synod of Chanforans (1532); in effect, becoming a Reformed Protestant sect. Today, this small Protestant sect still has about 20,000 members, centered chiefly in the Piedmont area of northern Italy.

16 The heresies of Protestantism were condemned by the Council of Trent (1545-1563), which was confirmed by Pope Pius IV on January 26, 1564.

17 Wycliff promoted the reading of the Bible in common languages, was against priestly celibacy, and was for the confiscation of all Church property by the secular authorities.

18 Msgr. Patrick F. O'Hare (LL. D.), *The Facts About Luther,* TAN Publishers, 1987, p. 24.

19 Heiko A. Oberman, *Luther: Man Between God and the Devil,* Image Books Doubleday, 1989, p. 92.

20 O'Hare, p. 51.

21 E. Michael Jones, *Degenerate Moderns,* Ignatius Press, 1993, p. 246.

22 Oberman, p. 155

23 Hebrews 10:38.

24 Luther wanted to discard the entire Epistle of St. James because it preached faith and good works.

25 Luther's writings were filled with scatological language. One of his favorite words he loved to call people was "dung." Another was "ass." See Oberman, pp. 106-110.

26 O'Hare, p. 113.

27 Jones, p. 246.

28 O'Hare, p. 109.

29 Ibid., p. 115.

30 Romans 6:1-2.

31 Romans 7:7-12.

32 Oberman, p. 39.

33 The German princes protested against papal taxes, the Turkish crusade fund, and the peddling of indulgences.

34 Oberman, p. 289.

35 Ibid.

36 Jones, p. 249.

37 O'Hare, p. 139.

38 Oberman, p. 294.

39 Ibid., p.5.

40 William Cobbett, *A History of the Protestant Reformation,* TAN Books and Publishers,1988, p. 41.

41 Ibid., p. 40.

42 Alison Weir, *The Six Wives of Henry VIII,* Grove Press, 1991, p. 231.

43 *Catholic Encyclopedia,* 1999.

44 *Chronicle of the World,* Ecam Publications, 1990, p. 491.

45 Ibid.

46 Cobbett, p. 84.

47 *Chronicle of the World,* p. 495

48 Cobbett, p. 145; *Chronicle of the World,* p. 503.

49 *Chronicle of the World,* p. 491.

50 Cobbett, p. 96.

51 Ibid., p. 65.

52 *Catholic Almanac,* 1991, p. 136.

53 Gorton Carruth, *The Encyclopedia of World Facts,* Harper Collins, 1993, p. 224.

54 Seymour's body was mutilated to save the baby boy.

55 Weir, p. 530.

56 Ibid.

57 I Kings 21:19.

Chapter 3: Our Lady of Guadalupe

1 Daniel Lynch, *Our Lady of Guadalupe and Her Missionary Image*, 1993, p. 3.

2 *Chronicle of the World*, p. 435.

3 Francis Johnston, *The Wonder of Guadalupe*, TAN Books and Publishers, 1981, p. 23.

4 Ibid., pp. 14-15.

5 *Chronicle of the World*, p. 490.

6 Ibid.

7 Ibid., p. 500.

8 Luke 14:23; *Chronicle of the World*, p. 505.

9 The temple of the terrible god Huitzilopochtli in Tenochtitlán was eventually replaced by the church of Santiago del Tlaltelolco in 1978.

10 Lynch, pp. 9-10.

11 Johnston, p. 33.

12 A larger chapel, the *Second Hermitage,* was constructed on Tepeyac in 1533, and a third in 1556.

13 *Catholic Almanac,* 1999.

14 Johnston, p. 130.

15 The Italian liner *Andrea Doria* collided with the Swedish liner *Stockholm* on July 25, 1956 off Nantucket, Massachusetts, killing 52 people. Twelve divers have perished since 1981 while diving for treasures in the sunken shipwreck.

16 Gorton Carruth, *The Encyclopedia of World Facts*, p. 240.

17 Johnston, p. 60.

18 Ibid., pp. 137-140.

19 Ibid., p. 72.

20 Ibid., p. 78.

21 Ibid.

22 Ibid., pp. 84-85.

23 For more information on Mary's apparitions in Guadalupe, read Francis Johnston's *The Wonder of Guadalupe* by TAN Publishers, one of the best books written on the subject.

Chapter 4: Our Lady of the Miraculous Medal

1 *The Portable Enlightenment Reader,* edited by Isaac Kramnick, Penguin Books, 1995, p. xiii.

2 Paul Fisher, *Behind the Lodge Door,* TAN Books and Publishers, 1988.

3 Kramnick, p. xvi.

4 Voltaire, Letter to d'Alembert, November 1762.

5 Other notable "Philosophers of the Enlightenment" were Beccaria, Priestly, Bentham, Mozart, Lord Herbert of Cherbury ("the Father of Deism"), Descartes, Hume, Kant, Spinoza, Hobbes, Bayle, D'Alembert, Lessing, Price, Hartley, La Mettrie, Condorcet, Godwin, Adam Smith, Benjamin Franklin, Thomas Jefferson, James Madison, and Thomas Paine.

6 *Chronicle of the World*, 1990, p. 756.

7 Fr. John Laux (M.A.), Church History, TAN Books and Publishers, Inc., 1989, p. 523.

8 Ibid.

9 The Jacobins got their name because they first met in a Dominican convent (Dominicans were often called Jacobins in France because they housed pilgrims on their way to visit the shrine of St. James in Spain).

10 *Sans-culottes* means "without breeches," which were popular with the aristocracy.

11 Rousseau, who fathered five children by his mistress and then put them in orphanages, went insane 10-15 years before he died in 1778.

12 Laux, p. 523.

13 *Chronicle of the World*, p. 780.

14 Laux, p. 523.

15 *Western Civilizations: Their History and Their Culture*, Burns, Learner and Meacham, (9th ed.), W.W. Norton & Co., 1980, p. 611.

16 *Chronicle of the World*, p. 774

17 John Delaney, *A Woman Clothed with the Sun*, Image Books, 1960, p. 66.

18 Ibid., pp. 72-74.

19 Catherine M. Odell, *Those Who Saw Her*, Our Sunday Visitor, 1986, pp. 51-52.

20 John J. Delaney, *A Woman Clothed with the Sun*, Image, 1990, pp. 77-78.

21 Bob and Penny Lord, *The Many Faces of Mary: A Love Story*, Journeys of Faith, 1987, pp. 58-60.

Chapter 5: Our Lady in Tears

1 Peter and Fiona Somerset Fry, *A History of Ireland*, Barnes & Nobles Books, 1993, pp. 230-233.

2 Delaney, pp. 93-95.

3 Recall the horrible American Civil War during the early 1860's and the murderous revenge killings by those such as Quantrill's raiders, and the equally devastating conflicts in Europe.

4 From the 1878 text written down by Mélanie and published at Lecce on November 15, 1879—with the "imprimatur" of Bishop Zola—and reprinted "ne varietur" at Lyons in 1904. Taken from Fr. Paul Gouin, *Sister Mary of the Cross: Shepherdess of La Salette*, 101 Foundation, pp. 63-69.

5 Psalms 8:3.

Chapter 6: Our Lady of Lourdes

1 An earlier Solemnity of the Immaculate Conception was observed in the East by the eighth century, in Ireland by the ninth, and then later on in European countries.

2 Darwin was studying to be a minister before he lost his faith in God and Christianity.

3 Karl Marx developed the philosophy of "dialectical materialism," which maintains that the material basis of a reality is constantly changing in a dialectical process and

that matter takes priority over mind. The atheistic philosophy of materialism, therefore, helped give birth to Marxism.

4 Agnostics won't come right out and say that there is no God, but that there is no way of knowing there is a God.

5 Darwin believed in the superiority of some races over another, and that natural selection would weed the bad races out. Hitler, of course, was a big fan of Darwin, as were Marx and Lenin.

6 Published *On the Origin of Species by Means of Natural Selection* (1859), arousing a storm of controversy; *The Variation of Animals and Plants under Domestication*, setting up provisional hypothesis of pangenesis (1868); *The Descent of Man and Selection in Relation to Sex*, deriving the human race from an animal of the anthropoid group (1871); *The Expression of the Emotions in Man and Animals* (1872); a series of supplemental treatises on cross—fertilization and self-fertilization, ecology, climbing plants, etc.; and a biography of Erasmus Darwin (1879).

7 Darwinian evolutionists who say that man is only an intelligent monkey are gravely mistaken. Man is a creature made in the image and likeness of God; that is, he has an immortal soul capable of intelligence and reason. Yes, man also has an "animal" body created from the dust of the earth which could have evolved from lower anthropoids who had no souls, but there is no way to prove or disprove the theory of evolution. The story of the creation of Adam and Eve as the first human beings to receive an immortal soul and an intimate knowledge of God is not inconsistent with the paleontological discoveries of science. After all, if Adam was the first and only human, as biblical fundamentalists argue, who did Cain marry and who were all those people who saw the mark of God's curse on Cain's forehead as he wandered about the earth? (Genesis 4:11-17.)

8 Delaney, pp. 122-123.

9 Ibid., pp. 124-125.

10 Abbé François Trochu, *Saint Bernadette Soubirous*, Tan, 1957, p. 223.

11 Ibid., pp. 378-379.

12 Ibid., p. 153.

13 Catherine Odell, *Those Who Saw Her*, OSV, 1986, p. 92.

Chapter 7: Our Lady of Hope

1 *The Chronicle of the World*, p. 963.

2 The apparition in Pontmain has further significance in that it occurred just before the Catholic Church was attacked in Germany by Chancellor Otto von Bismarck. Anti-Catholics in Bismarck's government protested the First Vatican Council's passage of the dogma *Pastor Aeternus* on July 18, 1870, which declared that the pope, when he speaks ex cathedra as "Shepherd and Teacher of all Christians," enjoys infallibility in defining doctrine on faith and morals. In the *Kulturkampf*, or conflict of beliefs, Bismarck published a set of new laws which forbade the Catholic Church to intervene in the affairs of German government, the clergy to discuss politics in church, and forbade the teaching of Catholicism in German state schools. But Bismarck's suppression of the Catholic Church backfired on him because many loyal Catholics living in Germany demanded that he rescind his anti-Catholic laws, which he did.

Chapter 8: Our Lady of Silence

1 Peter and Fiona Somerset Fry, *A History of Ireland*, Barnes and Nobles Books, New York, 1988, p. 33-34.

2 *Funk and Wagnalls Encyclopedia*, 1996.

3 William Cobbett, *The History of the Protestant Reformation in England and Ireland*, TAN Books and Publishers, pp. 175-176.

4 Fry, p. 141.

5 Cobbett, pp. 280-285.

6 Fry, pp. 116-136.

7 Ibid., p. 124.

8 *Chronicle of the World*, p. 541.

9 Cobbett, p. 251.

10 Ibid., p. 300

11 Fry, p. 158.

12 *Chronicle of the World*, p. 641.

13 Ibid., p. 643.

14 Ibid., p. 654.

15 Ibid., pp. 664-665.

16 Protestant Orangemen in Northern Ireland still celebrate the Battle of the Boyne in 1690 where William of Orange defeated his father-in-law, James II, and drove him into exile in France.

17 Fry, p. 164.

18 Cobbett, pp. 358-360.

19 Fry, p. 195.

20 Ibid., p. 231.

21 Ibid., pp. 233.

22 Carleton Beals, *Brass-Knuckle Crusade: The Great Know Nothing Conspiracy: 1820-1860*, Hasting House, New York, 1960.

23 Regarding political and religious acts of violence and terrorism in Ireland today, be they from the Catholic Republicans (IRA) or the Protestant Unionists, the Catholic Church has resolutely condemned the use of violence for political ends.

24 Revelation 22:18.

25 Revelation 1:3.

26 The English word "knock," according to Merriam-Webster's Collegiate Dictionary, is derived from the ME word *knoken,* fr. OE *cnocian;* akin to MHG *knochen,* "to press." According to Gramadach's Lexicon, "knock," in Irish Gaelic, is *cnag.* Not to be confused with the Gaelic word *cnoc,* pronounced "crock," which means hill or knoll. In Greek, knock is *krouo,* in Hebrew *dapaq,* in Latin *caedo.*

27 Revelation 3:20.

28 Luke 11:9.

Chapter 9: Our Lady of the Rosary

1 Amos 3:7.

2 Frère Michel de la Sainte Trinité, *The Whole Truth About Fátima: Science and the Facts,* (Vol. I), Immaculate Heart Publications, New York, 1989, p. 7.

3 Lucifer's name means "bright, shining one."

4 2 Corinthians 11:3-15.

5 *Chronicle of the World,* p. 289.

6 Ibid., p. 291.

7 Ibid., p. 296.

8 Ibid., p. 299.

9 Ibid.

10 Ibid., p. 303.

11 Ibid., p. 302.

12 Ibid., p. 336.

13 For example, Osama bin Laden and his "Foundation of Islamic Salvation," which has openly declared a jihad on the U.S. and Israel, and which is suspected in numerous Muslim terrorist acts in the U.S., Israel, Algeria, Asia, Afghanistan, Pakistan, Egypt, Somalia, Bosnia, Chechnya, Kenya, Tanzania, and a host of other countries. Bin Laden, the son of a rich Saudi oil magnate with inexhaustible revenues, says he makes no distinction between military personnel and innocent civilians when it comes to terrorist targets. He is believed to be behind the terrorist attacks on the World Trade Center bombing in New York in 1993, the plots to assassinate President Clinton and Pope John Paul II in 1995, the Marine Corps barracks bombing in Riyadh, Saudi Arabia in 1995, the murder of Americans at the U.S. consulate in Pakistan in 1995, the truck bombing of Marine Corps barracks in Dhahran, Saudi Arabia in 1996, the murder of Americans in Pakistan in November of 1997 in retaliation for the convictions of Mir Aimal Kasi (CIA attacker) and Ramzi Yousef (Trade Center bomber), the U.S. embassy bombings in Nairobi and Dar es Salaam in August of 1998, and has been foiled in his plot to blow up the U.S. embassy in Albania in 1998. Lord knows how many more of Osama bin Laden's terrorist attempts have been foiled by Western intelligence agencies.

14 Frère Michel de la Sainte Trinité, *The Whole Truth about Fátima: The Secret and the Church,* (Vol. II), Immaculate Heart Publications, 1989, pp. 305-308.

15 Ibid., pp. 308-312.

16 Ibid., p. 314. Declaration to the Congress of Free Thought, March 26, 1911.

17 Ibid., p. 315.

18 The date of Mary's first appearance to the three children in the Cova da Iria, May 13, has historical significance. On May 13, 610, Pope Boniface IV had consecrated a pagan Roman temple, the Pantheon, to the Mother of God and all martyrs. May 13 was also the Feast of Our Lady of the Blessed Sacrament and the day King John I of Portugal dedicated all Portuguese cathedrals to Mary.

19 Frère Michel de la Sainte Trinité, *The Whole Truth about Fátima: The Third Secret,* (Vol. I), Immaculate Heart Publications, 1990, pp. 181-182.

20 One book often quoted by Protestants as proof that the Catholic doctrine of Mary was adopted from ancient Babylonian pagan religions is Alexander Hislop's *The Two Babylon's or The Papal Worship Proved to be the Worship of Nimrod and His Wife,* (2nd ed.), Loizeaux Brothers, New Jersey, 1959.

21 The first two secrets were the revelations of hell and the designation of the Immaculate Heart of Mary as the remedy offered by God for the salvation of souls.

22 Frère Michel, (Vol. I), p. 342.

23 *O Seculo,* October 15, 1917.

24 Frère Michel, (Vol. I), p. 324. From Avelino de Almeida, *Illustracao Portuguesa.*

25 Both, by the way, knew beforehand the day that they would die.

26 Frère Michel, (Vol. II), pp. 116-117.

27 Ibid., p. 247.

28 Ibid., pp. 265-266.

29 Matthew 12:36-37.

30 Frère Michel, (Vol. II), pp. 464-465.

31 Jonathan Luxmore, *Our Sunday Visitor,* November 12, 1995.

32 Warren Carroll, *70 Years of the Communist Revolution,* Trinity Communications, 1989, p. 37

33 *Time,* June 11, 1979, p. 54.

34 Carroll, p. 83.

35 Ibid., p. 84.

36 Ibid., p. 87.

37 Ibid., pp. 90-91.

38 Francis McCullagh, *The Bolshevik Persecution of Christianity,* New York, 1924, p. 73.

39 Like Christ, "Lord" Lenin's mother was named Maria and his grandmother Ann.

40 Frère Michel, (Vol. II), p. 452.

41 Edvard Radzinsky, *Stalin,* Doubleday Publishers, New York, 1996, p. 201.

42 Carroll, pp. 141-142.

43 Pope Pius XI in a letter to Cardinal Pompli, dated February 2, 1930.

44 Heller and Nekrich, *Utopia in Power,* p. 265.

45 Alexander Solzhenitsyn, *Gulag Archipelago,* II, 52n (quoted from an eighteenth-century manuscript called "The lives of the Solovetsky Fathers").

46 Adam Hochschild, *The Unquiet Ghost: Russia Remembers Stalin,* Viking, 1995, p. xi.

47 Radzinsky, p. 29.

48 Ibid., p. 12.

49 Ibid., pp. 36-37.

50 Ibid., p. 37.

51 Funk and Wagnalls New Encyclopedia, 1996.

52 He called himself Stalin instead of Koba because it sounded like Lenin.

53 Radzinsky, pp. 576-577.

54 Frère Michel, (Vol. II), p. 665.

55 Simon Wiesenthal Resources at http://motlc.wiesenthal.com/resources/questions/#3

56 Frère Michel (Vol. III), pp. 182-190.

57 Pope Pius XI had soundly condemned communism as "barbarous," "intrinsically perverse," and "diabolical" in his 1937 encyclical *Divini Redemptoris.*

58 Frère Michel, (Vol. III), p. 183.

59 Frère François de Marie des Agnes, *Fátima: Tragedy and Triumph,* (Vol. IV), Immaculate Heart Publications, 1991, pp. 27-29.

60 Carroll, p. 215.

61 Ibid., pp. 252-253.

62 Hungary Network at http://www.hungary.com/corvinus/humis/humis13.html

63 Fatima Network: Our Lady's Library Online.
http://www.fatima.org/library/cr27pg37.html

64 Carroll, pp. 255-256.

65 Ibid., pp. 260-261.

66 Ibid., p. 330.

67 Malachi Martin, *The Keys of This Blood*, Touchstone, Simon & Schuster, New York, copyright 1990, p. 96.

68 Carroll, p. 332.

69 Ibid., p. 330.

70 Ibid., p. 331.

71 Ibid., pp. 358-359.

72 Ibid., p. 359.

73 Ibid., pp. 482-487.

74 Father Fernando of Fátima, *Fátima: A World-Shaking Message*, Vantage Press, 1987, pp. 41-43.

75 Carroll, pp. 496-500.

76 Ibid., pp. 520-522.

77 *The Soviet War in Afghanistan: History or Harbinger of Future War?* From the U.S. Army Foreign Military Studies Office.

78 Martin, p. 60.

79 Tad Szuic, *Pope John Paul II,* Scribner, 1995, p. 34.

80 Martin, p. 501.

81 Ibid., p. 504.

82 Ibid., p. 514.

83 *Chronicle of the World*, p. 628.

84 Bernstein and Politi, *His Holiness: John Paul II and the Hidden History of Our Time,* Doubleday, New York, 1996, p. 38.

85 Martin, p. 543.

86 Ibid., p. 549.

87 Szulc, p. 103.

88 Martin, p. 548.

89 Carroll, p. 216.

90 Martin, p. 551.

91 Szulc, pp. 310-313. From the archives of the Central Committee of the Soviet Communist Party in Moscow, released in 1994.

92 Martin, p. 627.

93 *La Croix*, August 17, 1981, as cited in Abbe Daniel Le Roux, *Peter, Lovest Thou Me?* (Australian: Instauratio Press, 1989), p. 18.

94 Prayer card commemorating the visit of Pope John Paul II to Fátima on May, 13, 1982.

95 *Time,* May 25, 1981, p. 21.

96 Paul B. Henze, *The Plot to Kill the Pope,* Charles Scribner's Sons, New York, 1983, p. 199.

97 *Time,* March 14, 1983, p. 39.

98 Carroll, pp. 542-545.

99 Ibid., p. 543.

100 *Time,* January 3, 1983, pp. 54-55.

101 *Time,* June 17, 1985, World Notes page.

102 *Time,* June 10, 1985, p. 51.

103 Henze, p. 30.

104 But John XXIII did institute the Feast of Our Lady of the Rosary on December 13, 1962.

105 Frère François, p. 159.
106 Ibid., p. 160.
107 *Time,* December 28, 1981, p. 8.
108 *Time,* February 24, 1992, p. 30.
109 Bernstein and Politi, p. 266-167.
110 *Time,* February 24, 1992, p. 32.
111 Martin, p. 421.
112 Gorton Carruth, *World Facts and Dates,* Harper Collins, 1993, p. 947.
113 Ibid., p. 984.
114 Andrei Codrescu, *The Hole in the Flag: A Romanian Exile's Story of Return and Revolution,* W. Morrow, New York, 1991. Edward Behr, *Kiss the Hand You Cannot Bite: The Rise and Fall of the Ceausescus,* Villard Books, New York, 1991.
115 Home of the infamous Vladimir Dracul, also known as "Vlad the Impaler," or just simply "Count Dracula."
116 Carruth, p. 997.
117 Ibid., p. 1010.
118 Luke 4:6-8.
119 "Goodbye, Gorbachev," Peter McGrath, *Newsweek* magazine, p. 18, December 23, copyright © 1991. All rights reserved. Reprinted by permission of Newsweek, Inc.
120 "I Want to Stay the Course," John Kohan and Strobe Talbott, *Time* magazine, December 23, 1991, p. 24.
121 Judith 13:18.
122 If you look closely at the picture in this book of Judith slaying Holofernes you will see a bloodstained spot on the bed sheet below Holofernes's head that looks remarkably similar to the port-wine birthmark on the forehead of Gorbachev, which is a physical clue to the First Beast's identity, the mighty beast who lived by the sword yet was slain by a woman.
123 *World,* March 6, 1992.
124 The family name "Romanov" is derived from the word "Roman."
125 Rome and Constantinople being the first two capitols of the ancient Roman Empire.
126 Josyp Terelya with Michael Brown, *Witness: An Autobiography of Josyp Terelya,* Faith Publishing, 1991, pp. 2-5.
127 Terelya, pp. 302-315.
128 Ibid., pp. 114-123.
129 Ibid.
130 Ibid., pp. 120-141.
131 Ibid., 302-324.
132 In the Bible, the head is frequently used as a sign of a person's honor and glory or his shame, humiliation, and defeat. Gold crowns indicated a king's glory; a mitre, a priest's high position; and long hair, a maiden's beauty. As a symbol of shame and repentance, Old Testament Jews shaved their heads and threw ashes on their bald tops, and as a symbol of grief they would wail and throw dirt on their heads. Heaping "live coals" on a person's head was metaphoric, biblical language for vindication. An enemy's head was customarily cut off and paraded around or put on a spike or wall as a sign of victory over an enemy. Young David slew Goliath with a single rock to the forehead from

his slingshot, and then cut off his head. King Uzziah (2 Chron. 26:18) was struck with leprosy in the forehead for his disobedience to God.

It is not beyond possibility that God marked Gorbachev with a physical sign on his forehead to symbolize Mary's victory over communism. Cain, who committed the first homicide, was marked with a sign on his forehead so that no one would slay him. The prophet Ezekiel (593-571 B.C.) had a vision where an angel marked with an X the forehead of all those in Jerusalem who cried out over the abominations practiced within it (Ezek. 91:6). The devil spiritually marks his subjects with the sign of the beast on the right hand and forehead (Rev. 13:16, Rev. 14:9, Rev. 17:5), and likewise, God marks his followers on their foreheads with his seal and name (Rev. 7:3, Rev. 9:4, Rev. 14:1, Rev. 22:4).

133 God wants us to grow in our knowledge and probe the mysteries of the universe so that we love and admire him that much more, not to grow in our pride and deny his existence. Science without religion is blind, religion without science is dumb.

134 Roman slaves were stamped on their right hand and forehead with their owners' mark.

135 Genesis 3:1-13.

136 From the 1942 lecture of John Maynard Keynes, a distinguished economist and Newton scholar, to the Royal Society Club, after Keynes reviewed a collection of Newton's papers, which he purchased at Sotheby's. Excerpted in Michael White's *Isaac Newton: The Last Sorcerer*, Addison Wesley, 1998, p. 3.

137 There is sufficient evidence to suggest that the story of Newton's apple is not a myth but a reality. The first account comes from William Stukeley, who said that after dining with Newton in Kensington on April 15, 1726, Newton related to him the story of the apple: "The weather being warm, we went into the garden and drank tea, under the shade of some apple-trees, only he and myself. Amidst other discourses, he told me, he was just in the same situation, as when formerly, the notion of gravitation came into his mind. It was occasion'd by the fall of an apple, as he sat in a contemplative mood. Why should the apple always descend perpendicular to the ground, thought he to himself. Why should it not go sideways or upwards, but constantly to the earth's centre." (*Memoirs of Sir Isaac Newton's Life*, pp. 19-20.)

The second account comes from John Conduitt, who was married to Newton's niece: "In the year 1666 he [Newton] retired again from Cambridge... to his mother in Lincolnshire & whilst he was musing in a graden it came into his thought that the power of gravity (which brought an apple from the tree to the ground) was not limited to a certain distance from the earth but that this power must extend much farther than was usually thought. Why not as high as the moon said he to himself & if so that must influence her motion & perhaps retain her in her orbit." (Keynes Collection, King's College, Cambridge, MS 130.4 pp. 10-12).

A third account comes from Voltaire, who published a couple of accounts in the eighteenth century about Newton's apple. First, in the *Essays on the Civil War in France* (1727) Voltaire stated that "Sir Isaac Newton walking in his Garden had the first thought of the System of Gravitation, upon seeing an apple falling down from the tree." Second, Voltaire referred in *Letters Concerning the English Nation* (1733) to "a fruit falling from a tree [of Newton's]." Voltaire was given this information from Catherine Barton, Newton's niece and John Conduitt's wife.

A fourth account comes from Henry Pemberton, editor of Newton's monumental book, *Principia Mathematica*: "The first thoughts, which give rise to his *Principia*, he had, when he returned from Cambridge in 1666 on account of the plague. As he sat alone in the garden, he fell into a speculation on the power of gravity." (Pemberton, *A View of Sir Isaac Newton's Philosophy*, London, 1728, preface.)

138 The test code name for the Manhattan Project which developed the first atomic bomb was "Trinity." Trinity College is where Newton studied; he went there even though he didn't believe in the trinity of God.

139 Alchemy, in its purest form, was the medieval attempt to transmute base metals into gold, but also involved secret, mystical arts to produce magic elixirs, the universal cure for diseases, the "fountain of youth," and the philospher's stone. During the seventeenth century, it was considered by scientists of that period to be pseudoscience.

140 Michael White, p. 2.

141 Frank Manuel, *A Portrait of Isaac Newton*, Harvard University Press, 1968, pp. 79-80; 361-380.

142 Ibid., p. 80.

143 Michael White, p. 2.

144 Ibid., p. 153.

145 Ibid., p. 156.

146 Ibid., pp. 359-360.

147 Ibid.

148 Manuel.

149 Michael Hart, *The 100*, London: Simon & Schuster, 1993.

150 Alan Freedman, *The Computer Desktop Encyclopedia*, Amacom, 1996, p. 26.

151 This is not to imply that Steve Jobs and Steve Wozniak, the founders of Apple Computer, are evil. This is only to underscore the fact that knowledge is power and can be used for good or evil purposes

152 Columbine, by the way, means "dove-like."

153 Matthew 7:13.

154 I don't blame them for relocating: an address like 666 can be unnerving.

Chapter 10: Our Lady of Beauraing and Banneux

1 The later gas extermination camps were the inspiration of SS Police Inspector Christian Wirth.

2 The date of Crystal Night (November 9-10) had special significance for Hitler because it was the birthday of two of his favorite heroes, Martin Luther and Baron Rudolf von Sebottendorff, the man who founded the Thule Gesellschaft—the secret, mystical, occult society that later evolved into the Nazi Party. Crystal Night also occurred on the day the Second Reich collapsed (November 9, 1918), and was the day Hitler lost his eyesight for the second time in WWI, and the same day that, while in the Pasewalk sanitarium, voices inside Hitler's head told him that he was selected to be the new German Messiah. November 8-9 was also the date of Hitler's Beer Hall Putsch in 1923, and was the date of the foiled assassination attempt on Hitler's life at a meeting commemorating the Putsch.

3 Hitler's father, Alois, was the illegitimate son of Maria Anna Schicklgruber, whom,

legend has it, became pregnant by a Jew. However, no documents have been found to support Hitler's Jewish ancestry.

4 Konrad Heiden, *Der Fuehrer: Hitler's Rise to Power*, Boston, Houghton Mifflin, 1944.

5 It is a recurring irony that the antichrists of this world hate their father, unlike Jesus who loved his father.

6 Wagnerian operas glorified medieval Germanic chivalry, Nordic mythology, neo-paganism, the search for the Holy Grail, and the greatness of the Aryan race—that's why Hitler loved them so much.

7 Joseph J. Carr, *The Twisted Cross*, Huntington House Publishers, 1985, p. 36.

8 Peter Levenda, *Unholy Alliance*, Avon Books, 1995, pp. 33-35.

9 Some historians say *Protocols* originated as a plot between czarist police and occult circles operating in Paris and St. Petersburg to smear Jews and Freemasons.

10 Carr, p. 116.

11 It is ironic that Hitler would consult the prophecies of a Jewish soothsayer about his future.

12 A few interesting facts: Hitler was Nazi No. 555; Hister is an old name for the Danube River; Hitler was born in Braunau, Austria in an inn across from the Inn River, which stems from the Danube; soon after his birth, Hitler's family moved to Linz, Austria, which sits on the Danube; in 1907, Hitler studied in Vienna, Austria, which is next to the Danube; in 1913, Hitler moved to Munich, Germany, which sits on the Isar River that stems from the Danube.

13 Millie Ridge, *Nostradamus: An Illustrated Guide to His Predictions*, (III:35), Ottenheimer Publishers, 1994, p. 36.

14 Ibid., (II:24), p. 34.

15 Robert G. L. Waite, *The Psychopathic God—Adolph Hitler*, Basic Books, New York, 1977.

16 Ibid.

17 Ibid.

18 Carr, p. 38.

19 Some evidence suggests Eva took cyanide.

20 Hitler's Lebensborn Project bred genetically superior SS men to racially pure Germanic women.

21 Nietzsche's namesake, King Friedrich Wilhelm IV of Prussia, also went insane.

Chapter 11: Our Lady of Mount Carmel

1 Wayne Thompson, *Western Europe: 1995*, 14th Edition, Stryker-Post Publications, p. 470.

2 Ibid.

3 Ibid.

4 Warren Carroll, *70 Years of the Communist Revolution*, Trinity Communications, 1989, p. 189.

5 Ted and Maureen Flynn, *The Thunder of Justice*, MaxKol Communications, 1993, p. 161.

6 Roman Pérez, *Garabandal: The Village Speaks Out*, (2nd ed.) The Workers of Our Lady of Mount Carmel, Inc., 1985, pp. 50-51.

374 THE WOMAN AND THE DRAGON

7 Ibid., p. 51.
8 Ibid., pp. 51-52.
9 Ibid., p. 54, Conchita in an interview with *Needles,* February 9, 1975.
10 Ibid., p. 56, Mari Loli to Mrs. Herrero de Gallardo, October 7, 1972.
11 Ibid., p. 56.
12 Ibid., pp. 57-58.
13 Ibid., p. 58.
14 Ibid., p. 36.
15 Ibid., pp. 36-37.
16 Ibid., p. 31.
17 Flynn, pp. 169-170.
18 Perez, p. 32.
19 Flynn, p. 163.
20 Ibid., p. 166.

Chapter 12: Our Lady of All Peoples

1 Father Teiji Yasuda, *Akita: The Tears and Message of Mary,* 101 Foundation, Asbury, New Jersey, 1992, pp. 132-133.
2 Ibid., pp. 77-78.
3 "A Hill of Redemption," video by Westernhanger Productions.
4 Yasuda, p. 135.
5 "A Hill of Redemption."
6 Ibid.
7 Miraculously, a group of Jesuits living near ground zero survived unscathed.
8 From the benediction prayer: "Blessed be Jesus Christ, True God and True Man."
9 Yasuda, p. 20.
10 Ibid., p. 21.
11 Ibid., p. 34.
12 Ibid., p. 35.
13 Ibid., p. 36.
14 Ibid., p. 54.
15 Ibid.
16 Ibid., pp. 62-63.
17 Ibid., pp. 77-78.
18 Ibid., p. 101.
19 Ibid., p. 109.
20 Ibid., p. 130.
21 Ibid., p. 148.
22 Ibid., p. 178.
23 Ibid., p. 10.

Chapter 13: The Mother of the Word

1 Catherine M. Odell, *Those Who Saw Her,* (rev. ed.), Our Sunday Visitor Books, 1995, p. 210.

2 Ibid.
3 Ibid., p. 212.
4 "Kibeho Africa," video by Marian Communications, Ltd.
5 Odell, (rev. ed.), p. 213.
6 "Kibeho Africa" video.
7 Odell, (rev. ed.), p. 219.
8 Ibid., p. 214.
9 "Kibeho Africa" video.
10 Odell, (rev. ed.), p. 215.
11 Ibid., p. 217.
12 "Kibeho Africa" video.
13 Odell, (rev. ed.), p. 216.
14 Flynn, pp. 27-28.
15 Ibid.
16 *UN Chronicle,* December 1994, v31n4, pp. 4-9.
17 *Christian Century,* March 8, 1995, p. 264.
18 *Christian Century,* February 22, 1995, p. 212.
19 Nancy Jones, Concentric Internet Services, April 26, 1996.
20 One in ten Central Africans is expected to die from AIDS within the next decade.
21 *Kansas City Star,* February 11, 1995, p. A-17.

Chapter 14: The Queen of Peace

1 Excerpted from *Spark from Heaven,* by Mary Craig, p. 13. Copyright © 1988 by Mary Craig. Used with permission of Ave Maria Press, P.O. Box 428, Notre Dame, Indiana 46556.
2 Ibid., p. 16.
3 Sister Emmanuel, *Medjugorje: The War Day by Day,* The Florida Center for Peace, 1993, p. 85.
4 Referenced from Stella Alexander, *Church and State in Yugoslavia Since 1945,* Cambridge University Press, 1979.
5 Craig, p. 31.
6 Ibid., p. 30.
7 Sister Emmanuel, p. 50.
8 Craig, p. 33.
9 Warren Carroll, *70 Years of the Communist Revolution,* Trinity Communications, 1989, pp. 252-253.
10 Craig, p. 46.
11 Ibid., p. 47.
12 Ibid., p. 56.
13 Ibid., p. 62.
14 Ibid., pp. 63-64.
15 *Kansas City Star,* August 17, 1997.
16 Another "Mir" became famous when the Pakistani Mir Aimal Kasi killed two CIA employees outside of CIA headquarters in Virginia in 1993. Kasi was convicted on November 10, 1997. Four U.S. citizens were gunned down in Karachi, Pakistan on November 12, 1997 in retaliation for Mir's conviction. Yet another "Mir" made head-

lines on May 30, 1999 when a deadly stampede in a Minsk, Belarus tunnel occurred during a rock concert celebrating the two-year anniversary of the radio station "Mir," trampling 54 drunken youths to death who were seeking shelter from a sudden downpour and hailstorm.

17 Craig, p. 66.

18 Ibid., p. 63-65.

19 Ibid., p. 107.

20 Ibid., p. 108.

21 Ibid., p. 71.

22 Ibid., p. 72-73.

23 Ibid., p. 76.

24 Ibid.

25 Ibid., p. 78.

26 The visionaries, like everyone else, thought that Mary's birthday was September 8: little Jakov greeted Mary with a happy birthday wish on September 8, 1981. August 5, by the way, is dedicated to St. Mary Major in Rome, the largest and most important Marian basilica in the world. August 5 is also the feast day of Our Lady of Snows, in which snow fell in Italy on August 5 centuries ago. August 5 is also the Patronal Feast Day of the Congregation of Sisters of Our Lady of Mercy, whom Sister Faustina Kowalska belonged to.

27 Sister Emmanuel, p. 126.

28 Michael O'Carroll's *Medjugorje: Facts, Documents, Theology*, Veritas, 1989, p. 73.

29 Ibid., p. 109.

30 Bosnia incorporated the principality of Herzegovina, which means "the dukedom," in the fourteenth century.

31 Craig, p. 96.

32 Ibid., p. 111.

33 Ibid.

34 Ibid., p. 102.

35 Pavao Zanic, *Posizione attuale...* "The Present Position (Non-Official) Of The Bishop's Curia Of Mostar With Regards To The Events In Medjugorje," October 30, 1984. Reprinted in its entirety in Michael O'Carroll's *Medjugorje: Facts, Documents, Theology*, Veritas, 1989, pp. 79-103.

36 Craig, p. 113.

37 Ibid.

38 Ibid., p. 114.

39 Peter Hebblethwaite, *National Catholic Reporter,* June 3, 1988, *Medjugorje: a 'pious fraud,'* p. 9.

40 Craig, p. 113.

41 René Laurentin (with Ljudevit Rupcic), *Is the Virgin Mary Appearing in Medjugorje?* The Word Among Us Press, Washington, 1984.

42 Craig, pp. 121-122.

43 Ibid., p. 145. Referenced from R. Laurentin's *Denieres Nouvelles de Medjugorje*.

44 Craig, p. 124.

45 Ibid., p. 144.

46 Ibid.

47 Ibid., p. 145.
48 Ibid., p. 144-145.
49 Ljudevit Rupcic, *The Truth about Medjugorje*, Ljubuski-Humac 1990, p. 134.
50 Craig, p. 127.
51 Ibid., p. 154.
52 Ibid., p. 174.
53 Ibid., p. 184.
54 Ibid., p. 124.
55 Ibid.
56 Craig, p. 154. Referenced from Lucy Rooney (S.N.D.), and Robert Faricy (S.J.), *Medjugorje Unfolds: Mary Speaks to the World,* Fowler Wright Books 1985.
57 Hebblethwaite, p. 9.
58 The Worldwide Church leaders call for the expulsion of the Serbian Orthodox Church from the World Council of Churches in December of 1994 for their unrelenting attacks on religious property.
59 The Croats made up 17% of the Bosnian population, while the Serbs made up 31%.
60 Sister Emmanuel, p. 13.
61 Ibid., p. 17.
62 Ibid., p. 19.
63 Ibid., p. 21.
64 Ibid., p. 57.
65 Ibid., p. 27.
66 Ibid., p. 67.
67 Ibid., p. 69.
68 Ibid., p. 135.
69 René Laurentin, *War—Love Your Enemies—Medjugorje 12 Years Later,* Queenship Publishing, p. 76.
70 Sister Emmanuel, p. 98.
71 Laurentin, *War—Love Your Enemies—Medjugorje 12 Years Later,* p. 76.
72 Sister Emmanuel, pp. 66, 118.
73 Laurentin, *War,* p. 27.
74 Ibid.
75 Sister Emmanuel, p. 145.
76 ABC World News Tonight, March 9, 1995.
77 Sister Emmanuel, p. 77.
78 Ibid., p. 82.
79 Ibid., p. 78.
80 Ibid., p. 79.
81 René Laurentin and Professor Henri Joyeux, *Scientific & Medical Studies on the Apparitions at Medjugorje,* Veritas, 1987, p. 12.
82 Ibid., pp. 16-17.
83 Ibid., p. 45.
84 Ibid., pp. 13-14.
85 Ibid., pp. 14-15.
86 Ibid., p. 17.
87 Craig, p. 152.

88 Laurentin and Joyeux, p. 18.

89 Ibid., p. 12.

90 Hebblethwaite, *Medjugorje: a 'pious fraud.'*

91 Thomas C. Fox, *National Catholic Reporter,* January 15, 1988, *Medjugorje; Miracle or Hoax.*

92 Hebblethwaite, *Medjugorje: a 'pious fraud.'*

93 Fox, *Medjugorje; Miracle or Hoax.*

94 Father M. O'Carrol (C.S.S.), *Medjugorje: Facts, Documents, Theology,* (4th ed.), Dublin: Veritas, 1989, p. 238.

95 The bishop was having heart trouble and he underwent open heart surgery in 1993.

96 June 1986, papal advice to 12 Italian bishops seeking advice on pilgrimages to Medjugorje.

97 April 21, 1989, to Bishop Paul Hnilica (S.J.), Auxiliary Bishop of Rome.

98 June 17, 1992, meeting with Father Jozo.

99 February 1995, to Archbishop of Asuncion, La Paz, Bolivia.

100 Pope John Paul II to a group of Italian physicians on August 1, 1989, as reported by Bishop Paul Hnilica (S.J.), Auxiliary Bishop of Rome.

101 Pope John Paul II to Korean Archbishop Kwangju, *L'Homme Nouveau,* February 3, 1991.

102 René Laurentin, *Medjugorje-13 Years Later,* The Riehle Foundation, 1994, p. 46.

103 Thomas Petrisko, *Call of the Ages,* Queenship Publishing, 1995, p. 67.

Epilogue

1 Diary of Sister Faustina Kowalska, *Divine Mercy in My Soul,* Marian Press, Stockbridge, Massachusetts, copyright © 1987 Congregation of Marians of the Immaculate Conception, pp. 24-25. All world rights reserved; printed with permission.

2 Ibid., p. 44.

3 Ibid., p. 139.

4 Ibid., p. 190.

5 Ibid., p. 42.

6 Ibid., pp. 198-199.

7 Ibid., p. 264.

8 Ibid., p. 282.

9 Ibid., p. 320.

10 Ibid., p. 404.

11 Ibid., p. 296-297.

12 Ibid., p. 333.

13 Ibid., pp. 374-375.

14 Ibid., p. 420.

15 Ibid., pp. 297-298.

16 Ibid., p. 612.

17 Maria Valtorta, *The End Times,* Éditions Paulines, Centro Editoriale Valtortiano, 1994, p. ix.

18 Maria Valtorta Research Center, Univ. of Sherbrooke, Quebec, Canada, 1989.

19 Ibid.

20 Ibid.
21 John 10:27.
22 Maria Valtorta, *The End Times*, Éditions Paulines, Centro Editoriale Valtortiano, 1994, p. 1.
23 Ibid., p. 5.
24 Ibid., p. 6.
25 Ibid., pp. 15-16.
26 Ibid., p. 16.
27 Ibid.
28 Ibid., p. 25.
29 Ibid., pp. 41-42.
30 Ibid., pp. 99-100.
31 Ibid., p. 69.
32 Ibid., pp. 75-76.
33 Ibid., p. 79.
34 Ibid., pp. 114-115.
35 Ibid., pp. 118-119.
36 Ibid., pp. 146-147.

Appendix A

1 *Critique of Hegelian Philosophy*, 1844.
2 Ibid.
3 *On the Jewish Question*, 1844.
4 *Feuerbach*, 1888.
5 *Funeral oration for Marx*, March 17, 1883.
6 Ibid.
7 *Introduction to Socialism, Utopian and Scientific*, 1900.
8 *New Life*, December 16, 1905.
9 *Religion*, 1905.
10 *Complete Works, (French Edition)*, Vol. XVIII, p 361.
11 *Goerges Seldes, The Great Quotations*, 1960.
12 *C.L. Sulzberger, N.Y. Times*, June 11, 1956 (see Fátima prophecies about the fate of Russia in the end).
13 Ibid.
14 *Socialism and Religion*, 1905.
15 *Religion*, New York, 1933.
16 Ibid.
17 *Time* magazine, October 15, 1990.
18 Credo of *Red Sword*, organ of the Special Corps of the Cheka.
19 Letter to the head of the Cheka (Dzherzhinsky) by T. Samsonov, December 4, 1920.
20 Stalin, on being asked to encourage Catholicism in Russia by way of conciliating the pope. May 13, 1935.
21 Stalin, to the first American labor delegation to Russia, September 9, 1927.
22 *Problems of Leninism*, 1929.
23 Malachi Martin, *The Keys of This Blood*, p. 416.

24 Khrushchev, stated at reception for Wladyslaw Gomulka at the Polish Embassy, Moscow, November 18, 1956.
25 Khrushchev speech, 1955.

Appendix B

1 *The Gay Science,* [125], 1882.
2 *The Gay Science,* Book V, [343], 1887.
3 *Thus Spoke Zarathustra,* part 2.
4 *Thus Spoke Zarathustra,* part 3, [11].
5 *The Antichrist,* [62], 1888.
6 *The Antichrist,* [20], 1888.
7 *The Antichrist,* [42], 1888.
8 *The Antichrist,* [2], 1888.
9 *The Antichrist,* [7], 1888.
10 *Thus Spoke Zarathustra,* part 2, chapter on the Immaculate Perception.
11 *The Dawn,* [202], 1881.
12 *The Gay Science,* Book III, [116], 1882.
13 *Twilight of the Idols or How One Philosophizes with a Hammer,* chapter on the Four Great Errors, [6], 1888.
14 *The Antichrist,* 1888.
15 *The Antichrist,* [51], 1888.
16 *The Antichrist,* [14], 1888.
17 *Thus Spoke Zarathustra,* part 1, [2-3], 1883.
18 *The Antichrist,* [5], 1888.
19 *The Antichrist,* [3], 1888.
20 Letter to Peter Gast, 27 October 1887.
21 *The Antichrist,* [6], 1888.
22 *The Twilight of the Idols,* 1889.
23 *Beyond Good and Evil,* [212], 1886.
24 Ibid.
25 *Ecce Homo,* 1888.
26 *The Gay Science,* [125], 1882.
27 "Why I Am a Destiny," [1].

Bibliography

Bernstein, Carl and Marco Politi, *His Holiness: John Paul II and the Hidden History of Our Time* Doubleday Publishers, New York, 1996.

Carr, Joseph J., *The Twisted Cross*, Lafayette, Louisiana: Huntington House Publishers, 1985. (Phone # 1-800 749 4009)

Carroll, Warren H., *70 Years of the Communist Revolution*, Manassas, Virginia: Trinity Communications, 1989.

Carruth, Gorton, *The Encyclopedia of World Facts*. Harper Collins, 1993.

_____, *Catholic Almanac:1991*, Huntington, Indiana: Our Sunday Visitor, Inc., 1990.

_____, *Catholic Encyclopedia*, Huntington, Indiana: Our Sunday Visitor, Inc., 1991.

_____, *Chronicle of the 20th Century*, Mount Kisco, New York: Chronicle Publications, 1987.

_____, *Chronicle of the World*, Mount Kisco, New York: Ecam Publications, 1990.

Cobbett, William, *A History of the Protestant Reformation in England and Ireland*, Rockford, Illinois: TAN Books and Publishing, Inc., 1988.

Craig, Mary, *Spark From Heaven*, Notre Dame, Indiana: Ave Maria Press, 1988.

Delaney, John, (Editor), *A Woman Clothed with the Sun*, New York, New York: Doubleday, 1960.

de la Sainte Trinité, Frère Michel, *The Whole Truth About Fátima*, (Vols. I-III), Buffalo, New York: Immaculate Heart Publications, 1983-85.

de Lubac, Henri, *The Drama of Atheistic Humanism*, San Francisco, California: Ignatius Press, 1995.

de Marie des Agnes, Frère François, *Fátima: Tragedy and Triumph, (Vol. IV)*, Immaculate Heart Publications, 1994.

_____, *Dictionary of Mary*, New York, New York: Catholic Book Publishing Company, 1985.

Dillon, Mgr. George E. (D.D.), *Freemasonry Unmasked: As the Secret Power Behind Communism*, Palmdale, California: Christian Book Club, 1950.

Emmanuel, Sister, *Medjugorje: The War Day by Day*, Miami, Florida: The Florida Center for Peace, 1993.

Faricy, Father Robert (S.J.) and Sister Lucy Rooney (S.N.D), *Mary Queen of Peace*, Alba House, 1984.

Feeney, Robert, *Mother of the Americas,* Aquinas Press, (2nd edition), 1993.

Fernando, Father, *Fátima: A World-Shaking Message,* New York, New York: Vantage Press, 1987.

Flynn, Ted and Maureen, *The Thunder of Justice,* MaxKol Communications, Inc., 1993.

Fox, Rev. Robert J., *Rediscovering Fátima,* Huntington, Indiana: Our Sunday Visitor, Inc., 1982.

Fry, Peter and Fiona Somerset, *A History of Ireland,* New York, New York: Barnes and Nobles Books, 1988.

Fukushima, Francis Mutsuo, *Akita: Mother of God as Co-Redemptrix, Modern Miracles of Holy Eucharist,* Santa Barbara, California: Queenship Publishing Company, 1994.

Gouin, Fr. Paul, *Sister Mary of the Cross: Shepherdess of La Salette,* Asbury, New Jersey: 101 Foundation, (P. O. Box 151, Asbury, New Jersey, 08802-0151).

Graham, Robert A. (S.J.), *The Vatican and Communism During WWII: What Really Happened,* San Francisco, California: Ignatius Press, 1996.

Heller, Mikhail and Aleksandr M. Nekrich, *Utopia in Power: The History of the Soviet Union From 1917 to the Present,* Summit Books, New York, 1986.

Henze, Paul B., *The Plot to Kill the Pope,* Charles Scribner's Sons, New York, 1983.

Hochschild, Adam, *The Unquiet Ghost: Russia Remembers Stalin,* Viking, New York, 1994, p. xi.

Johnston, Francis, *The Wonder of Guadalupe,* Rockford, Illinois: Tan Books and Publishers, Inc., 1981.

Kaufmann, Walter, *The Portable Nietzsche,* New York, New York: Penguin Books, 1982.

Keating, Karl, *Catholicism and Fundamentalism,* San Francisco, California: Ignatius Press, 1988.

Kennedy, Joseph S., *Light of the Mountain: The Story of La Salette,* McMullen Books Inc., 1953.

Kondor, Fr. Louis (S.V.D.), *Fátima in Sister Lucia's Own Words,* Still River, Massachusetts, 1989.

Kowalska, Sister M. Faustina (Congregation of Sisters of Our Lady of Mercy), *Divine Mercy In My Soul: Diary of Sister M. Faustina Kowalska,* Stockbridge, Massachusetts, copyright 1987, Congregation of Marians of the Immaculate Conception; all world rights reserved; printed with permission.

Kraljevic, Svetozar (O.F.M.), *The Apparitions of Our Lady at Medjugorje,* Edited by Michael Scanlan, (T.O.R.), Chicago, Illinois: Franciscan Herald Press, 1984.

Kramnick, Isaac, (Editor), *The Portable Enlightenment Reader,* New York, New York: Penguin Books, 1995.

Laurentin, René, *Medjugorje—13 Years Later,* Milford, Ohio: The Riehle Foundation, 1994.

Laurentin, René and Henri Joyeux, *Scientific & Medical Studies on the Apparitions at Medjugorje,* Veritas Publications, 1987.

Laurentin, René, *War, Love Your Enemies: Medjugorje 12 Years Later,* Santa Barbara, California: Queenship Publishing Company, 1993.

Laux, Fr. John (M.A.), *Church History,* Rockford, Illinois: TAN Books and Publishers, Inc., 1989.

Levenda, Peter, *Unholy Alliance: A History of Nazi Involvement with the Occult,* New York, New York: Avon Books, 1995.

Lynch, Daniel J., *Our Lady of Guadalupe and Her Missionary Image,* St. Albans, Vermont, 1993. The Missionary Image of Our Lady of Guadalupe, Inc., Route 36, East Fairfield, Vermont 05448.

Manuel, David, *Medjugorje Under Siege,* Orleans, Massachusetts: Paraclete Press, 1992.

Martin, Malachi, *The Keys of This Blood,* Touchstone, Simon & Schuster, New York, copyright 1990, p. 96.

Michalenko, Sister Sophia, (C.M.G.T), *Mercy My Mission: Life of Sister Faustina H. Kowalska, S.M.D.M.,* Marian Press, Stockbridge, Massachusetts, 1995.

_____, *The Life of Sister Faustina Kowalska,* Servant Publications, Ann Arbor, Michigan, 1999.

_____, *The New American Bible,* Thomas Nelson Publishers, 1978.

_____, *The New Unger's Bible Dictionary,* Chicago, Illinois: Moody Press, 1988.

Oberman, Heiko A., *Luther: Man Between God and the Devil,* New York, New York: Doubleday, 1992.

O'Carrol, Father Michael (C.S.S.), *Medjugorje: Facts, Documents, Theology,* (4th ed.), Dublin: Veritas, 1989.

Odell, Catherine M., *Faustina: Apostle of Mercy,* Our Sunday Visitor Publications, Huntington, Indiana, 1998.

_____, *Those Who Saw Her,* Huntington, Indiana: Our Sunday Visitor, Inc., 1986.

_____, *Those Who Saw Her,* (rev. ed.), Huntington, Indiana: Our Sunday Visitor, Inc., 1995.

O'Hare, Msgr. Patrick F. (LL.D.), *The Facts About Luther,* Rockford, Illinois: TAN Books and Publishers, Inc., 1987.

_____, *The Oxford Companion to Philosophy,* New York, New York: Oxford University Press, 1995.

Pelletier, Joseph A. (A.A.), *The Queen of Peace Visits Medjugorje,* Worcester, Massachusetts: Assumption Publication, 1985.

Perez, Ramon, *Garabandal: The Village Speaks,* (2nd ed.), Lindenhurst, New York: The Workers of Our Lady of Mount Carmel, 1985.

Petrisko, Thomas W., *Call of the Ages,* Santa Barbara, California: Queenship Publishing Company, 1995.

Radzinsky, Edvard, *Stalin,* Doubleday Publishers, New York, 1996, p. 201.

Ridge, Millie, *Nostradamus: An Illustrated Guide to His Predictions,* Ottenheimer Publishers, Inc., 1994.

Rodriguez, Cardinal Caro y, *The Mystery of Freemasonry Unveiled*, Palmdale, California: Christian Book Club of America, 1992.

Rose, Frank, *West of Eden: The End of Innocence at Apple Computer*, Hutchinson, 1989.

Szulc, Tad, *Pope John Paul II*, New York, New York: Scribner, 1995.

Tindal-Robertson, Timothy, *Fátima, Russia & Pope John Paul II*, Augustine Publishing Co., 1992.

Trochu, Abbé François, *Saint Bernadette Soubirous*, Rockford, Illinois: TAN Books and Publishers, Inc., 1957.

Valtorta, Maria, *The Book of Azariah*, Italy: Centro Editoriale Valtortiano, 1993.

_____, *The End Time*, Italy: Éditions Paulines, Centro Editoriale Valtortiano, 1994.

_____, *The Notebooks:1943*, Italy: Centro Editoriale Valtortiano, 1996.

_____, *The Poem of the Man-God*, (Vols. I-V), Italy: Centro Editoriale Valtortiano, 1989.

Waite, Robert G. L., *The Psychopathic God: Adolph Hitler*, New York, New York: Basic Books, 1977.

Wayne, Thomas, *Western Europe: 1995*, (14th ed.), Stryker-Post Publications.

_____, *Western Civilizations*, (9th ed.), New York, New York: W. W. Norton & Company, 1980.

White, Michael, *Isaac Newton: The Last Sorcerer*, Helix Books, 1998.

_____, *Words From Heaven: Messages of Our Lady from Medjugorje*, Birmingham, Alabama: Saint James Publishing, 1990.

Yasuda, Fr. Teija (O.S.V.), *Akita: The Tears and Message of Mary*, Asbury, New Jersey: 101 Foundation, Inc., (P. O. Box 151, Asbury, New Jersey, 08802-0151).